语言学及应用语言学名著译丛

沉默的句法
截省、孤岛条件和省略理论

〔美〕贾森·麦钱特 著

张天伟 译

THE SYNTAX OF SILENCE

SLUICING, ISLANDS, AND THE THEORY OF ELLIPSIS

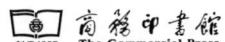

The Syntax of Silence: Sluicing, Islands, and the Theory of Ellipsis was originally published in English in 2001. This translation is published by arrangement with Oxford University Press. The Commercial Press is solely responsible for this translation from the original work and Oxford University Press shall have no liability for any errors, omissions or inaccuracies or ambiguities in such translation or for any losses caused by reliance thereon.

《沉默的句法——截省、孤岛条件和省略理论》英文版最早于 2001 年出版。此中译本经牛津大学出版社授权出版。商务印书馆对中译本负有全部责任,牛津大学出版社对其中的任何错误、遗漏、不准确或含糊之处,以及由此而造成的损失,概不负责。

根据英国牛津大学出版社 2001 年英文版译出

作者简介

贾森·麦钱特（Jason Merchant, 1969— ）

芝加哥大学语言学系洛娜·帕特卡默·斯特劳斯（Lorna P. Straus）冠名教授，现任学校学术事务与研究生教育副教务长。1991年在耶鲁大学获得语言学学士学位，1999年在加州大学圣克鲁斯分校获得语言学博士学位，而后在美国西北大学和荷兰格罗宁根大学从事博士后研究，于2001年加入芝加哥大学。曾任 *Natural Language and Linguistic Theory* 副主编，*Linguistic Inquiry* 等期刊编委，芝加哥大学语言学系主任、人文学院副院长。2012获得 Quantrell 本科生教学杰出贡献奖。在省略等相关语法现象的形式句法和语义研究方面成就卓著，特别是对德语和希腊语的研究。

---- 译者简介 ----

张天伟 北京外国语大学中国外语与教育研究中心教授、博导，入选北京外国语大学卓越人才支持计划。主要研究领域为句法学、语言政策。在《外语教学与研究》《外国语》《现代外语》等刊物上发表论文多篇，并被《中国社会科学文摘》、人大复印资料《语言文字学》全文转载。出版专著《跨语言视角下的英汉省略限制条件研究》、译著《语言规划与语言教育》等。

语言学及应用语言学名著译丛
专家委员会

顾　问　胡壮麟

委　员（以姓氏笔画为序）

　　　　马秋武　　田海龙　　李瑞林

　　　　张　辉　　陈新仁　　封宗信

　　　　韩宝成　　程　工　　潘海华

总　　序

商务印书馆出版的"汉译世界学术名著丛书"在国内外久享盛名，其中语言学著作已有10种。考虑到语言学名著翻译有很大提升空间，商务印书馆英语编辑室在社领导支持下，于2017年2月14日召开"语言学名著译丛"研讨会，引介国外语言学名著的想法当即受到与会专家和老师的热烈支持。经过一年多的积极筹备和周密组织，在各校专家和教师的大力配合下，第一批已立项选题三十余种，且部分译稿已完成。现正式定名为"语言学及应用语言学名著译丛"，明年起将陆续出书。在此，谨向商务印书馆和各位编译专家及教师表示衷心祝贺。

从这套丛书的命名"语言学及应用语言学名著译丛"，不难看出，这是一项工程浩大的项目。这不是由出版社引进国外语言学名著、在国内进行原样翻印，而是需要译者和编辑做大量的工作。作为译丛，它要求将每部名著逐字逐句精心翻译。书中除正文外，尚有前言、鸣谢、目录、注释、图表、索引等都需要翻译。译者不仅仅承担翻译工作，而且要完成撰写译者前言、编写译者脚注，有条件者还要联系国外原作者为中文版写序。此外，为了确保同一专门译名全书译法一致，译者应另行准备一个译名对照表，并记下其在书中出现时的页码，等等。

本译丛对国内读者，特别是语言学专业的学生、教师和研究者，以及与语言学相融合的其他学科的师生，具有极高的学术价值。第一批遴选的三十余部专著已包括理论与方法、语音与音系、词法与句法、语义与语用、教育与学习、认知与大脑、话语与社会七大板块。这些都是国内外语言学科当前研究的基本内容，它涉及理论语言学、应用语言学、语音学、音系学、词汇学、句法学、语义学、语用学、教育语言学、认知语言学、心理语言学、社会语言学、话语语言学等。

尽管我本人所知有限，对丛书中的不少作者，我的第一反应还是如雷贯耳，如 Noam Chomsky、Philip Lieberman、Diane Larsen-Freeman、Otto Jespersen、Geoffrey Leech、John Lyons、Jack C. Richards、Norman Fairclough、Teun A. van Dijk、Paul Grice、Jan Blommaert、Joan Bybee 等著名语言学家。我深信，当他们的著作翻译成汉语后，将大大推进国内语言学科的研究和教学，特别是帮助国内非英语的外语专业和汉语专业的研究者、教师和学生理解和掌握国外的先进理论和研究动向，启发和促进国内语言学研究，推动和加强中外语言学界的学术交流。

第一批名著的编译者大都是国内有关学科的专家或权威。就我所知，有的已在生成语言学、布拉格学派、语义学、语音学、语用学、社会语言学、教育语言学、语言史、语言与文化等领域取得重大成就。显然，也只有他们才能挑起这一重担，胜任如此繁重任务。我谨向他们致以出自内心的敬意。

这些名著的原版出版者，在国际上素享盛誉，如 Mouton de Gruyter、Springer、Routledge、John Benjamins 等。更有不少是著名大学的出版社，如剑桥大学出版社、哈佛大学出版社、牛津大学出版社、MIT 出版社等。商务印书馆能昂首挺胸，与这些出版社策划洽谈出版此套丛书，令人钦佩。

万事开头难。我相信商务印书馆会不忘初心，坚持把"语言学及应用语言学名著译丛"的出版事业进行下去。除上述内容外，会将选题逐步扩大至比较语言学、计算语言学、机器翻译、生态语言学、语言政策和语言战略、翻译理论，以至法律语言学、商务语言学、外交语言学，等等。我也相信,该"名著译丛"的内涵,将从"英译汉"扩展至"外译汉"。我更期待,译丛将进一步包括"汉译英""汉译外",真正实现语言学的中外交流,相互观察和学习。商务印书馆将永远走在出版界的前列!

胡壮麟

北京大学蓝旗营寓所

2018 年 9 月

汉译版序

我很高兴能够在本书中文译本出版之际撰写此序。张天伟博士非常专业地译介了此书,在此我向他致以诚挚的感谢。张天伟博士在过去几年,包括在芝加哥的一年多时间里,承担了大量辛苦的学术工作,他与我们院系学者的合作也极其愉快。

本书源自我的博士论文,经过稍许改动后于2001年由牛津大学出版社出版。自那以后,本书如我所愿发挥了有益的作用,它将疑问句中的省略现象作为待解释的核心领域,对人类语言如何运作进行了理论性说明。在近20年后的今天,我们所知已远超当时,而且出现了许多极富见地的著作,涉及多种语言,包括中文。在本书的诸多不足中,我认为最需要补救的是对中文这类"疑问词原位滞留"(wh-in-situ)语言的忽略。我仅在第二章的一个简短附录里提到过这些语言,概述了我当时所想到的能够处理这些语言中类似截省结构的几种分析方法。幸运的是,在随后几年里,来自中国和其他地方的许多有能力的研究人员填补了更多的空白。

本书试图将句法分析和语义分析结合起来,这是一种合乎读者心意的方式。对分析者而言,在处理复杂的省略现象时,真正重要的是掌握所有必要的方法,并且能够论证一种语言现象应该从句法还是语义途径加以分析。对分析方法进行区分是一项困难的工作,我们永远无法提前知晓其边界在何处。但是不充分了解这两种方法的人是很难严谨地研究这些问题的,因为很明显,在分析全部语料时都要涉及这两套体系。当然,这并不代表所有研究工作都必须在句法和语义接口进行。虽然人们已经努力阐释这一界面,但语法和语义两个系统的本体论是截然不同的。毫无疑问,不同的语言和认知对象需要采用不同的操作方案和约束手段。我们应该清楚，有许多省略现象值得完全从句法或完全从语义界面来处理，研究者们在这两个领域都取得了很大进展。

我还想就语料来源说几句。尽管书中有不少验证过的例句是我在近几年的阅读过程中积累的，但绝大多数例句是在数百个语料采集点收集到的，是从母语者那里获得，或者是与他们一起或我独自测试得到的。正如精细的实验工作所示，这种方法除了成本低、速度快之外，还很稳妥可靠。虽然许多为统计检验提供数据的实验方法也具备上述优点，但这些技术却难以复制，其研究设计也常常得不到充分的论证。尤其是在E类代词回指、范围和可能的解读方面，其语义数据是可靠的，并且实际上在此后的许多研究论文中都得到了验证。我之所以指出这一点，是因为这些有关意义的语料——尽管简明易懂——却无法通过典型的实验范式，在受控的语境中从母语者那里轻易获得。语言学的语料库很可能是认知科学中最强大的数据集，如果我们不承认，甚至不称道这一事实，那会是非常不明智的。

我非常高兴看到这本书激发了人们对该领域的兴趣，并催生了研究省略现象的一些新的和意想不到的方向，以及对其分析主张的一些重大改进。本书追求的是新颖的实证内容和精确的分析过程，力求在它寻求解决的问题上充分见证和回应前人的所有研究。我很高兴这本书能拥有一个中国读者群，我也相信他们将为我们理解中文和其他语言中的省略现象做出新的重要贡献。

贾森·麦钱特
2020年7月于芝加哥

目　　录

原版丛书总序 ··· 1
前言 ··· 2
缩略词 ··· 6

导论 ··· 1
    全书概述 ··· 7
    阅读提示 ··· 9

第一章　省略中的同一性：焦点和同构 ······························· 10
  1.1　语义背景 ··· 11
  1.2　焦点和同构条件 ··· 13
  1.3　同构条件存在的问题 ··· 20
  1.4　修正的焦点条件和省略给定 ····································· 28
      1.4.1　动词短语省略中的省略给定 ······························ 28
      1.4.2　截省中的省略给定 ·· 32
  1.5　小结 ·· 41

第二章　截省的句法 ··· 42
  2.1　外部句法：作为一种疑问 CP 的截省 ························· 43
      2.1.1　选择 ·· 44
      2.1.2　数的一致 ·· 45
      2.1.3　格 ··· 46
      2.1.4　位置分布 ·· 49
      2.1.5　德语中的 wh- 重音转移 ···································· 55

ix

　　　　2.1.6　小结 ··· 58
　　2.2　内部句法：截省的隐藏结构 ··· 59
　　　　2.2.1　IP 省略的允准条件 ··· 60
　　　　2.2.2　截省中的 COMP 域 ··· 67
　　2.3　小结 ··· 92
　　附录：疑问词原位语言 ··· 93

第三章　孤岛和形式同一性 ·· 95
　　3.1　截省中的句法（"强"）孤岛 ··· 95
　　3.2　形式同一性概括 ··· 98
　　　　3.2.1　格匹配 ··· 98
　　　　3.2.2　介词悬置 ··· 101

第四章　删除的诞生与消亡 ··· 119
　　4.1　罗斯（Ross 1969）：删除和孤岛问题 ································· 119
　　4.2　假截省句 ··· 127
　　　　4.2.1　初步思考 ··· 128
　　　　4.2.2　反对等式"截省句 = 假截省句" ······························ 132
　　　　4.2.3　小结 ··· 141
　　4.3　截省 ≠ 疑问算子 + 复述 ·· 141
　　　　4.3.1　初步思考 ··· 143
　　　　4.3.2　复述性与格 ·· 145
　　　　4.3.3　结论 ··· 160
　　4.4　钟等（Chung et al. 1995）：IP 复制、合并和萌生操作 ············ 162
　　4.5　IP 复制与 A′ 链一致性 ·· 168
　　4.6　小结 ··· 175

第五章　删除的复活 ·· 176
　　5.1　PF 孤岛 ·· 180
　　　　5.1.1　左分支提取 ·· 180

5.1.2 COMP 语迹效应 204
5.1.3 派生位置孤岛：话题化和主语 206
5.1.4 并列结构限制（一）：并连语条件 215
5.1.5 小结 224
5.2 截省下的 E 类型照应 224
5.2.1 问题：截省下的 A′ 语迹 224
5.2.2 解决办法：载体转换和 E 类型代词 228
5.2.3 小结 232
5.3 命题性孤岛 233
5.3.1 关系从句 233
5.3.2 附加语和句子主语 247
5.3.3 并列结构限制条件（二）：并连语中的提取 249
5.4 选择性（"弱"）孤岛 253
5.5 小结 256

结语 257

参考文献 259
语言索引 281
姓名索引 283
主题索引 289
译后记 296

原版丛书总序

牛津理论语言学研究系列丛书的理论重点，是关注人类语法系统子成分之间的界面以及与语言学不同分支学科之间的界面密切相关的领域。"界面"概念已成为语法理论（如乔姆斯基最近提出的最简方案）和语言实践的中心：句法与语义、句法与形态、音系与语音等之间的界面研究，使我们对特定的语言现象和思维或大脑涉及的语言成分的结构有了更加深入的了解。

本丛书将涵盖语法核心成分之间的界面问题，包括句法与形态、句法与语义、句法与音系、句法与语用、形态与音系、音系与语音、语音与语音处理、语义与语用、语调与话语结构，以及涉及这些界面区域的语法系统在使用中习得和配置方式的问题（包括语言习得、语言功能障碍和语言处理）。我们希望，它将有益于这一议题：更好地理解特定的语言现象、语言、语族或语言内部变异，都需要考虑界面问题。

本丛书对所有理论派别和各思想流派的语言学家的作品开放。丛书对作者的主要要求是：所写内容应该让语言学相关分支领域的同事和同源学科的学者能够理解。

我们很高兴推出了该系列丛书的第一卷。贾森·麦钱特考察了省略结构，重点讨论了截省现象，并且提出了一个涉及句法与语音形式以及句法与语义界面的视角。他指出，涉及语义同一性下语音形式删除的理论能够解释很多跨语言语料。

戴维·阿杰（David Adger）
哈吉特·博雷尔（Hagit Borer）

前　言

本书是我博士论文的修订版，主要写于 1997—1999 年，并于 1999 年 6 月提交给加州大学圣克鲁斯分校。本书得以出版，我首先要感谢我的导师 Jim McCloskey 和 Bill Ladusaw。在审阅书稿和讨论中，Jim 提出了不少富有启发性的见解，这表明他能力超群，能够洞察论点的核心并对之加以阐释，并且对文献的掌握也很令人惊叹。我与 Bill 的面谈和讨论对于本书所提观点的完善也至关重要。若非他具有将形式敏锐性和语言洞察力结合起来的能力，本书将会失色不少。我也受益于 Sandy Chung 敏锐的头脑与合理的质疑。我还必须特别感谢上述三位的是，他们愿意大度接受并积极鼓励本文所示的截省分析，尽管这种分析与他们自己的分析背道而驰。很少有答辩委员会成员会受到如此挑战，我确信没有人能以更多的风度和热情来应对这一挑战。

总之，我怀疑倘若没有圣克鲁斯语言学研究的激励氛围，这本书是否还可以完成。与这个学术共同体每个人的互动都让我受益匪浅，我还特别要感谢 Judith Aissen、Chris Albert、Daniel Büring、Donka Farkas、Ted Fernald、Jorge Hankamer、Junko Ito、Chris Kennedy、Armin Mester、Line Mikkelsen、Eric Potsdam、Geoff Pullum、Jaye Padgett、Peter Svenonius 和 Rachel Walker。

在撰写和修改本书过程中，我收获了来自全世界同行的大量帮助，感谢他们的宝贵意见、建议、反馈和支持。我要感谢在荷兰的 Norbert Corver、Marcel den Dikken、Jeroen Groenendijk、Jack Hoeksema、Helen de Hoop、Josep Quer、Henk van Riemsdijk、Eddy Ruys、Yoad Winter、

Jan-Wouter Zwart 和 Frans Zwarts。我要感谢在德国的 Kerstin Schwabe、Satoshi Tomioka、Chris Wilder、Susanne Winkler 和 Niina Zhang。我要感谢在美国和其他地方的 Mike Dickey、Edit Doron、Hana Filip、Danny Fox、Dan Hardt、Hajime Hoji、Norbert Hornstein、Kyle Johnson、Mika Kizu、Anne Lobeck、Taisuke Nishigauchi、Maribel Romero 和 Uli Sauerland。此书的许多改进都是基于与 Daniel Büring 和 Chris Kennedy 的讨论以及他们的评论而做出的。

我还要特别感谢 Anastasia Giannakidou，几年来她的评论、想法与合作对本书的完善至关重要。

如果没有大量语料提供者和讨论者的积极参与，这一著作永远不可能完成，因为它面对的是传统语法中所未知的结构。我要感谢下述各位对他们的母语做出的讨论，他们的帮助是不可或缺的。他们在判断我所关注的众多例句时做出了艰辛但很耐心的解答，很遗憾这样一份列表不能够将这些完全反映出来。

1. 阿拉伯语（摩洛哥）：M'hamed Bennani-Meziane、Mohamed Damir
2. 巴斯克语：Arantzazu Elordieta
3. 保加利亚语：Sevdalina Dianova、Lily Schürcks-Grozeva
4. 加泰罗尼亚语：Josep Quer
5. 汉语（普通话）：Niina Zhang
6. 捷克语：Hana Filip、Anna Pilátová
7. 丹麦语：Line Mikkelsen
8. 荷兰语：Norbert Corver、Jelle Gerbrandy、Herman Hendriks、Petra Hendriks、Jack Hoeksema、Bart Hollebrandse、Iris Mulders、Henk van Riemsdijk、Rob van Rooy、Eddy Ruys、Frans Zwarts
9. 芬兰语：Dan Karvonen
10. 法语：Caroline Féry、Paul Hirschbühler、Marie Labelle
11. 弗里斯兰语：Jelle Gerbrandy、Ger de Haan、Jarich Hoekstra、Oebele

Vries

12. 德语：Daniel Büring、André Meinunger、Armin Mester、Hans Rott、Patrick Schindler、Susanne Winkler；瑞士德语，Philip Spaelti

13. 希腊语：Yoryia Agouraki、Artemis Alexiadou、Elena Anagnostopoulou、Kostis Danopoulos、Anastasia Giannakidou、Anna Roussou、Athina Sioupi、Melita Stavrou

14. 印地语：Rajesh Bhatt

15. 希伯来语：Edit Doron、Danny Fox、Adam Sherman、Yoad Winter、Shalom Zuckerman

16. 匈牙利语：Donka Farkas、Genoveva Puskás

17. 冰岛语：Höskuldur Thráinsson

18. 爱尔兰语：Jim McCloskey

19. 意大利语：Maria Aloni、Gloria Cocchi、Paola Monachesi

20. 日语：Motoko Katayama、Mika Kizu、Kazutaka Kurisu、Junko Shimoyama、Satoshi Tomioka

21. 挪威语：Peter Svenonius

22. 波斯语：Behrad Aghaei

23. 波兰语：Dorotha Mokrosinska、Adam Przepiórkowski

24. 罗马尼亚语：Carmen Dobrovie-Sorin、Donka Farkas、Alexander Grosu

25. 俄语：Sergey Avrutin、Dasha Krizhanskaya

26. 塞尔维亚－克罗地亚语：Svetlana Godjevac

27. 斯洛文尼亚语：Tatjana Marvin

28. 西班牙语：Rodrigo Gutierrez、Juan Mora、Josep Quer

29. 瑞典语：Kerstin Sandell、Peter Svenonius

30. 土耳其语：Dilara Grate

31. 索西语：Judith Aissen

32. 意第绪语：Jerry Sadock、Elisa Steinberg

前　言

本书的部分内容已经在格罗宁根、巴黎、柏林、塞萨洛尼基、图宾根、乌得勒支、莱顿、奥斯汀、洛杉矶、圣克鲁斯、芝加哥、温哥华、埃文斯顿和圣地亚哥等地的学术论坛上展示过，本书也得益于各地听众的反馈和评论。

这项研究的大部分内容得到了乌得勒支大学和阿姆斯特丹大学富布赖特奖学金，以及加州大学圣克鲁斯分校校长论文奖学金的资助。书稿编写的最后阶段得到了西北大学梅隆博士后奖学金和格罗宁根大学 NWO（荷兰研究理事会）博士后奖学金的支持。谨在此致以诚挚谢意。

最后，我要深深地感谢父母多年来的支持，还有 Anastasia，为了她，我可以付出所有。

贾森·麦钱特

缩略词

以下是语料注解中使用的缩略词：

1	1st person 第一人称	lit.	literally 字面上
2	2nd person 第二人称	LOC	locative 处所格
3	3rd person 第三人称	NEG	negative (marker) 否定（标记）
ACC	accusative 宾格（受格）	NOM	nominative 主格
AGR	agreement 一致	PFV	perfective 完成时（完成体）
AUX	auxiliary 助动词	pl	plural 复数
CL	clitic 附着形式	PRES	present 现在时
DAT	dative 与格	PROG	progressive 进行时（进行体）
ENC	enclitic 前附着形式	PRT	(modal) particle 情态助词
ERG	ergative 作格	Q	question particle 疑问词
FIN	finite 定式的	REFL	reflexive 反身代词
FUT	future 将来时	sg	singular 单数
GEN	genitive 属格	SUBJ	subjunctive 虚拟式
INSTRA	instrumental 工具格	TOP	topic 话题

献给我的夫人阿纳斯塔西娅

导　　论

> 沉默是快乐最完美的宣告
> （《无事生非》，2.1.286）

当代理论语言学的首要目标是发展一套声音（或手势）和意义两者之间对应的理论。但是，这种声音和意义的对应在省略中则消失殆尽了。自然语言中存在着各式各样的省略，本来应该由语言符号展现的词和短语就这么无踪无影了。这可能吗？

这是可能的，因为省略基于冗余而存在，如维特根斯坦所述："对不必谈论的内容您可以保持沉默"。省略过程利用特定上下文中某类信息的冗余性，通过删除原本用于表达这些信息所需要的语言结构成分来实现表达的经济性。

这种冗余性是生物系统中的一般特性，在许多其他系统中也有使用（压缩算法就是当前的一个例子）。但是在表达的经济性（基于说话人的最小付出原则）和输出表达如预期（基于听话人的最小付出原则）的可用性（即可理解性）要求之间总是存在着竞争。从说话人的角度看，无论我们想要采取何种标准来衡量经济性（说到"付出"，无论如何定义，一般指词、短语等成分的使用数量问题），使用省略的方式显然都更加经济。同样，对于听话人而言，解读省略性话语也意味着需要更多的工作，因为必须要从非显性语言符号中推导出其中的意义。

对语言系统的这些竞争性要求，可以确保语言系统与其他各种为优化资源分配而选取的系统相类似。从这一点看，自然语言广泛使用省略是自然而然且可预见的：一种保持可用性的同时，又利用了系统中冗余性的明显方法。

在许多语言中，语法信息以各种方式被冗余地编码。一个简单的例子就是主谓一致问题，例如，英语中的动词在主语已明确为第三人称的情况下仍旧进行第三人称标记：$She_{3sg}\ is_{3sg}$ smart。许多语言要在句中各类成分上标注相同的语法信息：芬兰语中的数既标注在否定助动词上也标注在动词性分词上，达嘎瑞语（Dagaare）中的体被冗余地标注在了连动结构（serial verb construction）中每一个动词中心语上，阿肯语（Akan）中连动结构的每个动词上都出现时和否定标记，等等（例子引自 Niño 1997）。

这些事实表明，尽管表达中的冗余信息可能是允准语言结构省略的必要条件，但它肯定不是充分条件。事实上，不同语言在允准通过语法手段来系统地减少冗余方面是很不相同的。正因如此，可否省略，无论是针对特定语言还是特定结构，都不能单单归因于信息冗余这一整体原则，在语法中还必须以某种方式对可能出现的省略进行编码。这里涉及两个问题，即常说的"允准"（licensing）和"识别"（identification）。允准指的是对结构省略的局部限制条件，而识别指的是对那些本该由显性结构所呈现的信息的恢复。

允准理论与那些可能颇为有限的事实有关，而这些事实均是关于局部结构及其所涉语类特征的。我将在第二章中讨论这一问题。乍一看，识别问题似乎更加棘手，这是因为我们直接回到了从无声表达中生成意义这一令人困惑的问题。

仅此一点就引发了过去三十年来有关省略的大量研究，这也是省略作为一个活跃的研究课题不断困扰和挑战研究者们的主要原因。省略研究多集中在英语动词短语省略上，这是由基南（Keenan 1971）和萨格（Sag 1976a）及后续著作所取得的显著成果推动的结果。他们给出了一个可信的结论：动词短语省略（简称 VP 省略）对语义条件很敏感，而并非人们通常假定的那样只是简单的短语结构的省略。

尽管英语中基于 VP 省略的研究成果丰硕，但研究范围却极其有限。由于一些尚不清楚的原因，VP 省略尽管很可能与助动词系统的某些特殊属性密切相关，但英语中的 VP 省略现象在世界语言中似乎相当罕见。鉴于必要语料的细微差别（许多文献特别关注省略可能带来的照应关系问题），大多数关于 VP 省略的研究，以及后来关于省略的研究，都是由英语母语者开展的。虽然这对以英语为母语的研究者来说不失为一大便利，但也存在这一领域的理论研究唯英语一家独大的局面。毋庸置疑，这种局限性让我们无从知晓英语 VP 省略的研究结论是否具备跨语言检验的适用性。

幸运的是，许多语言中都存在比 VP 省略更为普遍的其他类型省略现象，本书的目标就是研究一些语言中的某种省略结构所具有的特定特征，而引起我们关注的这种省略现象就是**截省**（sluicing）。

截省是罗斯（Ross 1969）[①] 对（1）和（2）中所列现象的命名——（2）中的疑问句被简化成了只包含 wh- 短语的句子。该 wh- 短语可能对应一个显性的关联成分（（1）中的斜体部分），或者没有可对应的关联成分（如（2））。

(1) a Jack bought *something*, but I don't know what.
    b *Someone* called, but I can't tell you who.
    c *Beth* was there, but you'll never guess who else.

(2) a Jack called, but I don't know {when/how/why/where from}.
    b Sally's out hunting—guess what!
    c A car is parked on the lawn—find out whose.

[①] 罗斯一向以善于提出术语而闻名，不过这次术语命名不如他许多其他命名那样通俗易懂。这一术语名称大概选取了动词 sluice 的意义（韦氏词典第二版给出了以下词源：源自荷兰语 *sluys*, *sluis* < 古法语 *escluse* < 晚期拉丁语 *exclūsa*，是拉丁语 *exclūdere* "排除，关在门外"的过去分词；牛津英语词典里的词源也类似)，意思是"用湍急的水流冲洗掉"，隐喻性地扩展为"冲走 wh- 短语之下的句子。一种更为奇异的解释是，从在 wh- 短语下失去 S 节点的意义上说，这一术语的起源可以追溯到与 sluicing 发音相似的"S-losing"（比较 S-lifting 'slifting' 和 wh-is 'whiz' 删除）。

这些句子似乎具有与（3）相类似的结构，其中被删除的屈折短语（Inflectional Phrase，简称 IP）部分说明疑问标句词短语（Complementizer Phrase，简称 CP）中的句子被部分省略了。

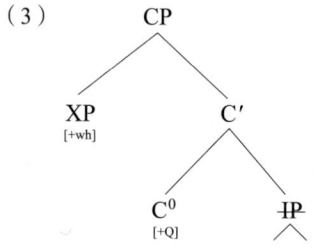

（3）

4　　尽管这种观点并未得到广泛认可，但截省也许可以看作是那些常被研究的省略结构中最重要的一个，其中一个原因是：可被截省的句子类别似乎是其所对应的非省略"无重音"句子类别中的真超集（proper superset）——下文中将提及这一点。

这与我们已经从 VP 省略中观察到的情况相反：许多属于 VP 省略的特性在去重音 VPs 中也有所体现；换言之，在 VP 省略中，省略情况构成了整个现象的一个真子集。这使得很多研究者，尤其是坦克雷迪（Tancredi 1992）、鲁思（Rooth 1992a）、乔姆斯基和拉斯尼克（Chomsky and Lasnik 1993）、富冈（Tomioka 1995, 1997）、阿舍等（Asher *et al.* 1997）、罗梅罗（Romero 1998）和福克斯（Fox 2000）认为，省略的同一性条件与特定语法环境中对焦点和平行性影响的更加全面的调查（全部或部分）不相符。（但要注意的是，早期研究者已经意识到，仅仅关注省略 VP 和先行 VP 同一性的理论，即谓项同一性理论是不够的：有学者（Prüst and Scha 1990a, b; Prüst 1993; Prüst *et al.* 1994）注意到，**子句平行性**（clausal parallelism）是关键要素，即使在省略位置之外也能限制量词互动）。因此，传统上用来分析省略的无中生义（*significatio ex nihilo*）问题，由于运用了句法同一性机制，似乎就成了一个次要问题：一旦我们明确了在非省略结构中允准去重音的条件，那么可以推测，我们可以将这些条件应用到省略的案例分析中，省略本身不过就是去重音的基本形式，即语音删除。

正是在这种情形下,关于截省的共识性看法日益凸显,尽管关于省略的一般文献忽略了这一点。这种共识性看法源自罗斯(Ross 1969),据我所知这是毋庸置疑的。在对这一领域的最初调查中,罗斯注意到截省所留下的 wh- 短语表面上违反了他的孤岛限制条件,如(4a)和(4b)间的对比所示((4b)中的斜体部分表示被去重音的成分会呈现低平 F_0 语调特征)。

(4) a They want to hire someone who speaks a Balkan language, but I don't remember which.
 b *They want to hire someone who speaks a Balkan language, but I don't remember which *they want to hire someone who speaks*.

钟等(Chung et al. 1995)格外关注了这种对孤岛条件不敏感的现象,这种不敏感性是将省略结构从句法上单纯简化为去重音结构的主要绊脚石。如果我们假设含有孤岛提取成分句子可接受度的降低是用于阻止这种非约束依存关系的句法原则所导致的,那么(4a)和(4b)间的对立就难以理解了。若采用删除法,在语音形式(Phonological Form,简称 PF)上操作,(4a)由(4b)通过纯粹的语音删除而得。如果使用纯句法手段来解释孤岛,这种情况下,语音形式上的操作应该与提取无法进行无关。

对此,一种观点认为孤岛本质上是 PF 现象,正如文献中经常提到的那样(文献和新近研究路径见 Kluender 1998),也许看作一种(关于记忆及联想辖域的)加工限制条件更为合理。如果孤岛落在省略位置内部且在 PF 层被删除,则不会发生任何违规现象。这基本上就是罗斯的建议——这些违反孤岛现象通过推导(整体上)得以解决,保留在语音层面的被提取的孤岛比被删除的孤岛更加糟糕。但是在显性提取而非省略的情况下,把违反孤岛条件的现象淡化为加工上的困难当然还需要一些原则性方法来区分显性语言符号的加工与必须为省略结构赋予意义的加工。如果人工在线语言处理可以反映任何关于句子实际理解的问题——因为如果它真的有这方面的优势,它就势必如此——那么这种差异就是完全出乎意料且极度令人担忧的。

然而，即使这种差异可以得到解决，总体策略也将失效，因为在某些情况下，孤岛会出现在省略位置内部且保持其效力。比如（4a）是不可能发生 VP 省略的：

（5） *They want to hire someone who speaks a Balkan language, but I don't remember which they do [$_{VP}$ want to hire someone who speaks].

反对所有孤岛都是 PF 现象这一观点的另一主要原因是，有证据显示隐形移位遵守某些类型的孤岛条件（见 Huang 1982, Nishigauchi 1986；可进一步参考 May 1991）——包括（4b）中的关系从句。因此我们可以放弃将所有孤岛都简化成 PF 限制条件的做法（尤其是（4b）所代表的这类孤岛）。

那么，我们就只剩下（4）中通过对比所引发的问题：为什么截省看上去能够使孤岛条件无效？尽管迄今为止，对这些事实最成功的解释（即 Chung et al. 1995）依赖于逻辑形式（Logical Form，简称 LF）复制机制，并附加各种匹配和修复操作以做补充，但这里我将证明这些事实实际上也与一种严格基于删除的省略研究方法相一致，这种方法对被删除成分的焦点结构的部分新条件很敏感（Rooth 1992b 针对 VP 省略概括性地提出过这一点，Romero 1997a，1998 继续探讨过截省问题）。换言之，我接下来的目标是重塑截省的删除路径解读。

人们通常假定，删除解读要求在被删除结构和某一先行项之间拥有一种形态句法同一性的条件。然而，这绝对不是一个必要的假设，我也不会采纳这个假设。事实上我们将看到，任何像这样的句法同构要求在截省和 VP 省略中都会遇到严重的问题，并且在任何情况下都必须予以避免。删除路径和句法同构之间的这种历史联系很容易被割裂：建立一个将语义同一性要求施加于 PF 操作上的省略理论不存在任何内在矛盾；事实上我们将看到，这种理论提供了一种将句法（允准）和语义（识别）要求联系起来的直接方法。

但是，如果省略部位的结构是小句的常规句法结构，这是此处要捍卫的一个主要主张，那么我们就回到了明显的孤岛不敏感问题上。某些类型的截省对孤岛不敏感这一事实，要求我们修正对某些句法孤岛的本质的理解。特别是，我将论证某些孤岛确实是 PF 现象，而像上文（4）中关系从句那样的孤岛则不是。这意味着并非所有孤岛都是平等创建的：我们需要一个多元化的孤岛观。截省可能出现在像（4a）这类例句中的这一事实具有误导性：我认为，绝对没有理由认为在被删除的 IP 中存在一个对应的孤岛，也没有理由认为在没有该孤岛的情况下可以生成所观察到的解读。

我们一开始就提出，在省略情况下如何克服声音和意义之间惯有相关性的缺失这一问题。当所涉及的词项具有语音（或手势）外在形式时，通常可以给上述问题一个更为通俗的答案：这种相关性是由句法调节的。然而，这些情况下的句法事实上没有语音外在形式，因而其研究难度增加了。但目前看来，任何其他的选择都不太可能被证明是正确的。本研究的目标就是论证在沉默中确实存在句法结构这一结论。

全书概述

我将在这里捍卫这样一个观点：句子（1）和（2）的推导基于两个部分：从疑问结构的 IP 中提取 wh- 短语的一般移位规则，以及对由移位所导致的剩余 IP 部分的删除操作。这种观点给出了一个最为简单的句法规则，因为它恰好是 wh- 小句一般的句法结构。

我在第一章首先回顾我们目前对省略的理解，主要基于对英语 VP 省略的理解。我证明了，即使对于最简单的截省情况，人们通常在被删除结构上使用的结构同构条件假设（是对用于去重音的一般焦点条件的补充）也会遇到许多严重问题。此外，它还遇到了一个大家熟悉的问题，即省略下的照应问题，这一点被菲恩戈和梅（Fiengo and May 1994）称之为"载体转换"（vehicle change）。然后，我在省略位置上定义了一个新的焦点条件，它构建于双向的隐含关系中，这使我们能够放弃额外的结构同构条件，解决了截省的问题，而且不再需要一个独立的"载体转换"理论。这些一般性条件对 VP 省略和截省都适用，也为接下来的语料分析奠定了基础。

第二章考察用于解释截省的结构条件，并探究截省的外部和内部结构。我明确了截省涉及一个省略了 IP 的 CP，并且在洛贝克（Lobeck 1995）研究的基础上讨论了空形式 IP 的允准条件。我证明了这些条件可以在 PF 删除路径下得到解释，其基础是某一单一特征触发了删除，这一特征又进一步为第一章所阐述的语义条件的应用提供了位置。最后，我记录了关于在截省句 C 辖域（C-domain）中可能出现的成分的新颖概括，并建议其遵循对删除和经济性的自然解读，以及关于能跟随标句词（complementizer）的空形式成分类别的一般原则。

在第三章中，我把注意力转向本研究的核心新语料，这些新语料来自对 24 种语言的调查。我首先梳理了相关的孤岛事实，这些事实主要是从文献中获取的。接下来我做出了一个新的概括，这对第四章和第五章的研究至关重要。这个新的概括与被截省的 wh- 短语及其先行项之间所要求的形式同一性（form-identity）有关，特别是与 wh- 移位导致的介词悬空的跨语言适用性有关。

在第四章中，我探讨了当今学界对截省现象的五种代表性解释方法。结果显示这些解释均不能为孤岛不敏感问题或第三章的形式同一性概括问题提供解决方法。

最后，在第五章中，我着重谈了我对形式同一性概括的看法，指出截省的删除解释路径抓住了这些事实，一般情况下的孤岛不敏感问题可被解释清楚，只留下了没有句法孤岛条件被违反的情况。这表明该分析方法支持区别对待句法孤岛条件（如关系从句和附加语）和 PF 效应问题（如 COMP 语迹现象、某些并列结构以及左分支效应）。删除路径对截省的解释力间接说明用 LF 复制法来解决省略问题的最佳论据之一（或者实际上是更加抽象的语义研究路径）瓦解了。从目前的理论视角来看，这种结论还具有使得截省不再那么神秘的可喜结果。我希望这一结果能使截省在省略类型学中受到和 VP 省略一样的重视。

阅读提示

  首先值得强调的是，对省略理论研究所涉及的大量研究语料感兴趣的读者会在本书中发现很多乐趣，但对于主要关注英语 VP 省略以及对严格与宽泛同一性这一长久以来的问题感兴趣的读者不会如此。换句话说，一方面，由于时间和空间要求，截省足够复杂，需要单独处理，使能更好理解所有过程的最终完善的统一解释成为可能。因为第一章中提出的统一解释是一般性的、笼统的，但很多问题，尤其是 VP 省略所特有的问题仍有待从这一角度进行深入研究。另一方面，很难在截省下研究严格与宽泛同一性问题，因为说话人一致认为截省下的宽泛解读是极难达到的。①

  有鉴于此，我将着重讨论关于省略的最新理论研究，暂且把 VP 省略放到一边，而集中探讨截省问题。

---

① 尽管罗斯（Ross 1969）给出了一个在截省下相当容易接受的宽泛同一性解读例句，但即使是对更大范围内的情况做最粗略的考察，也会发现其中涉及与 VP 省略大为不同的内容。下面的例句得到了三位发言者的检验，在这些例句中很难得到宽泛解读（检验结果有一些变化，但是在"不可能"到"非常边缘化"的范围内）。

  (i) a Abby said she'd stop smoking tomorrow, but Beth wouldn't say when.
    b Alex said someone would visit him after Ben wondered who.
    c Abby knew how fast she'd run, but Beth had to ask how fast.
    d Abby knew how fast she'd run, but Beth even had to ask how far.
    e Abby already knew which students were enrolled in her seminar, but Beth didn't even know how many.
    f Abby knew who she saw, and Beth said she knew who, too.

这些例句应该与下面对应的 VP 省略例句进行比较，VP 省略例句完全可以得到宽泛解读。我们可以对上述例句进行类似的对比，对比结果是十分显著的。

  (ii) a Abby told us when she'd stop smoking, but Beth didn't.
     b Abby already knew which students were enrolled in her seminar, but Beth didn't.

相关讨论及关于 VP 省略下宽泛同一性的大量文献，见 Tomioka 1996, 1999；在一个扩展领域的相关讨论，见 Hoji and Fukaya 1999 和 Hoji（出版中）。

第一章

省略中的同一性：焦点和同构

尽管本书的主要目的是研究截省句，但任何对省略普遍性条件的讨论都必须从研究得最为成熟的英语动词短语省略入手。因此我也从动词短语省略问题入手，概述该领域研究所得出的基本结论，进而考察这些结论对于截省句的应用和解释力，最后再简要地回到对动词短语省略问题的探讨上。

众所周知，自坦克雷迪（Tancredi 1992）和鲁思（Rooth 1992*a*）起，对英语动词短语省略条件的探究就一直伴随英语动词短语去重音或省音条件的研究而展开。这两个问题似乎都与制约焦点分布的一般性条件密切相关。有几位作者已经阐释并确定了适宜的、用来约束去重音和省略的焦点条件。虽然这种统一的解释路径并非毫无争议（反对意见参阅 Winkler 1997, López 2000），但它是建立在人们对语言的直觉之上的，该解释似乎也非常有希望能够探索和分析上述两个问题之间的联系。尽管如此，如下文所示，即使确定了动词短语去重音的条件，也无法解答与动词短语省略条件相关的所有问题——动词短语省略还受到附加的、通常是结构性限制条件的制约。

在这一章中，我将概述去重音的一般性条件以及附加的结构性限制条件的证据。我将阐明这种附加的限制条件在动词短语省略，尤其是截省句等不同领域中造成的许多问题。（这些问题中最广为人知的也许就是被菲恩戈和梅（Fiengo and May 1994）称为"载体转换"的问题，该理论的重要内容是提出一系列条件，依据这些条件，在同一性下代词和指称语可以被删除）随后我将提出一个改进版的焦点条件，它能够解决一般的焦点条件处理起来较为棘手的问题，并可以让我们抛掉问题重重的一般性焦点条件，即结构同构限制条件（且不必采取单独的"载体转换"理论来解释这些情况）。最后，我将阐释改进后的焦点条件是如何应用到截省句等一系列核心语料上的，从而为接下来的研究打好基础，特别是为第五章中要展开的分析做好铺垫。

接下来，我将对后续几章中的一些结论先做简要概述，并将支配残余 wh- 短语的成分视为 CP，缺失部分视为 IP，将省略的推导过程视为删除。这些术语的选择后文中将会全面论证，在此提及只是为了方便讨论。

1.1 语义背景

在本节中，我非常简要地列举一些下文中会用到的相关背景概念和假设。这些假设均为标准假设，熟悉语义学的读者可直接进入下一节。

我假设在 LF 中存在一种受类型驱动的短语标记转换，这些短语标记将对决定句法结构意义的所有相关属性（取决于上下文）进行编码。LF 层面的运算把短语标记转换编码到逻辑语言 L 中（对于 L，我们采用标准的谓词运算），L 的这些运算根据表述功能而被评估，表述功能 $[\![\cdot]\!]$ 与模型 M 和赋值函数 g（暂不考虑内涵性（intensionality）问题）有关，写作 $[\![\cdot]\!]^{M,g}$。

相关定义见（1）。

（1）使 $M = \langle E, I \rangle$，E 是个体域，I 是表述功能，I 给 L 中的每个常量（个体或谓词）在 E 中指派一个外延（extension）。

若 c 是个体常量，则 $I(c) \in E$。若 P 是 n 元谓词，则 I 将 P 映射到 E 中元素的一个有序 n 元组上。例如，对于一个 $\langle e, t \rangle$ 型一元谓词 P 和一个〈e〉型常量 c 来说，当且仅当 I(c)∈I(P) 时，P(c) 在 M 中为真，如例（2）中所示。

（2）Let $M_1=\langle E, I\rangle$，其中
$$E = \{abby, ben\}$$
$$I = \begin{bmatrix} a \to abby \\ b \to ben \\ sing \to \{abby\} \end{bmatrix}$$

此时，$[\![sing(a)]\!]^{M_1,g} = I$ iff $[\![a]\!]^{M_1,g} \in [\![sing]\!]^{M_1,g}$，即 iff abby ∈ {abby}，这就是（2）中模型所示的情况。

该模型对仅包含常量和谓词（以及各种逻辑连接词，此处不做详细讨论）的公式来说非常有效，但还需对用作移位和代词语迹转换形式的变项做进一步阐释。具有自由变项的公式是根据赋值函数来评估的。就本书而言，变项仅为〈e〉型，赋值函数 g 是域 E 中从变项到个体的函数。详例见（3）中的函数 g_1。

（3）$g_1 = \begin{bmatrix} x \to abby \\ y \to ben \\ z \to charlene \end{bmatrix}$

通过此赋值函数，我们可以评估 **sing**(y) 这样的公式。当且仅当 g 返给 y 的值是 I(**sing**) 给定集合中的一个元素时，有关 M 和 g 的公式才为真。以 M_1 和 g_1 为例，我们可以得到 $[\![sing(y)]\!]^{M_1,g_1} = I$ iff $[\![y]\!]^{M_1,g_1} \in [\![sing]\!]^{M_1,g_1}$；因为 $g_1(y)=$ ben，且 ben ∉ {abby}，因此该公式在 M_1 和 g_1 下为假。

须注意，$[\![sing(y)]\!]^{M_1,g_1}$ 和 $[\![sing(b)]\!]^{M_1,g_1}$ 之间没有区别。下文将会看到，这一简单的事实将会是消除"载体转换"核心案例之一的关键。

通常来说，与模型 M 和赋值函数 g 有关的 $[\![\cdot]\!]$ 的语义学递归定义如（4）所示。

（4）若 α 是个体常量或谓词，则 $[\![α]\!]^{M,g} = I(α)$。

若 α 是变项，则 $[\![α]\!]^{M,g} = g(α)$。

上述简要概述应能满足本书目的。

1.2 焦点和同构条件

鲁思（Rooth 1992a）基于菲恩戈和梅（Fiengo and May 1994）早期的研究，区分了被省略的动词短语（elided VP，简为 VP_E）与其先行项（VP's antecedent，简称 VP_A）间的两种不同关系，示意图如（5）所示，其中 VP_E 和 VP_A 先后顺序不相关。

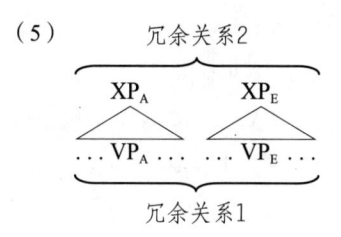

（5）

$$\underbrace{\overset{XP_A}{\triangle}\quad\overset{XP_E}{\triangle}}_{\text{冗余关系1}}\;\;\text{冗余关系2}$$

…VP_A…　…VP_E…

上述作者声称，冗余关系 1 是句法性的：尤其是菲恩戈和梅所提出的"重构"（reconstruction），我们马上会接触到这一概念。鲁思接受这一假定，但他更关注冗余关系 2。菲恩戈和梅（Fiengo and May 1994）声称冗余关系 2 可以归到他们的依附理论（本质上是通过平行结构来阐释句法同构，即取模指数）。鲁思表示，冗余关系 2 实际上是一种语义关系，与他所提出的 ~ 算子（operator）一致（见 Rooth 1985, 1992b, 1996）。~ 算子依附于逻辑形式成分 α，要求有一组与 α 类型相同的选项。此处不做详述，读者请参考布林（Büring 1997）对鲁思的焦点理论所做的清晰阐述。

鲁思的假设如下：

> 省略只有在具有以下特点的构型中才能出现：
> 1. 动词短语能够被句法重构，且
> 2. 被重构短语或支配被重构部位的短语同先行结构或支配先行结构的短

语之间存在~算子关系……(Rooth 1992a: 18)

根据鲁思假设中的2,(5)中的模式需要满足 $XP_A \sim XP_E$。为明确这一点,我们将该条件重述为(6)所示(按以往惯例:见 Johnson 1997, Romero 1997a)。

(6) 动词短语省略的鲁思焦点条件(鲁思版本)
当且仅当存在一个先行 XP_A,且 XP_A 与省略短语 XP_E 相同,或蕴涵省略短语 XP_E 时,XP_E 中的动词短语 α 才能被删除。①

鲁思的观点也可以基于施瓦茨柴尔德(Schwarzschild 1999)对"给定"(GIVEN)的定义,用施瓦茨柴尔德的焦点理论加以解释。

(7) 给定(Schwarzschild 1999)
1. 若成分 α 不承担焦点标记,那么 α 一定是给定的。
2. 当且仅当表达式 E 有一个凸显的先行词 A,且有 ∃ 类型替换②取模时,A 蕴涵 E 的焦点闭包(F-closure),表达式③ E 为给定。

(8) 焦点闭包
α 的焦点闭包写作 F-clo(α),是通过适当的 ∃ 约束变项替换 α 的焦点标记部分而得到的结果(∃ 类型替换取模)。

此处,我不会向读者全面展示施瓦茨柴尔德的理论,而是通过不同的例句来说明该理论如何运作。

(9) 动词短语省略的施瓦茨柴尔德焦点条件(施瓦茨柴尔德版本)
当且仅当 α 或包含 α 的成分为给定时,动词短语 α 才可以被删除。

让我们用例句加以阐释。

---

① 简单地说,$[\![α]\!]^o$ 是 $[\![\ ]\!]$ 返给 α 的常值;$[\![α]\!]^f$ 是 α 的焦点值,是 α 选择的对象集,是通过用适当类型的变量替换 α 中的所有焦点标记成分,从而从 α 中推导出的。
② ∃ 类型转换是一种类型转换操作,使话语提升至 ⟨t⟩ 类型,并约束着未填充论元。
③ 我用"表达式"(expression)这一术语来替代施瓦茨柴尔德的"话语"(utterance),目的是将史瓦西涉及的、但与本研究不相关的一些复杂难题排除出去;见 Schwarzschild 1999。

（10） a Abby sang because [Ben]$_F$ did.
　　　b
```
             IP
            /  \
          IP₁   because IP₂
          /\           /\
      Abby sang  [Ben]_F did [_VP sing].
```

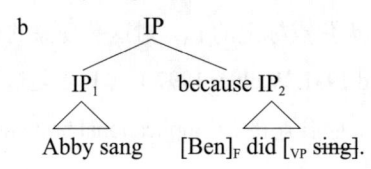

（10b）是（10a）的逻辑形式，其中删除部分是语音层面上未发音的读音符号（我认为导致语音层面删除的特征存在于逻辑形式层面；见 2.2.1 节中的论述）。

鲁思的焦点条件要求 $[\![IP_1]\!]^0 \in [\![IP_2]\!]^f$，即 $\lambda w.sing_w(a) \in \{\lambda w.sing_w(x): x \in D_e\}$。后面的集合等同于 M_1 中的 $\{\lambda w.sing_w(a), \lambda w.sing_w(b)\}$。（此处及后述整个论述过程中，我将忽略时和体。）

施瓦茨柴尔德的焦点条件也得到了满足：删除的动词短语是给定的，因为通过 ∃ 类型替换，先行项 *Abby sang* 蕴涵被删除的动词短语：$\exists x.sing(x)$。同样，我们可以通过屈折短语（IPs）的比较，用 ∃ 约束变项 $\exists x.sing(x)$ 替换 IP_2 中的焦点 [Ben]$_F$。

现在来看例句（11a），我们把其中的代词 him_2 替换为变项 x_2。

（11） a Abby saw him after [Ben]$_F$ did.
　　　b
```
             IP
            /  \
          IP₁   after IP₂
          /\           /\
      Abby saw him₂  [Ben]_F did [_VP see him₂].
```

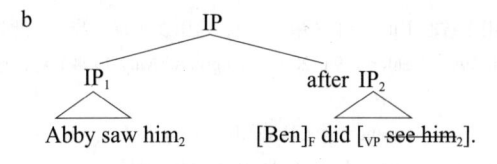

当且仅当 $[\![Abby\ saw\ x_2]\!]^0 \in [\![[Ben]_F\ saw\ x_2]\!]^f$，即当 $\lambda w.see_w(a, g(x_2)) \in \{\lambda w.see_w(y, g(x_2)) | y \in D_e\}$ 时，（11b）中的逻辑形式才能满足鲁思的焦点条件。当且仅当 IP_1 蕴涵 $\exists x.see(x, g(x_2))$ 时，且 $see(abby, g(x_2))$ 为真时，该逻辑形式才能满足施瓦茨柴尔德的焦点条件。

众所周知，某些类型的动词短语在满足一定焦点条件时，可以去重音，但在相同条件下却不能被删除。例如（12）和（13）中前行小句提供了合适的先行项，所以后行句中动词短语可以去重音。此处，大写字母表示焦点重读，斜体字表示去重音（即无焦点标记的 F_0，对这一现象的详细考察与重要说明见 Hirschberg and Ward 1991, Winkler 1997）。（13）是这一现象中较为极端的案例，被鲁思称之为"隐含连接"（implicational bridging）。

（12） a Abby was reading the book while BEN *was reading.*

b Abby ate a sandwich after BEN *ate.*

c Abby left the party because BEN *left.*

d Abby sang her hymn louder than BEN *sang.*

（13） a Abby called Chuck an idiot after BEN *insulted him.*

b Abby ate a sandwich after BEN *had lunch.*

c Abby left the party because BEN *took off.*

上述例句中的先行项都隐含着一个命题，该命题包含去重音动词短语的焦点值，满足鲁思的焦点条件。[①]（12a）的情况如（14）所示：

（14） $[\![\text{Abby was reading the book}]\!]^0 \to [\![\text{Abby was reading}]\!]^0$ 和

$[\![\text{Abby was reading}]\!]^0 \in [\![\text{BEN}_F \text{ was reading}]\!]^f$

同样，由于蕴涵[②]被纳入施瓦茨柴尔德对"给定"的定义中，该句的逻辑

[①] 类似的观点也适用于省略下的被动—主动变换，这引发了许多难题，此处我将暂避不谈。已有文献（见 Hardt 1993; Kehler 1993, 2000; Fiengo and May 1994）对这些问题做了广泛讨论。试比较：

(i) a First, Abby picked Ben, and then CHARLIE *was picked.*

b *First, Abby picked Ben, and then CHARLIE *was fired.*

c *First, Abby picked Ben, and then CHARLIE *was.*

[②] 这里"蕴涵"（entailment）的意思是"语境蕴涵的一种，假定存在一定的背景信息"（Schwarzschild 1999: 151），与预设的标准概念有明显的联系。我认为，如施瓦茨柴尔德所说，这种较为宽泛的蕴涵概念将允许文中例句所示的删减所必需的等同关系。例如，只有当语境支持 Abby 午餐吃的三明治（Abby ate sandwich for lunch）这一"蕴涵"（或（可以调整为）预设）时，（13b）才合法。（13）中其他例句需要较少的语境支撑，因为"离开"（leave）在相关意义上总是蕴涵着"走掉"（take off），如果你叫某人白痴，几乎可以肯定你已经侮辱了他（除非他真的是个白痴）。

运算可直接表述为：

（15） *Abby was reading the book* 蕴涵 ∃x.x **was reading**

这些例句应与下述例句进行比较。在下述例句中，先行项不隐含包含去重音动词短语焦点值的命题。用施瓦茨柴尔德的术语，即先行项不蕴涵去重音动词短语所在的 IP 的焦点闭包（只有在评价性语境中，主句谓词蕴涵或隐含从句谓词时，下述例句才合法，比如在某个范例中，if *x* reads the book, *x* coughs）：

（16） a *Abby was reading the book while BEN *was coughing*.

　　　b *Abby ate a sandwich after BEN *coughed*.

　　　c *Abby left the party because BEN *coughed*.

　　　d *Abby sang her hymn louder than BEN *coughed*.

（17） a *Abby called Chuck an idiot after BEN *coughed*.

　　　b *Abby ate a sandwich after BEN *coughed*.

　　　c *Abby left the party because BEN *coughed*.

然而，对（12）和（13）中去重音的论证不能用来解释动词短语省略。对于动词短语省略，仅靠隐含的解释是不够的；确切地讲，正如许多作者以不同形式所提出的那样（最新方法和文献见 Hardt 1992, 1993），我们似乎需要意义上的同一性。以（18）和（19）中的动词短语省略为例，省略的动词短语不允许具有与（12）和（13）中动词短语等同的解读。

（18） a Abby was reading the book while BEN was.

　　　b Abby ate a sandwich after BEN did.

　　　c Abby left the party because BEN did.

　　　d Abby sang her hymn louder than BEN did.

（19） a Abby called Chuck an idiot after BEN did.

b Abby ate a sandwich after BEN did.
c Abby left the party because BEN did.

相反，在上述各例中，省略的动词短语在意义上必须与先行项保持一致。所以，只有当本（Ben）正在读书（Ben was reading the book），而非只是读某些东西（Ben was reading something）时，（18a）才为真。[①]由此可见，上述焦点条件适用于动词短语去重音和动词短语省略（也是造成辖域平行的原因等；尤见 Tomioka 1995, 1997; Asher et al. 1997; Fox 2000），然而省略结构似乎还遵守额外的、更为严苛的限制条件。

一般认为，这个更为严苛的条件是一种结构的同构性（structural isomorphism）。该观点进一步认为这个条件要求存在一个在句法结构上完全相同的先行项——该先行项不仅要具有与删除目标相同的意义，而且要具有完全相同的结构（实际上在这种路径中意义并不起直接作用，大多数情况下只不过是结构同一性的副产品）。如果没有结构相同的先行项，就不可能有删除。菲恩戈和梅（Fiengo and May 1994）的"重构"概念就是这一主张准确的表达。他们将"重构"定义为"一组符号结构，出现于终端词汇的给定（次）短语标记上"（第191页）；删除的短语必须是重构结构中的一部分。因此，省略理论中的结构部分包含省略短语必须有结构相同的先行项这一要求。我把这一观点称为省略的同构条件。

让我们来看一下同构条件如何应用到上述例句中。例如，（18a）的结构如（20）所示。

[①] 这些事实说明为何上述条件是删除的必要条件而非充分条件；如果我们只将这些条件应用到去重音上，而不应用到删除上，则这些条件可能会被强化成双条件（biconditionals）。

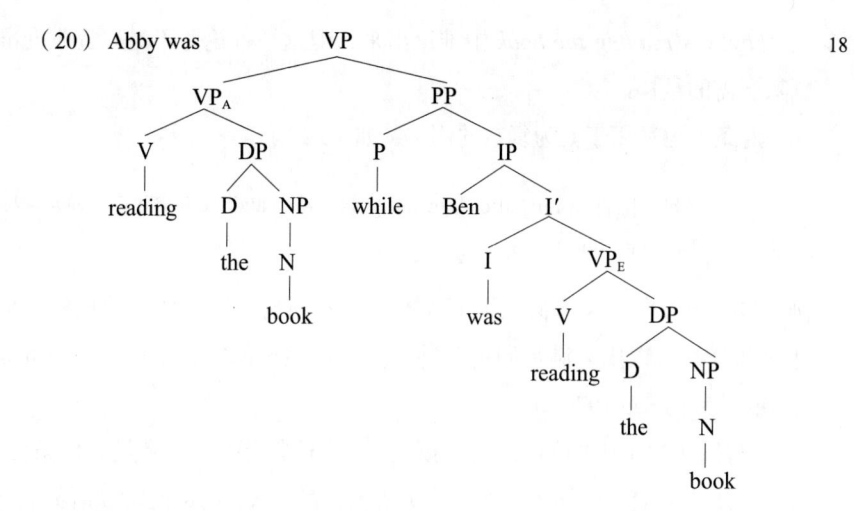

（20） Abby was [VP [VP_A [V reading] [DP [D the] [NP [N book]]]] [PP [P while] [IP Ben [I' [I was] [VP_E [V reading] [DP [D the] [NP [N book]]]]]]]]

在这一结构中，先行项 VP_A 和省略短语 VP_E 具有相同的结构。根据同构条件，VP_E 可以删除。

正如所预期的，同构条件不允许像（12a）这类结构中的内嵌式动词短语的删除。该例句的结构如（21）所示（假设不及物的 *read* 的隐性不定宾语不出现在句法结构中）：

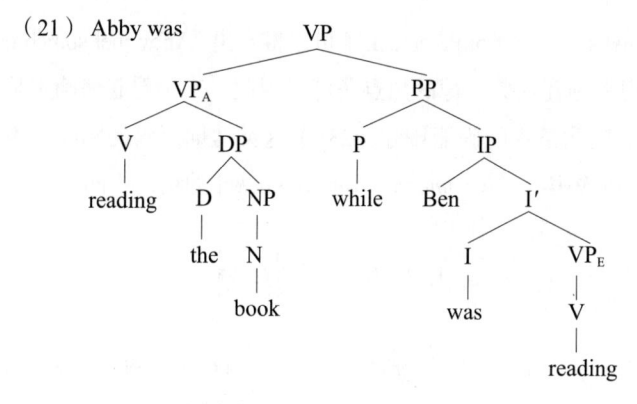

（21） Abby was [VP [VP_A [V reading] [DP [D the] [NP [N book]]]] [PP [P while] [IP Ben [I' [I was] [VP_E [V reading]]]]]]

由于 VP_A ≠ VP_E，故删除不被允许。

因此，关于删除的同构条件成功地解释了上述基本事实。但须注意的是，推论可行性总则在这里似乎并未起到作用；尽管 *Abby was reading* 可

从 *Abby was reading the book* 中推论出来，但这一推论并不足以提供允准删除所需的结构。

此条件也适用于更为复杂的例句，如（22）。

（22）Abby [$_{VP1}$ [$_{VP2}$ left] after Ben did [$_{VP3}$ leave]], and Carla did [$_{VP4}$ ~~leave after Ben did~~] too.

例（22）中 VP$_3$ 与 VP$_2$ 同构，而 VP$_4$ 与 VP$_1$ 同构。这表明，动词短语的任何部分都可以用来满足同构条件（支持该结论的完整论证见 Merchant 2000*b*；另见 Sag 1976*b*）。

当然，（22）中的例句不能用来证明以下推论：如果满足同构条件，就可以忽略一般的附加语。如（23）所示，最小 VP 内部的附加语不能被忽略。（23）中的例句只有（a）中的解读，即名词性附加语位于省略部位，而不能有（b）中忽略附加语的解读。

（23）Abby [$_{VP}$ met [$_{DP}$ [$_{DP}$ someone] from Kentucky]], and then Ben did.
 a =⟨meet someone from Kentucky⟩
 b ≠⟨meet someone⟩

因为由 ⟦Abby met someone from Kentucky⟧ 可以推导出 ⟦Abby met someone⟧，（23b）满足鲁思和施瓦茨柴尔德的焦点条件，因此（23）看起来确实是同构条件的结果。同构条件的确能排除（23b）这类动词短语的删除，因为该短语与先行动词短语 [*meet someone from Kentucky*] 的结构不同。

1.3 同构条件存在的问题

尽管同构条件成功地解释了上述现象，但它很快就遇到了一些问题。本节将列举其中的部分问题，有些问题可能比其他的更为严重，但这些均可为下文的语义研究路径做铺垫。

最明显的一个问题源自于简单的带隐性关联词（implicit correlates）

的截省句，如（24）。

（24） a Abby was reading, but I don't know what.
　　　 b Ben called—guess when!

（24a）先行 IP 和 CP 中的相关部分如（25）所示。

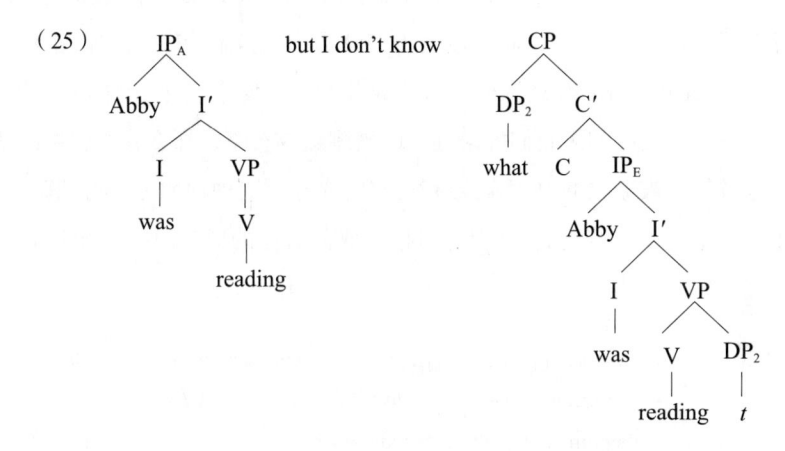

（25）
```
     IP_A              but I don't know      CP
    /   \                                   /  \
  Abby   I'                               DP_2  C'
        /  \                               |   /  \
       I    VP                           what  C  IP_E
       |    |                                    /  \
      was   V                                  Abby  I'
            |                                       /  \
         reading                                   I    VP
                                                   |   / \
                                                  was V  DP_2
                                                      |   |
                                                   reading t
```

在上文中我们看到，*read* 的不及物用法不能满足其及物用法下动词短语省略的同构条件。及物用法下动词短语省略必须包括一个直接宾语。显然，这同样适用于 IP 省略，此时 IP$_A$ ≠ IP$_E$。假设附加语 wh- 短语生成于 IP 内部（令人信服的论证见 Johnston 1994），那么（24b）会遇到同样的问题。

针对这一语料，我们可能会说，wh- 短语移位产生的语迹不会结构性地存在于逻辑形式中，而同构条件是在逻辑形式层面起作用的。这一观点使人联想到为消除逻辑形式中间语迹而提出的各种语迹修剪算法（如 Lasnik and Saito 1984）。但是消除逻辑形式结构中的语迹首先就直接违背了存在逻辑形式这一常理：如果语迹不出现在逻辑形式结构中，我们又怎么知道 wh- 短语所需的变项应该移到哪里？及物动词——如（24a）中的 *read*——对成分的要求如何得到满足？我们还必须提供另外的解释来说明那些切实表明语迹在逻辑形式中结构性存在的语料，特别是关于重构效应研究的语料（Romero 1997b, Fox 1999; 另见 Sauerland 1998, Merchant 2000a）。总的来说，此类观点把清晰的逻辑形式搞得一团糟，使同构条件沦为空谈。

然而，即便在截省句中，也有确凿证据表明，移位成分的语迹对省略起着重要的作用。荷兰语就是一个佐证。荷兰语是 V_2 型语言，最高动词前置至标句词位置（C），同时短语（XP）须前置至标句词短语的指示语位置（SpecCP）。在 V_2 结构中，这些成分的移位使它们在 IP 中对应的位置变为空壳，因此如果它们的语迹可以被删除或忽略，那么我们就可以认为，截省句中被删除的 IP 不需要有对应的成分。这种预期无法得到验证。下述例句中，只有当先行 IP 中有与移位成分对应的成分时，被删除的 IP 才能有合理的解读，这也是唯一合乎句法的可能情形：

(26) a [$_{CP}$ Nu gaat [$_{IP}$ zij t_{nu} t_{gaat}]], maar ik weet niet waarom.
          now goes she   but I know not why
    'She's going now, but I don't know why.'
   b *...waarom [$_{IP}$ zij]
   c =...waarom [$_{IP}$ zij nu gaat]

(27) a [$_{CP}$ Gisteren heeft [$_{IP}$ hij $t_{gisteren}$ met iemand gesproken t_{heeft}]],
          Yesterday has   he   with someone spoken
    maar ik weet niet met wie.
    but I know not with who
    'He spoke to someone yesterday, but I don't know who.'
   b *...met wie [$_{IP}$ hij met iemand gesproken]
   c =...met wie [$_{IP}$ hij gisteren heeft gesproken]

（当然，如果采用复制移位理论，上述反驳力度就会大大减弱。采用复制理论，在这种情况下，问题就变成了在何种语境下移位成分可以被忽略，而且如上所述，什么时候成为省略解决方案必不可少的一部分？）

同构条件在截省句中的第二个问题来自罗马尼亚语。如多布罗维耶-

索林（Dobrovie-Sorin 1993）和格罗苏（Grosu 1994: 224）所述，在某些（语篇关联的）wh- 短语疑问句中，附着成分复现现象（此处附着成分 l-'him'）是强制性的，如下例中的 care 'which'：[①]

（28） Pe   care   băiat *(l-)   ai   văzut?
　　　ACC   which   boy   him   have.2sg seen
　　　'Which boy did you see?'

尽管如此，如多布罗维耶-索林（私下交流）所提到的，在截省句中删除的 IP 可以与先行 IP 中非附着复现的关联成分对应：

（29） Am   văzut pe   un băiat dar nu știu   pe care.
　　　I.have   seen ACC   a boy   but not I.know ACC which
　　　'I saw a boy, but I don't know which.'

此句中已移位的 wh- 短语 pe care 应该有一附着复现成分，但已被删除，而先行 IP 中并没有与之对应的附着复现成分，因此不符合同构条件。

　　另一潜在的问题源于（30）至（32）中的截省，其中大部分都是被删除的不定式与其他类型的结构相对应：动名词，表将来时的助动词，表否定可能的助动词，现在和过去分词，例外成分，施事名词以及祈使语气动词。

（30） Decorating for the holidays is easy if you know how!
　　　a　≠ *... how [decorating for the holidays]
　　　b　= ... how [to decorate for the holidays]

[①] 瓦克纳格尔附着成分是雅各布·瓦克纳格尔（Jackob Wackernagel）在 1892 年发现的那些轻韵律成分（通常是附着成分），它们总是出现在小句的第二位置，主要来自希腊语和拉丁语。但是目前这一术语已经得到了扩展，它包括各种类型的"第二位置"附着成分或单词，而这就是本书所提到的内容。几乎所有分析都认为，这些附着成分对语音语境很敏感，而且可能被语音语境所驱动。我们也可以称它们为"像瓦克纳格尔所研究的那种附着成分"。——译者

(31) I'll fix the car if you tell me how.
   a ≠ . . . how [I'll fix the car]
   b = . . . how [to fix the car]

(32) a 'I can't play quarterback: I don't even know how.' (Bart, *The Simpsons*, 'Homer Coaches Football' episode)
   b Invest now! We'll tell you how! (BankOne advertisement)
   c Eat (something), if you figure out what!
   d Two or three men were crying. Others couldn't remember how. (O'Brien 1994: 103)
   e George . . . suffer[ed] . . . the very same sort of guilt trip he'd inflicted on countless others since he first learned how. (Brin 1991: 316)
   f He put his feet in the drawer, resting them on somebody's paper. He didn't look to see whose. (Dexter 1988: 58)
   g 'Cut it loose,' she said.
      'I don't know how.' (Dexter 1988: 203)
   h 'Do you know who the forger is?'
      'I talked to Seth Frank. Apparently Whitney learned how in prison.' (Scott Glenn in *Absolute Power*, 1997 US film)
   i 'Nobody'll talk to you, except for old Wakasha. I have no idea why.' (from the context it's clear that this means 'I have no idea why old Wakasha will talk to you') (Graham Greene in *Thunderheart*, 1992 US film)

（33）和（34）中的例句存在类似的问题。（33）中，动名词 *meeting him* 允准定式小句 *I met him* 的删除。同样，例句（34）已被证实（与 W. Klein 1993 中的例句类似），虚拟助动词 *würden* 'would' 似乎等同于情态动词 *sollten* 'should'，因为德语疑问句中 wh- 短语后不能直接跟不定式（参考（34a）），且情态助词 *gern* 不能出现在被删除的 IP 中（（34）不能有（34b, c）中给出的解读，只能解读为（34d））。

(33) I remember meeting him, but I don't remember when. [=I met him]

（34）Politiker   würden   gern helfen aber sie wissen nicht, wie.
　　　 Politicians would.SUBJ PRT help but they know not how
　　　 (*Die Zeit*, 31 Aug. 2000)
　　　 'Politicians would like to help but they don't know how.'
　　　 a ≠ ... * wie [zu helfen].
　　　　　　　　 how to help
　　　 b ≠ ... wie [sie gern helfen würden].
　　　　　　　　 how they PRT help   would
　　　 c ≠ ... wie [sie gern helfen sollten].
　　　　　　　　 how they PRT help   should
　　　 d = ... wie [sie helfen sollten].
　　　　　　　　 how they help   should

考虑到同构条件遇到的这些困难，有人也许会提出，基于上述讨论的原因，同构条件也许只适用于动词短语省略，而不适应截省。① 但是，那些使我们得出动词短语省略遵守同构条件的事实同样也存在于截省中。特别是，IP 去重音的可能性和制约因素与上述动词短语去重音是一样的。因此，（35a）和（35b）是可接受的，因为它们的意义被第一个 IP 所蕴涵，（36）是不可接受的，其情况与（16）和（17）中的动词短语相同。

（35）a Abby called Ben an idiot, but I don't know who else *she called an idiot*.
　　　 b Abby called Ben an idiot, but I don't know who else *she insulted*.

（36）*Abby called Ben an idiot, but I don't know who else *she dated*.

同样，（37）中的截省也不能有（37a）中的结构，而只能是（37b）。

（37）Abby called Ben an idiot, but I don't know who else.
　　　 a *Abby called Ben an idiot, but I don't know who else she insulted.

---

① 但是请特别参阅哈尔特（Hardt 1993），本着与我们这里对屈折短语省略结构分析同样的精神，哈尔特记录了一系列先行项与被省略动词短语之间存在着明显结构差异的语料。

25

b Abby called Ben an idiot, but I don't know who else ~~she called an idiot~~.

由此可见，我们采用同构条件解决的、动词短语省略中遇到的难题，同样存在于截省中。

关于同构条件，最后一个，也许是最重要的一个问题来自于省略，包括截省（见5.2节）和动词短语省略中（可能是复杂的）指称语和代词之间的等同性，如（38）所示。目前的研究只针对动词短语省略讨论过这一问题，所以这里我以动词短语省略为例。

（38） a They arrested Alex$_3$, though he$_3$ thought they wouldn't.
b They arrested [the guy who lives over the garage]$_3$, though he$_3$ thought they wouldn't.

正如菲恩戈和梅（Fiengo and May 1994）所指出的，如果被删除的动词短语和先行动词短语完全等同，那么我们会错误地预测出（38）应与（39）相同。

（39） a *He$_3$ thought they wouldn't arrest Alex$_3$.
b *He$_3$ thought they wouldn't arrest [the guy who lives over the garage]$_3$.

在（39）中，限定词短语 *Alex*$_3$ 和 *[the guy who lives over the garage]*$_3$ 被同标代词 he$_3$ 成分统制在各自小句中，这违反了约束三原则C，如（40）所述（见 Chomsky 1986*b*）。

（40） 约束三原则 C
带下标 *i* 的指称语 α 不能被任何带下标 *i* 的短语 β 成分统制，其中 β 处于论元位置。

显然（38）中的例句是合法的，并未违反约束三原则C。菲恩戈和梅（Fiengo and May 1994）提出"载体转换"操作，该操作允许与名词性成分相关的代词特征值在"重构"过程中发生变化。他们这一提议的有些细节并不完全清楚（尤见前一文献第218及后续页），但这些细节在此处并不重要（相关讨论见 Kennedy 1997, Giannakidou and Merchant 1998, Potts 1999, Safir 1999, 以及 5.2 节）。就我而言，他们发现的是，先行项中的指称语可以允准省略部位中代词的删除。参照手头的例句，这意味着被删除的动词短语并非如（41a, b）所示，而是（41c）。

（41） a *[$_{VP}$ ~~arrest Alex$_3$~~]
　　　 b *[$_{VP}$ ~~arrest [the guy who lives over the garage]$_3$~~]
　　　 c [$_{VP}$ ~~arrest [him]$_3$~~]

但是此类删除也会违反同构条件，因为被删除 VP 和先行 VP 的终端词汇是不同的。（为了确切地描写，有人或许会提出这是证明代词具有内部结构的间接证据：代词具有复杂内部结构，其内部结构根据语境需求而变化。但我认为这是在没有独立证据证明这种内部结构时的归谬法（*reductio*），在任何情况下都不可能拓展到称谓词的案例中。① 相关讨论和文献见 McCawley 1998: 第 11 章）。

那么，代词和指称语之间的这种不等同关系是如何满足我们上文所述的结构同构条件的呢？菲恩戈和梅是唯一严肃对待这一问题的作者，他们保留了同构条件，并提出为了能结构性比较，像 [代词性] 这种特征值可被视为"等价类"。也就是说，当省略部位确定包含一个结构上和词汇上都相同的指称语时，该指称语不会引发违反约束理论（约束三原则 C）的行为，因为该指称语（仅在省略部位时）被允许具有 [+代词性] 特征。这与其显性对应词不同，显性对应词必须具有 [-代词性] 特征。为了实现省略，我们假设，这种特征的错配，也就是"载体转换"的核心，因为删除的原因可以被忽略。尽管这种分析是可行的，而且菲恩戈和梅强调并严肃对待这一问题本身就是很大的贡献，但它并没有极大提高我们对这一

---

① 同样的问题也出现在含有复杂先行项的截省句中的简单疑问词上。

　（i）He talked to somebody from the Finance Department, but I don't know who.

此处，[who] 将不得不在结构上与 [somebody from the Finance Department] 同构。

现象的理解，也没有阐释为什么"载体转换"只出现在省略中（而不能出现在去重音中，否则去重音应该会表现出与省略相类似的特点）。认为通过"载体转换"就足以基于同构条件提出省略理论的做法，是混淆了诊断和治疗的区别。

1.4 修正的焦点条件和省略给定

此处要探究的另一种可能的路径，是修正或拒绝将结构同构作为省略的条件。最强硬、最有趣、但也最具挑战的观点认为省略的同构条件根本不存在。由于同构一说遇到了大量问题，我认为卓有成效的做法是彻底放弃同构说，尝试采用另外的方式来对这些语料做出解释，这是一种不迫使我们修改特征恒定的观点或不违反 wh- 移位的句法条件的方式。下文所提出的理论仅依赖省略的语义条件而非结构条件，这种做法与许多研究者的目标一致，他们也都追求纯粹的语义路径，如达尔林普尔等（Dalrymple *et al.* 1991）、哈尔特（Hardt 1993, 1999）、普鲁斯特（Prüst 1993）、普鲁斯特等（Prüst *et al.* 1994）、希伯等（Shieber *et al.* 1996）、阿舍等（Asher *et al.* 1997）、亨德里克斯和胡普（Hendriks and de Hoop, 出版中）等等。然而，此处所提出的观点具有独创性，与大多数明确假设省略部位存在句法结构的观点不同。

1.4.1 动词短语省略中的省略给定

尽管我此处的目的并不是提出一套完整的动词短语省略理论，但仍会提出一个修正的焦点条件，这一条件能够解释目前给出的所有语料。然而，我首要的目标是用这个新的焦点条件阐释下文 IP 省略的条件。该条件基于（42）中省略给定的定义，如（43）中所述。

（42）省略给定

当且仅当表达式 E 有一个凸显的先行项 A，且 ∃ 类型转换取模中

(ⅰ) A 蕴涵焦点闭包（E）①，且

(ⅱ) E 蕴涵焦点闭包（A）时

表达式 E 可被视为省略给定（e-GIVEN）

（43）动词短语省略的焦点条件

只有当动词短语 α 为给定时，α 才能被删除。

这里可以进行一些简化，但为了表述清楚暂先略去。应该说明清楚的是，该定义中唯一创新的内容是（42ii），由此可以轻易地将这一严格应用于省略部位的条件与上文讨论的更为普遍的条件区分开来。上文的那些理论与我这里的理论基础相同，但在某些方面更为简单，因为上文 1.2 节中更为普遍的焦点条件当然也适用于包括省略在内的结构。可为了简洁，我把省略结构的两个限制条件（更为普遍的焦点条件和（42ii））整合成一个定义——这允许我们谈到某个结构时，可以说仅满足省略的给定限制条件就够了，但细心的读者也许要记住这一定义的合并。

首先，让我们来看一下如何用（43）解释（18）和（19）中的例句，例句重述如下，同构条件正是基于此类例句提出的。

(44) a Abby was reading the book while Ben was.

　　b Abby ate a sandwich after BEN did.

　　c Abby left the party because BEN did.

　　d Abby sang her hymn louder than BEN did.

(45) a Abby called Chuck an idiot after BEN did.

　　b Abby ate a sandwich after BEN did.

　　c Abby left the party because BEN did.

以（45）为例，此处的关键是，根据我们对（45a）可能语义的直觉，确

---

① 当然，一般来说，也许在原则性的基础上（相关讨论见 5.2.1 节），一个被删除成分不会包含任何被焦点标记的内容；相反，从省略部位提取的内容就算不总是，但也经常是被焦点标记的。如上所述，我将假设，为了满足各种焦点条件，从省略部位所移出的成分的语迹会是 ∃ 约束的。

保（45a）中省略的动词短语源自（46a），而非源自（46b）。

（46） a ＝ ... after BEN did ~~call Chuck an idiot~~.
　　　 b ≠ ... after BEN did ~~insult Chuck~~.

首要任务是弄清（46a）中省略的动词短语是如何"给定"的。这里的先行项是第一小句中的动词短语 [$_{VP}$ call Chuck an idiot]。该动词短语有一个与主语相对应的开放变项（open variable），所以必须运用 ∃ 类型替换，从而得到（47）（（47）中 α' 表示将 ∃ 类型替换运用到 α 得到的结果）。

（47） VP_A' = ∃x.x called Chuck an idiot

现在第一个问题是通过 ∃ 约束变项，VP_A' 是否蕴涵被删除 VP 焦点标记部分的替换。让我们假设主语 BEN 在被删除 VP 内部的语迹也是被焦点标记的，这一点我认为无比重要。用 ∃ 约束变项替换该语迹，可以得到（48）：

（48） F-clo(VP_E) = ∃x.x called Chuck an idiot

那么很显然，VP_A' 蕴涵焦点闭包（VP_E）。第二个问题是 VP_E' 是否蕴涵 VP_A 的焦点闭包，如（49）所示。由于左右两边一致，所以答案是肯定的。

（49） F-clo(VP_A) = ∃x.x called Chuck an idiot

现在看例句（46b）。焦点闭包（VP_A）不变，但被删除的动词短语本身不同——对主语的语迹进行 ∃ 约束变项替换，得到（50）：

（50） VP_E' = ∃x.x insulted Chuck

现在第二个问题的答案发生了变化：VP_E' 不蕴涵焦点闭包（VP_A），因为你在侮辱某人的时候不一定非要称他或她为傻瓜，所以根据（42ii），（46b）中的动词短语不是给定的。因此，该动词短语不满足（43）中修正的焦点条件，不能删除。同样的道理也适用于（44）中的例句。

同构条件的取消，可以解决如（38）（重述如下）这样存在问题的案

例,(38)是促使载体转换提出的依据,而现在我们可以认为,被删除 VP 只是包含了一个常规代词:

(51) a They arrested Alex$_3$, though he$_3$ thought they wouldn't ~~arrest him~~$_3$.
     b They arrested [the guy who lives over the garage]$_3$, though he$_3$ thought they wouldn't ~~arrest him~~$_3$.

来看一下(51a)中的句子,被删除的动词短语满足焦点条件吗?当 *him* = *Alex* 的时候,是满足的。这是因为当 *him*(x_3)通过赋值函数被赋予与 Alex 相同的值,二者表示同一个体时,先行项 VP 通过 ∃ 类型替换取模,如(52a)所示,蕴涵被删除 VP 的焦点闭包,如(52b)所示。(Schwarzschild 1999: 154 也注意到了这一结果——当某一代词有一个同标的先行项时,该代词将被视为给定的。因为对任何 g 来说,⟦John$_i$⟧^{g} = ⟦he$_i$⟧^{g},所以可以允准谓词和代词之间去重音的等同关系。)当然,这正是我们所期望的结果。

(52) a VP$_A'$ = ∃x.x arrested Alex
     b F-clo (VP$_E$) = ∃x.x arrested him

第二个条件,即被删除 VP 的 VP′ 蕴涵先行 VP 的焦点闭包(VP),也同样得到满足。(有些复杂但能在与对认识兼容性和预设有关的自然假设下被解决的问题,如(51b)中所描述的,我在此不做探究,我也将避开第 16 页脚注 ① 中所提到的与语态(主动/被动)变化相关的问题。)

(43)中的焦点条件解决了触发载体转换① 的语料,同时也排除了缺

---

① 至少对菲恩戈和梅(Fiengo and May 1994)中考查得最好的"载体转换"背后的机制(指称语和代词之间的等同关系)来说是这样的。然而,"载体转换"这一术语在上述著作中使用广泛,在第 201—230 页中被以 12 种不同的方式加以应用,来解释省略中的非显著性变体。这些非显著性变体是否都能或都应采取同样的方式加以阐释须在将来的研究中加以探讨。须注意,目前的路径也体现了贝克和布雷姆(Baker and Brame 1972: 62)、萨格(Sag 1976a)所注意到的否定极性词(negative polarity items)和不定指短语在 VP 省略中的等同关系,菲恩戈和梅(Fiengo and May 1994)也将其列为"载体转换"中的一员。

失 VP 中不合法的"隐含连接"现象。① 我们的下一个问题是这一焦点条件是否能够同样成功地应用到截省句的分析中。

1.4.2 截省中的省略给定

要回答这个问题需要有更多的背景知识。特别是，它要求我们对问题的替代方案做一些具体的假设，以便确定什么应该算作"给定"。这里我采用罗梅罗（Romero 1998）的研究结果②，他表明，（6）和（9）中所展示的更为普遍的焦点条件可以卓有成效地应用到 IP 去重音和截省句中，以解释更多和范围更广的语料，尤其关于先行项的本质和辖域平行（这些问题在很大程度上与我们无关，尽管 5.4 节会简要地回应其中的某些问题）。就我们的目的而言，她的基本分析就足够了。其基本思想是，（53）中的所有问题都应该看作是彼此的替换。

(53) a (know③) which P are Q
  b (know) how many P are Q
  c (know) whether any P are Q

---

① 这也将确保在像（i）和（ii）这类情况中残余成分 XP 的对应成分必须承担着焦点（其中（ii）是假空缺（pseudogapping）的一种，我赞同许多研究者的观点，认为此结构涉及 VP 省略——参阅 Kennedy and Merchant 2000a）：
  (i) I saw [Abby]$_F$, but [Bart]$_F$, I didn't.
  (ii) I want to see [the Simpsons]$_F$ more than I do [the X-Files]$_F$.
例如在（i）中，VP$_E$'=∃x∃y[x saw y]，F-clo(VP$_A$) = ∃x∃y[x saw y]。须注意，此处 VP$_E$' 不蕴涵 VP$_A$'，VP$_E$'=∃x[x saw Abby]。如果 VP$_A$ 中的 Abby 没有焦点标记，焦点闭包（VP$_A$）就不会被 VP$_E$' 所蕴涵，VP$_E$ 也不能被删除。被删除 VP 所在的小句中也应会包含某些显性成分，以表明先行项中焦点闭包的可能性；相关讨论见 Fox 2000。
② 页码和例句编号引自书稿 1998 年版的第二章，我还没得到完成后的完整书稿。
③ 此处及后文，我用 know 作为嵌入谓词，假设由此例得出的结论可以得到推广（例如从语义上说，wonder 类的谓词会有一些等同于 know——'want to know' 之类的成分）；见罗梅罗的论述。用 I know ... 之类的表达作为先行项和包含截省的 CP 的导入结构（leader），可以让我们避免对评估给定条件来说十分必要的 ∃ 类型转换进行多重应用。虽然这些应用是常规情况，但它们也会把公式弄得极其混乱。

第一章 省略中的同一性：焦点和同构

罗梅罗进一步采纳了施瓦茨柴尔德的给定条件，并将其应用到包含 IP 省略的成分上（她表明鲁思的版本也同样适用，此处暂不谈及）。通过用"IP"替代"VP"来修改前文所提到的（9），得到（55）中的限制条件（为了方便，给定的定义重述如下）。

(54) 给定（Schwarzschild 1999）
当且仅当表达式 E 有一个凸显的先行词 A，且有 ∃ 类型替换取模时，A 蕴涵 E 的焦点闭包，表达式 E 为给定。

(55) IP 省略的施瓦茨柴尔德焦点条件（施瓦茨柴尔德版本）
当且仅当 α 或包含 α 的成分是给定时，IP α 才能被删除。

具体来说，假设这将允许空 IP，如（56）所示：

(56) I know how MANY politicians she called an idiot, but I don't know WHICH (politicians)[①].

在这种情况下，就会有如（57）所示的备选问题。

(57) a (know) which politicians she called an idiot
b (know) how many politicians she called an idiot
c (know) whether she called any politicians an idiot

通过 ∃ 约束变项，同类别替换缺失 IP 所在的 CP 的焦点标记部分，得到（58）；此处我用 Q 来代表疑问限定词的变项（见 Romero 1998: 18–22）。[②]

(58) ∃Q[I know [Q-politicians she called an idiot]]

[①] 大多数情况下，我忽略了 which 等之后的 NP 省略如何得到解决这一独立问题。
[②] 如果采用鲁思的限制条件，假设 E^f = 〖WHICH$_F$ (politicians) she called an idiot〗^{f} = {which politicians she called an idiot, how many politicians she called an idiot, whether she called any politician an idiot}，且 A = *how many politicians she called an idiot*，那么也会得到相同的结果。因此，正如所要求的，$A \in E^f$。详细例证见 Romero 1998。

在下述例句中，类似的运算为我们提供了预期的结果：

（59） I know she called some politician an idiot, but I don't know WHICH.

因为知道她叫某些政客傻瓜蕴涵知道她是否把任何一个政客叫作傻瓜（也就是说，"知道她是否把任何一个政客叫作傻瓜"是给定的），因此施瓦茨柴尔德焦点条件将得到满足。

但这还不足以达到我们的目的：使用（54）给定定义中的单向蕴涵会允准（60）中不合法的 IP 省略。

（60） *I know how many politicians she called an idiot, but I don't know WHICH (politicians) [$_{IP}$ she insulted t]

同样，这也是因为叫某人傻瓜在相关意义上蕴涵着侮辱某人。因此罗梅罗与她之前的学者一样，采取了逻辑形式同一性对焦点条件加以补充，从而排除上述类型的省略。但我们已经看到这种与 IP 省略同构限制条件相关的困难。与上述对动词短语省略的分析一样，我们可以通过放弃同构条件，采用上文中修正的焦点条件来解决 IP 省略这一问题。（42）中省略给定的定义复述如下。

（61） 省略给定

表达式 E 为给定，当且仅当表达式 E 有一个凸显的先行项 A，且∃类型替换取模中

（i）A 蕴涵焦点闭包，且

（ii）E 蕴涵 A 的焦点闭包。

根据此省略给定条件，我们现在提出 IP 省略的焦点条件：

（62） IP 省略的焦点条件

当且仅当 α 为省略给定时，IP α 才可以被删除。

来看一下这一限制条件是如何应用到下面例句中的。

（63） I know how MANY politicians she called an idiot, but I don't know WHICH (politicians).

首先，我们需要决定如何处理被删除 IP 和先行 IP 中 wh- 移位的语迹（同样，我暂时只关注 IP 内部没有焦点标记的情况，下文再回过头来讨论其他的情况）。问题与 VP 内部主语语迹一样，我采取与前文相同的做法，把这些语迹视为简单的存在约束变项。这种方便的过度简化的做法会使论述更加清楚，但应该记住，有确凿证据表明语迹具有比这种符号标示更多的结构（实际上，这一事实对某些案例的解释十分重要，此处不详叙；见 Romero 1997b, Sauerland 1998, Fox 1999, Merchant 2000a）。

基于此，可以得出（64），$IP_A{}'$ 蕴涵焦点闭包（IP_E），因此满足省略给定限制的第一部分。

（64） a F-clo(IP_E) = ∃x.she called x an idiot
b $IP_A{}'$ = ∃x.she called x an idiot

其次，$IP_E{}'$ 蕴涵焦点闭包（IP_A），满足省略给定限制的第二部分。因此，根据（62）中的焦点条件，IP_E 可以被删除。

以下例句也同样适用：

（65） I know she called some politician an idiot, but I don't know WHICH.

我们可以得出 IP_A 和 IP_E，满足（42i），如（66）所示。

（66） a $IP_A{}'$ = F-clo(IP_A) = ∃x.she called x an idiot
b $IP_E{}'$ = F-clo(IP_E) = ∃x.she called x an idiot

由于 IP_A 和 IP_E 完全相同，（42ii）也得到满足。

但须注意，（42ii）将会排除上文所讨论的那些原来焦点条件允准的例句：

（67） *I know how many politicians she called an idiot, but I don't know WHICH (politicians) [IP she insulted t]

现在我们可以得到：

（68） a F-clo(IP$_A$) = ∃x.she called x an idiot
　　　 b IP$_E$′ = ∃x.she insulted x

33 由于（68a）产生了（68b）所没有的蕴涵（因为 she insulted x 不蕴涵 she called x an idiot），基于（42ii），IP$_E$ 不是省略给定。因此，根据（62），IP$_E$ 不能被删除。

这些定义在解释钟等（Chung et al. 1995）发现的范例（其文中的（21））时有着令人满意的额外效果，如（69）所示：

（69） a *She served the soup, but I don't know who(m).
　　　　　（比较 She served the soup, but I don't know to whom.）
　　　 b She served the students, but I don't know what.

钟等（Chung et al. 1995）采用的是通过逻辑形式复制（LF-copying）来实现结构同构的方法，提出通过逻辑形式层面"萌生"（sprouting）操作的限制条件来阐释（69a）和（69b）中的不同。本质上，他们提出"萌生"是"由先行 IP 中特定论元结构的外延所允准的"（第 262 页），见莱文和拉帕波特（Levin and Rappaport 1988）对论元结构的表述：

（70） a $serve_1$: server ⟨meal (diner)⟩
　　　　　　　　　　　　　DP　　PP$_{to}$
　　　 b $serve_2$: server ⟨diner (meal)⟩
　　　　　　　　　　　　　DP　　DP

后面我会在 4.4 节中讨论他们的论述。但他们最根本的见解——截省句中不可能出现论元结构变换——在此处所提出的系统里也可以得到解释。在该系统下，假设（70）中的是词条，那么问题是：为什么这两个动词在允准未直接表述出论元的截省方面，其允准的能力是不同的？在已有的解释中，这一反差必须依附于那些未直接表述出的论元在其存在的可推理性方面的差异（句法–词汇界面是如何处理的似乎与此无关）。事实上，这种预期的反差的确存在。请注意下面两句连贯性的不同：

（71） a I served₁ the food, but there were no guests.

　　　 b #I served₂ the guests, but there was no food.

例句（71b）是矛盾的，因为使用 serve₂ 时，即使没有可选论元，句中也蕴涵一个主题论元。另一方面，由（71a）的合法性可见，serve₁ 不能蕴涵一个目标论元的存在（我可能只是单纯把食物放在桌上的盘子里）。这些事实也说明了（72）中不能去重音的原因：

（72） *She served₁ the meal, but I don't know WHO *she served₁ it to*.

　　　（比较 She served₁ the meal, but I don't know who *she served₁ it* TO.)

（72）中的介词不能去重音，因为它不是给定的。相关运算如（73）所示：34

（73） a IP$_A$ = she served the meal

　　　 b F-clo(IP$_E$) = ∃x[she served the meal to x]

根据焦点条件，IP$_A$ 必须蕴涵 IP$_E$ 的焦点闭包。既然事实并非如此，那么（72）中的 IP 就不能去重音。更不必说，IP 也不能被删除，如（69a）所示。因此，这一被注意到的差异也可以放到现有系统之中。

在继续讨论之前，我们必须考虑并排除最后一种可能性。钟等正确地观察到，截省情况下 *serve*₁ 不等同于 *serve*₂，这在我们现在的系统中如何处理？换句话说，是什么排除了（74）这种推导结果？

（74） *She served₁ the meal, but I don't know WHO$_i$ ~~she served₂ t$_i$ the meal~~.

　　　（比较 She served₂ someone the meal, but I don't know who$_i$ ~~she served₂ t$_i$ the meal~~.)①

---

① 须注意，正如登迪肯（M. den Dikken）向我指出（私下交流）的那样（本质上与 Baker and Brame 1972: 62 对其例句（31）的分析相同），第二个例句的合法性表明经常被提及的双宾语结构中第一宾语提取的限制（如（i），见 Fillmore 1965, Kuroda 1968）必须在 PF 界面起作用，不能被置入句法中的提取机制中。

　　（i） ??Who$_i$ did she serve t$_i$ the meal?

同样，该问题的答案取决于先行 IP_A 和被删除 IP_E 各自所产生的蕴涵，如（75）所示。

(75)　a　IP_A = she served the meal
　　　b　F-clo(IP_E) = ∃x[she served x the meal]

如上所见，$serve_1$ 不蕴涵存在一个食物接收者（供餐接收者）。但是在被删除 IP_E 中，IP 的 ∃- 闭包蕴涵存在一个与移位 wh- 短语相对应的接收者，因此先行 IP_A 必须用这一蕴涵时，省略才能被允准。

钟的研究让我注意到一个相关问题，涉及（76）这样的例句：

(76)　*Someone shot Ben, but I don't know by who(m) [$_{IP}$ Ben was shot t]

如果主动及物动词 shoot 的主语引发了 by 短语的宾语不能引发的与之意义相关的蕴涵，那么该句就会被排除。尽管此刻很难给出具体的细节，但不论这仅仅是基于观察得出的（论述与文献见 Dowty 1991），还是的确在词汇蕴涵中发现的，主动式/被动式的区别似乎可能与意义上的区别相对应。然而，这些区别已被特征化，省略给定条件似乎对这些区别很敏感。（上文已部分注意到，进一步的难题出现在动词短语省略中；然而还须注意的是，假空缺句表现出与（76）类似的情形：*Abby shot Ben {before / and} Chuck was by Dara.）

到目前为止，我们集中探讨的是那些先行 IP 中不包含焦点标记的例句。但对下面两种情况的考察也很有启发意义。

第一种情况可以通过（77）这类例句加以说明：

(77)　She called Ben an idiot, but I don't know who else [$_{IP}$ she called t an idiot].

如果先行 IP 中没有焦点标记，就违反了（42）的第（ii）条，因为被删除 IP 中自由变项的简单的存在性闭包可以使我们得到 IP_E' = ∃x.she called x an idiot。但 F-clo(IP_A) = She called Ben an idiot，不是 IP_E' 的蕴涵。这会违反（42ii），IP 删除被排除，但实际情况恰恰相反。

但当我们把必要焦点标记考虑进去，问题就解决了。请思考（78）中这一对句子的解读：

（78） a ABBY$_F$ called Ben an idiot, but I don't know who else.

　　　 b Abby called BEN$_F$ an idiot, but I don't know who else.

对（78a）和（78b）中截省的解读分别如（79a）和（79b）所示：

（79） a ... but I don't know who else called Ben an idiot.

　　　 b ... but I don't know who else Abby called an idiot.

这种分配与焦点条件所预测的完全一致。请根据（42ii）来详细考察（78a）。（80）中给出了用于比较的相关要素。

（80） a IP$_E'$ = ∃x.x called Ben an idiot

　　　 b F-clo(IP$_A$) = ∃x.x called Ben an idiot

由于两个等式相同，因此相关的蕴涵一致（即 IP$_E'$ → F-clo（IP$_A$））。但如果先行 IP 是（78b）中的第一个 IP，情况就不一样了，因为在那种情况下，F-clo(IP$_A$) = ∃x.*Abby called x an idiot*。对于（78b）而言，反之亦然：*Ben* 的焦点标记确保截省只能源于（79b），而不能源于（79a）。(*else* 的隐性论元在这些情况下必须被当作焦点标记成分，这一事实是根据 *else* 的自然语义（如 Romero 1998: 31（81））和更为普遍的焦点条件所得出的，推理过程与上文提到的代词的相同。)

　　第二种焦点标记在截省句中起作用的情况如（81）所示，我们可称之为"对比性"截省。

（81） a She has five CATS, but I don't know how many DOGS.

　　　 b The channel was 15 feet wide, but I don't know how deep.

　　　 c Abby knew which of the MEN Peter had invited, but she didn't know which of the WOMEN.

　　　 d We know which streets are being repaved, but not which avenues.

  e Max has five Monets in his collection, and who knows how many van Goghs.
  f There are nine women in the play, but I don't know how many men.
  g I know how many women are in the play, but I don't know how many men.
  h She's an absolute idiot: unaware of who she is, or where. (Wallace 1986)

请思考（81a）。我们可以假设（81a）的结构如（82）所示。

（82） She has [five CATS]$_F$, but I don't know how many DOGS [$_{IP}$ ~~she has t~~].

其相关运算如（83）所示，满足（42ii）。

（83） a $IP_E' = \exists x.\text{she has } x$
    b $\text{F-clo}(IP_A) = \exists x.\text{she has } x$

  如果我们只看 IP_A，而不能把与 wh- 短语中描述性内容 DOGS 相对比的成分提取出来，我们就会错误地预测删除不可能发生，因为 IP_E' 不蕴涵 *she has five cats*。与一般的 NP 省略一样，在 wh- 短语中没有对比成分的情况下，更为普遍地采用给定条件的焦点条件能够确保正确的描述内容得到理解（如 Romero 1998 所示）——只有在 wh- 短语中有对比成分的情况下，（42）中公式的必要性才得到充分体现。[1]

---

[1] 必须牢记更为重要的限制条件：焦点标记必须与从删除 IP 中提取的 wh- 短语中的成分进行对比，因此必须避免（i）这类例句：
  （i）A：Who did Abby see?
     B：*Abby [$_{VP:A}$ saw BEN$_F$], and Carla did [$_{VP:E}$ ~~see someone~~] too.
假设第一并列分句中 BEN 的焦点标记是由特殊疑问句所允准的，则 $\text{F-clo}(VP_A) = \exists x \exists y [x \text{ saw } y]$，$VP_E' = \exists x \exists y [x \text{ saw } y]$，因此如果没有更多的内容要说，删除可以被允准。到目前为止，为了便于呈现，我们忽略了一个事实：焦点标记必须是照应性的，省略给定条件对这些相互照应的关系必须是敏感的；有关如何对此进行编码的讨论和假设，见 Schwarzschild 1999, Schwabe 2000。在其余章节我将假设这种理论可以成功应用，且截至目前仍然是最简便的算法，请将这一点牢记于心。

1.5 小结

本章考察了一些省略的一般性条件，尤其是 VP 和 IP 去重音的限制条件是否与 VP 和 IP 省略的限制条件相同这一问题。虽然更为普遍的焦点条件仍适用于不同的省略结构，但我们发现，省略部位的解读所受到的制约远远超过与其对应的去重音的情况。

虽然大多数研究者已假设或论证，认为省略的这些额外的限制反映了结构同构限制条件，但我已证明这种限制条件在许多领域都存在很多问题，甚至在简单截省句中也失败了，没能就省略部位中的代词和与其对应的先行项中的指称语之间的等同关系，给我们一个满意的解释。相反，我通过采用施瓦茨柴尔德（Schwarzschild 1999）给定条件的扩展定义，此处称之为省略给定条件，对语料做了适当的区分。

基于这一修正的定义，我提出了一个简单的省略部位限制条件，它是对 VP 和 IP 省略的概括，如下所示：

（84） 省略的焦点条件
只有当成分 α 为省略给定时，α 才可被删除。

因为省略给定条件包含双向蕴涵限制（即，对照被删除 XP 的蕴涵核查先行 XP 的蕴涵，反之亦然；将观察到的由焦点成分引起的复杂问题进行取模（modulo）），与去重音不同，省略中的先行项与省略部位必须保持一致。

这一系统成功地解释了那些驱使结构同构条件提出的语料。因为它在本质上是语义性的，所以当焦点条件满足时，允许省略部位存在句法变异。这使该理论从整体上得到了重要简化，不再需要任何额外的理论来解释，特别是对截省的解释，如"载体转换"理论，或在截省语境下其他需要用来解释偏差的结构同一性理论。

第二章

截省的句法

本章将考察截省的结构条件，并探究其内部与外部的句法。第一个问题是外部句法，目前比较容易解决，且答案也很直接："截省"是一个CP。第二个问题则需要通过更间接的方式来考察省略的结构——隐性句法，所以也更加困难。这里要论证的是，省略部位具有和显性句法相类似的句法结构。

本章大致按照分析的难度展开。我们一开始先分析一个简单的问题，即通过考察截省句中 wh- 短语的外部分布来确定截省句的类型。结论非常清楚：截省表现为 CP。由此结论可以推导出一个假说：截省句包含着一个 CP，这一 CP 中的句子性部分，即 IP，被省略掉了。基于这一假说，我把目光转向更为复杂的问题，即什么样的句法机制允准了 IP 的省略。我们将会看到，这些允准条件的范围相当有限，仅限于这个空 IP 的 C 姐妹节点上的某些特征组合。为了找出这些限制条件，我提出了一个基于向 C 特征移位而触发语音形式省略的机制。通过解决由 2.2.2 节中创新性归纳所引起的令人困扰的分析性问题，我将得出以下结论：在截省句中，只有 wh- 短语能显性地出现在标句词（COMP）的域内。我认为这一事实与其他的、可能是韵律上的、对各种空成分的限制有关，这些空成分可以直接跟在标句词后面。

2.1 外部句法：作为一种疑问 CP 的截省

我将先考察截省成分的外部句法，即截省句中的 wh- 短语与其周围的句法成分是何种关系？本节整合选择性事实、数、格、句法位置和韵律等所呈现的论证，支持关于这一问题的普遍看法（opinio communis）——表面上单一孤立的 wh- 短语实际上是一个 CP。虽然这并不是令人惊异的结论，但却一直被质疑，所以在我们讨论由其引发的省略问题之前，必须先明确这一观点。

很多论点均来源于罗斯（Ross 1969）对截省所做的开创性的研究。因为很多文献都直接采纳了他的结论，我在此不再赘述。但有时学者会就截省是否必须包含 CP 而进行争论，范里姆斯迪克（van Riemsdijk 1978）认为截省不一定包含 CP，金兹伯格（Ginzburg 1992）在某种程度上也持这种观点。关键问题是，像（1）这样的截省句是含有（2）中所示的 CP，还是含有如（3）所示更为简单的结构，即 wh- 片段是基础生成的，在这里做动词 know 的补足语。范里姆斯迪克（van Riemsdijk 1978）认为是后者，而我支持前一观点。

（1）Anne invited someone, but I don't know who.

（2）疑问 CP 截省：

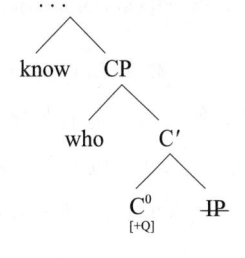

```
         ...
        /   \
     know   CP
            / \
          who  C'
               / \
              C⁰  I̶P̶
             [+Q]
```

（3）"wh- 片段"截省：

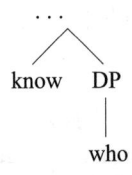

```
        ...
       /  \
    know   DP
            |
           who
```

接下来我们很快会看到，不管以什么标准来检验，截省的 wh- 短语都不是内嵌谓词的直接论元，而是一个完整的疑问 CP。

2.1.1 选择

正如罗斯（Ross 1969）所指出，关于什么样的谓词能允许其补足语截省，什么样的不能允许截省，可以概述如下：

（4）所有且只有语义选择（s-select）问句和范畴选择（c-select）CP 的谓词，才能允准 wh- 短语截省。

尽管例（1）中的 *know* 允许的补足语 CP 既可以是疑问句，也可以是非疑问句，但当我们进一步考察像 *wonder* 这样只能带疑问补足语的动词时，如（5a）和（5b）间的对比所示，我们就会发现像例（6）中的截省是成立的。

（5）a *I wonder {the time/the answer/the question}.
  b I wonder {what time it is/what the answer is/what Ben asked/who's coming}.

（6）a Ben wanted to ask something. I wonder what.
  b Abby said someone's coming to dinner. We're all wondering who.

的确，我们考察一些词汇义上有歧义的谓词时，例如 *know* 或 *remember*，发现其截省解读通常是在给定语境下唯一可能的解读。尽管如例（7）中所示，*know* 和 *remember* 可以选择 DP 做其宾语，也可以如例（8）所示选择 CP 做其补足语，但当语境要求截省时，原本的歧义就不复存在了，只有内嵌 CP 的解读，如例（9）所示。

（7） a Jack knows Guard Mulligan.

　　　b Jill remembers the important announcement from yesterday.

（8） a Jack knows which guard was present.

　　　b Jill remembers what I told you yesterday.

（9） a He claimed one of the guards had been present. Who knows which?

　　　b I told you something important yesterday. Which of you remember what?

在给定语境下,（9a）只能被解读为包含截省 CP 的（10a）,而不可能是如（10b）所示的多重 DP 疑问句。换句话说,对（9a）可能的回答是（11a）中的那些句子,而不是（11b）。

（10） a （9a）= Who knows which guard he claimed had been present?

　　　 b （9a）≠ Who knows which guard?

（11） a Jack does. /Jack knows which.

　　　 b #Jack knows Guard Mulligan, Bill knows Guard Keeley, etc. /#Everyone knows the guard outside his cell.

这些所谓谓词中 wh-DP "宾语" 的截省解读和那些常规的、真正的宾语之间的区别,在范里姆斯迪克的理论下完全是神秘的,这两者的区别不复存在。相反,例（9a,b）的相关解读表明我们处理的是这些动词的一般性 CP 补足语。

2.1.2　数的一致

罗斯（Ross 1969）提出的第二点是,带截省 wh- 短语的主动词,与 CP 主语保持数的一致,与 wh- 短语自身数的标记没有关系。正如例（12a）所示,CP 主语要求动词必须是单数形式（见 McCloskey 1991c 和其中的文献）,同样,例（12b）中截省的复数 wh- 短语也要求动词必须为单数形式。

（12） a [$_{CP}$ Which problems are solvable] {is/*are} not obvious.

　　　 b Some of these problems are solvable, but [which problems] {is/*are} not obvious.

2.1.3 格

罗斯赞同乔治·威廉姆斯（George Williams）的观点，"疑问词必须和前行小句中的某一 NP 保持格一致"（1969: 253）。他用动词 *schmeicheln* 'flatter' 和 *loben* 'praise' 来阐释这一观点，在德语中，*schmeicheln* 赋予其宾语与格，*loben* 赋予其宾语宾格，如（13）和（14）。

(13) Er will   jemandem   schmeicheln, aber sie wissen nicht,
he wants someone.DAT flatter   but they know   not
{wem   /*wen}
who.DAT who.ACC
'He wants to flatter someone, but they don't know who.'

(14) Er will   jemanden   loben, aber sie wissen nicht,
he wants someone.ACC praise but they know   not
{*wem /   wen}
who.DAT who.ACC
'He wants to flatter someone, but they don't know who.'

这些例子也表明，即便内嵌句中的谓词能赋格，截省的 wh- 短语的格也和该谓词对其宾语所赋的格无关。如例（15）所示，*wissen* 'know' 作为及物动词时，赋予其宾语宾格。然而如例（13）所示，如果省略部位具有像 *schmeicheln* 这样的动词的解读或理解，截省的 wh- 短语不能是宾格。

(15) Sie   wissen {*der Antwort /   die Antwort} nicht.
they know   the answer.DAT the answer.ACC not
'They don't know the answer.'

下面希腊语的例子也表明相同的观点。在（16a）中，主语必须是主格。与之相对照的（16b）中，动词 *ksero* 'know' 通常赋宾格。

(16) a Kapjos   irthe, alla dhe ksero   {pjos /   *pjon}.
someone came, but not know.1sg who.NOM who.ACC
'Someone came, but I don't know who.'

b Dhe ksero   {*i apantisi   / tin apantisi}.
   not know.1sg   the answer.NOM   the answer.ACC.
   'I don't know the answer.'

英语中也有类似的语言事实，即代词性属格（prenominal genitives）：

（17） Somebody's car is parked on the lawn, but we don't know {whose/*who}.

但是仅凭 whose，我们还不能断定我们所讨论的就是一个具有格标记的 wh- 短语，因为此句更像是 NP 省略，如 [whose [$_{NP}$ car]] is parked on the lawn? 和 [Ben's [$_{NP}$ car]] is parked on the lawn（见 Lobeck 1995）。但是这一点并不受隐形裹挟式移位（pied-piping）的影响，即 wh- 短语的格必须和它的先行项（（17）中的 somebody's）的格保持一致，不能变化。我们在第三章中再来探讨这些事实。

然而 wh- 短语的格与其先行项"一致"，并不是全部内容，以上谈到的仅仅是**有**先行项的情况。当 wh- 短语缺乏显性先行词时，截省 wh- 短语的格特征也不是自由的，必须完全独立于内嵌谓词所能赋予名词性宾语的格。截省 wh- 短语的格总是与其在完整 CP 中未被省略的对应成分一致。此关联性如（18）中所述：

（18） wh- 短语只能从省略的 IP 内部格位置显示出格标记，而非内嵌句的谓词。

通过考察例（19）这样没有 DP 先行项的例子，我们可以看出此关联性：

（19） A car is parked on the lawn, but we don't know {whose/*who}.

有些动词既可以赋予宾语某一特定格，也可以作为不及物动词出现。这类动词也可以体现上述关联性。如德语中的 helfen 'help' 可以赋予其宾语与格。

（20） Er meinte, er hätte, geholfen, aber wir wüßten nicht,
he thought he had.SUBJ helped but we knew.SUBJ not
{wem /*wen}.
who.DAT who.ACC
'He claims he helped, but we wouldn't be able to say who.'

所有这些例子中截省 wh- 短语的格都是由省略的谓词赋予的，或者由其在省略小句中的功能所决定的，而不是由内嵌句的谓词来赋予。

另一个反驳光杆补足语分析法的论据，来自于在一定条件下可以带内嵌疑问句的形容词，如 *obvious*、*clear*、*certain* 等（从本质上说，这些形容词允许其后出现 CP 补足语，这些 CP 补足语的合法言外之力由其主句特点决定：见 Adger and Quer 1997 及其中的文献）。例（21）是其中一个例子：

（21） Somebody had called, but it wasn't clear who (had called).

然而按照标准假说，这些形容词并不能赋格，这可以解释例（22a）的不合法性。事实上，即使在被认为格不起作用的结构中，如（22b）这样的 *there* 插入结构，*clear* 也不可能带 DP 补足语。

（22） a *It wasn't clear his idea(s).
b *There weren't clear his ideas.

例（21）中的截省句与这些句子的对比反驳了 wh- 片段分析法。即使像 *worth* 这样可以赋格的形容词，也不能允准 CP 补语，所以也不能允准截省。

（23） a The watch is worth five dollars.
b *The watch isn't worth which bonds he cashed in.
c *He cashed in some bonds, but I don't think the watch is worth which.

以上所有例句都表明，截省的 wh- 短语的格必须从被省略 IP 的内部赋格者处获取，而不是从内嵌句的谓词处获取。

2.1.4 位置分布

另外一个证明截省是 CP 的强有力论据是不同语言中截省 wh- 短语的位置分布,基本可以概括为(24):

(24) 被截省 wh- 短语的残余部分可能出现的位置,与完整 CP 问句可能出现的位置总是相同的,而不可能出现在未移动的 wh- 短语的位置上。

罗斯(Ross 1969)考察了英语中的外置结构(extraposition),他的发现将会在接下来的小节中讨论。在 2.1.4.2 中,我将从德语、荷兰语、爱尔兰语和印地语中找出相似的语言现象,提供更多论据。

2.1.4.1 英语的外置结构

罗斯(Ross 1966)发现,如果截省的 wh- 短语不是被 CP 支配的话,像(25)和(26)之间的对比就会变得扑朔迷离。在(25)中,我们发现,形容词性谓词 *clear* 不允准 DP 论元的"外置"。

(25) a The correct approach wasn't clear.
　　　b *It wasn't clear the correct approach.

然而,这一模式似乎可以与截省的 wh-DP 一同出现,如(26b)所示。

(26) a One of these approaches is correct, but [which of them] is not clear.
　　　b One of these approaches is correct, but it's not clear [which of them].

当然,按照 CP 来分析,这只是简单地反映了疑问式 CP 可以作为主语,或者在外置结构中出现:

(27) a [$_{CP}$ Which of these approaches is correct] is not clear.
　　　b It's not clear [$_{CP}$ which of these approaches is correct].

罗斯还给出了 wh- 介词短语和副词性短语的例子,这两种类型的短语都不能做 *clear* 的论元:

（28） a　*{With Bob/Quickly} wasn't clear.

　　　 b　*It wasn't clear {with Bob/quickly}.

但这两种类型的 wh- 短语都可以出现在截省中：

（29） a　We know that he was eating, but {with whom/how rapidly} isn't clear.

　　　 b　We know that he was eating, but it isn't clear {with whom/how rapidly}.

如果认为 wh- 短语直接作为 *clear* 的论元生成的话，以上这些模式就会变得难以捉摸。

2.1.4.2　$SO_{DP}VO_{CP}$ 语言

位置分布的另外一个论据来自于名词性论元（包括 wh- 短语）出现在谓词的一侧，而小句性论元（包括疑问式 CP）出现在另一侧的语言。德语、荷兰语、印地语和爱尔兰语具有这一特点：就名词性论元而言，在某些特定情况下，都是 SOV 结构（在德语和荷兰语中，名词性论元仅出现在内嵌小句中；在爱尔兰语中，名词性论元仅出现在非限定小句中），但通常情况下，CP 论元都必须出现在动词的右侧（或者是我们将会看到的话题化情况）。把这一语言现象纳入到我们对截省的两种分析方法中，会得出不同的预测：如果截省的 wh- 短语，像其他非小句性论元那样，只是在小句中基础生成的 wh- 片段，那它应该出现在动词的左边（在中场[①]）。如果 CP 分析是正确的，被截省的 wh- 短语应该出现在动词的右边（在后场[②]）。这里我们先聚焦于德语，荷兰语和德语的语料在这一点上是类似的，最后我们会讨论印地语和爱尔兰语。

在德语中，wh- 短语可以出现在多重疑问句内部，如例（30）：

[①]　原文为 in the Mittelfeld，指德语句子的框形结构以内的位置。——译者

[②]　原文为 in the Nachfeld，指德语句子中框形结构的第二个成分之后的区域。在德语句子为正常语序时不被占据，破框结构时有些句子成分进入后场。——译者

(30) Wann hat Elke gestern　　[was/ welches Auto] repariert?
　　　when has Elke yesterday　what/ which　car　repaired
　　　'When did Elke fix {what/which car} yesterday?'

通常认为，这些 wh- 短语不能像 DP 那样可挪移（Fanselow 1990; Müller and Sternfeld 1993），这就产生了（31）中的对比。在（31a）中，我们可以看出，宾语 DP 可以挪移到主语和副词的前面，但在（31b）中，相应的 wh- 短语则不能。①

(31) a　Wann　hat　[das Auto]$_1$　Elke　gestern t_1　repariert?
　　　　when　has　the car　　Elke yesterday　repaired
　　　　'When did Elke repair the car yesterday?'
　　 b　*Wann　hat　[{was/ welches Auto}]$_2$ Elke　gestern t_2　repariert?
　　　　When has　what/which　car　Elke　yesterday repaired
　　　　（'When did Elke fix {what/which car} yesterday?'）

例（32）中的语料表明，DP 出现在最后动词的右边会降低句子的可接受度；任何 wh- 短语出现在此位置，比定指短语 *das Auto* 的可接受度还要差（比较英语中相似的重 XP 转移）。

(32) a　*Wann　hat　Elke　gestern t_1　repariert　[das Auto]$_1$?
　　　　when　has　Elke yesterday　repaired　the car
　　　　（'When did Elke fix the car yesterday?'）

---

① 这一论断多少有些过于简略：就挪移来说，wh- 短语似乎表现出与不定指成分相同的特点。见（i）中一个经论证的例子（出自 *Die Zeit*, 2000 年 10 月 12 日，第 47 页）。

(i)　...gründlicher　ist wissenschaftlich notiert worden, wer　wann　was　wie
　　　more.rigorouly is scientifically　　noted　been　who when what how
　　lange sieht.
　　long　watches
　　'...it has been more rigorously scientifically recorded who watches what when for how long [on TV].'

更多的例子见 Beck 1996。

b *Wer hat gestern t_2 repariert [welches Auto]$_2$?
     who has yesterday   repaired which car
     ('Who fixed which car yesterday?')

另一方面，完整的内嵌疑问式 CP，不能出现在小句内部——它们要么如（33a）那样外置于小句，要么像（33b）那样出现在 CP 指示语位置（Spec-CP）（参阅 Büring 1995 和 Müller 1995 的论证：CP 在小句内部生成，通过移位移至所显示的位置）①：

（33） a Wir haben nicht gewußt, [welches Auto Elke repariert hat].
         we have not known, which car Elke repaired has
       b *Wir haben [welches Auto Elke repariert hat] nicht gewußt.
       c *Wir haben nicht [welches Auto Elke repariert hat] gewußt.
       d [Welches Auto Elke repariert hat] haben wir nicht gewußt.
         'We didn't know which car Elke repaired.'

同样情况也适用于印地语（感谢巴特（R. Bhatt）与我讨论并提供语料）：

（34） a Mujhe nahīī pataa   [ki Gautam ne kis se baat kii   thii].
         I.DAT NEG knowledge that Gautam ERG who with talk do.PFV PAST
       b *Mujhe nahīī [ki Gautam ne kis se baat kii thii] pataa.
       c *Mujhe [ki Gautam ne kis se baat kii thii] nahīī pataa.
       d [Gautam ne kis se baat kii   thii], mujhe (yeh) nahīī pataa.②
         Gautam ERG who with talk do.PFV PAST I.DAT it$_{CP}$ NEG knowledge
         'I don't know who Gautam talked to.'

至关重要的是，在德语和印地语中，被截省的 wh- 短语和内嵌的

---

① 应该注意，在这一方面，内嵌疑问句和内嵌命题的表现有所不同。内嵌命题可能出现的位置由内嵌谓词决定。(见 Webelhuth 1992, Büring 1995)。

② 因为一些相对独立的原因，标句词 ki 不会出现在前置的定式小句中：
  (i) *[ki Gautam ne kis se baat kii   thii], mujhe (yeh) nahīī pataa.
      that Gautam ERG who with talk do.PFV PAST I.DAT it$_{CP}$ NEG knowledge
      ('Who Gautam talked to, I don't know.')

[+wh]CP 出现的位置相同，而不会像原位 wh- 短语那样出现在小句内部：

（35） [Daß Elke ein Auto repariert hat] haben wir gewußt, aber...
that Elke a car repaired has have we known but
'We knew that Elke repaired a car, but...'
a wir haben nicht geahnt, [welches].
   we have not suspected which
b *wir haben [welches] nicht geahnt.
c *wir haben nicht [welches] geahnt.
d [welches] haben wir nicht geahnt.
   'we had no idea which.'

（36） Gautam ne kisi se baat kii thii, lekin
Gautam ERG someone with talk do.PFV PAST but
'Gautam talked with someone, but...'
a mujhe nahīī pataa [kis se].
   I.DAT NEG knowledge who with
b *mujhe [kis se] nahīī pataa.
c *mujhe nahīī [kis se] pataa.
d [kis se] (yeh) mujhe nahīī pataa.
   'I don't know with who.'

（35）和（36）中的语料完全符合截省的 wh- 短语居于完整 CP 指示语位置这一假设，而不符合 wh- 短语仅仅是在主句中基础生成的推断。

相同的论据也存在于爱尔兰语中。尽管爱尔兰语在这方面的语言事实不如德语和印地语那样丰富，但在某些环境下，CP 补足语和 DP 补足语占据不同位置（感谢麦克洛斯基（J. McCloskey）提供的语料）。在非定式（限定）小句中，DP 宾语必须出现在动词前面，如例（37）。

（37） Rinne sé socrú le duine den dís,
made he arrangement with person of.the two
a ...ach níl sé sásta [rud ar bith] a inseacht dúinn.
but not.is he willing anything tell[-FIN] to.us

53

b ... *ach níl sé sásta a inseacht dúinn [rud ar bith].
　　'He made an arrangement with one of the two people, but he won't tell us anything.'

但内嵌的 CP，必须出现在小句末尾：

（38）a ... *ach níl　　sé sásta　[caidé a tá ar bun]　a inseacht　dúinn.
　　　　　　but not.is　he willing　what C is going-on　tell[-FIN]　to.us
　　b ... ach níl sé sásta a inseacht dúinn [caidé a tá ar bun].
　　'... but he won't tell us what's going on.'

同样地，被截省的 wh- 短语出现在 CP 所能出现的位置上，即小句末尾，而不是像 DP 论元那样出现在小句内部：

（39）a ... *ach níl　　sé sásta　[céacu ceann]　a inseacht　dúinn.
　　　　　　but not.is　he willing　which of.them　tell[-FIN]　to.us
　　b ... ach níl sé sásta a inseacht dúinn [céacu ceann].
　　'... but he won't tell us which of them.'

这些语料再次证明了截省的 wh- 短语和 CP 之间的同一关系。[①] 我们也应注意，这些语料表明，无论是何种因素制约着这些语言中 CP 小句的

[①] 朱迪丝·艾森（Judith Aissen）向我提及（私下交流），索西（Tzotzil）语中一些附着成分附加在语调短语的右边缘。基于这种分布，似乎也可以得出相似的论点，即是 CP 而不是 DP，才可以外置，进而产生这种词序 ...enclitic CP 而不是 *...enclitic DP。在这一点上，截省的 wh- 短语应该表现得像一个完全的、外置的小句，而不是一个 DP。下面是她提供的假想的语料：

（i）[Someone left ...]
　　a　pero mu sna'　li Xun-e　buch'u (ibat).
　　　but NEG he.knows the Juan-ENC who　left
　　b *pero mu sna'　li Xun buch'u-e.
　　　but NEG he.knows the Juan who-ENC
　　'but Juan doesn't know who (left).'

如果这些语料是正确的，就表明截省的 wh- 短语位于 CP 的内部。关于前附着形式更多的讨论，见 Aissen 1992。

边缘特性，仅仅诉诸于语音重量（phonological weight），通过音节的数目或者相类似的方法来解释是不够的。相反，这些语料清楚地表明，若像常规假定的那样，这些语言成分出现的位置是由韵律原因驱动的，那么这些韵律规则应该对更高一级的韵律结构敏感，而不一定会对（例如音节）容量敏感。换句话说，如果是语调短语必须外置，但可能不是更小的韵律短语，那么句法范畴 CP 必须凭借自身的句法结构直接投射语调短语。这对我来说是一个喜闻乐见的结论，尽管从句法范畴到韵律阶（prosodic exponence）的推导过程，我在这里并不会深入探究。

2.1.5　德语中的 wh- 重音转移

我的最后一个论据是基于德语 wh- 短语的重音对比。霍勒（Höhle 1983）注意到了这一现象，赖斯（Reis 1985）对此也曾予以探讨。这些作者指出，在主句的 SpecCP 位置上，某些多音节的 wh- 词重音是可变的，如（40）和（41）；重音既可落在 wh- 词（$wV-$）的算子部分，也可落在非算子部分（本质来讲是嵌入的介词）。但是在内嵌小句中，重音只能出现在 wh- 词的非算子部分，如（42）和（43）所示。我并非要解释这一对比，而仅仅想说明，截省的 wh- 短语和内嵌环境下的 wh- 短语具有类似的特点。

（40）a　Warúm ist Elke gekommen?
　　　b　Wárum ist Elke gekommen?
　　　　 why　　is　Elke　come
　　　 'Why did Elke come?'

（41）a　Worán hat Elke gedacht?
　　　b　Wóran hat Elke gedacht?
　　　　 what-on has Elke thought
　　　 'What was Elke thinking about?'

（42）a　Wir haben nicht gewußt, [warúm Elke gekommen ist].
　　　b　*Wir haben nicht gewußt, [wárum Elke gekommen ist].
　　　　 we　have　not　known　why　Elke　come　　is

'We didn't know why Elke came.'

(43) a Wir wollten gerne wissen, [worán Elke gedacht hat].
     b *Wir wollten gerne wissen, [wóran Elke gedacht hat].
       we would gladly know what-on Elke thought has
       'We'd love to know what Elke was thinking about.'

请注意，这种重音上的差异和内嵌深度有关，而不仅仅和句首位置有关，因为出现在话题化 CP 的指示语位置上的 wh- 短语仍然不能允许词首重音：

(44) a [Warúm Elke gekommen ist] haben wir nicht gewußt.
     b *[Wárum Elke gekommen ist] haben wir nicht gewußt.
       why Elke come is have we not known
       'Why Elke came, we didn't know.'

(45) a [Worán Elke gedacht hat] wollten wir gerne wissen.
     b * [Wóran Elke gedacht hat] wollten wir gerne wissen.
       what-on Elke thought has would we gladly know
       'What Elke was thinking about, we'd love to know.'

词首重音有时也可以出现在小句内部的 wh- 短语上（恕与 Reis 1985 看法不同）。例如，在回声多重疑问句中可以发现这一重音模式：

(46) a Wer will wohín fahren?
     b Wer will wóhin fahren?
       who wants where.to to drive
       'Who wants to go where?'

(47) a Wer ist warúm gestorben?
     b Wer ist wárum gestorben?
       who is why died
       'Who died for what reason?'

即使在 wh- 虚位结构[①]中（见 McDaniel 1989, Müller 1995），可能在逻辑形式层面位于句首 SpecCP 位置，但拼读时不出现在此位置的 wh- 词，也不能带词首重音：

（48） a   Was hast du nochmal gesagt, worán ich dich erinnern sollte?
       b *Was hast du nochmal gesagt, wóran ich dich erinnern sollte?
          what have you again said   what-on I you remind should
         'What did you say again that I was supposed to remind you about?'

非常重要的一点是，在内嵌小句中，截省结构中的 wh- 短语只能带词尾重音，如（49）和（50）；即使如（50）和（52）所示前置，也只能带词尾重音：

（49）Elke ist gekommen, aber wir haben nicht gewußt
       Elke is come   but we have not known

[①] 越过 wh- 虚位本身的截省是不可能的，即使其对应的问句形式合乎语法也不行，如例（ii）：
   （i）*Du hast mir gesagt, ich sollte dich an jemanden erinnern, aber ich weiß
        you have me told I should you on someone remind but I know
     nicht mehr, [was^x [du~~ mir gesagt hast, an wen* ich dich erinnern sollte~~]]
     not longer what you me told have on who I you remind should
     ('You told me to remind you about someone, but I can't remember who.')
   （ii）Was^x hast du mir gesagt, an wen^x ich dich erinnern sollte?
       What have you me told,   on who I   you remind should
     'Who did you tell me to remind you about？'
导致这一现象的原因可能是被截省的 wh- 短语的残余部分承担着焦点信息，但 wh- 虚位成分，以及一般的虚位成分，都不能是焦点。对比（iii）的例子：
   （iii） a *IT was raining.
        b *THERE are prisoners in the yard.
        c *IT is obvious that I'm right.
        d *WAS hast du gesagt, an wen ich dich erinnern sollte?
          what have you said   on who I you remind should
        ('Who did you say I should remind you about?')

　　　　a　[warúm].
　　　　b　*[wárum].
　　　　　　why
　　　　'Elke came, but we didn't know why.'

（50）Elke ist gekommen, aber
　　　　Elke is come　　　but
　　　　a　[warúm] haben wir nicht gewußt.
　　　　b　*[wárum] haben wir nicht gewußt.
　　　　　　why　　have　we　not　known
　　　　'Elke came, but we didn't known why.'

（51）Elke hat an etwas　　gedacht, und wir würden gerne wissen
　　　　Elke has on something thought and we would PRT know
　　　　a　[worán].
　　　　b　*[wóran].
　　　　　　what.on
　　　　'Elke was thinking of something, and we'd love to know what.'

（52）Elke hat an etwas　　gedacht, und
　　　　Elke has on something thought and
　　　　a　[worán]　würden wir gerne wissen.
　　　　b　*[wóran] würden wir gerne wissen.
　　　　　　what.on whould we　PRT　know.
　　　　'Elke was thinking of something, and what, we'd love to know.'

以上语料再次证明截省的 wh- 短语位于内嵌 CP 的指示语位置，否则将很难解释上述差异。

2.1.6　小结

由以上所见五点原因，我们可以相信：截省的 wh- 短语是 CP 中可辨别的一部分，CP 的句域被省略，而这些被截省的短语，并不像范里姆斯迪克（van Riemsdijk 1978）所说的那样，仅仅是一个片语，由语法直接生成，并插入到 CP 位置。在本书其余部分，我们可以断定，截省至少有如（53）所示的结构。这一结构假定 wh- 短语出现在 CP 指示语位置上，但基于上文所考察的语言中的疑问式结构的显性表征，我认为这是一个无效假设。对于这种移位是否必须是显性的这一问题，我们在接下来考察 wh- 原位语言时会进行探讨，但总的来说，我将基于 wh- 残余部分直接由 CP 来支配这一假设进行研究。

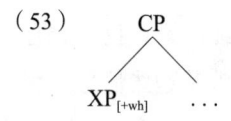

（53）
```
        CP
       /  \
  XP[+wh]  ...
```

既然截省的外部句法结构已经建立，那么我们接下来将探讨更为复杂的内部句法问题。

2.2　内部句法：截省的隐藏结构

探究截省的内部句法，意味着要探究无声现象中隐性的结构：为了生成可以被理解的省略短语，我们要确定什么样的结构必须出现。众所周知，关于省略解读的任何理论的当务之急，是为解读提供合适的语料。在此书所建立的理论框架下，这预示着要给 LF 层面提供合理的结构，不过这些自然会由不依赖于结构条件的解释性机制来补充。

尤其是对于截省，这意味着，缺失的 IP 必须在句法层面上解释：要么是出现在整个句法推导过程中，最后在语音形式层面被省略；要么是通过逻辑形式上的短语标记复制。本书中所提供的语料清楚地表明省略是**有结构的**——省略部位包含与显性句法类似的句法结构，这一点再怎么强调也不为过。

这是极为重要的基础。有些研究者试图抛开这一点来进行研究（如见 Ginzburg 1992, 出版中），但抛开省略部位具有句法结构这一基础，将会导致句法-语义接口的复杂化：在解读某些依赖语境（如指示语、直指、等级形容词等）来诠释其意义的成分时，明显需要句法-语义接口；但在解读省略时，却不太清楚是否需要句法-语义接口。与被经常讨论的 VP 省略相比，截省尤为明显地表现出句法依赖性，某些没有语音形式的成分，在句法上必须出现。

　　截省部位不存在句法结构的假设会增加语义解释的负担，这些解释信息包括特殊的赋格，以及一种语言是否允许介词悬置（preposition stranding）等，这些细节问题我们将在下一章详细讨论。我认为有必要构建一种理论，在这一理论中，狭义的语义不会涉及这些信息，它们直到后期逻辑层面的句法推导才出现。这样我们又回到了之前得出的结论——如果省略部分的确存在句法结构，那么我们有两种选择：要么按常规处理，句法提供结构，然后语法进行某些特殊处理（即语法发布指令，不要对省略部分进行发音）；要么为音系提供输入的结构，因为其自身在省略部位没有相关的音系材料，需要在拼读之后，在推导的逻辑形式上被提供出来。正如文献中所注意到的那样（讨论和文献见 Lobeck 1995），前一种观点需要在语音形式和逻辑形式这两个互不相同的层面建立一种交流，看起来会有些问题。但不管怎样，在解释去重音现象分布时，这种"交流"是有必要的，在这种情况下，诉诸复制程序在原则上是不相关的。[①] 在后续篇幅的讨论中，采用复制还是删除的分析方法并不重要，因为所给的证据对于两种方法都适用。但是在后面几节，考虑到后面几章的语料和结论，我将采用语音形式上的删略路径进行概括和后续分析。

2.2.1　IP 省略的允准条件

　　罗斯（Ross 1969）的一些文献早已注意到，截省的 IP 只有在一定的

[①] 这一"交流"也可以用来解释语义焦点与音高的关联性，总的来说，来解释声音与意义的相关性。

环境下才被允准。通常情况下，IP 做标句词 that 的补足语时，不能省略，如（54）所示。①

（54） a She was there, but Ben didn't know [CP that [IP she was there]].
    b *She was there, but Ben didn't know [CP that [IP e]].

例（54a）中内嵌的 IP，在发音时倾向于读成"低平"调，这是英语中重复成分的语调特征。通常认为这种去重音的语调本质上是完全音系缩减的自由变异，即省略。去重音在这里是可能的，但省略却不可能。这意味着我们必须为这种省略提供附加的句法限制条件，而不仅仅从音系上将某些结构随意解读为"去重音的"或"不发音的"。

在所有其他语境下，that 的表现与上述特点完全一致：

（55） a It was painted, but it wasn't obvious [CP that [IP it was painted]].
    b *It was painted, but it wasn't obvious [CP that [IP e]].

（56） a It was painted, but [CP that [IP it was painted]] wasn't obvious to the casual observer.
    b *It was painted, but [CP that [IP e]] wasn't obvious to the casual observer.

（57） a She had arrived, but [CP that [IP she had arrived]], they didn't tell us.
    b *She had arrived, but [CP that [IP e]], they didn't tell us.

正如罗斯（Ross 1969）所指出的，标句词 whether 和 if 也不能允准空 IP 补足语：

（58） *The Pentagon leaked that it would close the Presidio, but no-one knew for

---

① 当然，这点只适用于（54b）中的标句词 that，而不适用于指示代词 that。在一些语言，比如希腊语中，这两类词并不是同音异义词，因此相关的例子无疑不符合语法（oti 是标句词 that，而 afto 是指示代词）：

（i） a *Itan ekei, alla o Petros dhen iksere [CP oti [IP e]].
    b Itan ekei, alla o Petros dhen iksere [CP oti [IP itan ekei]].
    was there but the Petros not knew that was there
    'She was there, but Peter didn't know she was there.'

sure [$_{CP}$ {whether/if } [$_{IP}$ e]].

洛贝克（Lobeck 1995: 46）指出，标句词 *for* 同样也不能允准空 IP 补足语：

（59） *Sue asked Bill to leave, but [$_{CP}$ for [$_{IP}$ e]] would be unexpected.

洛贝克修改了乔姆斯基（Chomsky 1986*a*）的 CP 投射，为截省提供了如（60）所示的结构：

（60）
```
          CP
         /  \
   XP[+wh]   C′
            /  \
       C⁰[+Q]   IP
```

洛贝克（Lobeck 1995）进一步讨论了截省中空 IP 必须满足较为严格的允准条件和同一性限制的一些情况。首先，当被词汇管辖时，空 IP 不能出现，如（61）和（62）（Lobeck 1995: 56）：

（61） a *Even though Mary doesn't believe [$_{IP}$ e], Sue expects Hortense to be crazy.
　　　 b *John appears to be smart, and Mary also seems [$_{IP}$ e].
　　　 c *Mary doesn't expect Bill to win, but she wants [$_{IP}$ e].

（62） a *John talked to Bill, but before [$_{IP}$ e], Mary called.
　　　 b *Mary ate peanuts during the game, and while [$_{IP}$ e], the home team made four runs.

洛贝克认为，空 IP 必须被与其一致的中心语适当地中心语管辖，此处是 C^0，它必须具有 [+wh] 特征。这就准确地排除了"部分"截省的情况，如（63）（洛贝克第 56 页的例（54）），因为内嵌的 C^0 不具有 [+wh] 特征。

（63） I know someone likes Mary, but
　　　 a *who do you think [$_{CP}$ *t* [C^0 [$_{IP}$ e]]]?
　　　 b who do you think [$_{CP}$ *t*′ [C^0 *t* likes her]]]?

但是即使内嵌的标句词有 [+wh] 特征，这种部分截省也是不可能的：

（64） *They wondered if Marsha would invite someone, but I don't remember who they wondered whether [$_{IP}$ e].

（比较？Who did they wonder whether Marsha would invite?）

洛贝克通过假定允准的 C^0 必须与 Spec-CP 上词汇性的 wh- 短语同标，排除了以上句子。但是即使满足这一条件，正如威廉姆斯（Williams 1986）指出的那样，内嵌的截省可能仍然不可行①：

（65） *John knows how to do something, but I don't know what he knows how [$_{IP}$ e].

（即 ... I don't know what he knows how to do.）

例（64）和（65）中的"部分"省略接受度的降低，似由一种不太可能的省略限制条件造成：（64）和（65）中的"部分"省略，要求冗余成分应该以非重读的形式与省略部位连接在一起。这一不管本源在何处的限制条件②，

---

① 这里我不会详细讨论威廉姆斯对于这一例子不合法性的解释，因为该假设是建立在一个错误的假设之上，即具有区别性特征的算子不会约束一个省略位置，来源见 Williams 1977 和 Sag 1976a。这种在字母变异上的限制会错误地排除像（i）中的句子：

(i) I know what I like and what I don't.

② 这一在"部分"删除上的限制，即在 wh- 算子和去重音的混合省略上的限制，也会扩展到坦克雷迪（Tancredi 1992: 123）所讨论的有疑问的例子中（独到的观察和讨论见 Hirschbühler 1978, 1981；坦克雷迪的例子相当于 Hirschbühler 1981: 139 中的（14））。

(i) A: I wish I knew who brought what to the party.
  B: I wish I did too. I have no IDEA a *who did.
                    b who brought what (to the party).

基于下面 VP 省略的合法性，像坦克雷迪所假定的那样，将这一限定条件限制在与 wh-算子的互动上，似乎是必要的：

(ii) a Abby knew that he had quit, but Beth didn't *know that he had*.
   b Abby asked if he had quit, but Beth didn't *ask if he had*.

对某些说话者来说，这些例子可以与省略部位包含被前置附加语 when 的初始位置的例句进行比较。

(iii) a ??Abby knew when he had quit, but Beth didn't *know when he had*.
    b ??Abby asked when he had quit, but Beth didn't *ask when he had*.

对于去重音、省略和 wh- 提取之间的互动，这些对照语料提出了有趣的问题。但是在这里我并不打算仔细讨论这些问题。感兴趣的读者可以参阅相关讨论（Lobeck 1995: 6.3; Johnson 1997; Winkler 1997）。我先把这些问题放在一边，主要关注任何 IP 省略理论都应该进行探究的核心语料。

可能是导致像例（66b，d）这样不寻常的语言现象的关键原因。

(66) a Ben knows who she invited, but Charlie doesn't.
　　　b ?? Ben knows who she invited, but Charlie doesn't *know who*.
　　　c Ben knows who she invited, but Charlie doesn't *know who she invited*.
　　　d ?? Ben knows who she invited, but Charlie doesn't *know who she did*.

下面回到截省中 C 系统的条件：与 CP 指示语位置上 [+wh] 算子简单的一致关系是不足以允准空 IP 的，因为在关系从句中截省是不合法的（例（67c）是洛贝克书中第 57 页的例（57b））。

(67) a *Somebody stole the car, but they couldn't find the person who.
　　　b *The judge gave five years each to the adults who participated in the riot, but she hasn't yet sentenced the minors who.
　　　c *Although the place where is unclear, the time when the meeting is to be held is posted on the door.

洛贝克引用里齐（Rizzi 1990）的观点认为，有着显性关系算子的关系从句中的标句词具有 [-wh] 特征。这使她确信，强特征（值）[+wh] 能够允准并识别空 IP。但事实上，里齐（Rizzi 1990）的体系和洛贝克略有不同，尽管它通过简单修改可以达到洛贝克的目的。对于里齐来说，关系从句中的标句词，既可以与显性的 wh- 关系算子共现，具有 [+wh] 特征，也可以和空算子（null operator）共现，具有 [-wh] 特征。前者在英语中总是空的，而后者有不同的变化，这些变化受一定条件的限制，这些不在此处所讨论的范围内。

与其仅仅依靠 [wh] 特征的 [±] 值来建立特征核查机制，我们不如设法找到问句中（即截省句中）出现的特殊标句词，并把这一标句词和其他类型的标句词，如关系从句中的显性关系代词区别开来。幸运的是，我们很容易就能找到所感兴趣的这一标句词，它完全可以由特征 [+wh, +Q] 来确定，这两个特征通常被认为只能一同出现在构成成分疑问句中的标句词上。这样我们就可以修正洛贝克的理论体系，认为：只有疑问句中带有

[+wh, +Q] 的空 C^0，才能允准空 IP。

相似的推论也可以扩展到例（68）的分裂句中①：

（68） a *We thought it was Abby who stole the car, but it was Ben who.
　　　 b *Somebody stole the car, but no one knew that it was Ben who.

　　洛贝克早期关于允准和同一性条件要求的理论假设和空语类原则（Empty Category Principle）有很多相同点，因此很大程度上依赖于中心语管辖的概念。在最近一次对这些省略要求的研究中，洛贝克（Lobeck 1999）提出，空语类（null category）有一个到允准中心语的指示语的移动。这同最简方案一样，都把消除管辖作为一种理论手段。她的讨论主要限于动词短语省略：在这一设想中，空动词短语（最大和最小的空成分类似于 pro）移位到 TP 的指示语位置（SpecTP），来核查强一致性特征。因为根据假说，特征核查需要一个指示语–中心语构型（spec-head configuration）。她假设，TP 指示语位置未被其他成分占据，自由允许该动词短语移入，主语位于 AgrP 指示语（SpecAgr$_s$P）位置。无论这一分析方法有何优势，有一点是确定的，即该分析方法无法扩展到截省中。因为在截省中，wh- 短语占据着 CP 指示语位置，阻止了空 IP 的移位。

　　如果摒弃管辖的最简方案框架，来考察管辖路径背后的机制，我们应

---

① 有趣的是，假分裂句（pseudocleft）似乎在某种程度上允许截省：
　　（i） a ?Ben stole something—[what] was a car.
　　　　 b ?He left, and when was yesterday.
在下列组合中，为了避免形式分散，我使用 [wh- 词组]—[中枢词（pivot）] 这一顺序：
　　（ii） a What did Ben steal? A car is what! *What is a car.
　　　　　b What's he doing? Dancing a jig is what! *What is dancing a jig.
希金斯（Higgins 1973）和登迪肯等（den Dikken et al. 1998）提出，假分裂句的截省，取决于是否有一个"自答"（self-answering）问句，或者取决于不那么自由的关系从句；自由关系从句，像常规的关系从句那样，不可以允准截省：
　　（iii） *He's up to something again, and I don't like [what]!

60

能确定允准的标句词中心语和被删除的 IP 之间存在必要的局部关系，它不是指示语-中心语关系（spec-head relation），而是中心语-中心语关系（head-head relation）。① 我们可以应用洛贝克所确定的关于截省的允准条件，但是需要把它们重新构建为一种在中心语-中心语关系中的特征匹配条件。中心语-中心语关系是特征核查的另一种结构关系。

我们需要的是，屈折中心语 I 具有某一特征，这一特征只能被一个带有 [+wh, +Q] 特征的标句词中心语进行核查，并由此触发 IP 语音形式上的省略。我们可以把这个特征叫作 E。E 沿着上面所讨论的路径，从 I 移动到 C，并在 C 中被核查。② E 为了分解和生产，释放指令给语音形式，令其越过补足语。③ 这里我假设在语音形式上有一个严格地从左到右的算法：每个句法节点上的特征都触发语音成分上的操作，无论是词汇插入还是韵律范畴的建构，或其他类似的操作。例如，像 2.1.4 节所讨论的那样，一个 CP 节点，无论其内部有多少音节，都必须映射到某些更高一层的韵律范畴上（可能是一个语调短语）。有些节点上的特征可能会显示出来，并在韵律上嵌入它们的姊妹节。但是 E 特征恰恰相反，在韵律上，它的姊妹节根本不会并入到 PF 结构上。

我将忽略如何通过运用语义组合来建立模型以解决复杂中心语的一系列独立问题，但我们可以赋予 E 语义内容：在第一章，我们定义了焦点条件，而从本质上来看，E 是附加于焦点条件中的一个特征。设想 E 将会和 IP 合并（C 独立行使的日常功能是如何实现的，则是另一个问题，不局限于当前话题），那么最简单的实现方法，是把因没有遵守焦点条件而导致的省略失败归结为一种预设失败。在这一方法的指导下，我们可以得

---

① 或者是特征-特征关系（feature-feature relation）。在一定程度上这些是有所不同的。

② 与之等价的是，这一特征也可以起初就在 C 上，并不是从别的地方移动过去的。在这种情况下，我们可以把 E 的特征核查条件理解为一种特征兼容性限制条件。

③ 另一种可能性是对 E 敏感的删除设立一个普遍的限制条件，见肯尼迪（Kennedy 2000）对此所做的探索。

到 E 语义的部分同一性函数（这里采用 Heim and Kratzer 1998: 244 对于 φ 特征的运算）：

（69） ⟦E⟧ = λp: p is e-GIVEN.p

通过赋予 E 语义，省略的允准（E 的局部特征要求）和识别（E 对其补足语施加的语义限制）限制条件第一次直接地联系起来。

省略机制这一观点，保持了管辖路径的优势，即要求在核查 E 特征的中心语（用传统术语，就是"允准"省略）和受 E 影响的语类之间维持一种局部关系，与此同时，句法对可能运用的关系提出更具限制性的要求，而这一局部关系符合这一要求。我们可以注意到，这一特定的操作为弄清特征核查的精确本质和数量，以及被核查的 E 特征的要求，留下了很多空间，如果需要的话，还允许这一范围的跨语言变异。这一解释会遭到批评似乎可以预料，但是它却为洛贝克的"强一致"假设的重新构建提供了一种路径。

然而到目前为止，我们仍然没有什么具体的经验证据，能够确定在这里所研究的一般性方法中，哪种更受欢迎。目前所见的语料证据，既支持省略部位是一种句法上的空语类，也支持省略是 PF 删除的结果。

2.2.2 截省中的 COMP 域

本节主要考察传统上称为 COMP 的结构：由 CP 支配，但在 IP 之外的成分，如（70）所示：

（70） [$_{CP}$ XP$_{[+wh]}$ C^0 [$_{IP}$ ...]]
            ⏟
         'COMP'

哪些成分，在什么情况下出现在 COMP 范围内，很多语言都不大一样。我不打算就各语言在这方面的差异和不同模式做详细综述。此处的目标主要是考察在截省的情况下，COMP 范围内的表现情况，以及引出在分析截省的句法时所要呈现出的语料的重要性。我所呈现的语料可以用一个非常简单却让人惊讶的概述来描述，如（71）所示：

(71) **截省 COMP 概述**
在截省中，非算子成分不能出现在 COMP 中。

如（70）所示，我们可以把"算子"理解为"句法的 wh-XP"。至于（71）中的"成分"，可以简单地理解为任何发音的成分，包括标句词、动词、附着成分、一致语素，诸如此类。只有那些直接和句法算子即 wh-XP 相联系的分段，才能在截省的疑问式中显现。

以上归纳包含两个单独的子情况，我将在下文分别考察。第一种子情况涉及这样一种语言成分：它们经常被分析为来源于 IP 内，然后移位到 COMP 或是寄生附着在 COMP 基础生成的成分上，包括日耳曼语言中的 I^0 至 C^0 的动词移位、标句词一致、南部斯拉夫语和其他巴尔干语言的瓦克纳格尔附着成分（Wackernagel clitics），以及各种一般意义上的"第二位置"现象。第二种子情况通常被认为是在 COMP 系统上基础生成的成分，即标句词本身（以及一些语言中的 wh- 虚位成分，见第 57 页脚注①，和约束复述代词（resumptive pronoun）的 wh- 算子，见 4.3 节）。

我们得到的结论是：尽管这一部分中（已经被讨论）的语言事实本用于支持空语类解释路径，而非删除路径，但深入探究，会发现它们其实完全适用于删除路径，而且还可能为特征驱动移位的本质提供基础。最后，最好将截省成分的限制条件视为 PF 接口上的检测手段，在某种程度上类似于 COMP 语迹效应。

2.2.2.1 COMP 中的非算子外来元素

本节首先考察英语、荷兰语、德语和丹麦语中主句截省的语言事实（据我所知，其他斯堪的纳维亚语也一样）。众所周知（讨论和文献见

Vikner 1995），所有这些语言在非内嵌疑问句中都展现了第二动词（V_2）特征，如（72）所示。尽管这些语言在非疑问主句中是否需要 V_2 方面上有所不同，但我们对这些结构并不感兴趣，因为截省仅限于疑问结构中。

（72） a Who   has   Max   invited?   ［英语］
　　　 b Wen   hat   Max   eingeladen?   ［德语］
　　　 c Wie   heeft Max   uitgenodigd?   ［荷兰语］
　　　 d Hvem   har   Max   inviteret?   ［丹麦语］

如（73）中的英文语料所示，对此标准的分析是从 I^0 到 C^0 的移位。（为简单起见，我假定这种移位是替换而不是附加；复杂中心语内部屈折性成分的排序由形态原则决定，而非由附加的方向性决定）：

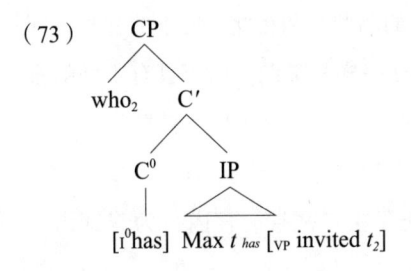

（73）
　　　　　　　　CP
　　　　　　／　　＼
　　　who$_2$　　　C′
　　　　　　　　／　＼
　　　　　　 C^0　　IP
　　　　　　　|
　　　[$_I{^0}$has] Max t_{has} [$_{VP}$ invited t_2]

基于（73）中的结构，我们可以预测，在这些语言中，主句截省由 wh-XP 和其后某一移位后的动词组成，特别是如果截省中的 IP 省略只是 PF 层面上的语音删除。但是这一猜测并没有得到证实。

（74） a A: Max has invited   B: Really? Who (*has)?   ［英语］
　　　 someone.
　　　 b A: Max hat jemand   B: Echt?   Wen (*hat)?   ［德语］
　　　 eingeladen.
　　　 c A: Max heeft iemand   B: Ja?   Wie (*heeft)? ［荷兰语］
　　　 uitgenodigd.

d A: Max har inviterert en　B: Ja?　Hvem（*har）?　［丹麦语］
　　　　eller anden.

有人可能怀疑，这些结构是否是截省。毕竟片语问句在回声功能中是明显存在的，而且甚至不需要有 wh- 形式，尽管这肯定也是可能的。

（75） A: Superman tricked Mr Mxyzptlk.
　　a B: Who?
　　b B: Mr who?
　　c B: Superman tricked Mr who?

但我们很容易看出，这种光杆反问 wh-XP 与（74）中的主句截省大不相同。首先，（75a）中 wh- 短语的语调调型和（75b、75c）的调型相同……是升调（L*H；更为全面的描述见 Gunlogson 即将出版的著述）。然而，（74a）中被截省的 wh- 短语的调型，和在此语境下的完整疑问句的调型一致：和问句 *Who did he trick*? 一样是降调。由于具有不同的音高调型，像（75a）那样的光杆 wh-XP 回声句和（74）中（被截省的）主句疑问句是明显不同的。

我们也须注意，例（74）中先于主句截省的言内行为修饰语 *really*，不能出现在回声疑问句的前面：

（76） A: Superman tricked Mr Mxyzptlk.
　　　　　　L*H
　　B: #Really? Who?

这是因为，*really* 在这里表示 B 已经接受了 A 的表达内容，并达成共识（尽管可能表示出惊讶）。但是如果 B 不理解 A 所表达的内容，如同上升调型所显示的那样，那就不可能使用 *really*。

第二，将主句截省和片语 wh- 疑问句区别开来的句法证据来自于英语中截省的 wh- 短语可以和介词倒置（"附带结构"（swiping）），对此麦钱特（Merchant，出版中）将会有详述。^① 我们可以从例（77）中观察到，在英语中，一些 wh- 算子可以和管辖它的介词颠倒位置：

（77） Lois was talking (to someone), but I don't know [who to].

在非截省疑问句中这是不可能的：

（78） a *I don't know [who to] Lois was talking.
　　　 b *[Who to] was Lois talking?

这种倒装可以看作是截省所独有的，但是我们不关注其原因。重要的是，这种倒装也可以出现在主句截省中：

（79） A: Lois was talking (to someone). B: Really? Who to?

但这种倒装不可能出现在 wh- 片语回声句中：

（80） A: Lois was talking to Mr Mxyzptlk.
　　　　　　L*H

---

① 限于篇幅，在这里我无法对这种现象展开充分的讨论。但是我注意到，在一些斯堪的纳维亚语中，也存在这种现象（感谢 P. Svenonius 提供挪威语语料以及 L. Mikkelsen 提供丹麦语语料）：

（i） Per har　 gått på kino,　　 men jeg vet　 ikke hvem med.　［挪威语］
　　 Per er　　 gået i　 biografen, men jeg ved　 ikke hvem med.　［丹麦语］
　　 Per has/is gone to cinema　 but　 I　 know not　 who　 with
　　 'Per went to the movies but I don't know who with.'

至少在英语中，这种倒装仅限于"最小"的 wh- 算子中，如 who、what、where 和 when。尽管如此，这种倒装并不是由（或仅仅由）韵律所造成的，因为尽管 which 和 where 不能倒装——如伊藤（J. Ito）所指出的那样（私下交流）——由 the hell 组成的复合词则是可以倒装的（尽管在通常情况下并不出现在截省中，见 4.2.2 节中的（35））：

（ii） a　 He was talking to one of those guys, but I don't know which (*to).
　　　 b　 He was talking to somebody's mom, but I don't know whose (*to).
　　　 c　 He was talking, but God knows who the hell to.

最充分的解释似乎是把这些 wh- 词当作提升到 P 上的中心语（"最小的最大" X，像附着成分，这里采用乔姆斯基的术语（Chomsky 1995: 249））。中心语到中心语的移位可以准确地区别出这一类别（排除 which，假设并入是不允许的）。更多语料见 4.2.2 节；关于附带结构的详细讨论，见 Merchant（出版中）。

a B: To who?
       L*H
   b B: *Who to?

因为在倒装中，C 上不可能出现移位的助动词，与上面的（74a）相同：

（81） A: Lois was talking (to someone). B: Really? Who to (*was)?

以上简要讨论仅证明了一点，即截省也可以发生在主句中。这一点和罗斯（Ross 1969）以及克莱因（M. Klein 1977）的观点相左，但和贝克霍弗（Bechhofer 1976a, b, 1977）的看法一致（进一步的证据见后者）。这也证明，（74）中的模式需要一个解释。

一个同样令人困惑的问题来自于南部斯拉夫语言，如斯洛文尼亚语、保加利亚语、塞尔维亚－克罗地亚语和马其顿语等。这些语言中都有"瓦克纳格尔"附着现象，即语言中某些类型的成分，如助动词、否定词和一些代词性成分在分布上受到位置限制，必须附加在 wh- 短语上。简单来说，这些成分像 V_2 语言中主句屈折动词一样，必须出现在"第二"位置。这里的"第二"位置可以是韵律上相对于第一韵律词而言，也可以是句法上相对于第一个句法成分而言。（讨论见 Rudin 1985；最近有新的研究路径试图把 V_2 现象纳入到讨论范围内，见 Anderson 1996, 2000。）这一现象的解释以及变体与我们的讨论关系不大。我们感兴趣的是，在一些条件下，这些词可以出现在 CP 系统的复杂 wh-XP 之中或之间。例（82）是斯洛文尼亚语的例子，出自马文（Marvin 1997）。在例（82）中我们可以看出，体助词 je 必须附着于内嵌的 wh- 短语上。（对塞尔维亚－克罗地亚语的研究，另见 Browne 1974, Bošković 1995；对马其顿语和保加利亚语的研究，另见 Legendre 1999）：

（82） Peter se   je spraševal, kako$_1$, je Špela popravila t_1 [斯洛文尼亚语]
       Peter REFL AUX asked   what   AUX Špela fixed.
       'Peter wondered what Spela fixed.'

这一现象也存在于多重前置 wh- 短语中。在这些句子中，助动词 *je* 附着在第一个 wh- 短语上：

（83）a Nisem   vprašal, kaj₁ je komu₂ Špela kupila *t₁ t₂*.
         NEG.AUX.1SG asked   what AUX who.DAT Spela bought
         'I didn't ask what Spela bought for who.'
      b *Nisem vprašal, kaj₁ komu₂ je Špela kupila *t₁ t₂*.

但在截省的情况下，这种 *je* 附着绝不会出现（感谢马文对此的判断）：

（84）a Špela je   popravila nekako,   a nisem   vprašal, kako (*je).
         Spela AUX fixed   something but NEG.AUX.1SG asked   what AUX
         'Spela fixed something, but I didn't ask what.'
      b Špela je   kupila nekaj   nekomu,   a nisem
         Spela AUX bought something someone.DAT but NEG.AUX.1SG
         vprašal, kaj   (*je) komu.
         asked   what AUX   who.DAT
         (lit.) 'Spela bought something for someone, but I didn't ask what for who.'

一些语言提供了另外一类语料，人们发现在这些语言的 C 系统中，非 wh- 一致有各种表现。这种标句词一致体系在日耳曼语族的语言中得到很好的体现。"标句词一致"（complementizer agreement）这一术语，与日耳曼语言文献中所使用的一样，仅指标句词与内嵌主语的某些特征一致的现象，不要与爱尔兰语的那种标句词和 wh- 短语一致的现象相混淆。日耳曼语的标句词一致现象的具体细节不是我关注的重点（讨论和文献见 Zwart 1993: 3.3）；此处所关注的是，当 SpecCP 上出现 wh- 短语时，这种一致现象依然存在，如（85）（卢森堡语，出自 Zwart 1993: 163）和（86）（巴瓦兰语，出自 Lobeck 1995: 58）所示：

（85）... mat wiem (datt) s   de spazéiere ganng bas.   ［卢森堡语］
         with who that 2sg you walk   gone are.2sg
         '... with whom you went for a walk.'

(86) Du woidd-st doch kumma, owa mia wissn ned wann-st
　　 you wanted-2sg PRT come   but we know not when-2sg
　　 (du) kumma woidd-st.　　　　　　　　　　　　　［巴瓦兰语］
　　 you come wanted-2sg
　　 'You wanted to come, but we don't know when you wanted to come.'

洛贝克（Lobeck 1995: 59）指出，如果没有显性标句词，标句词一致标记可以在语音上附着在 SpecCP 中的 wh- 短语上。虽然这些方言中大都存在截省，但这种一致关系却不能出现在截省结构中（洛贝克的例（65））：

(87) Du woidd-st doch kumma, owa mia wissn ned wann(*-st).
　　 you wanted-2sg PRT come   but we know not when-2sg
　　 　　　　　　　　　　　　　　　　　　　　　　　　　［巴伐利亚语］
　　 'You wanted to come, but we don't know when.'

她把这一事实和另一个语言事实联系起来，即当具有匹配一致特征的动词不出现时，如在比较短语中，标句词一致标记同样不能出现。下面的语料出自拜尔（Bayer 1984）：

(88) a Der Hans is gresser (als) wia-st du bist. ［巴伐利亚语］
　　　　the Hans is taller than how-2sg you are-2sg
　　　　'Hans is taller than you are.'
　　 b Der Hans is gresser (als) wia(*-st) du.
　　　　the Hans is taller than how-2sg you
　　　　'Hans is taller than you.'

洛贝克根据挪威语标句词 *som* 的分布，提出了相似的观点。在挪威语中，*som* 必须与主语提取一同出现在内嵌疑问句中，如（89a）所示。（出自 Rizzi 1990: 57, 稍有改动；见 Taraldsen 1986, Vikner 1991；丹麦语中的 *der* 在口语中也类似，如果 *der* 确实在 C 上的话[①]）：

[①] 感谢米克尔森（L. Mikkelsen）提供的丹麦语语料。

（89）a Vi vet hvem *(som) snakker met Marit. ［挪威语］
b Vi ved hvem ??(der) snakker met Marit. ［丹麦语］
we know who C⁰ talks with Marit
'We know who is talking with Marit.'

洛贝克指出，*som* 不可能出现在截省结构中，如（90a）所示（她的书中第 60 页，例（68））。她认为，这是由于 *som* 必须和 INFL 一致（为允准主语的语迹），但在截省中 INFL 消失了。例（90a）中没有上面提到的标句词一致，这种偏差印证了洛贝克的想法。（90b）中丹麦语的例子也可以看出这种对比来（同样地，如果 *der* 的确是在 C 位置）。

（90）a Noen snakker met Marit, men vi vet ikke hvem (*som). ［挪威语］
b En eller anden snakker met Marit, men vi ved ikke hvem (*der). ［丹麦语］
someone talks with Marit but we know not who C⁰

如果关于 *som*（和 *der*）与 INFL 间关系的本质的假设是正确的，这就为我们提供了另一例证，即一个 C 系统内的成分与被省略 IP 内部的某一位置或成分之间存在不合法的非算子依存关系。

本章给出的所有语料都有一个共同点：在通常的设想下，出现在 C 系统的非算子成分在小句内部生成。看看我们上面提到的第一个例子，也是最熟悉的例子：日耳曼语言中主句疑问句的 V₂ 现象，标准分析认为，前置的成分在 IP 内部生成，要么在 I⁰ 处（如英语的情态动词和助动词 *do*），要么在更低一层的 VP 生成，然后提升到 I⁰（例如英语的 *have* 和 *be*；在其他语言中，几乎所有动词都可以提升）。在不同语言中，V₂ 现象发生在不同层次构型中（在包括英语在内的所有语言的主句中，对于英语来说，发生在主句问句、祈使句、否定倒装，以及其他非常具有限制性语境的情况下）——此处至关重要的是，这种前置是 I⁰ 到 C⁰ 的提升（或者不管什么中心语的投射，只要在这些语言中它的指示语是 wh- 移位的落点就行）。标句词一致，通常也会被分析为涉及功能中心语或者功能中心语的某些特征从 IP 内到 C^0 的移位（Hoekstra and Marácz 1989 认为是 I^0；Zwart 1993 认为是 $Agrs^0$）。（挪威语中的 *som* 是否符合这一分析路径还不清楚，这里的问题可能与下一节中描述的事实有关。）最后，出于句法目的，瓦克纳格尔附着成分明显必须在 IP 内生成：代名词性成分满足选择性限制条件，而助动词决定其动词补语的形式。这些附着成分如何出现在它们被观察到的位置并不重要，可能通过句法机制（如通常所认为的中心语移位），或是通过语音机制。

对于上述成分都不可能出现在截省当中这一现象，如下是几种可能的解释。

正如洛贝克（Lobeck 1995: 58-60）从挪威语和巴伐利亚语所得出的结论那样，第一种解释认为，这些语言事实支持句法中的空 IP 是空语类。同样扩展到 V_2 现象，她的推理十分直接：在句法中，I^0 中只有 $[_{IP}\,e]$，因此这些成分从一开始就不能提升。这一推理也同样适用于 C 一致现象。如她所述，如果"COMP 形态上的一致……取决于与内嵌 INFL 的一致"（第 60 页），这里"取决于"直接对应那些用 V_2 和 C 一致关系来表达中心语移位至 C^0 平行关系的路径。相同的推断对南部斯拉夫语的瓦克纳格尔附着成分的分布也适用：这些附着成分在 IP 内部生成，根据假设，如果 IP 是空的，那么这些成分都无法进行句法或语音操作。

尽管这一论据似乎合理，但它建立在一种很难成立的假设之上。我们可以回想一下，在空结构路径下，wh- 短语是在 SpecCP 上基础生成的，在 S 结构式上不约束任何成分（或者可能约束 IP 空语类本身，延伸到艾克（Haïk 1987）的主张，即在涉及先行项的删除中，被删除的先行项的相关算子约束 VP 空语类：讨论见 Kennedy and Merchant 1997, 1999）。但是，如果情况确实如此，是什么阻止了非算子成分原位生成于其着陆位置，即 IP 之外的"移位"位置呢？就像与 wh- 短语的情况那样。这样的话，我们必须假设在 S 结构式中无效的算子约束（或者是受艾克约束的在范畴上有显著区别的空语类）和中心语约束（主要指 V2、标句词一致以及南部斯拉夫语的瓦克纳格尔附着成分）之间存在区别。

但是这种区别大都缺乏动因。有人可能认为，这种不同不在于范畴本身，而在于范畴层级：wh- 短语是一个 XP，根据假设，它约束空 XP（IP），然而中心语 X^0 却不能约束空 XP。但是如果是这样的话，结合对 VP 省略的分析，VP 省略也包含一个空 VP（$[_{VP}\ e]$），那么我们可能会期待，VP 省略不能有一个在 I^0 上"被提升的"助动词。如果有人设想这些成分是 I^0 上例外基础生成的中心语（当然，通常情况下，我们所讨论的助动词——体动词 have 和进行时、过去式及系动词 be——必须生成在更低一层的 V^0 中），这是不正确的：

(91) a I've been writing, and Bill has, too.
  b Frank is learning Swahili because Marsha is.
  c Max was arrested, but Andy wasn't.
  d Cathy is a doctor, and so is her husband.

根据这种分析，例(92)应该有如下结构：

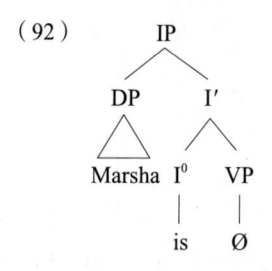

(92)
```
         IP
        /  \
       DP   I'
       |   / \
    Marsha I⁰ VP
           |  |
           is Ø
```

但这一反驳微不足道，因为很明显，对于(91)的句子来说，(92)的结构是不正确的。洛贝克(Lobeck 1995)令人信服地指出，这些句子应该是由下面的结构推导出来的（尤见 Potsdam 1996: 83–88）：

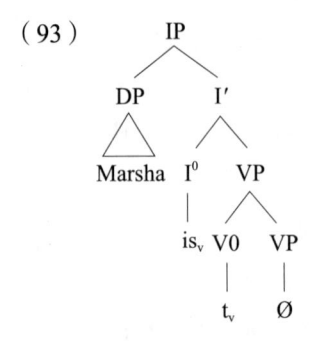

(93)
```
         IP
        /  \
       DP   I'
       /\   /\
    Marsha I⁰ VP
           |  /\
          is_v V0 VP
               |  |
               t_v Ø
```

71　但是，麦克洛斯基（McCloskey 1991a）所讨论的爱尔兰语的例子（还有 Doron 1990, 1999 中关于希伯来语的例子）确实存在异议。麦克洛斯基指出，爱尔兰语具有谓词省略现象，这与英语的 VP 省略类似。两者的不同在于，爱尔兰语的主语处在比较低的位置（不在 SpecIP 位置），而动词却提升了（如升至 I⁰）。这种结构中的 VP 省略，很明显会产生只有动词的句子，如例（94）：

(94) Cheannaigh siad teach?
　　 bought   they house
　　 'Did they buy a house?'
　a Cheannaigh.
　　 bought
　　 '(Yes.) They did.'
　b Níor   cheannaigh.
　　 NEG.PAST   *bought*
　　 '(No.) They didn't.'

麦克洛斯基认为，这些省略的答句有（95）所示的结构（为了反映他 1996 年的论点，麦克洛斯基略微更新了他的建议（McCloskey 1991a），即一个 VP 外部主语和句子 *There were rabbits in the garden today, though there weren't yesterday* 在某些方面相似，尽管还不清楚一个被省略的 VP 内部主语是否无论如何都不能避免显性的提升）：

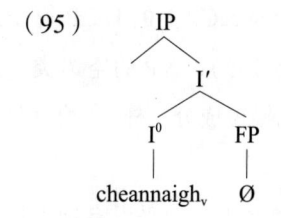

(95)
```
        IP
        |
        I′
       / \
      I⁰   FP
      |    |
  cheannaigh_v  Ø
```

如果这种"错位的"(displaced)中心语在 LF 重构前,需要约束一个空成分,那么必须承认一个最大(空)语类的中心语约束关系。如果这种中心语约束不是必须的,要是只有真算子在推导的每个阶段必须约束一个空语类(见 Koopman and Sportiche 1982),那么上面提到的截省例子的不合法性就不能从这一论据中推导出来。

另一种可能的策略认为,虽然这种中心语约束是合法的,但在截省中,却有超过一个成分——wh- 短语和中心语成分(head-material)——必须同时约束空 IP 语类。无论哪种版本的库普曼和斯波尔蒂什的双射原则(Koopman and Sportiche's Bijection Principle)都会排除掉这种多重"错位"(displacements)。但是,鉴于肯尼迪和麦钱特的例子(Kennedy and Merchant 1997, 1999),这一逻辑也有行不通的时候。例(96a)表明,比较结构中的假空缺结构(pseudogapping)是合法的,(96b)为其可能具有结构(残余部分和空 VP 的顺序并不重要):

(96) a Jack read a longer magazine than Abby did a book.

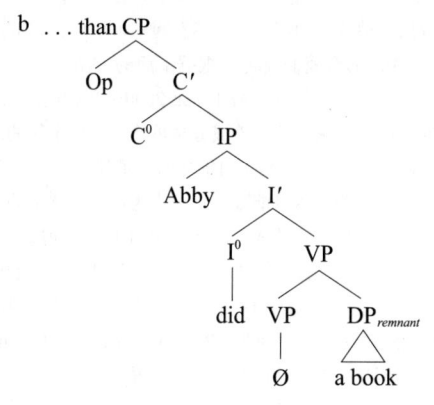

b ... than CP
```
          than CP
         /    \
        Op    C′
             /  \
            C⁰   IP
                / \
              Abby  I′
                   / \
                  I⁰  VP
                  |  /  \
                 did VP  DP_remnant
                     |     △
                     Ø   a book
```

79

按照省略是基础生成的观点,这意味着,位于 SpecCP 上的 DegP 算子约束 VP 的空语类的同时,VP 外部残余部分也必须约束 VP 的空语类(这一论点基于:"错位的"残余部分,要像其他的错位成分一样,"约束"省略部位,这和上面提到的截省的中心语类似)。

综上所述,在标准的空 IP 语类截省分析路径下,似乎没有理由相信无论什么样的机制去允准 SpecCP 上基础生成的 wh- 短语,以及其后随之而来的该 wh- 短语的约束条件的满足(按照标准假设,在 LF 层上),该机制不能也允准以同样方式出现在"错位的"位置上的中心语、一致关系和瓦克纳格尔附着成分。①

另一方面,按照这里采取的删除路径,语料可以通过一个有序的方案来解决:如果 IP 成分的删除在中心语移位和韵律重新排序操作之前,这些成分就都不会出现,韵律重新排序操作造成了 C 系统中 IP 内部形态的出现。那么问题就是,是否有一种原则性的方式来推导出这种排序,而不仅仅是规定这种排序。一些观点认为的确有这样一种方式。首先,对于这些现象,许多文献都有一个普遍的看法,即这种韵律重新排序操作似乎是一种非常"迟的"(late)操作,由句法所回馈,但不一定由句法生成(最明显的例子就是附着成分,尽管相同的想法也适用于 I

---

① 瓦克纳格尔附着成分表现出一种特殊的情况。既然看起来很明显,调节这些附着成分顺序的机制是语音的而不是句法的,那么我们就可以根据下面的方法,用一个独立的论证,来把它们从截省结构中排除出去。假定安德森(Anderson 2000)和勒让德尔(Legendre 2000)是正确的:语音形式上的对齐限制要求这些附着成分尽可能地接近小句的左边缘;与此同时另一个约束条件,使一个韵律词或者一个 XP(可能更普遍的是,一个韵律短语)离开实际所在的左边缘位置,从而使附着成分"尽可能地接近"成为可能。这个韵律材料由句法所提供;但是,根据假设,句法不会强加给这些成分任何特定的顺序,使这些顺序超出助动词、否定词和论元的需要。如果情况确实如此,那么,在截省的条件下,我们应该使这些成分(我认为是中心语,而不是短语)基础生成于 IP 外部。鉴于附接成分的限制条件,这意味着这些成分应该出现在 C^0 上或附接在其上,因为 CP、IP 或 SpecCP 上的 wh- 短语这些最大投射,对于一个中心语来说,都不是一个合法的附接成分位置。

到 C 移位）。

理论上讲，这似乎反映了经济原则（推导的经济性和表征的经济性，只要这两者是可区分的）。简而言之，对于这些成分来说，如果删除可能发生就倾向于删除。通常认为 I 到 C 移位是由 C 上的某些强势特征驱动的，这些特征必须由 I 上的匹配特征进行核查（如见 Holmberg and Platzack 1995）。在正常条件下，当该特征是弱特征时，从 I 到 C 的移位可以是非显性的（发生在 LF 层上）—— 在这种情况下，只有特征自身会在 LF 层移位，因为 PF 的裹挟式移位（pied-piping）不起作用。在这一理论下，当一个强特征被核查时，PF 会强制"裹挟式移位"。通常认为其原因在于光杆特征在 PF 层不能被拼读，但也可能是缺少一个与 I 上残留的特征束相对应的项而导致的 PF 崩溃，而现在缺少移位的特征。上述两种解释难以抉择。

我们再回到省略。有一种方法可以解释上面提到的语言事实，它与 I 到 C 移位的标准分析路径一致，认为的确是残余特征束导致了 PF 的崩溃。在 IP 省略的情况下，从 I 到 C 的最小特征移位可以不导致裹挟式移位，因为 I 中残余特征束并不需要发音；这一点已隐含在上面提到的省略特征 E 中。注意，这是对乔姆斯基的"特征"（feature）裹挟式移位的一种创新：正是残余部分触发了 PF 的崩溃，而不是本身没有任何语音内容的光杆特征。这种分析方法也与乔姆斯基（Chomsky 1995）提出的关于 I 到 C 的移位发生在 PF 层的一般看法一致。

和标准分析相反，对于这些语言事实的另一种解释是 I 上的强特征驱动了 I 到 C 的移位（在英语中，可能只有某些种类的主句标句词 C 可以核查这一特征）。由于未被核查的强特征会导致 PF 的崩溃，在正常情况下，这将迫使 I 向 C 的明显移位。但是一个有趣的例外再次出现在省略中：如果 IP 被删除了，那么 I 上的强特征不会到达 PF 接口，从而避免了 PF 的崩溃。（第五章中的好几个例子都会用到这一逻辑。）我认为现阶段没有令人信服的理由来确定采取哪种分析方法，两种分析方式似乎同样可行，我将不做结论。①（类似结论另见 Lasnik 1999。）

综上所述，通常出现在 C 系统的 IP 内部成分，在截省结构中却不会出现在该位置。这种语言事实和我们所提倡的删除路径是兼容的，而不支持经常提到的那种空语类的分析路径。

2.2.2.2 基础生成的 COMP 内部成分

上述成分会移动到 C 系统的这种逻辑，不会扩展到本节所考虑的语料中。本节我将探讨那些通常认为是在标句词上，即 C^0 中心语上基础生成的成分。因为英语受双重标记语填入过滤条件制约，所以英语语料在这里并不适用。我们将考察那些不遵守此条件的语言，即允许一个显性的标句词和 wh- 短语同时出现在 SpecCP 上的语言。下面荷兰语的一些方言变体可以作为例子（例（97a）是根据 Bennis 1986: 234 修改而来，例（97b）是根据 J. Hoekstra 1993 和 Zwart 1993: 169 修改而来；另见 den Besten 1978: 647, 1989）。

(97) a Ik weet niet, wie (of) (dat) hij gezin heeft. ［（尤其南部）荷兰语］
      I know not who if that he seen has
      'I don't know who he has seen.'
   b Ik wit net wa (of) *('t) jûn komt. ［弗里斯兰语］
     I know not who if that.CL tonight comes
     'I don't know who's coming tonight.'

例（97a）有如（98）所示的结构（被错位的 *wie* 是否经过 *dat* 的指示语位置并不重要，这里，尽管从兹瓦尔特（Zwart 1993: 5.2.2）的证据来看，它并没有经过）。在这个树形图中，为了简明，我使用了递归的 CP

---

① 注意，为触发已被验证的 wh- 移位，至少 $C^0_{[+wh]}$ 必须出现；如果 C 上的 [+wh] 是强特征（一般来说，对英语是这么认为的），我们就有证据证明，删除是以 IP 为目标的，而不是 C'……如果 C' 是目标，那么驱动移位的 [+wh] 特征会在触发 wh- 移位至 SpecCP 之前就被消除了。

标签。这两个不同的投射被确认为是 WhP 和 TopP（见 J. Hoekstra 1993, Müller and Sternefeld 1993, Zwart 1993, Rizzi 1995, 以及下文）。

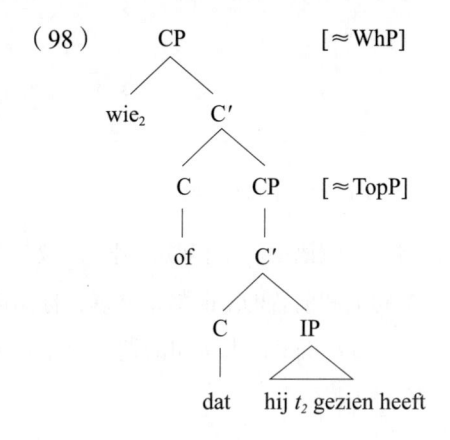

（98）
```
          CP            [≈WhP]
         /  \
       wie₂   C'
             /  \
            C    CP       [≈TopP]
            |   /  \
            of  C'
                /  \
               C    IP
               |    /\
              dat  hij t₂ gezien heeft
```

根据这个结构，我们可能会预想，要么是由 dat（TopP）做中心语的 CP，要么是 dat 的 IP 补足语可以被省略。如果就像通常认为的那样，例（97）中的 of 是英语中空标句词 C^0[+wh, +Q] 的对应成分，那么它就应该带有所有相关可以允准其补足语省略的一致特征。与之类似，如果 wie 移动时经过 dat 的指示语位置，那么我们可以预想，它也应带有所有相关可以允准其补足语省略的一致特征。但是，正如我们在（99）和（100）中看到的那样，这两种可能性都没有得到证实；合语法的截省只有仅剩 wh-短语的结构（J. Hoekstra, J. Gerbrandy, 私下交流）：

（99） Hij heeft iemand gezien, maar ik weet niet　　　［荷兰语］
　　　he has someone seen but I know not
　　a　wie.
　　b　*wie of.
　　c　*wie dat.
　　d　*wei of dat.
　　　 who if that
　　　'He saw someone, but I don't know who.'

83

(100) Ien   komt   jûn,   mar ik wit   net   [弗里斯兰语]
     someone comes tonight but I know not
     a wa.
     b *wa of.
     c *wa   't
     d *wa of 't
        who if that.CL
     'Someone's coming tonight, but I don't know who.'

马文（Marvin 1997）讨论过斯洛文尼亚语中一个相似的例子。像荷兰语一样，斯洛文尼亚语也可以允许标句词和前置的 wh- 短语共现；标句词是疑问式 C *ali* 'whether' 还是陈述式 C *da* 'that'，由主句的谓词决定。下面的例子出自马文（Marvin 1997: 50）。

(101) a Rad   bi   vedel, koga   da   je   Peter videl.
         glad SUBJ know   whom   C[-wh] AUX Peter seen
         'I would like to know who Peter saw.'
     b Sprašujm se,   koga   ali   Špela ljubi.
         I.ask   REFL   whom   C[+wh] Spela loves
         'I wonder who Spela loves.'
     c Nisem   ga vprašal, komu kaj   da   zameri.
         NEG.AUX.1sg him asked   whom what C[-wh] blames
         'I didn't ask him who he blames for what.'

但这些标句词均不能与截省后残余的 wh- 短语共现（T. Marvin，私下交流）：

(102) a Peter je   videl nekoga   in rad   bi   vedel, koga (*da).
         Peter AUX seen   someone and glad SUBJ know who   that
         'Peter saw someone and I would like to know who.'
     b Špela ljubi nekoga, a   nisem   vprašal, koga (*ali).
         Spela loves someone but NEG.AUX.1sg asked   who   if
         'Spela loves someone, but I didn't ask who.'

c Nekomu   nekaj   ocita,   a   nisem   ga vprašal,
   *someone.*DAT *something he.blames but* NEG.AUX.*1sg him asked*
   komu   kaj   (*da).
   *who.*DAT *what   that*
   'He blames someone for something, but I didn't ask him who he blames for what.'

爱尔兰语也同样允许标句词和算子共现（J. McCloskey，私下交流）：

（103）Cheannaigh sé leabhar inteacht ach níl   fhios   agam céacu
      bought   he book   some   but not.is knowledge at.me which
      ceann (*a /   *ar).
      one C_{trace} C_{pro}
      'He bought a book, but I didn't know which.'

至于丹麦语（有些出现在丹麦语使用的不同语域中）中堆叠的标句词 77（L. Mikkelsen，私下交流），我标注为"C"（见 Vikner 1991；Mikkelsen，出版中）：

（104）Vi ved   hvem (som) (at) der snakker med Marit. ［丹麦语（口语）］
      we know who   C   C   C talks   with Marit
      'We know who is talking with Marit.'

（105）En eller anden snakker med Marit, men vi ved   ikke
      someone   talks   with Marit but we know not
      a hvem.
      b *hvem som.
      c *hvem som der.
      d *hvem at.
      e *hvem at der.
      f *hvem som at der.
      'Someone is talking with Marit, but we don't know who.'

洛贝克分析巴伐利亚语或挪威语所采用的路径，即认为这些非算子成分生成于 IP 内部，对于这些例子明显行不通。

根据 CP 分裂理论假说，洛贝克式分析会出现两个问题：第一，为什么不能省略 Top 的 IP 补足语，留下 WH^0、Top^0，或者两个都留下呢？第二，为什么只有 C [+wh] 为空时，Top 短语才能省略？

在洛贝克系统下，第一个问题的答案来自一个假设，即一个可以允准空 IP 代词的中心语，必须与在其指示语位置上的一个 wh-XP 一致：由于这些例子中的 wh-XP 不会经过 SpecTopP，就不可能建立必要的指示语-中心语关系，Top 的中心语就不会有合适的特征来允准一个空补足语。

第二个问题的答案更复杂。如果我们假设功能性结构的投射在不同语言中都是相同的（如在 Cinque 1999 中），那么我们对于截省结构的设想就太简单了。（106）和（107）是我们为截省的短语结构提出的两种可能选择：

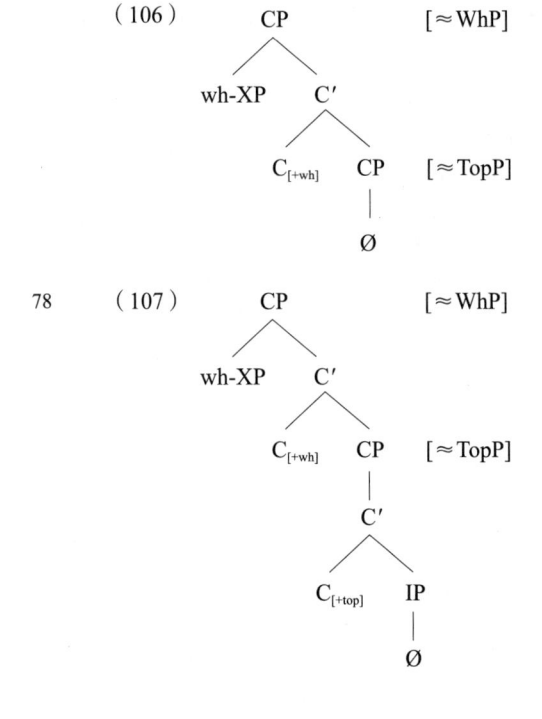

（106）

```
         CP                [≈WhP]
        /  \
    wh-XP   C'
           /  \
      C[+wh]   CP          [≈TopP]
               |
               Ø
```

（107）

```
         CP                [≈WhP]
        /  \
    wh-XP   C'
           /  \
      C[+wh]   CP          [≈TopP]
               |
               C'
              /  \
         C[+top]  IP
                  |
                  Ø
```

（107）中的第二个结构，与截省的传统分析结构有很多相似之处，如前面（2）所示，因为这一结构假设存在一个空的 IP 节点。但是，如果 wh-XP 移位时不经过 SpecTopP，那么这种空成分就不会被允准。

当然这时一个附带的问题出现了：前置至 SpecTopP 的话题短语 XP，是否能允准这样一个空补足语呢？这个问题回答起来非常复杂，一般而言，那些可以为这一短语结构提供最好的证据的语言（大陆西日耳曼语族的变体），其话题化成分并不能够和前置的 wh-XP 共现：

（108） a *Wann   {hast} den Wagen {hast} du gemietet?   ［德语］
       b *Wanneer {heb} de auto   {heb} je gehuurd?   ［荷兰语］
          when   have the car   have you rented
       （'When did you rent the car?'）

（在德语的例子中，我用了一个弱代词主语来确保宾语不会跨越主语挪移；在荷兰语中，宾语跨越主语挪移现象通常在任何情况下都不会发生。）由于在这些语言中，SpecWhP 和 SpecTopP 处都不能出现显性成分，所以上面那个子问题无法得到回答，至少基于荷兰语和德语来看是这样的。

而且，由于荷兰语、弗里斯兰语和斯洛文尼亚语没有双重标记词填入过滤条件，这使（99）、（100）和（102）中的不合法性变得难以理解。一种可能的解释是，此类例子的不合法性与（109）中所示的经典 COMP 语迹效应有联系或事实上完全相同。

（109） a *Who did Lex say that __ kidnapped Lois?
       b *Which guy did Jimmy wonder if __ had tipped Lois off?

如果如一些证据所表明的那样（见 5.1.2 节），COMP 语迹效应是一种语音形式层面的效应，那么截省结构将会如（109）那样违反语法规则。具体而言，让我们假设有一个过滤公式，如（110）所示，但也需考虑这一公式的局限性（在英语主语关系从句中的局限性，这一公式不适用于代词脱落（pro-drop）类语言，等等；见 Perlmutter 1971）。①

（110） *[$_C$ α] [$_x$...]，其中，α 有语音阶，且 x 是不含语音阶的韵律成分。

初看起来，这一公式对荷兰语和弗里斯兰语似乎是起作用的，（111）中的句子完全不合法。

（111） a *Wie vraag je je af of ＿ hem heeft gezien ?　　［荷兰语］
b *Wa fregest dy ôf oft ＿ hem sjoen hat?　［弗里斯兰语］
   who ask you REFL PRT if him has seen has
('Who were you wondering if ＿ saw him?')

但遗憾的是，（111）中的偏差与德语等语言并无不同。在这些语言中，从内嵌疑问句中任何位置提取论元，都会导致比英语程度更为严重的偏差：

（112） a *Wie vraag je je af of zij ＿ heeft gezien?　　［荷兰语］
b *Wa fregest dy ôf oft se ＿ sjoen hat?　［弗里斯兰语］
   who ask you REFL PRT if she has seen has
('Who were you wondering if she saw ＿?')

实际上，当非 wh CP 的主语提取时，荷兰语和弗里斯兰语并没有表现出典型的 COMP 语迹效应：

（113） a Wie denk je dat ＿ komt?　　　　　　［荷兰语］
b Wa tinkst   dat ＿ komt?　　　　［弗里斯兰语］
   who think.2sg you that comes
'Who do you think that ＿ is coming?'

---

① 另见凯恩（Kayne 1994: 94）的建议，类似 COMP 语迹效应的内容可以用来排除阿姆哈拉语（Amharic）和其他名词末位关系从句语言中关系从句中显性的 C_s（凯恩认为，其结构为 [$_{IP2}$ [$_{the}$ [$_{CP}$ [$_{NP}$ picture] [C [$_{IP}$ t_2]]]]]，IP 补足语经过限定短语的中心语前移至 C）。但遗憾的是，这一建议与他在 53 页对末位标句词的分析是相冲突的，他将像日语这样的语言中的 [IP C] 顺序分析为是 IP 移位到 SpecCP 的结果：[$_{CP}$ IP$_2$ [C [$_{IP}$ t_2]]]。在这些例子当中，C 可以，而且有时候必须，是显性的。

这一解释在斯洛文尼亚语中也遇到了相同的问题,斯洛文尼亚语也缺少 that 语迹效应(Marvin 1997: 51):

(114) Kdo je Peter mislil, da je prišel?
who AUX Peter thought that AUX come
'Who did Peter think that __ came?'

通过限定这一过滤公式只适应于 [+wh] 标句词,可以挽救这一路径:

(115) *$C_{[+wh]}$ [x ...],其中,$C_{[+wh]}$ 有语音阶,且 x 是不含语音阶的韵律成分。

这样就可以准确地排除所有想要排除的例子,而且可以额外应用于像(111)这样的情况。

另外一种可能性是,诉诸于 C_s^0 上固有的附着性特征:如果可以证明这些成分的右侧必须附着语音成分,那么例(99)(100)(102)不符合语法的原因就会有独立的解释。毫无疑问,标句词对与其后管辖域的韵律合并表现出高度的敏感性,至少右分支语言是这样的(见 Shlonsky 1988 和 McCloskey 1996 分别对希伯来语和爱尔兰语的标句词管辖域的右向依存的讨论)。①

须注意的是,这两种解释路径都是把截省条件下带标句词的例句的不合语法性置于语音形式层面。② 第一个路径将其等同于某种类型的 COMP

---

① 这也使人回想起时常被提及的一个建议(最近版本见 Lightfoot 2000),即英语中被减缩的助动词,在形态句法上附着于其右侧(尽管在韵律上附着于其左侧),这解释了为什么它们在省略和移位部位前不可共现。关于(i)中对比所表现出来的复杂性,见 Pullum and Zwicky 1997:

(i) a He is SO going!
b * He's SO going!

② 这几种解释方法附带着令人欣喜的效应,或许可以帮助我们对其后紧跟着有些成分的"if/whether"截省有更为清晰的认识,如(i)所示,这个例子来自于温克勒(Winkler 1997: 30 (33c))(另见 W. Klein 1993),此处稍微做了修改,以及詹纳基杜和麦钱特(Giannakidou and Merchant 1998)所分析的"逆向"截省,如例(ii)所示。

81 语迹效应，可能会延伸到前面章节中所讨论的大部分语料。尽管还需要更深入的研究来确定这些提议是否能够独立且卓有成效地解释这里讨论的问题，但在我看来，即使现在暂时还不能形式化地表达，这些方法也已把问题纳入到了正确的领域上来，因为对于语音形式接口上的操作过程，我们还需要更多的信息。比起结构上的解决路径，我认为这些方法可能更正确。结构上的解释路径会规定截省删除的是 C′，而不是 IP，因为很难找出其他的以最大投射为目标的例子。另外，这些提议还可以有效减少对 C 系统中成分本质的要求：与洛贝克（Lobeck 1995）的观点不同，我们不需要规定 SpecCP 必须被显性成分填充。

在本节的结尾，我简要评论一下我所知的匈牙利语中的一个例子，这个例子是唯一一个（71）中描述的截省 COMP 概述的潜在反例。在匈牙利语的 wh- 问句中，wh- 短语不会显性移位到 SpecCP 处，而是出现在紧接在动词之前的焦点位置（讨论和文献见 Puskás 1999；在这里我仅考虑非多重 wh- 问句）。如例（116）所示，这一 wh- 短语可以和标句词"that"共现（感谢 D. Farkas 和 G. Puskás 所做的判断）：

（116） Nem emlékszem, (hogy) kivel találkoztak a gyerekek.
　　　　not　I.remember　that　who.with　met　　the　children
　　　　'I don't remember who the kids met.'

从上面的观点来看，多少有些令人惊讶的是，相同的选择也出现在截省中：这一标句词可以省略，也可以保留：

（接上页）
　　（i） Bitte　laß mich hören, wie Ralf reagiert und ob *(überhaupt).
　　　　 please let me hear how Ralf reacts and if at.all
　　　　 'Please let me know how Ralf reacts, if (he reacts) at all.'
　　（ii）Magdalena worried about whether and how to break the news to her father.
　　　　 (Giannakidou and Merchant 1998: 239 (18a))
这些语言事实让人想起 COMP 语迹效应的"副词干涉"改进机制；见 5.1.2 节。

(117) A gyerekek találkoztak valakivel de nem emlékszem,
the children met someone.with but not I.remember
(hogy) kivel.
that who.with
'The kids met someone, but I don't remember who.'

因此，乍看上去，匈牙利语代表着（71）中截省 COMP 概述的一个反例——似乎没有理由认为（117）中的 hogy 不在正常的标句词位置上。这一例句和以上所讨论的那些例句之间的区别在于，例（117）中的 wh- 短语不在 COMP 位置上，它在结构中位置较低，可能和例（116）中相同。这似乎说明只有当 wh- 短语移动到 SpecCP 位置时，截省 COMP 概述才起作用。但是应该注意，如果上面提到的两种韵律分析方法有一个正确的话，那么这种状态正是我们所期待的。因为，在匈牙利语中，（被截省的）wh- 短语出现在标句词的后面，满足上面提到的限制条件之一。特别值得注意的是，截省中对标句词的限制，似乎与这些标句词会附加到省略部位这一事实有关联，而匈牙利语却不是这样。①

---

① 印地语的情况似乎更为复杂——尽管像匈牙利语那样，wh- 短语也出现在动词前的"焦点"位置，但却像英语、丹麦语那样，不允许标句词出现在截省结构中。另外更为复杂的一点是，标句词的隐现并不完全是可选择的，这一点与匈牙利语不同。印地语中内嵌的 CP，像德语那样，可以外置，出现在小句末尾，也可以话题化，出现在小句句首，见 2.1.4.2 节。标句词 ki 更加倾向于出现在句尾位置，而不可能出现在句首。在（ib）中，前置的截省 CP 不能允准 ki，这一点不足为奇，但是在（ia）中，句末截省也禁止 ki，这一点却出乎意料。

(i) a Gautam ne kisi se baat kii thii lekin mujhe nahīĩ pataa
Gautam ERG someone with talk do.PFV PAST but I.DAT NEG knowledge
[(*ki) kis se].
that who with

b Gautam ne kisi se baat kii thii lekin [(*ki) kis se]
Gautam ERG someone with talk do.PFV PAST but that who with
mujhe nahīĩ pataa.
I.DAT NEG knowledge

'Gautam talked with someone, but I don't know who.'
感谢巴特提供的这些语料和相关讨论。

2.3 小结

　　从本章中我们可以得出两个重要的结论。首先，出现在截省中的 wh- 短语并不是一个飘忽不定的幽灵，一个神秘的 XP 片语，以某种奇怪而新颖的方式与周围句法结合在一起。相反，截省中的 wh- 短语是在其常见的位置上，即 SpecCP 位置，而且就出现在我们所期待的疑问式 CP 应出现的环境中。这一结论使我们得出第二个结论，即在截省中有一个消失的 IP，而且这个 IP 内部存在句法结构——CP 必须支配 IP，而且 wh- 短语必须来源于某处。第二个结论要求我们建立一个关于这种空 IP 分布的理论——允准理论。我们可以看出，IP 省略的限制条件对该 IP 的统制姐妹节点上的特征很敏感。尽管这种关系通常被看作是管辖，基于局部特征分布的解释方案（由基础生成或特征移位/中心语移位实现）同样允许我们从 PF 层面删除的路径来诠释省略理论，进而解决问题，我们也将会看到这一理论有很多令人满意的结果。而且令人高兴的是，通过一种特征来表述允准条件，可以使我们把语义结合起来，将允准限制条件和同一性限制条件第一次统一起来。最后，我们发现了一系列新的语言事实，它们可以被截省 COMP 概述解释：在截省中，非算子成分不能出现在 COMP 中。这一令人惊喜的事实看起来与这里所提倡的省略观点完全相符：韵律限制条件与经济原则限制条件共同限定省略部位外部成分、省略部位附着成分和省略部位成分本身等类别。

附录：疑问词原位语言

疑问词原位语言引出了另一个明显的问题。这类语言在形式上是否也存在我们一直关注的在 wh- 移位语言中所发现的截省现象？如果有，是什么机制驱动了满足删除要求的移位？为什么只有在截省下才可以看到这种移位（因为在这些语言中，wh- 移位通常不会以显性形式发生）？尽管这些问题很有趣也很重要，但对这些问题更为深入的探讨已超出目前研究的范围。有关这些问题的研究文献主要集中在日语方面，现已有几种用于解释相关语料的方法。艾瑞喜（Ai）[①] 提供了一个关于日语"截省"的例子；显然，这类语料是由井上（Inoue 1976, 1978）首次提到的。

（AI） Abby-ga   dareka-o   mi-ta   ga, watashi-wa dare ka wakaranai.
       Abby-NOM someone-ACC see-PAST but I-TOP   who Q   know.not
       'Abby saw someone, but I don't know who.'

已有好几种方法可以用来解释这类语料。高桥（Takahashi 1994）提出日语中有一种特殊的 wh- 移位（"挪移"至标句词短语（CP）的指示语位置），经过删除，可以得到基本上等同于英语截省句的结构。然而，他的分析受到了广泛批评，这些批评既有来自遵循 LF 或后 LF 复制法的学者（Nishigauchi 1998；对某一种特定截省的讨论见 Fukaya 1998, Hoji and Fukaya 1999），也有来自那些支持"截省"是一种简化的分裂结构的学者（Shimoyama 1995, Kuwabara 1996, Nishiyama *et al*. 1996, Kizu 1997, Merchant 1998；对另一种截省的讨论见 Hoji and Fukaya 1999；关于这种方法对英语不成立的原因，见 4.2 节）。

我自己对日语和汉语中这类语料的有限探索也得出了类似的结论——

[①] 这里指 Ai, Ruixi Ressy. 2006. Elliptical Predicate Constructions in Mandarin. PhD dissertation, Harvard University. ——译者

这些语言中看似是截省的结构，实际上是某些操作的结果，这些操作不同于那些具有显性 wh- 移位语言中所发现的移位 + 删除的推导。这也与西山（Nishiyama et al. 1996）和木津（Kizu 1997）对韩语和汉语所做出的结论相吻合。

匈牙利语、印地语和土耳其语这类语言中的情况有些不太明晰。这些语言中 wh- 短语出现在与动词邻近的特定位置；对于印地语和土耳其语等代表性 SOV 语言而言，这就意味着 wh- 短语通常会出现在小句内部，紧随句内其他成分之后。在这方面，我所得到的语料是有限的、混杂的。虽然印地语似乎的确具有至少在表面上与英语截省句相似的结构（见如 2.1.4.2 中的语料），但木津（Kizu 1997）表示土耳其语中缺少这些结构，取代它的是某种形式的系动词。我自己有限的信息收集工作表明，尽管这种类分裂结构（cleft-like structures）明显更可取，但尚不清楚与英语截省句更为相似的结构是否完全不可接受。例如，对于多重截省（multiple sluicing）而言（简要讨论见 4.1 节），系动词可以缺省。

一种可能性是，印地语和土耳其语中的截省结构，在一定程度上与像英语这样具有显性 wh- 移位至 CP 指示语位置的语言中的截省结构一样，都采取了一种挪移型移位，从而产生删除的输入结构，且不采用向 CP 指示语位置的"真正的"wh- 移位（例如，通过挪移成为 IP 的附加语，再将下面的 IP 片段删除）。另一种可能性是，任何阻止向 CP 指示语位置进行显性移位的限制都会因删除自身而得以改善，无论这种想法如何得以实现（例如，根据上述有关 I 到 C 移位的推理，一种可能是认为这些语言中 wh- 移位的语迹会触发某种能被删除修复的 PF 崩溃）。

这些问题在我看来是相当直接的事实和分析。很遗憾，我目前无法解决这些问题，只能把它们留给相关语言的专家；但重要的是，这些语言似乎与这里采用的总体方法不存在本质上的不兼容。

第三章

孤岛和形式同一性

前文已证实截省涉及 CP 和空 IP，现在我将在考察大量语料的基础上，探讨与之相关的两个问题：CP 指示语（SpecCP）上的 wh- 短语的原始位置在哪里，以及空 IP 是如何产生的。本章通过界定本书的核心、也是全新的研究难题，为第四章和第五章中将要进行的讨论奠定基础。我将展示大量证据，表明 wh- 短语并不是通过移位来占据标句词短语的指示语位置；也将展示大量明显的反例，表明 wh- 短语移位前的原始位置在空 IP 内部。这些证据可总结如下：截省不遵守孤岛条件，而截省中的 wh- 短语残余在语法形式上表现出语言特定的规律性。后面两章将详细考察这些实证性发现的理论价值。

3.1 截省中的句法（"强"）孤岛

罗斯（Ross 1969）注意到，截省可以改进他在 1967 年论文中所发现的一些孤岛条件。他着重给出了下面五个例句，本文将例句和他最初的判断转引于此。

（1）并列结构限制（Ross 1969（71b））

?? Irv and someone were dancing together, but I don't know who.

（2）复杂名词短语限制（Ross 1969（72b, d））

a ? She kissed a man who bit one of my friends, but Tom doesn't realize which one of my friends.

 b I believe (??the claim) that he bit someone, but they don't know who.

（3）句子主语限制（Ross 1969（73b））

 ??That he'll hire someone is possible, but I won't divulge who.

（4）左分支条件（Ross 1969（74b））

 *I know that he must be proud of it, but I don't know how.

如莱文（Levin 1982）指出，例（2b）和例（3）在句法上略微的降格是由无关因素引起的：即一个可以很容易被修复的语用冲突（见下文更典型的例句）。（2a）也是类似的情况：wh- 短语中 *one of my friends* 的重复稍显冗余；若去掉此部分，该例句就完全合法了。我会在第五章中重新讨论例（1）和例（4）的情况，其中部分判断确实经得起更仔细的检验（特别是例（4），它完全经得起检验）。

除这些例句外，截省似乎可以在更大范围内违反罗斯的孤岛条件和后续发现的其他孤岛条件。本小节的剩余部分列出了相关语料，后续章节会对此进行详细讨论。

此处我只讨论"强"孤岛，而将"弱"孤岛留到第五章讨论。我认为这些"强"孤岛在本质上是句法性的，也就是说，在这些孤岛提取上所发现的偏差并不仅仅源于解读方面的影响，但弱孤岛的情况确实如此。此处的例句均出自英语语料，尽管后续章节也会引入一些相关的跨语言语料。

第一种情况是下文所看到的关系从句孤岛。截省句和与其解读等同的未截省显性疑问句在合法性上形成了鲜明对比。

（5）关系从句孤岛

 They want to hire someone who speaks a Balkan language, but I don't remember which.

 （比较 *I don't remember which (Balkan language) they want to hire someone who speaks.*）

附加语孤岛中也发现了同样的差异。

（6）附加语

a Ben will be mad if Abby talks to one of the teachers, but she couldn't remember which.

比较 *Ben will be mad if Abby talks to one of the teachers, but she couldn't remember which *(of the teachers) Ben will be mad if she talks to.*

b Ben left the party because one of the guests insulted him, but he wouldn't tell me which.

下面的例句大多引自钟等（Chung *et al.* 1995）（下文简称 CLM）。在这些例句中，我没有提供不合法提取的对照例句，要靠读者自行补出这些众所周知的事实。

（7）名词的补足语（CLM（94c））

The administration has issued a statement that it is willing to meet with one of the student groups, but I'm not sure which one.

（8）句子主语（CLM（94b））

That certain countries would vote against the resolution has been widely reported, but I'm not sure which ones.

（9）内嵌疑问句（CLM（94a））

Sandy was trying to work out which students would be able to solve a certain problem, but she wouldn't tell us which one.

（10）并列结构限制

a ?They persuaded Kennedy and some other Senator to jointly sponsor the legislation, but I can't remember which one.（CLM（83b））

b Bob ate dinner and saw a movie that night, but he didn't say which (movie).

（11）标句词语迹效应（CLM（85），（86a））

a It has been determined that somebody will be appointed; it's just not clear yet who.

b Sally asked if somebody was going to fail Syntax One, but I can't remember who.

（12）左分支（定语性形容词）

They hired a tall forward for the team — guess how tall!

（13）派生位置孤岛（话题化、主语）

a A: A biography of one of the Marx brothers, she refused to read.
B: Which one?

b A biography of one of the Marx brothers {is going to be published/will appear} this year — guess which!

虽然我不会在这里进行展示，但文献中记录了许多其他类型的孤岛（相关概述见 Postal 1996）。我认为上述清单可以完全满足我们的目的，因为我将建议对这些项目进行分析，而无须对此处未加说明的其他类型孤岛进行修改。

单从这些语料来看，很显然，截省中的 wh- 短语并不是通过常规的移位机制从 IP 内部位置提升到 CP 指示语位置的。

3.2 形式同一性概述

本节的目标是证实两个密切相关的概述的有效性，一个与截省的 wh- 短语有关，另一个与截省中的介词裹挟式移位有关。这两个概述至关重要，能够制约下面章节的理论选择。

3.2.1 格匹配

第一个概述的部分内容在 2.1.3 节中已有所提及，并且可以追溯到罗斯（Ross 1969），他对截省的许多观察也是如此。本文将罗斯的语料转引为例（14）和（15），为了完整性，添加了主格形式 *wer*：

（14）Er will jemandem schmeicheln, aber sie wissen nicht,
　　　　he wants someone.DAT flatter　　but they know not
　　　　{*wer　　/*wen　　/wem}.
　　　　 who.NOM　who.ACC　who.DAT
　　　'He wants to flatter someone, but they don't know who.'

（15）Er will jamandem loben, aber sie wissen nicht, {*wer
　　　　he wants someone.ACC praise but they know not　who.NOM
　　　　/wen　　/*wem}.
　　　　who.ACC　who.DAT
　　　'He wants to praise someone, but they don't know who.'

　　动词 schmeicheln 'flatter' 赋予其宾语与格，loben 'praise' 赋予其宾语宾格。（14）和（15）中截省的 wh- 短语的格与它在非省略内嵌疑问句中关联成分的格相同，如（16）和（17）所示：

（16）Sie wissen nicht, {*wer　　/*wen　　/wem} er schmeicheln will.
　　　　they know not　 who.NOM　who.ACC　who.DAT he flatter　　wants
　　　'They don't know who he wants to flatter.'

（17）Sie wissen nicht, {*wer　　/wen　　/*wem} er loben will.
　　　　they know not　 who.NOM　who.ACC　who.DAT he praise wants
　　　'They don't know who he wants to praise.'

　　这些语料证实，至少在单一小句范畴内，假设截省的 wh- 短语存在关联成分，则二者的格必须一致。由于关于截省的文献主要关注英语语料，所以对这种格属性没有做更多的论述。实际上，我所考察过的每一个对 wh- 短语进行显性格标记的语言都有这种格匹配属性（德语、希腊语、俄语、波兰语、捷克语、斯洛文尼亚语、芬兰语、印地语、匈牙利语和巴斯克语；日语的情况稍微复杂一些——见第二章附录中的文献）。这类语料似乎为删除法提供了初步证据，因为在删除法下，（14）和（15）分别派生自（16）和（17）。

　　一个很明显的疑问是，这种格匹配在跨越孤岛时是否也成立？尽管据我所知这一问题从未被研究过，但显而易见，同样的格匹配要求在跨越孤岛时也确实成立。在这里，我用德语中关系从句孤岛中的截省①来说明这一点。在这些语料中，动词 *helfen* 'help' 和 *sehen* 'see' 分别赋予其宾语与格和宾格。

(18) Sie will jemanden finden, der einem der Gefangenen geholfen hat,
She wants someone find who one.DAT of.the prisoners helped has
aber ich weiß nicht, {*welcher /*welcher /welchem}.
but I know not which.NOM which.ACC which.DAT
'She wants to find someone who helped one of the prisoners, but I don't know which.'

(19) Sie will jemanden finden, der einen der Gefangenen gesehen hat,
She wants someone find who one.ACC of.the prisoners seen has
aber ich weiß nicht, {*welcher /welcher /*welchem}.
but I know not which.NOM which.ACC which.DAT
'She wants to find someone who saw one of the prisoners, but I don't know which.'

尽管我在说明这一点时用的是德语语料，但我也在其他九种格标记语言中验证过，这一概括同样成立（希腊语、俄语、波兰语、捷克语、斯洛文尼亚语、芬兰语、印地语、匈牙利语、巴斯克语）。由此可得出第一个形式同一性概括，如（20）所述：

(20) 形式同一性概述（一）：格匹配
截省的 wh- 短语必须与其关联成分具有同样的格。

---

① 此处及后文，我经常只阐释关系从句和 *if* 从句中的孤岛，因为这两种孤岛在跨语言中最为常见，说话者对这两种孤岛的判断也要比其他类型的孤岛更加确定。在如 *want* 这样的内涵性动词下关系从句对从言宾语的选择也使我们确信，孤岛的确在省略位置得到了解读：似乎没有比主句更小的命题范围可以用来清楚地解析省略现象了。因此，我将经常使用这两种从句以及条件句的前提分句（这似乎同样承认了在截省下没有其他合理的解读），因为要确保说话者能够对有歧义的截省句做出正确解读，会极大地增加判断任务的复杂性，可能会使语料太具干扰性而无法使用。

尽管这一概述在表述中明确提到有一个关联成分，但我们从前文 2.1.3 节可知，即使缺少关联成分，截省的 wh- 短语的格属性仍然完全由它在省略 IP 中的功能所决定。我在这里暂且不考虑缺少关联成分的情况，因为下文会提到，由于与辖域和焦点要求相关的独立因素，没有关联成分的 wh- 短语极难受孤岛影响。既然情况如此，我将保留（20）当前的形式，为了保持简洁，暂不提及介入的孤岛。但读者应该记住这是简化形式。

3.2.2　介词悬置

第二个概述关注的是介系词（adposition）和截省 DP 的分布，以及这种分布与显性 wh- 移位模式之间的联系。广义上讲，语言似乎是在两个简单的选项间进行选择，即是否可以把一个 wh-DP 从相关的介词处移走：可以或者不可以。事实上，第一种选项似乎很难得到证明：德莱尔（Dryer 1997）在 625 种语料的样本中发现，在日耳曼语族以外，找不到任何语言可以有效地允准这种移位。[①] 事实简单而明显：在英语、弗里斯兰语和斯堪的纳维亚语中，在所有标准的 wh- 移位环境下，比如疑问句、话题化、关系化（包括分裂句和假分裂句）和比较句，wh- 移位都可能会使介词悬置。在其他所有语言中，所采取的策略是介词必须连同所管辖的 wh-DP 一起移位，这一现象被罗斯（Ross 1967）称为"裹挟式移位"。

我们很容易把第二个形式同一性概括用最简单的形式表述出来，见（21）：

(21) 形式同一性概述（二）：介词悬置
当且仅当语言 L 在常规 wh- 移位下允准介词悬置时，L 才允许截省下的介词悬置。

这一概括是根据语料（22）至（45）得出的，其中（a）句为截省语

[①] 赫希比勒（P. Hirschbühler，私下交流）告诉我，法语的新斯科舍（Nova Scotian）方言也可以有效地允许介词悬置，这大概是和英语密切接触的结果。

料,(b)句为对照组。(除一个例句外,例句(23)至(45)中所有(a)句都是英语例句(22a)的翻译,(b)句都是(22b)的翻译,它们都带有一个悬置的介词。)

第一组语料来自介词悬置语言:英语、弗里斯兰语、瑞典语、挪威语、丹麦语和冰岛语。感谢汉恩(G. de Haan)、胡克斯特拉(J. Hoekstra)和弗里斯(O. Vries)提供弗里斯兰语语料,桑德尔(K. Sandell)和斯韦诺纽斯(P. Svenonius)提供瑞典语语料,斯韦诺纽斯提供挪威语语料,米克尔森(L. Mikkelsen)提供丹麦语语料,以及萨恩森(H. Thráinsson)提供冰岛语语料。

(22) 英语

    a Peter was talking with someone, but I don't know (with) who.[①]

    b Who was he talking with?

(23) 弗里斯兰语

    a Piet hat mei ien sprutsen, mar ik wyt net (mei) wa.
      Piet has with someone talked but I know not with who

    b Wa hat Piet mei sprutsen?
      who has Piet with talked

(24) 瑞典语

    a Peter har talat med någon; jag vet inte (med) vem.
      Peter has talked with someone I know not with who

[①] (22)中呈现的语料会使人们认为情况比较简单,英语语料实际上要比这稍加复杂一些。(i)中更加准确地陈述了实际情况:

    (i) Peter was talking with someone,
      a but I don't know who.
      b %but I don't know with whom.
      c ?but I don't know with who.

(ia)最为自然,在正常会话中将是首选。(ib)为正式形式,尤其是书面语体的英语——见下文讨论。(ic)是稍加标记的,本质上是一种语域冲突:在介词裹挟式移位的语体中,*whom* 这一形式是被强烈禁止的。

b Vem har Peter talat med?
　　　who has Peter talked with

（25）挪威语

　　a Per har snakket med neon, men jeg vet ikke (med) hvem.
　　　Per has talked with someone but I know not with who

　　b Hvem har Peter snakket med?
　　　who has Peter talked with

（26）丹麦语

　　a Peter har snakket med en eller anden, men jeg ved ikke (med) hvem.
　　　Peter has talked with one or another but I knwo not with who

　　b Hvem har Peter snakket med?
　　　who has Peter talked with

（27）冰岛语

　　a Pétur hefur talað við einhvern en ég veit ekki (við) hvern
　　　Peter has spoken with someone but I know not with who

　　b Hvern hefur Pétur talað við?
　　　who has Peter talked with

第二组语料来自常规 wh- 移位下不允许介词悬置的语言，即（b）所示的例句不合法。此处的语料样本只限于那些表明 wh- 移位至小句句首位置的语言，排除了将 wh- 短语置于小句内部焦点位置的语言、仅通过挪移移位 wh- 短语的语言以及根本未表现出 wh- 移位的语言（见第二章附录中的简要讨论）。当然，传统语法中缺少截省语料，因此我所收录的语料只能来自于那些我有机会接触到的母语者。这在很大程度上使语料的样本库向欧洲和北非语言倾斜，令我无法给出任何充分的类型学主张。此处提供的语料来自 18 种语言，其中 15 种是印欧语：希腊语（希腊语支）、德语、荷兰语、意第绪语（西日耳曼语支）、俄语（东斯拉夫语支）、波兰语、捷克语（西斯拉夫语支）、保加利亚语、塞尔维亚—克罗地亚语、斯洛文尼亚语（南斯拉夫语支）、波斯语（印度－伊朗语支)、加泰罗尼亚语、西班牙语、法语和意大利语(罗曼语支)。另有 2 种是亚非语:希伯来语和摩洛哥阿拉伯语(闪语)。最后 1 种是巴斯克语(孤立语)。

希腊语语料经由阿古拉基(Y. Agouraki)、亚历克西娅杜(A. Alexiadou)、阿纳格诺斯托普洛(E. Anagnostopoulou)、达诺普洛斯(K. Danopoulos)、詹纳基杜(A. Giannakidou)和鲁苏(A. Roussou)核实。不同说话者不同时期的判断是一致的。

(28) 希腊语

 a I Anna milise me kapjon, alla dhe ksero *(me) pjon.
  the Anna spoke with someone but not I.know with who
 b *Pjon milise me?
  who she.spoke with

德语语料经由布林(D. Büring)、迈宁格(A. Meinunger)、梅斯特(A. Mester)、罗特(H. Rott)和温克勒(S. Winkler)核实。不同说话者在不同时期的判断是一致的。

(29) 德语①

 a Anna hat mit jemandem gesprochen, aber ich weiß nicht, *(mit) wem.
  Anna has with someone spoken but I know not with who
 b *Wem hat sie mit gesprochen?
  who has she with spoken

---

① 瑞士德语也一样,如(i)中的格拉鲁斯(Glarus)方言所示(感谢斯佩尔蒂(P. Spaelti)、黑伯利(E. Haeberli)告诉我,这些明确的判断对于其他瑞士德语方言也成立)。
 (i) a Dr Ruedi hät ds ganz Läbe vumene Land träumt, aber ich wäiss nüd *(vu) welem.
   *the Ruedi has the whole life of.a land dreamt, but I know not of which.*DAT
   'Reudi has dreamt his whole life of some country, but I don't know of which.'
  b *Welem Land hät dr Ruedi ds ganz Läbe vu träumt?
   which country has the Ruedi the whole life of dreamt
   ('Which country has Ruedi dreamt of his whole life?')

荷兰语语料①经由科弗（N. Corver）、格布兰迪（J. Gerbrandy）、亨德里克斯（H. Hendriks）、亨德里克斯（P. Hendriks）、霍克西马（J. Hoeksema）、霍利布兰德斯（B. Hollebrandse）、马尔德斯（I. Mulders）、范里姆斯迪克、范罗伊（R. van Rooy）和吕斯（E. Ruys）核实。

（30） 荷兰语②

---

① 这里有个值得注意的小问题。荷兰语、德语和瑞士德语允许介词与一小类成分悬置，这类成分被称为 R 代词（见 van Riemsdijk 1978）。然而这些成分并不会作为光杆残余成分出现在截省中，见（i）中的荷兰语语料（德语和瑞士德语也一样）。

（i） *Hij rekent ergens   op, maar ik weet   niet, waar.
    he counts something on but   I know not   what
    ('He is counting on something, but I don't know what.')

这大概是因为残余的 wh- 短语在这些环境下必须是焦点，第 57 页脚注 ① 对此已有提及。这一要求与这些成分不能被强调的事实相冲突：

（ii） a *Ik weet niet, WAAR hij op rekent.［只在 WAAR 上对比］
      b Ik weet niet, waar   hij OP rekent.
          I know not what   he on counts
          'I don't know what he's counting on.'

关于这些成分中重音位置的讨论，见古森霍芬（Gussenhoven 1983: 第 5 章）和胡克斯特拉（Hoekstra 1995）。

② 荷兰语的情况似乎是此处所考察语言中最不稳定的，例（30）中句（a）和（b）使用了各种标注就反映出了这一点，这些标注代表从受访者那里收集到的各种答复。许多受访者（十分之六）认为无介词的截省语句可以接受（有介词时所有人都认为可接受），有些受访者（十分之二）认为，尽管并非完全合法（主观因素可能影响了受访者对非省略测试语料的判断），(30b) 没有省略的疑问句中的介词悬置也是可以接受的。

一般来说，荷兰语似乎是一种过渡情况，比如，荷兰语允许介词悬置的范围比德语广，但受到的限制比弗里斯兰语多。即使在精心编写的文献中，规范上无法接受的 A' 移位下的介词悬置也得到了证实，请比较（i）中的例句（出自 Voskuil 1996: 65）：

（i） Onrechtvaardigheid wind ik me   over op.
    injustice   work I REFL about up
    'Injustice, I get worked up about.'

下面的光杆截省 wh- 短语也引自同一部文献，该 wh- 短语的对应在 PP 内部（Voskuil 1996: 31）：

（ii） De jongen leek   op iemand, maar hij kon niet bedenken wie.
     the boy   seemed on someone, but he could not think   who
     'The boy looked like someone, but he couldn't think who.'

鉴于目前荷兰语的使用情况不稳定，对截省例句的判断结果各异似乎并不完全出乎意料。

a Anna heeft met iemand gesproken, marr ik weet niet??/?/√
   Anna has with someone spoken   but I know not
   (met) wie.
   with who

b */??/?Wie heeft zij mee gesproken?
   who has she with spoken

意第绪语语料由萨多克（J. Sadock）和斯坦伯格（E. Steinberg）提供。

（31）意第绪语

a Zi hot mit emetsn geredt, ober ikh veys nit *(mit) vemen.
   she has with someone spoken but I know not with who

b *Vemen hot zi mit geredt?
   who has she with spoken

俄语语料由阿夫鲁京（S. Avrutin）和克里扎斯卡娅（D. Krizhanskaya）提供。

（32）俄语

a Anja govorila s kem-to, no ne znaju *(s) kem.
   Anja spoke with someone but not I.know with who

b *Kem ona govorila s?
   who she spoke with

波兰语语料由莫克罗辛斯卡（D. Mokrosinska）和普里齐奥科夫斯基（A. Przepiórkowski）提供。

（33）波兰语

a Anna rozmawiała z kimś, ale nie wiem *(z) kim.
   Anna spoke with someone but not I.know with who

b *Kim rozmawiała Anna z?
   who spoke Anna with

捷克语语料由菲利普（H. Filip）提供。

（34）捷克语

    a Anna mluvila s   někým, ale nevím   *(s)   kým.
       Anna spoke   with someone but not.I.know   with who

    b *Kým mluvila Anna s?
       who spoke   Anna with

保加利亚语语料由迪亚诺娃（S. Dianova）提供。

（35）保加利亚语

    a Anna e   govorila s njakoj, no ne znam *(s)   koj.
       Anna AUX *spoken with someone but not I.know with who*

    b *Koj e govorila Anna s?
       who AUX *spoke   Anna with*

塞尔维亚-克罗地亚语语料由戈杰瓦茨（S. Godjevac）提供。

（36）塞尔维亚-克罗地亚语

    a Ana je   govorila sa   nekim, ali ne znam   *(sa)   kim.
       Ana AUX *spoken with someone but not I.know with who*

    b *Kim je   govorila Ana sa?
       who AUX *spoken Ana with*

斯洛文尼亚语语料由马文（T. Marvin）提供。

（37）斯洛文尼亚语

    a Anna je govorila z   nekom, ampak ne vem   *(s)   kom.
       Anna AUX *spoken with someone but   not I.know with who*

    b *Kom je govorila Anna s?
       who AUX *spoken Anna with*

波斯语语料由阿盖伊（B. Aghaei）提供。

（38）波斯语

    a Ali bā   kasi   harf mi-zad,   ʔamā ne-mi-dan-am *(bā) ki.
       Ali with someone talk PROG-hit.3sg *but   not*-PROG-*know*-1sg *with who*

  b　*Ki　Ali bā　 harf mi-zad?
　　　　who Ali with talk PROG-hit.3sg

加泰罗尼亚语语料由克尔（J. Quer）提供。

(39)　加泰罗尼亚语
  a　L'Anna　va　parlar　amb algú,　però no sé　??(amb) qui.
　　　　the-Anna AUX speak with someone but not I.know with who
  b　*Qui va　parlar　l'Anna　amb?
　　　　who AUX speak the-Anna with

法语语料由费里（C. Féry）、赫希比勒（P. Hirschbühler）和拉贝尔（M. Labelle）提供。①

(40)　法语
  a　Anne l'a　offert　à quelqu'un, mais je ne sais pas *(à) qui.
　　　　Anne it-has offered to someone but I NEG know not to who
  b　*Qui est-ce qu'elle l'a　offert　à?
　　　　who Q　 she it-has offered to

西班牙语语料由古铁雷斯（R. Gutierrez）和克尔（J. Quer）提供。②

---

① 这些说话者的判断有些不同。尽管他们三人都认为正文中那样的例句不可接受，但其中有两位并不认为（ia）这样的例句有何偏差，如下所示。（ib）中带有重复介词的预期变式在所有说话者看来都是完全合法的。
  （i）a　Elle a　parlé　avec quelqu'un, mais je ne　sais　pas qui.
　　　　　She has spoken with　 someone but I NEG know not who
　　　　　'She spoke with someone, but I don't know who.'
　　　　　[三位说话者中有两位把此句标为"?"，一位标为"*"]
  　b　Elle a parlé avec quelqu'un, mais je ne sais pas avec qui.

② 古铁雷斯讲墨西哥语，克尔讲西班牙语。古铁雷斯认为，虽然带介词的截省不太可接受，但不带介词的截省变式大多可接受。然而他认为，（i）中不带介词的解释更不合语法。
  （i）Ana habló　con　 alguien,　pero *(con) quién, no sé.
　　　　Ana spoke with someone but　 with who not I.know
同样，莫拉（J. Mora）对（ii）中的例句给出了清晰的判断。

（41）西班牙语

    a Ana habló con alguien, pero no sé　　??(con) quién.
       Ana spoke with someone but not I.know　with who

    b *¿Quién habló　　con?
       who　spoke.3sg with

意大利语语料由阿洛尼（M. Aloni）、科基（G. Cocchi）和莫纳凯西（P. Monachesi）提供。三位说话者中有两位认为不带介词的变式几乎可以被接受。

（42）意大利语

    a Pietro ha parlato con qualcuno, ma non so　?(con) chi.
       Pietro has spoken with someone but not I.know with who

    b *Chi ha parlato Pietro con?
       who has spoken Peter with

希伯来语语料由多伦（E. Doron）、福克斯（D. Fox）和温特（Y. Winter）提供。他们的判断有较大差异，其中一人认为（43a）可接受，另一人认为不可接受，第三位介于两者之间。①

（接上页）

    (ii) a Me he bebido la cerveza de alguien, pero no sé *(de) quién.
        Me I.have drunk the beer of someone but not I.know of who
        'I drank up someone's beer, but I don't know whose.'

       b *¿Quién he bebido la cerveza de?
        who I.have drunk the beer of
        (Whose beer did I drink?)

目前我还没有办法解释这些判断上的差异。

① 多伦认为（43a）可接受，然而他提供了例句（i），认为该例句明显不合语法。在（i）中，介词 le 本质上是与格标记，经常被标示为与格标记。

    (i) Dani katav le-mišehu, aval ani lo yode'a *(le-) mi.
       Dani wrote to-someone but I not know to-who
       'Dani wrote to someone, but I don't know who.'

温特指出了宾格标记 et 可能出现的位置（比如部分不定词上），类似的对比呈现了出来：

    (ii) Ra'iti exad me-ha-yeladim, aval ani lo yode'a ??(et) mi.
       I.saw ACC one of-the-children but I not know ACC which
       'I saw one of the children, but I don't know which.'

(43) 希伯来语
　　a Adam diber 'im mišehu, aval ani lo yode ?('im) mi.
　　　　Adam spoke with someone but I not know with who
　　b *Mi Adam diber 'im?
　　　　who Adam spoke with

摩洛哥阿拉伯语语料由达米尔（M. Damir）和本纳尼－梅齐亚纳（M. Bennani-Meziane）提供。

(44) 摩洛哥阿拉伯语
　　a Driss tkəllem mᶜa ši wahəd, walakin ma ᶜraft š *(mᶜa) mən.
　　　　Driss talked with someone but not know NEG with who
　　b *Mən tkəllem Driss mᶜa?
　　　　who talked Driss with

巴斯克语语料由埃洛迪埃塔（A. Elordieta）提供。

(45) 巴斯克语
　　a Ana-k norbait-ekin hitzegin zuen, baina ez dakit nor-*(ekin).
　　　　Ana-ERG someone-with talk.to AUX but not know who- with
　　b *Nor hitzegin zuen -ekin?
　　　　who talk.to AUX with

这些语料代表的是最简单和最清晰的情况——单句范围内的介词短语论元。说话者对这种例句的判断是很有把握的。我的初步设想是，应该用核心的语法原则来解释这些核心语料。这并非无视或者否认当语料库扩展到其他类型的介词或介词的其他用法时（通常大致区分出"论元"和"附加语"这两种用法），语料会发生变化。在某些情况和某些语言中，说话者似乎可以接受用光杆 wh- 短语来代替介词短语，尽管我还不能足够清晰地断定在何种情况下这是可能的，或者这是否是某一类介词或语言的一个系统性的属性。例句（a）中偶尔使用"??"或"?"表明不同说话者之间的判断存在差异，选取的是受访者的平均判断情况。这种差异大多出现在那些显性格系统匮乏的语言中，在高度格标记语言里（德语、希腊语、俄语、捷克语、波兰语、塞尔维亚-克罗地亚语和斯洛文尼亚语），受访者的判断完全一致而且十分肯定。① 因此，我将主要关注后者，因为受访者的判断最为清晰。其他情况下判断出现变化可能有两个原因。

第一，我认为在许多情况下，因为我们首先处理省略结构，包容性强的说话者尤为愿意根据需要对省略进行解读，判断某一特定例句为"可接受的"。由于省略，"可接受的"往往意味着"可解读的"。在做出这些判断时，我经常发现说话者对建立必要的相关联系犹豫不决：毕竟在所有情况中，"I don't know who"这种带光杆wh-短语而非介词短语的句子是完全合乎语法且可解读的。② 当然这样做的目的是，如果作为省略源头的先行句紧接在前面，并且只有这一个句子出现时，带光杆wh-短语的句子就不合语法。在判断简单的介词悬置提取时，情况就并非如此：在这种情况下，没有发现来自线性同一的合法语句的干扰。因此，在判断截省时要像判断可能的约束关系和辖域时一样敏锐与克制——从一无所知的受访者那里收集到清晰的跨语言语料是极其困难的。然而，即使是有复杂语言背景的受访者，收集语料时也必须小心谨慎，因为截省并不是一个普通的研究领域，包容性是语料中真正的干扰源。对于省略结构而言尤其如此，做

---

① 这在印地语中也同样成立，尽管我在正文中没有讨论这一语言，因为印地语中wh-短语的位置不像上述语言一样位于小句边缘（它与土耳其语和匈牙利语的模式相同，倾向于把wh-XP放在动词前的焦点位置）。印地语的形式同一性效果如（i）所示（感谢巴特提供此语料）。

(i) Gautam-ne kisi se baat kii thii, lekin mujhe pataa nahīī kis *(se).
Gautam-ERG someone with talk do.PFV PAST but I.DAT knowledge NEG who with
'Gautam spoke with someone, but I don't know with who.'

② 特别是在那些没有显性形态学的格的语言中，我们可能要处理的是类似"… who it is"的截除现象。一些说话者也建议我这样做，对于带有这种后续成分的目标语句，他们只能给出非省略形式。大概在这些没有显性格标记的语言中，这种现象是可能的。但在有更明确格标记的语言中，这种现象是不可能的。因为在前者中疑问词的格不能完全确定，而后者中的wh-短语必须被标记为主格。

出预期的解读与判定某一例句合乎语法是同时进行的。很明显，受访者往往直到做出清晰的解读时，才会凭借自己所理解的，宣称该句"可接受"（当然，永远不可能在做出清晰解读之前宣称某句合乎语法，但合乎语法超越且不同于简单的可解读性）。这在一定程度是正确的，但并不是问题的全貌，因为在有些语言中，受访者的判断并无差异。这使我想到了第二个可能造成差异的原因。

很难相信显性形态上的格与介词悬置例句判断上的清晰度之间的关联完全是偶然的。很有可能，截省可以为我们展示一个在跨语言中探究控制介词悬置的窗口，这一机制在某些格和介词标记间存在较强联系的语言与联系较弱的其他语言之间并没有变异。尽管我无法解释介词悬置的成因（这是一个有名的、开放式的跨语言句法难题：语料及文献见 van Riemsdijk 1978, Takami 1992, J. Hoekstra 1995），但从一些绝对概念出发似乎不太可能是考察介词悬置的最有效的方法，比如介词是不是严格管辖者（Kayne 1981），或者与动词合并的能力（Hornstein and Weinberg 1981；反对的观点尤见 Takami 1992, Baltin and Postal 1996）。相反，采用传统的直觉性观点，把介词视为像格一样的语法功能标记，似乎最为合理（参看两者之间的普通历史性联系，在许多语言中，如芬兰语、匈牙利语和列兹基语，很难将两者区分开）。

我的基本思路是，各语言在语法关系标记方式的分析性上存在差异：在英语、弗里斯兰语和斯堪的纳维亚语中，介词与其名义上的宾语是可分的，因此这些语言极具分析性；而像列兹基语这样高度融合的系统，则是另一种极端，不允许对"介词"和附着在论元上表明语法角色的其他语素做任何区分。这种看法要求我们放弃以统一的分析尺度来对整个语言系统进行排序，并且把这种统一的分析尺度分解为不同领域中的一个分析功能。这些领域之间如何相关以及是否应该相关，是个很有意思的问题，当然也是个独立的问题。

这些论述只是为了解释上文中判断存在差异的原因：有些语言禁止介

词悬置，但在截省下会有明显的介词悬置现象，这种变化可能是在告诉我们这些语言中的一些分析机制。与德语和希腊语等在任何情况下介词都不能悬置的语言相比，这些语言就介词来说"不那么具有分析性"。再次说明，这些简要的论述不能被视为一种介词悬置理论，它只是呈现了一种可能用以解释上述事实的方法。

关于这些不同原因的干扰性因素，这里只是抛砖引玉，在每种语言中进一步对它们进行研究和完善肯定是必要的。不过我会记住这里仅做了简化处理，在本书的其余部分，我将专注于探讨本节所呈现的语料，主要对它们进行解释。

在继续考察新的语料之前，我要先为上面刚讨论过的那类语料提供一些更加详细的例句，这些例句都出自我接触较多并有一定了解的语言，以帮助完善实证语料。这些语料对上述概要性的语料做出了补充，也处理了个别讨论过的语言中的小问题。但目前我不会冒着逐渐偏离研究主线的风险，深入探究它们。不过我觉得在记录这些语料时，有必要比上文做得更加详细，以此作为进一步研究的起点。

首先，我提供了德语、希腊语、波兰语和俄语中其他类的介词短语的语料：这四种语言中被传递信息谓词选择的、以等同于"about"的词为中心语的介词短语，以及在德语中只被 *entscheiden* 'decide' 选择的、以 *für* 'for' 为中心语的介词短语。波兰语和俄语语料也可能排斥使用 *s/z* 'with' 一词，*s/z* 有很强的韵律依赖性，它和格标记没有什么区别（试比较在土耳其语、匈牙利语、芬兰语和列兹基语中，基于理论对二者进行区分的难度）；在这里，介词 *o* 'about' 至少自己形成了一个音节。

(46) 德语

  a Peter hat über jemanden aus deiner Klasse gesprochen—rate mal,
   Peter has about someone from your class spoken guess PRT
   *(über) wen.
   about who
  'Peter was talking about someone from your class—guess who.'

b Peter hat sich für ein amerikanisches College entschieden,
   Peter has REFL for a American college decided
   aber er wollte uns nicht sagen, *(für) welches.
   but he wanted us not say for which
   'Peter decided on an American college, but he wouldn't tell us which.'

(47) 希腊语
   I gonis tou pedhiou malosan gia kati, alla
   the parents of.the child argued.3pl about something, but
   arnite na ma pi *(gia) ti.
   refused.3sg SUBJ us tell about what.
   'The child's parents were arguing about something, but she refused to tell us what.'

(48) 波兰语
   Anna rozmawiała o czymś, ale nie wiem *(o) czym.
   Anna talked about something but not I.know about what
   'Anna was talking about something, but I don't know what.'

(49) 俄语
   Anna govorila o čëm-to, no ja ne pomnju *(o) čëm.
   Anna talked about something but I not remember about what
   'Anna was talking about something, but I don't know what.'

其次，我提供了这四种语言中介词短语做附加语的相关语料——德语和希腊语中的处所附加语，以及波兰语和俄语中的伴随附加语。

(50) 德语
   Anke ist in einem Seminar eingeschlafen, aber ich weiß nicht,
   Anke is in a class fallen.asleep but I know not
   *(in) welchem.
   in which
   'Anke fell asleep in a class, but I don't know which.'

(51) 希腊语

  I Anna apokimithike s'ena apo ta mathimata, alla dhe ksero *(se) pjo.
   the Anna fell.asleep in-one of the classes but not I.know in which
   'Anna fell asleep in one of the classes, but I don't know which.'

（52）波兰语

   Anna tańczyła z kimś, ale nie wiem *(z) kim.
   Anna was.dancing with someone but not I.know with who
   'Anna was dancing with someone, but I don't know with who.'

（53）俄语

   Pëtr tanceval s kem-to, no ja ne pomnju *(s) kem.
   Pëtr was.dancing with someone but I not remember with who
   'Petr was dancing with someone, but I don't remember with who.'

  尽管上述语料极大地扩充了截省的语料基础，因为以前的截省文献从未提到过这些语料，然而它们和上一节开始的语料具有同样的局限性：即所有语料都只涉及单句范围。（21）中的介词悬置概述似乎在"跨越"孤岛条件时也同样成立，后面几章所讨论的重要语料均来自于这一事实。下面的英语、德语、希腊语、波兰语和俄语语料证实，虽然截省的 wh- 短语必须要与孤岛"内部"的一个空缺具有明显联系，但也必须遵守该语言独特的介词悬置限制。

  当然，英语允许介词悬置，依靠介词短语内部不定指先行项而出现的截省无须把相关的介词一并移位。

（54） a Ben's mother will get angry if he talks with someone from his class, but I don't remember who.

    b Abby wants to interview someone who lived in one of the Balkan countries, but I can't remember which.

  与介词裹挟式移位的通常情况一样，英语中的介词裹挟式移位比单独移动 wh- 短语更糟糕（4.3 节中我会再次简要探讨这一点）。相反在德语、希腊语、波兰语和俄语中，介词悬置不可能发生，分别

沉默的句法

如（29）、（28）、（33）和（32）中的（b）句所示。下述语料显示，即使截省的 wh- 短语与孤岛有明显关联，介词悬置也不可能发生。我用一个关系从句孤岛和一个条件句的前提分句说明了这一点，如（54）中的英语例句。

德语

（55） Anke wird sich ärgern, wenn Peter mit einem der   Lehrer
      Anke will REFL upset if   Peter with one of.the teachers
      spricht, aber ich weiß nicht mehr, *(mit) welchem.
      speaks but   I know not more   with which
      'Anke will get upset if Peter talks to one of the teachers, but I don't remember which.'

（56） Anke will   jemanden heiraten, der   in einem bestimmten
      Anke wants someone marry who in a   certain
      mittel-europäischen Land   gewohnt hat, aber ich erinnere   mich nicht,
      central-European   country lived   has but I   remember REFL not
      *(in) welchem.
      in which
      'Anke wants to marry someone who has lived in a certain central European country, but I don't remember which.'

希腊语

（57） I mitera tou Gianni tha thimosi   an milisi me kapjon
      the mother of Giannis FUT get.angry if he.talks with someone
      apo tin taksi tou, alla dhe thimame   *(me) pjon.
      from the class his but not I.remember with who
      'Giannis's mother will get angry if he talks with someone from his class, but I don't remember who.'

（58） I Maria theli   na   milisi me kapjon   pu   na   exei polemisi
      the Maria wants SUBJ talk   with someone who SUBJ has fought
      s'enan apo tous Valkanikous polemous, ala dhen ksero *(se) pjon
      in-one from the   Balkan   wars   but not I.know in which

106

'Maria wants to talk to someone who fought in one of the Balkan wars, but I don't know which.'

波兰语

（59） Anna wścieknie się   jeśli Piotr zatańczy z   jedną z jej
      Anna angers   REFL *if   Piotr dances   with one of her*
      kolezanek i   Piotr chciałby wiedzieć *(z)   którą.
      friends   and Piotr wants   to. know   with which
      'Anna will get mad if Piotr dances with one of her friends, and Piotr wants to know which.'

（60） Piotr chciałby ozenić   się   z   kimś,   kto mieszka w
      Piotr wants   to.marry REFL *with someone who lives   in*
      jednym z krajów   bałkańskich, ale nie wiem *(w) którym.
      one   of countries Balkan   but not I.know in which
      'Peter wants to marry someone who has lived in a certain Balkan country, but I don't remember which.'

俄语

（61） Anna rasserditsja esli Pëtr budet tancevat' s   odnoj iz   eë
      Anna get.angry   if   Pëtr will dance   with one   from her
      podrug, no on ne pomnit   *(s)   kakoj.
      friends but he not remembers with which
      'Anna will get mad if Pëtr dances with one of her friends, but he doesn't remember which.'

（62） Pëtr xočet ženit'sja na ženščine kotoraja živët v odnoj iz
      Pëtr wants marry   on woman   who   lives in one   from
      balkanskix stran,   no ja zabyl *(v) kakoj.
      Balkan   countries but I forgot in which
      'Pëtr wants to marry a woman who lives in one of the Balkan countries, but I forgot (in) which.'

这些语料表明，无论省略位置内部（也就是说，在省略的 IP 解读中）是否有明显的孤岛，（21）中假设的第二个形式同一性概述（重复如下）107

都成立。

(63) 形式同一性概述 II：介词悬置
当且仅当语言 L 在常规 wh- 移位下允准介词悬置时，L 才允准截省下的介词悬置。

本章 3.2.1 和 3.2.2 节中呈现的语料显示，截省句中在 CP 指示语上的 wh- 短语的形式与 IP 没有省略时 wh- 移位下出现的 wh- 短语的形式有着密切联系。这两个事实，尤其是介词悬置的事实似乎表明，在某一特定语言中，影响非省略问句中 wh- 短语的赋格和决定 wh- 移位目标的常规机制，在截省中起到同样的作用。所有这些事实都充分表明，在截省中，发生了常规的 wh- 移位，IP 内部的 wh- 短语移到了 CP 指示语位置。①

这一结论与 3.1 节结尾所得出的结论产生了直接冲突，3.1 节中明显对孤岛不敏感的情况表明没有移位发生。本书其余部分将致力于解决这一冲突。

本章呈现的语料将有助于检验后文中与孤岛条件和省略相关的假说。在记录完这两个形式同一性概述的支撑性语料后，现在我将开始探讨它们的理论意义。

---

① 类似原因表明，剥落结构（stripping）、比较结构、片语答句、动词空缺残余和"省略连词"（elliptic conjunctions）（**除**短语等**外**）中各种相似的形式同一性效果可以用移位法解释，这些结构像截省一样，常常表现出对格和介词悬置的依赖性。

第四章

删除的诞生与消亡

本章将回顾现存的解决截省问题的代表性方法，并证明这些方法都未能处理截省明显的孤岛不敏感问题或第三章中记录的形式同一性语料事实。

与上一章中较简略的语料相比，本章发掘了更为丰富的语料，为解决一系列分析性问题奠定基础，这些分析性问题留待下一章详细讨论。

4.1 罗斯（Ross 1969）：删除和孤岛问题

罗斯（Ross 1969）提出了一种简单的删除法，认为内嵌疑问句句子成分的删除是通过与前行句采用相同的短语标记而得到允准的。我们并不关心罗斯给出的特定公式（尽管当时罗斯也承认该公式有不足之处），但其整体研究路径却奠定了我们目前对 PF 删除路径的理解。

对罗斯而言，与单纯的解释性论述相比，删除法最大的优势在于能够直接解释格匹配效应。尽管罗斯并未给出德语例句的实际推导情况（由于涉及到 V_2/V 末尾交替，截省句的特定公式在这些例句上遇到障碍），我们却能够看出这一推导会如何进行，只要限定同一性的条件并非罗斯所假设的表层结构短语标记同一性条件，而是第一章中所提出的条件即可。在此构想下，（1）中的截省只不过是从其对应的内嵌疑问句推导出来的（其中带删除线的文本表示删除的内容）。由于动词 *schmeicheln* 赋与格，因此残余的 wh- 短语只有与格这一种可能性。

(1) Er will   jemandem   schmeicheln, aber sie   wissen nicht,
    he wants someone.DAT flatter   but they know not
    {*wer   /*wen   /wem}   er t~wem~ schmeicheln will.
    who.NOM who.ACC who.DAT he   flatter   wants
    'He wants to flatter someone, but they don't know who.'

虽然罗斯并没有注意到删除法的这一结果，但删除法却直接预测到了介词悬置。在像德语这样缺少介词悬置的语言中，wh- 移位要想得到合乎语法的句子，唯一的方式就是将介词进行裹挟式移位。删除后的结构生产了（2）这唯一有可能合乎语法的截省结构。

(2) Anna hat mit jemandem gesprochen, aber ich weiß nicht,
    Anna has with someone   spoken   but I   know not
    [mit wem] sie t~PP~ gesprochen hat.
    with who she   spoken   has
    'Anna spoke with someone, but I don't know who.'

这一简单的事实是支持删除法的唯一强有力的论据。稍后我们将看到，这一事实也是大多数其他方法的主要绊脚石。

删除法还准确预测了另一事实，在有多重疑问词前移的语言中，应该可能有多于一个 wh-XP 残余的截省结构。保加利亚语就是这样的语言之一，如例（3）和（4）所示，它们分别对应主句疑问句和内嵌疑问句（见 Rudin 1985: 82ff., 1988；感谢 L. Schürcks-Grozeva 和 S. Dianova 为本节的保加利亚语例句做出判断）。

(3) a [~CP~ Koj kogo [~IP~ e   vidjal]]?
         who whom   AUX seen
       'Who saw who?'
    b *Koj e vidjal kogo?

(4) a Ne znam [$_{CP}$ koj kogo [$_{IP}$ e vidjal]].
    not I.know who whom AUX seen
    'I don't know who saw who.'
  b *Ne znam koj e vidjal kogo.

这种语言也允许截省下出现多个 wh- 短语，高桥（Takahashi 1994）称之为"多重截省"：

(5) Njakoj e vidjal njakogo, no ne znam [$_{CP}$ koj kogo [$_{IP}$ e vidjal]].
    someone AUX seen someone but not I.know who whom AUX seen
    'Someone saw someone, but I don't know who saw who.'

删除法更进一步的结果是，如果这些语言显示出优先效应，而且优先是推导性限制而非表征性限制的结果，则优先效应在截省下得到验证的事实，也支持在优先条件的限制下先发生 wh- 移位，然后发生删除。引自鲁丁（Rudin 1985: 115）的控制语料（6）表明，保加利亚语展示出了优先效应。（7）为对应的截省例句，可与（5）中合乎语法的对应例句进行比较。

(6) a Koj kogo e vidjal?
    who whom AUX seen
    'Who saw who?'
  b *Kogo koj e vidjal?

(7) *Njakoj e vidjal njakogo, no ne znam kogo koj.
    someone AUX seen someone but not I.know whom who
    ('Someone saw someone, but I don't know who saw who.')

然而实际情况十分复杂，似乎并非只有像保加利亚语这样有多重疑问词前移的语言才允许出现多个 wh- 残余。下面来自德语、荷兰语、土耳其语、希腊语和日语的语料分别表明①，这一现象也存在于其他没有多重疑问

---

① 感谢 A. Mester（德语）、H. Rullmann（荷兰语）、D. Grate（土耳其语）和 A. Giannakidou（希腊语）对这些以及下面不同语种的语料做出判断。

问词前移的语言中。

(8) a Jemand hat was gesehen, aber ich weiß nicht, wer was.
someone has something seen but I know not who what
(lit.) 'Someone saw something, but I don't know who what.'

b Iemand heeft iets gezien, maar ik weet niet wie wat.
someone has something seen but I know not who what
(lit.) 'Someone saw something, but I don't know who what.'

c Biri bir şey gördü ama, kim ne
someone something saw but who.NOM what.ACC
bil-mi-yor-um.①
know-NEG-PROG-1sg
(lit.) 'Someone saw something, but I don't know who what.'

---

① 土耳其语例句引出了许多有趣的问题，值得进一步考察。最有趣的是，(i) 中的非省略例句要求属格标记必须出现在内嵌的主语中（土耳其语中的内嵌式小句在诸多方面都和名词化十分相似）。

(i) Biri bir şey gördü ama, kim-*(in) ne gör-düğ-ünü bil-mi-yor-um.
someone something saw but who-GEN what see-DIK-ACC know-NEG-PROG-1sg
'Someone saw something, but I don't know who saw what.'

然而，这一格标记不能出现在"截省"句中，这时要求用主格，如 (8c)。

(ii) *Biri bir şey gördü ama, kim-in ne bil-mi-yor-um.
someone something saw but who-GEN what know-NEG-PROG-1sg
('Someone saw something, but I don't know who what.')

这些对比显示，土耳其语中的多重"截省"可能并不像我们第一次考察时所显示的那样，与其他语言中明显的多重截省有直接联系。有可能土耳其语中的多重截省实际上是某种删减后的并列结构。下面两个事实支持了上述猜想：其一，(8c) 中 *kim* 和 *ne* 之间要求有明显停顿，其二，(iii) 是合法的，或许是更加自然的变体。

(iii) Biri bir şey gördü ama, kim {ve/veya} ne bil-mi-yor-um.
someone something saw but who and/or what know-NEG-PROG-1sg
(lit.) 'Someone saw something, but I don't know who and/or what.'

比较刘易斯（Lewis 1967: 73）的例子 *neyi ve ne zaman yaptın* (lit.) 'What and when have you done?'（即 'What have you done, and when?'）。相关讨论见 Browne 1972, Bechhofer 1976b, Giannakidou and Merchant 1998, Merchant 1999a。

d Kapjos   idhe kapjon,   alla dhe ksero pjos   pjon.
  *someone.*NOM *saw   someone.*ACC *but not I.know who.*NOM *who.*ACC
  (lit.) 'Someone saw someone, but I don't know who whom.'

e Sono toki, dareka-ga   nanika-o   mise-ta. Sikasi,
  *that time someone-*NOM *something-*ACC *showed but*
  dare-ga   nani-o   ka omoidase-nai. (Nishigauchi 1998: 146 (70))
  *who-*NOM *what-*ACC *Q   remember-not*
  'At that moment, someone showed something (to me). (lit.) But I *can't remember who what.*'

甚至在英语中，尽管相关结构已经有些边缘化了（虽然在 Bolinger 1978①等中有提到），我们也发现了明显的"多重截省"例证。

（9） (?) Everyone brought something (different) to the potluck, but I couldn't tell you who what.

与（8）中的语言不同，在英语中，这种多重截省似乎仅在可以生成合适配对解读的环境中发生（相关讨论见 Nishigauchi 1998）——换言之，先行 IP 中的量词必须有一个是生成元。当有两个不定指词时，与（8）句类似的多重截省句不合语法，如：*Someone said something, but I couldn't tell you who what.（这并不表示，与（9）类似的例句在德语、荷兰语、希腊语、土耳其语和日语中被排除在外。相反，据我所知，这种例句是可能存在的，并表现出英语例句那样的解读限制，比如 Nishigauchi 1998 所注意到的日语语料。）

因此，"当且仅当存在显性多重前置时才产生的多重截省"这一形式并没有产生什么有意思的启示。尽管此处我无法详细探究这一现象的句法

---

① 亦可比较下面得到验证的例句。该例句出自保罗·波斯塔尔（Paul Postal）1975 年 10 月 20 日的一封信，为普鲁姆（Pullum 1991: 149）所引用。

(i) 'In French, we have noticed that some intransitive V permit Extraposition of Indefinite, while others permit Impersonal Passive. Which which?'

规则，但是在最简方案背景下可以有一种解读方式，即如果采用删除法，那么拖延原则就可以被推翻。（这表明在使用拖延原则时，并不把它作为一个普适性评估指标，而是作为局部性评估指标，它被通过删除而得到修复的语迹的某些特征所编码，这与第二章的讨论相符。）阿克玛和尼利曼（Ackema and Neeleman 1998）对 wh- 移位选择在跨语言中的验证提供了另一种可能性：如果阻止移位（约束（STAY））的限制不利于语迹在 PF 层出现，则包含结构的删除（此处指 IP）会完全满足便于多重移位的低级限制。此处的逻辑与下一章中多数情况下采用的逻辑相同：删除将一个原本次优的候选语句转变成了最优语句。肯尼迪（Kennedy 2000）富有洞见地将这一逻辑也应用到了比较结构和次比较结构中。①

总之，在那些存在优先效应的语言中，关于优先效应的预测是可以得以测试的。德语和荷兰语中的情况是由于主语的复杂性导致这些语言不是检测格的最佳语言。而在英语和希腊语中，优先效应能够在相对简单的单句中被清楚地检测到。

（10） a *I couldn't tell you what who brought to the potluck.
　　　 b *Dhen ksero   pjon   pjos   idhe. (on non-echo reading for *pjos*)
　　　　　 not   I.know who.ACC   who.NOM saw
　　　　　 ('I don't know whom who saw.')

---

① 有一点需要预先说明：目前尚不完全清楚，非句首残余的移位是否是普通 wh- 移位的结果，而不是某些其他类似移位操作（比如，空缺句或假空缺句中导致非句首残余撤换的操作）的结果。与上述语言中多重截省相关的一个重要事实是，这些截省往往不是由时态小句边界分隔开的（如 Takahashi 1994 所指出的那样），尽管这并非如我们有时候设想的那样绝对。比如在空缺句中，跨时态小句只有在内嵌句主语受主句主语约束时才合语法：
　　（i）[Everybody₁ said he₁'d bring something different to the potluck.] Jack₁ said he₁'d bring wine, Bob₂ ⟨ said he₂'d bring ⟩ beer, and Sam₃ ⟨ said he₃'d bring ⟩ whiskey.
　　（ii）[Everybody₁ said he₁'d bring something different to the potluck.] But I can't remember who what.
相关讨论尤见 Nishigauchi 1998，与空缺句有关的讨论见 Johnson 1997；关于多重截省和空缺句（可嵌入性、非并列性等）的某些差异的讨论，另见 Romero 1997a。

关键是，这些效应在相应的多重截省结构中也同样得到了验证：

(11) a *Everyone brought something (different) to the potluck, but I couldn't tell you what who.
 b *Kapjos idhe kapjon, alla dhe ksero pjon pjos.
   someone.NOM saw someone.ACC but not I.know who.ACC who.NOM
   (lit.) 'Someone saw someone, but I don't know whom who.'

如果优先条件是 wh- 移位的推导性限制的结果（例如，Chomsky 1995 认为是最小链接条件的结果；近期讨论另见 Hornstein 1995, Grohmann 1998, 2000, Pesetsky 1998*b*），且残余的 wh- 短语在到达截省结构表层位置时采用的是通常驱动显性 wh- 移位的过程，则以上语料中所呈现出来的模式就是预料之中的。由于这些语料经历了 wh- 移位，因此适用于优先条件并产生了预期结果。

尽管删除法有这些成功之处，但仍存在一个重要问题。如罗斯（Ross 1969）曾意识到的那样，删除法明显违反孤岛条件。在罗斯的方法下，（12a）和（13a）这样的例句派生自（12b）和（13b），（12b）和（13b）的 wh- 移位违反了孤岛条件，删除后孤岛被隐藏了起来。

(12) a They want to hire someone who speaks a Balkan language, but I don't remember which.
 b *I don't remember which (Balkan language) they want to hire someone [who speaks].
(13) a Ben will be mad if Abby talks to one of the teachers, but she couldn't remember which.
 b *Ben will be mad if Abby talks to one of the teachers, but she couldn't remember which (of the teachers) Ben will be mad [if she talks to].

罗斯对这一问题的解决办法是断定不合法性是跨越推导而得到推衍的，也就是说，普适性规则十分必要，它可以检视在较小的偏差标记出现时，是否存在违反孤岛条件的情况并判定孤岛是否通过删除得到了修复（是否"孤岛和形成节点不出现在表层结构中"（第 227 页））。拉科夫（Lakoff 1970, 1972）重申了这一结论。

除了这种评价指标模糊不清外（对立观点见 Baker and Brame 1972），依据经验也有充足理由放弃用这种方法来解释孤岛现象。正如"导论"中指出的那样，VP 删除没有修复被违反的孤岛条件，尽管罗斯的方法（或更新后的同类方法）期待会有类似的作用。

（14）[Everyone wants to hire someone who speaks a different Balkan language] *Abby wants to hire someone who speaks Greek, but I don't remember which (language) Ben does ~~want to hire someone [who speaks]~~.

（15）*Ben will be mad if Abby talks to Mr Ryberg, and guess who Chuck will be ~~mad [if she talks to]~~.

这些例句表明，至少对这些孤岛而言，对孤岛的修复效果是由于 wh- 移位跨越了孤岛边界而造成的，与孤岛诱导节点是否在 PF 层无关。乔姆斯基（Chomsky 1972）建议对这些事实进行再分析，贝克和布雷姆（Baker and Brame 1972）也重申了这一点，即跨越孤岛节点会给该节点标记上某些特征（Lakoff 1972 称之为"[＋坏（bad）]"），如果该节点未被删除，则会导致句子不合语法。但他们的分析也都由于同样的原因未能成功。①

---

① 这可能表明，文中的例句并非理想的考察对象，因为由于尚不清楚的原因，当 wh- 提取与先行句中的提取并行时，从 VP 省略部位进行 wh- 提取效果最佳，如（i）：

（i）We need to know which languages$_1$ Abby speaks t_1, and which$_2$ Ben does ⟨~~speak t_2~~⟩.

然而，如哈尔特（Hardt 1993, 1999）所述，当被提取部分的关联成分是主要焦点时，从 VP 省略部位进行 wh- 提取也可行；参照（ii）。

（ii）We know that Abby does speak [Greek, Albanian, and Serbian]$_F$—we need to find out which languages$_2$ she *doesn't* ⟨speak t_2⟩!

例句（14）和（15）的情况比（ii）这种不含孤岛且无平行提取的例句更加糟糕。另外，潜在的反对例证对于比较结构的解释并不适用，因为比较结构中并不需要"平行"提取：

（iii）Abby speaks more Balkan languages Op_2 than Ben does ⟨~~speak t_2~~⟩.

尽管如此，将这种省略位置内嵌到孤岛中是不合语法的：

（iv）*The University of Chicago hired a professor who speaks more Balkan languages Op_2 than Northwestern did ⟨~~hire a professor who speaks t_2~~⟩.

在这种情况下，基于"提取平行性"的潜在反对意见就失去了大部分影响力。

4.2 假截省句

面对这些困难,不久人们就建议重新分析罗斯的截省情况,认为截省并非对孤岛不敏感的 wh- 移位的结果,而是与一个完全不同的不包含孤岛的结构有关。埃尔特斯基克-希尔(Erteschik-Shir 1977)和波尔曼(Pollmann 1975)分别提出了这一建议。

埃尔特斯基克-希尔(Erteschik-Shir 1977: 107-108, 注释 4)在其论文最后一页的最后一个脚注中提出一个"有趣的替代截省的方法可能值得研究",(16a)这样的截省可能是由(16b)的底层结构通过删除主语 it 和系动词而派生出来的:

(16) a Someone just left—guess who.
　　　b Someone just left—guess who ~~it was~~.

她关注的正是我们一直在讨论的孤岛条件改良例句,并推测如果这一例句(她的例句(iii))只包含主句成分(*it will be*),则孤岛效应问题就不相关了。

(17) That he'll hire someone is possible, but I won't divulge who? (it will be).

波尔曼(Pollmann 1975)也提出了完全相同的建议,他制定了一种删除"[+pro, +def]$_{NP}$+ 系动词"的可选转换①,尽管他并没有意识到这也为孤岛问题提供了解决办法。

---

① 波尔曼的转换想要把 *dat* 'that' 和 *het* 'it' 也包含在内。克莱因(M. Klein 1977: 71(例(84))指出,这种做法错误地允准了(i)这种可能的简化方式;其英语译文也是如此。

(i) We hebben gisteren　Pollini horen spelen. Raad eens wie *(dat is).
　　we have　yesterday Pollini hear　play　guess PRT　who that is
　　'We heard Pollini play yesterday. Guess who *(that is).'

这两位作者都没有明确地表示，被认定成深层截省的简化结构与分裂句中所发现的结构有所关联，但认为二者密切相关的看法是合理的。实际上许多作者声称，日语中看似截省的结构正是从分裂句推导而来的（相关讨论和文献见 Merchant 1998）。换言之，(16b) 本身更像是分裂句的简化形式，该分裂句的中枢词（pivot）是被提取的 wh- 短语，如（18a）所示。我将这种省略称为"假截省"(pseudosluicing)，因为它所形成的结构和"真"截省看似没有区别（假设 wh- 片语是由更常见的疑问结构推导出来的，如（18b）所示）。

(18) a Guess who [it was ―― that just left].　　假截省句
　　　b Guess who [―― just left].　　截省句

换言之，两种推导方式都有可能产生已验证的语料。在下面几节中，我将提出一些诊断方法来区分二者，结论是无论以何种有趣的普遍方式，都极不可能将截省句简化为假截省句。下面几节重述了麦钱特（Merchant 1998）中呈现的许多观点，但也有一些是新观点。

4.2.1　初步思考

让我们首先考虑假截省的 CP 部分。如果把"it be XP"结构简化为"it be XP that ..."分裂结构的建议基本上是正确的，我们首先可能会想，是否有理由相信，分裂句的预设部分（类似于关系从句的部分）是可以被省略的。英语中似乎也会有这种"省略"，只要下列答语的简略形式确实是由未省略的对应语句转换而来的。试对比下述成对的问句和答句。

(19) a Q: Who knocked?
　　　　A: It was {Alex/me} (who knocked).
　　　b Q: What did they steal?
　　　　A: It was the TV and stereo (that they stole).
　　　c Q: Why is the bus late?
　　　　A: It's because of the traffic (that's it's late).

事实上，有时预设部分必须缺失：

(20) Q: Who's that?
     A: It's me (*that is that).

尽管这些结构存在某种关联，但这种"省略"的本质却和文献中通常讨论的中心词允准的省略（NP 省略、VP 省略、IP 省略）有所不同，这里"省略"的是 CP。实际上，有充分理由质疑这种形式的 CP 省略是否真的存在。让我们来考察两个最可能的备用语句。

英语中有其他两种情况似乎也涉及 CP 省略。其一是在对比小句中，如（21）所示。

(21) a More people came than we thought (would come).
     b He's sicker than the doctor {thought/expected/realized/admitted}
        (that he was).

鉴于感知上的解读，以及这些动词通常不允许空补足语（如 *I didn't expect *(that)*）的事实，似乎有理由假定（21）中的 CP 补足语已被省略了（也许通过某种普遍的比较删除方式）。但正如肯尼迪和麦钱特（Kennedy and Merchant 2000b）所证明的那样，这种假设是错误的。实际上，有充分理由相信（21）中的内嵌动词以 DP 而非 CP 做补足语。

有几条证据都指向这一结论，此处我只提及一个，即：DP 需要格，而 CP 不需要。注意当（21）中的动词为被动式时，例句便不合语法了。

(22) a *More people came than it was thought.
     b *He's sicker than it was {thought/expected/realized/admitted}.

这一效应也可以推广到以 CP 为补足语的形容词上：

(23) *Sally had a more serious problem than it was {evident/apparent}.

如果仅仅是缺失一个 CP 的问题，那么这些例句不合语法就很出人意料，尤其是 CP 出现时，语句反而合乎语法。

(24) a More people came than it was thought would come.
b He's sicker than it was {thought/expected/realized/admitted} that he was.
c Sally had a more serious problem than it was {evident/apparent} that she had.

如果（22）和（23）中的例句只是（24）中例句的省略版，则两者之间的差异就完全出人意料。相反，肯尼迪和麦钱特（Kennedy and Merchant 2000b）提出，（22）和（23）中缺失的成分是 DP 而非 CP，并且像所有论元 DP 一样，这个 DP 也需要格。这一方法得到了语言事实的支持，即当虚位主语省略时，DP 就可以移位到主语位置，并获得格变，例句（22）和（23）就可以得到改善。

(25) a More people came than was thought.
b He's sicker than was {thought/expected/realized/admitted}.
c Sally had a more serious problem than was {evident/apparent}.

因此我们可以推断，比较句中看似 CP 省略的形式实际上根本不包含 CP。

第二种情况是，当 CP 做某些特定动词的补足语时，CP 补足语似乎会缺失，如（26）：

(26) a A: They're late again. B: I know (that they're late again).
b A: Will she come? B: I don't know (if she'll come).

但同样，几乎不可能是 CP 省略这一句法操作在起作用。特定动词如 *know*、*insist* 和 *wonder* 不带补足语似乎是这些动词的一种特质（通常称为"空补足语照应现象"，参阅 Hankamer and Sag 1976, Fillmore 1986 等），需另做解释。须注意的是，如果从总体来看，补足语 CP 可以被删除，我们就需要采取一些方法来防止其应用到如（27）的情况中：

（27）a I {regret/arrested} *(that we bought the charcoal grill).

　　　b I {proposed/demanded} *(that we buy the charcoal grill).

因此，似乎没有理由认为英语中有独立的 CP 删除操作，并且与第一印象相反，*It's Bob* 这一形式的结构并不表示它就是句法上得到删减的分裂句。

然而即使为了使论证成立，假设英语**的确**可以允准 CP 省略，但假定分裂句中的虚位主语 *it* 和系动词（如果存在情态词，连同情态词一起）可以缺失，也同样难以令人信服，因为这些特性无法在英语中独立存在（换言之，英语既不是**主语脱落语言**，也不是空系动词语言）。埃尔特斯基克-希尔（Erteschik-Shir 1977）已经意识到了这一难题，他承认"［删除'it+be（带时态标记）'的删除转换］并非在所有情况下都能同样顺利地完成，调查这一删除转换所需的条件很有必要"（第 108 页）。

当然，一大难题是过度生成。赞同这种方法的人需要回答，为什么"it+be"删除不能适用于（28）一类的情况。

（28）a Q: Who knocked?

　　　　A: *(It was) {Alex/me} who knocked.

　　　b Q: What did they steal?

　　　　A: *(It was) the TV and stereo that they stole.

　　　c Q: Why is the bus late?

　　　　A: *(It's) because of the traffic that it's late.

实际上，片语答句通常没有像分裂句中枢词一样的特征，例如，它们不像分裂句中枢词那样强制要求穷尽性，也不能有同样的预设性。一般认为，分裂句有一个真实存在的预设（但 Prince 1978 和 Delin 1992 对这一概括性主张做出了附加说明：新信息有时可以出现在"预设"部分，尤其是在分裂结构的施为句中）。但是人们通常假定疑问句有一个关于某事物存在的会话隐涵义，它满足了疑问句的核心（见 Karttunen and Peters 1979 中的一系列文章）。此处用否定量化词来说明这一差异，带否定量化词的答句合乎语法，但分裂句中枢词带否定量化词却不合语法（因为断言与预设相矛盾）。

（29） a Q: What did the burglar take?
          A: Nothing.
       b #It was nothing that the burglar took.

（30） a Q: What did he do to help you?
          A: Nothing at all.
       b #It was nothing at all that he did to help us.

产生所假定的省略句需要一些操作，而上述初步思考严重质疑了这些操作的合理性。在下一节中，我展现了许多其他方面的差异，这让任何试图把截省句简化为假截省句的尝试都显得不太可能，因为在这种简化下，这些差异仍然无法得到理解。

4.2.2　反对等式"截省句 = 假截省句"

截省句和带 wh-XP 中枢词的分裂疑问句之间至少存在十个差异。我的目的不是解释或分析这些差异，而是表明这些差异的存在，因为正是存在这些差异，任何把截省句同化为省略的分裂句的做法都有问题。这些差异与截省句和 wh- 中枢词分裂句截然不同的表现有关，涉及附加语、隐性论元、韵律、强非语篇关联疑问词短语、"提及－部分"修饰语、"提及－全部"修饰语、else 修饰、附带省略（wh- 介词倒装）、带有限分裂策略或无分裂策略的语言、分裂句中带主格中枢词的语言以及左分支截省句。

1　附加语和隐性论元

区分截省句和分裂句的第一个原因是通过简单对比附加语和隐性论元在这两个结构中的表现所得出的。例如，（31）中的附加语语料（与 M. Klein 1977: 70 提供的语料类似）和（32）中的隐性论元语料表明，在英语中，带这些成分的截省句合乎语法，但当 wh- 附加语或隐性论元做光杆分裂句的中枢词时,语句可接受度会大大降低。(如果保留分裂句的预设部分,语句却会得到大幅改善,代价是语句会显得冗长。但这一事实的重要性难以估量,因为我们一开始就没能充分理解当 wh- 附加语和隐性论元做中枢词时,语句不合语法的原因是什么。)

(31) a He fixed the car, but I don't know how (*it was).

b He fixed the car, but I don't know why (*it was).

c He fixed the car, but I don't know when (*it was).

d He's hidden the jewels, but I don't know where (*it is).

e He served time in prison, but I don't know how long (*it was).

(32) a They served the guests, but I don't know what (*it was).

b He said they had already eaten, but I don't know what (*it was).

c They were arguing, but I don't know about what (*it was).

2 韵律

第二个差异与截省句的语调曲拱[①]有关。典型截省句要求最强的音高重音落在 wh- 短语上。相反,在 wh- 中枢词分裂句中,音高重音必须落在系动词上,如下列对比所示:

(33) Someone gave me a valentine, but

a I don't know WHO.

b I don't know who it WAS.

c *I don't know WHO it was.

(34) a Someone KISSED you, and you can't remember WHO?!?

b Someone KISSED you, and you can't remember who it WAS?!?

c *Someone KISSED you, and you can't remember WHO it was?!?

实际上这有些出乎意料,因为一般来说,分裂句中枢词必须包含音高

---

① 曲拱(intonational contour)是音系学中的一个术语,指一个语段中音高、声调或重音的一种独特的构型。——译者

重音。注意不能把上述对比单纯地简化为核心重音普遍喜欢落在话语的绝对结尾处，因为当内嵌的 CP 向左移位时，完全相同的判断也成立。

3 强非语篇关联疑问词短语

强非语篇关联疑问词短语（如在 Pesetsky 1987 中）通常不出现在截省句中①，尽管它们作为分裂句中枢词这一点无可非议：

(35) Someone dented my car last night—
　　a I wish I knew who!
　　b I wish I knew who the hell it was!
　　c *I wish I knew who the hell!

(35c) 的问题在于，没有强调 who the hell，(36) 所示为合乎语法的形式：

(36) Who the HELL do you think you are?!?

4 "提及-部分"修饰

由于中枢词有穷尽性的效果（见 Kiss 1998），只有"提及-全部"解读（相关论述见 Groenendijk and Stokhof 1997: 6.2.3 节）与中枢词里的 wh-短语兼容（感谢富冈建议做此检验）。因此，wh- 中枢词和 for example 这样明确要求"提及-部分"解读的修饰语不兼容。相反，截省句则允许有这种修饰语。例句 (37a) 和 (37b) 分别说明了内嵌句截省和主句截省的不同情况。

(37) A: You should talk to somebody in the legal department for help with that.
　　a B_1: Could you tell me who (*it is), for example?
　　b B_2: Who (*is it), for example?

---

① 这个规则的一个特例是附带省略结构（带倒装介词的截省结构），见第 71 页脚注① 和麦钱特（Merchant, 出版中）的讨论。

5 "提及-全部"修饰

对强制要求穷尽性的 wh- 修饰语 "all" 来说，情况正好相反，比如 *Who all was at the party?*（见 McCloskey 2000）。在某些例句的截省结构中，这类修饰语似乎会降级；关键是这种降级并不会延续到对应的分裂句中：

(38) A bunch of students were protesting, and the FBI is trying to find out who all *(it was).

6 *else* 修饰

同样，加修饰语 *else* 的特殊疑问词也可以出现在截省句中，但却不能出现在分裂句中。

(39) Harry was there, but I don't know who else (*it was).

7 附带省略结构（截省的 wh- 短语和介词倒装）

截省句和分裂句更进一步的差异源自一系列稍显复杂的情况，这些情况与英语截省结构中某些特殊疑问词和既定介词进行倒装的能力有关，我在麦钱特（Merchant，出版中）中将这一现象称为"附带省略"（swiping）（北日耳曼语中截省的 wh- 短语和介词倒装）（丹麦语和一些挪威语变体中也存在这一现象，但是瑞典语和弗里斯兰语中不存在这一现象）。

罗斯（Ross 1969）和罗森（Rosen 1976）注意到，在特定条件下，截省句允许看似"悬置"的介词。(40) 给出了附带省略例句。

(40) a She bought a robe, but God knows who for.
   b They were arguing, but we couldn't figure out what about.
   c This opera was written by someone in the 19th century, but we're not sure who by. (Chung *et al.* 1995: (4d))
   d He was shouting to someone, but it was impossible to tell who to.

e A: She's goinig to leave her fortune to someone.   B: Really? Who to?
f He'll be at the Red Room, but I don't know when till.
g She's driving, but God knows where to.

乍看上去，附带省略与西日耳曼语的 R 代词倒装类似（例如，van Riemsdijk 1978 和 Chung 1995 做出了这一判定）：众所周知，特定成分（即"R 代词"）能够和介词倒置，如（41a）和（42a）中所示的德语和荷兰语例句（例句 b 提供的是非倒装控制语料）：

（41） a Wo-r-an   denkst du   eigentlich?
         where-on think   you   actually
         'What are you thinking of, anyway?'
       b Du   denkst an dein Buch wieder!
         you think   on your book again
         'You're thinking of your book again!'

（42） a Waarover   praten zij?
         where-about talk   they
         'What are they talking about?'
       b Zij   praten over   het boek.
         they talk   about the book
         'They're talking about the book.'

与德语和荷兰语中的 R 代词倒装有些类似，附带省略也受到很多限制，但在可参与的特殊疑问词方面，附带省略要比 R 代词倒装的大陆变体更加自由（见 J. Hoekstra 1995 对诸多大陆方言的调查）。在英语中，只有某些"最小"的疑问算子才能倒装：*who*、*what*、*when* 和 *where*（对于某些人来说，*how long*、*how much* 可以，*how many* 或许也可以）。在这里我们可以注意到，无论这一限制的正确解释是什么，它绝不仅限于倒装的韵律条件，如下面带 *which* 的例句所示：

（43） a *She bought a robe for one of her nephews, but God knows which (one) for.

    b *They were arguing about animals, but we couldn't figure out what kind about.

    c *This opera was written by an Italian composer in the 19th century, but we're not sure which (one) by.

    d *He was shouting to one of the freshmen Republican senators supporting the bomber program, but it was impossible to tell exactly which (senator) to.

    e *He'll be at the Red Room, but I don't know what time till.

    f *She's driving, but God knows which town to.

然而，关键是附带省略中发现的倒装类型不可能出现在带有 wh- 中枢词的分裂句中：

（44） a It was [for Humphrey] that I voted.
        b [For who] was it that you voted?①
           *[Who for] was it (that you voted)?

（45） a It was [about the election] that they were arguing.
        b [About what] was it that they were arguing?
        c *[What about] was it (that they were arguing)?

同样，如果说截省句只是分裂句的一种特殊情况，那么截省句下介词短语中的特殊疑问词和做分裂句中枢词的特殊疑问词在表现上不对等就会让人感到意外。

8　带有限分裂策略或无分裂策略的语言

第八个论据源于有些语言只有非常有限的分裂策略，有的语言则根本没有任何类型的分裂结构，但是却允许有截省句。

---

① 规范而言，此处应该用 [for whom] 这一形式，因为包含裹挟式移位的语域也要求介词后用古体形式 whom。但没有在附带省略中发现这一形式：Peter went to the movies, but I don't know who(*m) with，这可能是因为，这种情况会涉及到语域之间的冲突：whom 属于英语书面语中（有时口语）最正式的语域，而附带省略表现出了极不正式的口语特征，甚至比非省略疑问句中的介词悬置更加不正式。

第一种语言可用德语来说明，德语中不允许介词短语做分裂句的中枢词（还有其他限制；见 Grewendorf and Poletto 1990）。但如我们上面所看到的，介词短语中的 wh- 短语可以做截省句的残余，甚至可以"位于孤岛中"。

（46） a *Mit wem war es, daß er gesprochen hat?
          with who was it that he spoken has
          'With whom was it that he spoke?'
       b Er hat mit jemandem gesprochen—rate mal mit wem!
          he has with someone spoken guess PRT with who
          'He spoke with someone—guess with whom!'

第二种语言的代表是罗马尼亚语和匈牙利语。下文格罗苏（Grosu 1994: 203-204；另见 Dobrovie-Sorin 1993）提供的语料显示，罗马尼亚语不允许像英语分裂句那样的结构存在。

（47） a *E Maria (că) vreau să întîlnesc.
          is Maria that want.1sg SUBJ meet.1sg
          ('It's Maria that I want to meet.')
       b *E Ion {ce/ care} a cîştigat premiul întîi.
          is Ion that/ who has won prize.the first
          ('It's Ion that won first prize.')
       c *E Ion pe care (l-) am întîlnit ieri.
          is Ion ACC who him- have.1sg met yesterday
          ('It's Ion who I met yesterday.')

不管对这一事实做出何种解释（Dobrovie-Sorin 1993 认为罗马尼亚语可能缺少合适的空算子），如果假截省句的假设成立，则该语言中缺少分裂结构就预示着罗马尼亚语也应该缺少截省结构。然而，这却是不正确的。

（48） a Vrea să întîlnească pe cine-va, dar nu ştiu pe cine.
          want.3sg SUBJ meet.3sg ACC someone but not I.know ACC who
          'She wants to meet someone, but I don't know who.'

b Cine-va a cîştigat premiul întîi—ghici cine!
　someone has won　prize.the first　guess who
　'Someone won first prize—guess who!'

c Am întîlnit pe unul diutre graţii tăi, dar nu ţin minte
　I.have met　ACC one among brothers you but not I.have memory
　pe care.
　ACC which
　'I met one of your brothers yesterday, but I don't remember which.'

类似论据也可从匈牙利语中得到，匈牙利语将动词前的位置作为识别焦点，但缺少英语的分裂结构。因此修改自基斯（Kiss 1998: 249 例句（8a））的例句（49a）与英语分裂句（即后面的翻译）相对应，但（49b）却不可能出现。①

（49）a Mari a kalapot nézte.
　　　　 Mary the hat.ACC looked.at
　　　　 'It was the hat that Mary was looking at.'

　　　b *Volt a kalap amit Mari nézte.
　　　　 it.was the hat.NOM which.ACC Mary looked.at
　　　　 ('It was the hat that Mary was looking at.')

不过匈牙利语允许相关形式的截省句。

（50）Mari nézett valamit, de nem emlékszem, mit.
　　　Mary looked.at something.ACC but not I.remember what.ACC
　　　'Mary was looking at something, but I don't remember what.'

9 在主格中带有分裂句中枢词的语言

反对将截省句同化为分裂句或类似分裂结构的第九个论据源自希腊语

---

① （49b）这样的结构是可能存在的，但会得到存在解读；（49b）中有定中枢词的使用排除了这种无关的可能性。感谢普斯卡斯（G. Puskás）的讨论。

这类语言。希腊语中的确既有截省结构，也有分裂结构，但也有明显可以区分的情况。在希腊语中，包括 wh- 中枢词在内的分裂句中枢词在与此讨论有关的情况中以主格形式出现。相反，截省的 wh- 短语的格必须与其对应成分的格相匹配（如前文 3.2.1 节中的讨论）。这就造成了（51a）和（51b）的差异（感谢詹纳基杜的判断）。

（51） I astinomia anekrine enan apo tous Kiprious prota, ala dhen ksero
the police interrogated one.ACC from the Cypriots first but not I.know
 a {*pjos /pjon}.
  which.NOM which.ACC
 b {pjos itan /*pjon itan}.
  which.NOM it.was which.ACC it.was
'The police interrogated one of the Cypriots first, but I don't know {which/which it was}.'

英语也存在相关的情况，将截省句同化为分裂句会产生下面这种不合语法的截省句：

（52） The police said that finding someone's car took all morning, but I can't remember who *(it was).

10 左分支截省句

最后，截省句可以违反左分支限制的某些情况，此处用定语性形容词来加以说明（关于这些情况的更多讨论见 5.1.1 节）：

（53） He married a rich woman—wait till you hear how rich!

但这些例句没有合乎语法的分裂句对应形式：

（54） a *How rich is it (that he married [a ___ woman])?
  b *He married a rich woman—wait till you hear how rich it is!

4.2.3 小结

本节给出了诸多理由，以说明对于任何试图将英语中的截省句简化为假截省句的尝试都应持怀疑态度。除了从句法上难以对缺失的系动词、虚位主语 *it* 和 CP 做出解释外，我也从附加语、隐性论元、韵律、强非语篇关联疑问词短语、"提及-部分"修饰、"提及-全部"修饰、*else* 修饰、附带省略现象（wh-介词倒装）、带有限分裂策略或无分裂策略的语言、在主格中带有分裂句中枢词的语言以及左分支截省句等方面提供了证据，以支持应该对疑问词做中枢词的分裂句和截省句加以区分这一结论。

4.3 截省 ≠ 疑问算子 + 复述

本节主要探讨是否有可能把违反强孤岛条件的截省例句归纳为通过复述策略得到挽救的非法移位构型。复述这种做法使我们能够维持对孤岛的标准解读，认为孤岛是通过非法移位操作产生的，因为疑问算子在不能发生移位的结构中可以约束复述代词（概述见 McCloskey 1990）。然而，如果仔细观察相关语料，就会发现这种方法是站不住脚的。

让我们先来考察，为什么将强孤岛中的截省简化为通过复述成分来形成算子和变项链的机制这种做法也许很有解释力。尽管这种方法在文献中从未得到过详细探讨①，不过基于某些分布上的相似之处，它还是很具启发性。试比较如下例句——（55）中的例句是强孤岛提取的标准示例，而在（56）中，句首的疑问算子可以与孤岛中的复述代词相关联。为了使术语简化，我把约束复述代词的疑问算子称为复述约束算子（resumptive-binding operator）（我会在下文中证明复述约束算子有许多跨语言特性，这些特性使复述约束算子区别于更为常见的语迹约束对应成分）。在（57）中，截省的疑问算子似乎约束着一个处于同样位置的变项。

---

① 绍尔兰（Sauerland 1996: 307-308）顺带提到过这一点。

（55） a *Who₁ did the Brazilian team improve after t_1 started playing for them?

b *What play₂ does he want to interview the woman who wrote t_2?

（56） a Who₁ did the Brazilian team improve after he₁ started playing for them?

b What play₂ does he want to interview the woman who wrote it₂?

（57） a The Brazilian team improved after somebody from Ajax started playing for them, but I can't remember who.

b He wants to interview the woman who wrote some play, but I can't remember what play.

我的基本想法是，截省例句并非推导自（55）中的移位变体，而是推导自（56）中它们的复述对应成分。既然语法上这一策略适用于任何情况，那么逻辑上就没有理由不采用这一策略。为使删除可以继续进行，平行条件必须允许先行小句中（约束变项的）不定词与被省略 IP 中的复述代词相同，而非与 wh- 移位的语迹相同。如第一章所示，这种做法没有坏处且在很多情况下都是必要的（见 5.2 节）；这种等同在省略下很普遍，而且自本课题研究伊始，就被认为是成立的，它被赋予了各种名称（Ross 1967 和 Bouton 1970 中的"宽泛同一性"；Fiengo and May 1994 中的"载体转换"）。

下表阐释了这种平行性：

（58）三种类型的算子-变项关联情况

	这种关联可否跨越强孤岛？
疑问算子和空缺（语迹）	否
疑问算子和复述代词	是
截省的疑问算子和"变项"	（很明显）是

这种平行性，尽管一开始很具吸引力，但不幸的是在很多地方都出现了问题，最终证明这只是一种表面上的平行。以下各节的目的就是要揭示这些问题。

4.3.1 初步思考

首先，有很多可能存在的 wh- 残余似乎没有现成可用的复述策略，如：when、where 和表示数量或程度的 how。① 尽管在英语中 then、there 和 that 是 when、where 和表示数量或程度的 how 对应的指示代词，但这些成分一般不起复述词的作用（最近的讨论和文献见 McCloskey 1990: 243, Finer 1997: 717）：

（59） a *Where$_1$ does he want to find a person [who camped (there$_1$)]?
      b *When$_2$ is she looking for journal entries [that describe a battle (then$_2$)]?
      c ??How much (weight)$_3$ did he promise to work out [until he lost (that much$_3$)]?

然而，如果关联词提供了宽域的地点、时间或数量变项，如（60）所示，则"对孤岛不敏感的" when、where 和 how much 就可能出现：

（60） a He wants to find a person who has lived somewhere specific in the Pacific, but I can't remember where.
      b She is looking for journal entries that describe a battle {at a certain time/in a certain year}, but I don't remember when.

---

① 我没有考虑表示方式的 how 和 why，因为它们没有对应的简单指示成分。这与文献中经常提到的一个事实有关，即 how 和 why 都是非语篇连接的，尤其是 why，它们不容易接受一种排序关系（见 Szabolcsi and Zwarts 1993）。因此，虽然可以用一个宽域不定词来说明一种方式或原因，但在这些不定词上的截省需要 DP 是 in what way 或 what reason，并且仍然不允许使用 why 或在小范围内允许使用 how，这种情况的原因目前尚不清楚。

（i） a She is practicing her serve so that she'll be able to hit the ball in a certain deadly way, but her trainer won't tell us {in what way/??how}.
    b He wants to interview someone who works at the soup kitchen for a certain reason, but he won't reveal yet {?what reason/*why}.

当然须注意的是，尽管我们可能认为（in）that way 和 for that reason 这种表达可能被认为在提取依存关系中能作为复核成分来替换 how 和 why，但这是不可能的：

（ii） a *How$_4$ did she practice her serve so much that she could hit the ball (that way$_4$)?
     b *Why$_5$ did you interview someone who quit the Red Cross (for that reason$_5$)?

当然，"不违反岛条件"的截省是可以用 how 和 why 的。

c He promised to work out until he lost a certain number of pounds, but I don't remember how much.

这一推论得到了爱尔兰语的证实,尽管爱尔兰语提供了一个极富成效的复述策略,但却缺少与 then 和 there 相对应的复述代词(McCloskey 1990: 243 注释 10)。如果这种成分通常不存在于复述成分系统中(大概是由于类型的原因,复述成分似乎只能是〈e〉类型),那么很难认为它们实际上可能存在,却在截省中只做空复述代词使用。[①]

爱尔兰语也会是一种可以从总体上考察出截省(至少表面上是对孤岛不敏感的变体)是否采用了复述策略的自然语言,因为爱尔兰语不仅像英语一样会标记出在基础位置出现的复述代词,还会标记出在标句词上出现的复述代词(见 McCloskey 1979, 1990)。但对于这一考察目的来说很不幸的是,如 2.2.2.2 节所述,截省绝不允许标句词和 wh- 残余同时出现,如(61)(该例句重抄自第二章的例句(103))。这里选取的语料来自(肯定式)过去时,因为在现在时中,标句词(对和语迹同时出现的标句词的辅音弱化(lenition)被标注为 C_{trace},对复述标句词的鼻音化被标注为 C_{pro})后动词的音变(mutation)是判断我们正在处理哪一标句词的唯一标志。当然,在截省中,相关动词是不发音的。但是在过去时中,复述标句词体现为 ar,而语迹标句词体现为 a(见 McCloskey 1979: 11)。

(61) Cheannaigh sé leabhar inteacht ach níl fhios agam
 bought he book some but not.is knowledge at.me

[①] 文献中也引用了一些处所复述词的例子:苏涅尔(Suñer 1998)提供了西班牙语和澳大利亚英语中限制性关系从句的例句,普林斯(Prince 1990)也提供了这类关系从句的例句(另见 Bissell 1999)。沃赫拜(Wahba 1984: 13-14)提供了埃及阿拉伯语话题化中的复述处所词例句,并论述了尽管这些复述代词不能出现在非孤岛语境中(只会出现一个空缺),但却可能出现在孤岛中。关键一点是,这些例句都没有涉及 wh- 疑问句(在埃及阿拉伯语中,对孤岛外的处所词进行提问会涉及疑问词原位滞留策略;见 Wahba 1984: 118-126),假如要把截省例句归纳为复述代词,就需要涉及 wh- 疑问句。有趣的是,时间复述代词甚至似乎在限制性定语从句中也不存在。

céacu ceann (*a /*ar).
which one C_{trace} C_{pro}
'He bought a book, but I don't know which.'

但是，爱尔兰语确实为反对将所有类型的截省都同化为复述行为提供了论据。此论据基于这样一个事实，即任何复述成分都不能在小句中作为最高主语出现（McCloskey 1979, 1990: 210）（希伯来语和阿拉伯语中也有同样的限制，这些语言中的截省语料与此处提供的爱尔兰语语料相似）。

（62）*an fear a raibh sé breoite
the man C_{pro} be.PAST he ill
(lit.) 'the man that he was ill'

假如截省结构仅仅是复述策略的结果，我们猜想爱尔兰语不允许在最高主语上出现截省。但这种截省却是完全合乎语法的（J. McCloskey，私下交流）：

（63）Tá duine inteacht breoite, ach níl fhios agam cé.
be-PRES person some ill but not.is knowledge at.me who
'Somebody is ill, but I don't know who.'

4.3.2 复述性与格

反对复述策略的另一重要论点来自于有格标记的语言。此处我将用英语中属格的例子加以说明，后文还有德语、俄语、波兰语、捷克语和希腊语中其他格的例句。这个论点的基本观点很简单：虽然移位的 wh- 短语一直携带着其在初始位置的格，但与复述代词相关的 wh- 短语却不必这样，通常也不能这样，相反如果可能的话，它会以某种默认的格出现。假如截省中残余的 wh- 短语约束着一个复述成分，我们猜想这个 wh- 短语的格就会是约束复述成分的 wh- 短语通常所采用的默认格。相反，如果 wh- 短语像在常规语迹约束构型中那样，实际上是移位的产物，则可以料到它会根据语境而采用合适的格。我将证明，实际情况显示后者才是事实。实际上，其中一些语言更加清楚地说明了这一点：看起来，对于各种各样的 wh- 短语而言，根本就没有可以采用的复述策略，但是这些相同的 wh- 短语完全可以很好地出现在截省中。无论缺乏复述性是不是所讨论语言的系统性特征（这是另一个问题，会在下一节中简要介绍），只要截省中可用的疑问算子的范围和用作复述约束算子的疑问算子的范围有一点不对等，都会让人质疑是否应该把前者归纳为后者。

自罗斯（Ross 1969）起，我们就知道格匹配效应在截省句中成立，如前文第二章和第三章所示。但是第二章乃至整个著作也讨论了一些例句，在这些例句中，带有格标记的 wh- 短语并不源自强孤岛（实际上，只讨论了有关格标记语言的单句例句），因此人们也许认为目前没有必要考虑这些例句。因为在这些例句中，截省内部都没有强孤岛，提倡删除 + 复述方法的人可能有理由认为，这些非孤岛例句在简单移位后进行了删除，并不需要复述策略。假设孤岛约束总体上控制着移位，只有当截省的 wh- 短语必须明显源自强孤岛内部时，才必须采用复述策略来挽救删除分析法。也就是说，我们希望对违反孤岛条件的截省例句进行简化，其中 wh- 短语基础生成于标句词短语的指示语位置（SpecCP），并且 IP 也随之得到了删除。该 IP 既包含孤岛，也包含受基础生成的疑问算子所约束的复述成分。

4.3.2.1 英语

为了验证这一假设是否违反了格标记的事实，我们必须要考虑涉及强孤岛提取的截省，如 3.2.1 所示。为了便于阐释，我先从英语疑问词系统中仅剩的一个格标记词开始，即表示属格的 *whose*。[①] 将 *whose* 截省句从

[①] 我没有顾及 *whom* 这一形式，（至少）在我的美式英语方言中完全没有出现 *whom*——这一形式完全是规定性的，像禁止"分裂不定指"一样必须被认为是一种语法外的附带现象，比如，禁止在 *to* 和其后的动词之间插入副词，如 *to boldly go* 等。这种规定性成分几乎不能显示出这一体系的底层结构；相反，它们反映了可以为这一体系带来哪些有意识的修改，类似于故意用口齿不清的方式说话等。虽然这种修改一般都可能会受底层语法规则的制约，但我还是会质疑对这些语料所做的任何判断是否可靠，因此会在下文中避免这种修改。

孤岛中提取出来是可以接受的，如（64）中的主语从句孤岛所示（此外它也违反了左分支限制条件）①：

（64） The police said that finding someone's car took all morning, but I can't remember
  a whose.
  b *who.

最关键的是，采用复述策略时，只能使用空疑问算子 who，如（65a）所示，不能使用带格标记的 whose，尽管 whose 和它所约束的复述代词 his 一样都是属格，如（65b）所示（（65b）中的例句在没有复述代词 his 时，也同样不合法，此外它也违反了左分支限制条件）。

（65） a Who$_1$ did the police say that finding his$_1$ car took all morning?
   b *Whose$_1$ did the police say that finding (his$_1$) car took all morning?

当然，这与（64）中的语料恰恰相反。假如将（64a）中截省的合法性归结为复述的原因，我们会得到恰好相反的判断，即与（65）中采用复述策略时相同的判断。②

---

① 我忽略了一个问题，即 whose 是否真的在形态上是 who 的带格标记的属格形式，或者仅仅是 D⁰ 中 who 带 's 的形式。与这一问题有关的证据是模棱两可的；本质上这一问题可以简化为如下问题：whose 是应该被同化成其他带格标记的代词，比如 his、its 等，还是像 who the hell's 这样可能出现的短语属格形式（如麦克洛斯基所指出的那样）。如果后者成立，那么文中的例句表明缺少与复述约束算子一起的裹挟式移位；如果前者成立，那么这些例句就表明复述约束算子缺少格标记（如果这实际上没有归纳为对裹挟式移位的限制的话）。在下面讨论的许多其他语言的语料中，这些问题都没有发生。

② 格罗苏（Grosu 1981: 25）也提到了类似的情况。他给出了以下例句，以此反对对"非标准关系从句结构"进行复制（移位）分析。

  （i）The man {who/*whom/*whose} I told you that his pants are always wet has been arrested by the police.

他提议，在关系从句中对此进行解释时，不要把（i）中的"who"分析成关系代词，而应该分析成基础生成的标句词。虽然这种分析方法可能在关系从句中有效，但还不清楚如何能够将它拓展到文中讨论的疑问句中的平行语料上。

英语中的 whose 允许省略的 NP 做补足语，如（66）所示，这一事实使上述语料变得稍显晦涩。

（66） Abby's car is parked in the driveway, but whose is parked on the lawn?

我们可以假设这个 whose 的结构为 [$_{DP}$ whose [$_{NP}$ e]]，无须详细探讨所涉及的 NP 省略（见 Lobeck 1995, Kester 1996）。实际上，很可能（64a）中的截省隐藏了一个省略的 NP，它也根本没有体现出真正的左分支提取（关于定语性形容词截省的例句见第五章）。但即便事实如此，它也不影响（64）和（65）之间的比较力度：（64b）不合法而（65a）合法这一事实已经破坏了使用复述策略和发生截省之间的任何双重条件关系。这对语料表明，在某些例句中，可以采用复述策略来使强孤岛失效，但其所对应的截省依然不合法。实际上，如果一种复述策略使用 whose car 这种复杂算子或者完整地说，使用 [$_{DP}$ whose [$_{NP}$ e]] 这种复杂算子的话，那么它本身就是不合法的：

（67） a *?[Whose car]$_2$ did the police say that finding it$_2$ took all morning?
b *I know that the police said they found Ben's car right away, but [whose e]$_2$ did they say that finding it$_2$ took all morning?

因此，我们无法以省略形式 [$_{DP}$ whose [$_{NP}$ e]] 为基础对（64）和（65）的对比提出反对意见。假如这一形式是（64a）合乎语法的全部原因，那么（67）中不能采用复述策略的事实仍然完全无法得到解释。

对属格截省中 whose 和 who 差异性的讨论以及对（67）中对比的讨论引出了另一个有趣的论点——复杂算子不能约束复述代词。比如，英语中复述-约束算子可能不会将介词短语裹挟式移位——复述约束算子必须是原形（即光杆形式）。[①]

---

① 复述约束算子不能裹挟式移位（包括指示语和介词裹挟式移位）似乎是一个跨语言的普遍特征，见下文和麦钱特（Merchant 1999c）的论述。实际上，不允许任何类型的复杂算子和复述词一起裹挟式移位；由于疑问句中（因此在截省中）的裹挟式移位相当有限，

(68) a (*For) which candidate$_2$ did they receive reports that more than 60 percent of eligible voters were planning to vote for him$_2$?

 b Lincoln was the candidate {who$_2$/OP$_2$ that/*for whom$_2$} they received reports that more than 60 percent of eligible voters were planning to vote for him$_2$.

(69) a (*Against) what measure$_3$ did they elect a candidate who made it clear that she was against it$_3$?

 b Proposition 209 was the measure {?which$_3$/OP$_3$ that/*against which$_3$} they elected a candidate who had made it clear that she was against it$_3$.

相反，无论有没有孤岛的干扰，带介词短语的截省的奇怪程度，似乎都与标准美式英语中的介词裹挟式移位的奇怪程度一样（相关讨论见 McDaniel *et al.* 1998）。我用 ® 来标记这种形式，表示它们受到了正式语体的限制。

(70) a ®For which candidate were more than 60 percent of eligible voters planning to vote?

 b More than 60 percent of eligible voters were planning to vote for one of the Red candidates, but I don't remember (®for) which.

 c They received reports that more than 60 percent of eligible voters were planning to vote for one of the Red Candidates, but I don't remember (®for) which.

我们将注意力转移到德语、俄语、波兰语、捷克语和希腊语这些有强

（接上页）因此这一点并不会造成分歧。但是在关系从句中可以清楚地看到这一点，尽管裹挟式移位在关系从句中更自由，但这种裹挟式移位也不可能和复述词一起发生：

 (i) a the president, a biography of whom she wrote ___ last year

 b *the president, a biography of whom he's married to the professor who wrote (it) last year

如果所有复述词实际上都被空算子所约束，这种现象就可以得到解释。这种空算子会被识别出来（正如需要被识别的小代词（pro）一样；见 Browning 1987, Grosu 1994），但当带有识别 φ 特征的 wh- 短语被嵌入时，空算子就无法获得允准。这一点究竟将如何延伸到英语疑问句上，还需进一步研究。

大格系统的语言上，可以避免英语中格和介词短语裹挟式移位来回变换的问题。

4.3.2.2 德语

德语有四个格：主格、宾格、与格和属格。德语在所有名词和形容词范畴中以多种方式对这些格进行了标记，尤其是在疑问代词和疑问限定词方面，而它们又与我们此处所讨论的截省有关（感谢罗特和温克勒，尤其感谢温克勒对本节中许多例句所做出的耐心判断）。下文给出了这些词中第一个词的格变化表（限定词 welcher 'which' 的词形变化与此类似，但它还有数和性的变化）：

（71）德语疑问代词 wer 'who' 的变格（declension）情况
主格　wer
宾格　wen
与格　wem
属格　wessen

回顾 3.2.1 节可知，德语中截省的 wh- 短语如果有先行项，就一定要与其先行项携带相同的格，即使在跨强孤岛时也是如此。这一事实使第一个形式同一性概述得以形成，此处重述为（72）：

（72）形式同一性概括 I：格匹配
截省的 wh- 短语必须与其关联词带同样的格。

将截省简化为复述的论述是直接从这一概述中推断出来的：复述约束算子的格应该与它所约束的复述代词的格相同。这大概是因为省略对源小句中关联词（的格）和目标（省略）小句中复述代词（的格）之间的对等性很敏感。

（73）*{Welchem Gefangenen$_1$ /wem$_1$}　will　sie　jemanden　finden,
　　　which.DAT　prisoner　　　　who.DAT　wants　she　someone　find

der ihm₁ geholfen hat?
who him.DAT helped has
('{Which prisoner/who} does she want to find someone who helped him?')

(74) *{Welchen Gefangenen₂ /wen₂} will sie jemanden finden,
which.ACC prisoner who.ACC wants she someone find
der ihn₂ gesehen hat?
who him.ACC seen has
('{Which prisoner/who} does she want to find someone who saw him?')

在这些例句中,尽管复述约束算子的格与复述代词的格相同,但语句却不合法。^①另一方面,它们可以与第三章中合法的截省例句(18)和(19)做比较,这两个例句重述如下:

(75) Sie will jemanden finden, der einem der Gefangenen geholfen
she wants someone find who one.DAT of.the prisoners helped
hat, aber ich weiβ nicht, {*welcher /*welchen /welchem}.
has but I know not which.NOM which.ACC which.DAT
'She wants to find someone who helped one of the prisoners, but I don't know which.'

---

① 在关系从句中也如此,尽管这些关系从句对于我们目前的研究目的来说没那么重要。德语没有空算子(比如"that")关系词,只允许带格标记的关系代词(der、das、die、die 等)。因此,任何复述词都不可能存在:

(i) *Peter ist der Gefangene, dem₁ sie jemanden finden will, der ihm₁
Peter is the prisoner who.DAT she someone find wants who him.DAT
geholfen hat.
helped has
('Peter is the prisoner that she wants to find someone who helped him.')

(ii) *Peter ist der Gefangene, den₁ sie jemanden finden will, der ihn₁
Peter is the prisoner who.ACC she someone find wants who him.ACC
gesehen hat.
seen has
('Peter is the prisoner that she wants to find someone who saw him.')

(76) Sie will jemanden finden, der einen der Gefangenen gesehen
she wants someone find who one.ACC of.the prisoners seen
hat, aber ich weiβ nicht, {*welcher /welchen /*welchem}.
has but I know not which.NOM which.ACC which.DAT
'She wants to find someone who saw one of the prisoners, but I don't know which.'

这两组语料之间的对比——一方面（73）和（74）中的复述策略不合法，另一方面（75）和（76）的截省合法——对于用复述法解释截省而言是一个无法解决的问题。

下述语料也表明，在附加语孤岛中的复述约束算子上也存在这种格匹配限制。

(77) a *Mit welchem Lehrer$_1$ wird Anke sich ärgern, wenn
with which.DAT teacher will Anke REFL upset if
Peter mit ihm$_1$① spricht?
Peter with him.DAT speaks

---

① 我在这里使用了规则的与格代词 ihm，取自德语中一组未简化的前置代词。德语中也有一组指示性代词，即直指（"deictic"），它们的形式和关系算子的形式一致，在文献中被称为"d 代词"。尽管这些词经常是前置的，但它们也可以在原位出现，尤其是在文中所讨论的那种上下文中，如（i）所示。

(i) Anke wird sich ärgern, wenn Peter mit dem spricht.
Anke will REFL upset if Peter with demonstrative.DAT speaks
'Anke will get upset, if Peter talks to that {one/guy}.'

尽管人们可能会认为，这些词与简单的代词系列相比，可以更好地充当复述成分，但实际情况却并非如此——(iia, b) 和（77）的情况一样：

(ii) a *Welchem Lehrer$_1$ wird Anke sich ärgern, wenn Peter mit dem$_1$ spricht?
b *Mit welchem Lehrer$_1$ wird Anke sich ärgern, wenn Peter mit dem$_1$ spricht?
('Which teacher will Anke get upset if Peter talks to that {one/guy}?')

我系统地测试了做复述词的 d 代词以及它们对应的简单代词，但文中所给出的语料仅限于后者。因为把所有这些额外的语料都公布出来，也不会增加论点的内容，而且读起来会很乏味，所以我在这里把它们省略掉了，因为它们无一例外地与其对应的简单代名词有着相同的模式。

b *Welchem Lehrer₁ wird Anke sich ärgern, wenn Peter mit
  which.DAT teacher will Anke REFL upset if Peter with
ihm₁ spricht?
him.DAT speaks
('Which teacher will Anke get upset if Peter talks to him?')

（78）*Wen₂   glaubst du, daβ Italien besser, spielt, seitdem sie
    who.ACC think you that Italy better plays since they
Ihn₂   in der Mannschaft haben?
him.ACC in the team   have
('Who do you think that Italy has been playing better since they have him on their team?')

但是同样，平行的截省例句是可以接受的（将（79）中必要的介词短语模数化，如前文 3.2.2 节中所述）：

（79）Anke wird sich ärgern, wenn Peter mit einem der   Lehrer
   Anke will REFL upset if Peter with one.DAT of.the teachers
spricht, aber ich weiβ nicht mehr, mit welchem.
speaks but I know no longer with which.DAT
'Anke will get upset if Peter talks to one of the teachers, but I don't remember which.'

（80）Er glaubt, daβ Italien besser spielt, seitdem sie einen   von
   he thinks that Italy better plays since they one.ACC from
Ajax in der Mannschaft haben, aber ich weiβ nicht mehr, wen.
Ajax in the team   have but I know no longer who.ACC
'He thinks that Italy is playing better now that they have someone from Ajax on their team, but I don't remember who.'

这些不平行之处表明，涉及孤岛提取的截省不能被归纳为复述性：这种归纳不能在合法的截省中生成合法的格匹配疑问算子。实际上，标准德语似乎根本没有英语中常见的那种复述策略（"插入性"复述），无论复述约束算子采用哪种格。尤其是，把主格当作"默认"格，任何"默认"格策略似乎都是不可能的（比如在悬置话题左错位结构中出现时，见 Vat 1981 和 van Riemsdijk 1997，并比较 Maling and Sprouse 1995 的论述）。下面的例句对这一点进行了阐释，（81）和（82）中是关系从句孤岛，（83）和（84）中是附加语孤岛。

(81) *{Welcher   Gefangene / wer}   will   sie jemanden finden,
      *which.*NOM *prisoner   who.*NOM *wants she someone   find*
      der   ihm   geholfen hat?
      *who   him.*DAT *helped   has*
      ('{Which prisoner/who} does she want to find someone who helped him?')

(82) *{Welcher   Gefangene / wer}   will   sie jemanden finden,
      *which.*NOM *prisoner   who.*NOM *wants she someone   find*
      der   ihm   gesehen hat?
      *who   him.*ACC *seen   has*
      ('{Which prisoner/who} does she want to find someone who saw him?')

(83) *{Welcher   Lehrer / wer}   wird Anke sich   ärgern, wenn
      *which.*NOM *teacher who.*NOM *will Anke* REFL *upset   if*
      Peter mit   ihm   spricht?
      *Peter with him.*DAT *speaks*
      ('{Which teacher/who} will Anke get upset if Peter talks to him?')

(84) *Wer   glaubst du,   daβ Italien besser spielt, seitdem sie
      *who.*NOM *think   you that Italy better plays since they*
      ihn   in der Mannschaft haben?
      *him.*ACC *in the team   have*
      ('Who do you think that Italy has been playing better since they got him on their team?')

为了使论述更加完整，我应该指出，如果复述代词是主格形式，复述性也同样不可接受，因为这使得格匹配要求和"默认"格在任何情况下都无法区分：

(85) *{Welcher　　　Gefangene / wer}　　will　　sie jemanden finden,
　　　 which.NOM　prisoner　　who.NOM　wants she someone　find
　　　 dem　er　　　geholfen hat?
　　　 who　he.NOM　helped　 has
　　　 ('{Which prisoner$_2$ / who$_2$} does she want to find someone who he$_2$ helped')

(86) *Wer　　　glaubst du,　daβ　Italien besser spielt,　seitdem er
　　　who.NOM　think　 you　that　Italy　 better　plays　since　he.NOM
　　　in der Mannschaft ist?
　　　in the team　　　 is
　　　('Who do you think that Italy has been playing better since he's been on the team?')

尤为异常的是下述例句的不合法性，这些例句中的复述约束算子是充当复述代词的疑问算子 wo（为方便起见，此处注释成"what"），有时人们认为它根本不需要任何形式的格（做状语时：见 Trissler 1993, Müller 1995）。在（87a）中，（尝试充当）复述成分是 [非疑问] 复述代词 da，注释成"that"。

(87) a *Wo$_1$　 glaubst du, wären　 alle　　 glücklich, wenn Peter
　　　　 what think　 you would.be everyone happy　 if　 Peter
　　　　 da$_1$mit　aufhörte?
　　　　 that-with stopped
　　　　 ('What do you think that everybody would be happy if Peter stopped doing it?')

　　 b *Wo$_2$　 glaubst du, wären　 alle　　 glücklich, wenn Peter
　　　　 what think　 you would.be everyone happy　 if　 Peter
　　　　 das$_2$　tun würde?
　　　　 that do　would
　　　　 ('What do you think that everybody would be happy if Peter would do it?')

拜尔（Bayer 1996）利用这类语料的孤岛敏感性来论证，实际上在（87a）这类例句中，算子 wo 源自介词短语内部。① J. 胡克斯特拉（Hoekstra 1995）得出了相同的结论。最重要的是，拜尔（引述了 Wiltschko 1993 的观点，与米勒（Müller）和特里斯勒（Trissler）的观点相左）认为复述 wo 和 da 必须有格的变化。这一结论似乎很合理，与上文出现的德语的复述情况相吻合。②

简而言之，尽管标准德语也有不少跨越强孤岛的截省，但似乎根本没有可采用的复述策略。很明显，任何试图将截省归纳为复述策略的论述都注定会失败。

4.3.2.3 斯拉夫语

斯拉夫语是另一个典型例证。我先从俄语入手，像德语一样，俄语也有丰富的格系统，俄语有六种格而德语只有四种（感谢阿夫鲁京对本

---

① 实际上他认为 wo . . . da 的结合是不可能的，因为 [+wh] wo 和 [-wh] da 两者之间在特征上不匹配，从而排除了这种结合。虽然在成对出现上，da . . . da 肯定要更好一些，wo . . . da 相对少见，但后者至少也是有一点可能性的，至少与简化的 d(r) 一起时是有可能的；奥本里德（Oppenrieder 1991）和特里斯勒（Trissler 1993: 265）都提供了一些例句：*Wo hast du dich den ganzen Tag drauf gefreut?*（lit. "What have you been looking forward to it the whole day?"）。

② 在这里，标准德语 wo（wo 是一个 XP）与关系词中发现的瑞士德语 wo 有区别，后者是对标句词（C）的实现（另见 Bayer 1984，其中巴伐利亚语的关系词（relativizer）wo 为此提供了论据）。这个 wo 可以和复述词共现，如下述例句所示（这些例句发表于 Demirdache 1991: 21，引自范里姆斯迪克 1988 年未发表的一篇手稿）。

(i) de vrund wo ich immer mit em gang go suufle
the friend that I always with him go go drink
'the friend that I always go drinking with'

(ii) s auto wo du gsäit häsch das es sich de Peter nod chönti läischte
the car that you said have that it REFL the Peter not could afford
'the car that you said that Peter couldn't afford'

在美式英语口语中也发现了这一策略，如下面已被证实的例句所示：

(iii) I've had dreams where he's been in them.（电视采访，《今晚娱乐》（*Entertainment Tonight*）节目，1999 年 1 月 1 日）

小节的例句做出判断)。(88) 给出了 kto 'who' 的变格情况；疑问词 čto 'what' 和疑问限定词、关系代词 ktoroj 'which' 的变格情况也与之类似。

(88) 俄语疑问代词 kto 'who' 的变格情况
    主格   kto
    宾格   kogo
    与格   komu
    属格   kogo
    工具格 kem
    处所格 kom

与德语一样，俄语也允许跨越强孤岛的截省，也遵循(72)中给出的第一个形式同一性概述。第三个有关的相似点是(88)中的算子不能约束复述代词，如下述语料所示。

(89) a *Kogo   ty   dumaeš' italjancy stali   lušče posle togo
     who.ACC you think   Italians became better after that
     kak oni vklučili (ego) v komandu?
     how they put   him in team
    b *Kto   ty   dumaeš' italjancy stali   lušče posle togo
     who.NOM you think Italians became better after that
     kak oni vklučili (ego) v komandu?
     how they put   him in team
     ('Who$_3$ do you think that the Italians became better since they put him$_3$ on the team?')

(90) a *Kto   ty   dumaeš' italjancy stali   lušče posle togo
     who.NOM you think Italians became better after that
     kak on v komandu?
     how he in team
     ('Who$_3$ do you think that the Italians became better now that he$_3$ is on the team?')

b *Čto   ty   dumaeš' italjancy stali   lušče posle togo kak
  what.NOM/ACC you think   Italians became better after that how
  oni uvideli (èto)?
  they saw   it
  ('What₂ do you think that the Italians became better since they saw it₂?')

c *Kakuju p'esu   Ivan xočet vstretit' ženščinu kotoraja
  which play.ACC Ivan wants meet   woman   who
  napisala (eë)?
  wrote   it

d *Kakaja p'esa   Ivan xočet vstretit' ženščinu kotoraja
  which play.NOM Ivan wants meet   woman   who
  napisala (eë)?
  wrote   it

  ('What play₂ does Ivan want to meet the woman who wrote it₂?')

波兰语中也有同样的情况，我不再一一说明（感谢莫克罗辛斯卡的判断）。和俄语一样，波兰语也有六种格，用这些格来标记疑问算子，允许跨越孤岛的截省和格匹配，但不允许有格标记的疑问算子充当复述约束算子。这里只对值得关注的最后一个特性进行说明：

（91）a *Która sztucę   on chce rozmawiać z kobietą
       which play.ACC he wants to.talk   to woman
       która (ją)   napisała?
       who   it.ACC wrote

     b *Która sztuca   on chce rozmawiać z kobietą
       which play.NOM he wants to.talk   to woman
       która (ją)   napisała?
       who   it.ACC wrote

       ('What play₂ does he want to talk to the woman who wrote it₂?')

与波兰语和俄语一样，捷克语也有六种格（感谢皮拉托娃（A. Pilátová）的判断）。尽管捷克语需要格匹配的截省，如（92）所示，但不能采用复述策略。

(92) Chce   mluvit s   tou ženou, která napsala nějakou
wants.3sg to.talk with the woman who wrote   some.ACC
hru,   ale nemohu   si   vzpomenout,
play.ACC but NEG.can.1sg REFL recall
{kterou   / *ktera}.   144
which.ACC which.NOM
'He wants to talk to the woman who wrote some play, but I can't remember which.'

(93) *{Kterou   hru   / ktera   hra}   chce   mluvit
which.ACC play.ACC which.NOM play.NOM wants.3sg talk
s   tou ženou, která napsala (tu)?
with the woman who wrote   it.ACC
('Which play does he want to talk to the woman who wrote it?')

4.3.2.4 希腊语

希腊语提供了进一步的语料证据（感谢詹纳基杜和阿古拉基的判断）。希腊语中有三种需要关注的格：主格、宾格和属格（此外还有呼格，但很明显，呼格不会出现在疑问算子上）。这些格在疑问代词/限定词 *pjos* 'who, which' 上的标记情况如下（这里我只提供了阳性形式）：主格 *pjos*，宾格 *pjon*，属格 *pjanou* 或 *tinos*。这些都不能作为复述约束算子出现——以下格匹配的（a）例句不合法，复述约束算子以"默认"主格形式出现的（b）例句也不合法。

(94) a *Pjon₁   psaxnun enan giatro pu na   (ton₁) voithisi?
who.ACC they.seek a   doctor that SUBJ him   helps
b *Pjos₂   psaxnun enan giatro pu na   (ton₂) voithisi?
who.NOM they.seek a   doctor that SUBJ him   helps
('Who are they looking for a doctor who can help him?')

(95) a {*Pjanou₁ /tinos₁} ipe i astonomia oti to na
who.GEN who.GEN said the police that the SUBJ
vroune to aftokinito (tou₁) dhiirkese olo to proi?
they.find the car his took all the morning

b *Pjos₂ ipe i astonomia oti to na vroune to
who.NOM said the police that the SUBJ they.find the
aftokinito (tou₂) dhiirkese olo to proi?
car his took all the morning

('Who did the police say that finding his car took all morning?')

但是当然，与这些例句相当的截省句的确表现出了与（72）中的概述相一致的格匹配效应：

(96) Psaxnun enan giatro pu na voithisi kapjon, alla dhen
they.seek a doctor that SUBJ helps someone.ACC but not
ksero {pjon /*pjos}.
I.know who.ACC who.NOM

'They are looking for a doctor to help someone, but I don't know who.'

(97) I astinomia ipe oti to na vroune to aftokinito enos
the police said that the SUBJ they.find the car of.one
apo tous ipoptous dhiirkese olo to proi, alla dhen
from the suspects took all the morning but not
thimame {pjanou /tinos /*pjos}.
I.remember who.GEN who.GEN who.NOM

'The police said that finding the car of one of the suspects took all morning, but I don't remember which one's.'

4.3.3 结论

总之，从这些语言中选取的语料有一个共同的作用，就是彻底打消人们想要以笼统的方式将截省归纳为一种复述策略的想法。如果这些语言确实全都缺少复述代词（比如 J. Hoekstra 1955 提出的西弗兰芒语和荷兰语），那么，它们应该也缺少截省现象，但这与实际情况不符。

特别是上文（58）中的表格，它是基于明显的孤岛敏感性不足而得出的，内容很简单，不够充分；下表展现出了全部内容：

（98） 三种类型的算子-变项关联情况

	关联能否跨越强孤岛？	是否有形式同一性效应
疑问算子和空缺（语迹）	否	是
疑问算子和复述代词	是	否
截省的疑问算子和"变项"	（很明显）是	是

这足以确立本节的主要论点——截省（尤其是"进入孤岛条件的截省"）通常不能被归纳为对复述成分的约束。（这一结论得到了截省中 wh- 短语解读上的支持——比如，截省中的 wh- 短语仍然可以得到功能性解读，但复述词却不可以；见 Doron 1982, Sells 1984。）

我们这里考察过的语料，以及麦钱特（Merchant 1999b, c）中讨论过的来自另外十种语言的语料，启发我们制定出了一个非常普遍的原则，如（99）所述：

（99） 格和复述约束算子概述
　　　 任何复述约束算子都不可以被格标记。

如果复述约束算子基础生成于标句词短语的指示语位置，就会直接发生（99）中的情况，且复述约束算子永远无法核查其格特征。须注意的是，这尤其适用于那些被孤岛把自身和所约束的复述代词分隔开的算子：当没有孤岛干扰时，各语言的差异体现在复述成分是否真的是拼读出来的（spell-out）移位语迹（近期论述见 Aoun and Benmamoun 1998）。（99）成立，至少对于进入孤岛的约束而言成立，这一事实提供了好几条论据，证实了孤岛内部的复述代词与通过移位而对它们进行约束的算子毫无关联（与 Pesetsky 1998a 等观点一致）。

截省句研究中最重要的一点是，(99)的成立排除了复述这种方法，复述法不能用来解决第三章中记录的明显的孤岛不敏感问题。

4.4 钟等（Chung *et al.* 1995）：IP复制、合并和萌生操作

为了解决孤岛不敏感问题，钟等（Chung *et al.* 1995）（后文记作CLM）提出，截省中的省略不是PF删除的结果。相反，他们按照赵（Chao 1987）和洛贝克（Lobeck 1995）等的做法，假设句法中有一个空IP范畴，如（100）所示，其中wh-XP基础生成于标句词短语的指示语（SpecCP）位置：

（100） Someone called, but I don't know [$_{CP}$ who[$_{IP}$ e]]. 拼读

然而，为了使解读在LF层可以继续进行，这个空语类必须被一个适当类型的句法结构所替代（即一个IP）。这个复制操作是一种应用在LF层的结构同构条件，通过复制短语标记词来实现。因此，第一章中针对这种结构同构解释法所提出的所有问题几乎都会给CLM造成困扰。唯一例外的是没有显性关联词的情况，为此他们提出了一种新的LF结构构建操作，并称之为"萌生操作"，后面我们再来讨论这一问题。我们先来考察一下他们的解释方法是如何在例句（100）上运作的。

在这一例句中，第一个IP可以充当省略的先行项，可以作为e被复制到第二个小句中，得到（101）（我用粗体字来表示LF复制的内容）：

（101） ... but I don't know [$_{CP}$ who[$_{IP}$ **someone called**]]. LF层IP复制后

CLM按照坎普（Kamp 1981）和海姆（Heim 1982）的做法，假设不定词不是量化的，而只是提供了一个（带有描述性内容的）变项，该变项被存在闭包的独立操作所约束，该操作可应用于结构中的不同位置，得出

不定词的变项辖域。① 按这种观点，(101) 中复制的不定词可以自由地被存在算子所约束，该存在算子也约束着标句词短语的指示语内 wh- 短语所引入的变项（同样也是不定词），CLM 称这一过程为"合并"(merger)。他们在 LF 层用上标来代表合并；(102a) 中合并的 LF 产物会通过标准操作，产生 (102b) 中内嵌式疑问句所需要的卡尔图宁式 (Karttunen-style) 解读。

(102) a ... [$_{CP}$ who^x [$_{IP}$ **someone**^{x} called]].　　　　　LF 层合并后
　　　 b ... $\lambda p[\exists x.[\textbf{person}(x, w_0) \wedge p(w_0) \wedge p=\lambda w. \text{call}(x, w)]]$

通过这样做，CLM 将截省的合法性建立在了可以在被复制 IP 中使用非约束变项（通常由不定词提供）这一基础上。如果找不到这种变项（比如，不存在不定词，或不定词已经被存在性地闭包在了 IP 内部，狭域不定词和否定极性词等的情况就是如此），截省就会失败。因此 CLM 正确地预测出，截省总是要求其所在小句中的关联词得到宽域解读，产生辖域平行（因为 wh- 短语本身在其小句上也有宽域）。

由于截省的 wh- 短语没有移位，预计孤岛限制条件不会成立。在 CLM 看来，(103) 这种例句的推导很简单。(104a) 中是它拼读出来的结构②，但经过 IP 复制和合并，其结构如 (104b) 所示。

(103) They want to hire someone who speaks a Balkan language, but I don't remember which.

(104) a ... [$_{CP}$ which [$_{IP}$ e]]
　　　 b ... [$_{CP}$ which^x [$_{IP}$ **they want to hire someone who speaks** [a Balkan language]^x]]

---

① CLM 解读法也可以用另一个理论来解释，该理论使用选择函数来解释不定词，如莱因哈特 (Reinhart 1995) 所示。

② 这里全篇都将忽略 which 短语中 NP 省略的问题——大概类似的机制会被用来检索合适的省略内容，就像用来解决 "one" 照应语一样。这是合并的一个方面，因此似乎是多余的，因为很明显，NP 省略的这种解释机制是被需要的，这一点与截省无关。

因为通过合并得到解释的截省仅仅是一种变项和约束关系，对 A′ 移位上的句法限制不敏感，因此预计它对孤岛也不敏感。相反，截省对关联词的辖域很敏感：如果这个不定词的辖域比截省所需要的辖域窄，截省就会失败。截省强制性地要求辖域平行，如（103）所示。第一小句中不定词 a Balkan language 的辖域只能在 want 之上，如（105a），不能在 want 之内，如（105b）。尽管在其他语境中，这句话完全可以有（105b）中的这种狭域解读，但当该小句用来充当截省下 IP 省略的先行项时，这种解读就被排除出去了。这是因为，用产生（105b）这种解读的 LF 来解决（103）第二个小句中的 IP 省略，会导致标句词短语指示语（SpecCP）中的存在算子出现空量化现象，因为与 a Balkan language 相关的必要变项已经得到了较低 ∃ 的约束。

（105） a ∃y.[Balkan-language(y) ∧ want(they, ∧[∃x.[person(x) ∧ speak (x, y) ∧ hire(they, x)]])]

b want(they, ∧[∃x.[person(x) ∧ ∃y.[Balkan-language(y) ∧ speak (x, y) ∧ hire(they, x)]]])

但是，当没有可用的显性关联词时，语句必须使用其他操作来为标句词短语指示语中基础生成的 wh- 短语提供被约束成分。这一操作就是"萌生操作"。他们假设"萌生操作"是形式链（FormChain）句法操作的一个实例，受孤岛限制，孤岛限制被认为是对 A′ 链形成的限制（与移位无关，最先由 Cinque 1990 提出）。除了这一方法的理论输入问题，仅仅通过在形式链上施加孤岛限制来对隐性关联词截省的局部限制做出解释有些过度概括。（106a）和（107a）中是合法的 A′ 链例句，但它们却不能产生合法的截省，如（106b）和（107b）所示。

（106） a When was no nurse on duty?

b *No nurse was on duty, but we don't know when.

（107） a When is a nurse rarely on duty?

b *A nurse is rarely on duty—guess when !

对 CLM 而言，例句（b）不合法是意料之外的，因为如例句（a）所示，其对应的 A′ 链是合法的。相反，阿尔伯特（Albert 1993）指出，"萌生操作"例句对选择性孤岛一律很敏感（Sauerland 1996 提出了类似的观点）。这可以再次简化为要求先行小句中的隐性量词和截省小句中与 wh-短语有关的量词之间具有辖域平行。比如在（106b）的第一个小句中，被隐性约束的时间变项相对于 *no nurse* 而言拥有狭域，如（108a）所示，也没有（108b）中所表达的解读。（106b）中的截省要想合乎语法，就必须得到这第二种解读。

（108） a ¬∃x[nurse(x) ∧ ∃t[**on-duty**(x, at t)]]
    b ∃t¬∃x[nurse(x) ∧ **on-duty**(x, at t)]

因此，没有理由对"合并"和"萌发操作"进行分析上的区分：一种有利的做法是，把两种情况都分析成要求在先行项中有一个未被约束的变项。它们唯一的区别是，隐性存在成分（无论是论元还是附加语）在小句中总是采取狭域，因此当其他算子介入时（比如在选择性孤岛中），它们不能为截省提供所需的开放变项。因此，我们可以假设"萌生"这一操作可以被取消，并把注意力集中在那些有显性关联词的例句上，因为这些例句可以（明显地）违反孤岛条件。

比如，当（103）中有显性关联词时，在那个先行项上可能出现的截省只受一种情况制约，即疑问句中不定词被约束的层级是否可以和解决省略问题所需的层级平行——在 LF 层需要复制的 IP 外部。因为只有在（特定类型的）显性不定词上才会发生这种宽域行为，只有在这些情况下才会出现孤岛不敏感的截省现象。

虽然对辖域平行进行解释是 CLM 体系的重要成就，但这并不是该体系所独有的。罗梅罗（Romero 1997a）已经证明，辖域平行即使与更普遍的焦点条件也不能相容；实际上，省略或去重音成分中的量化成分与其先行项中的量化成分之间具有辖域平行是一种相当普遍的特征，并不仅限于截省句中。有关 VP 省略的论述可见普鲁斯特和沙阿 (Prüst and Scha 1990*a*) 和福克斯（Fox 2000），涵盖截省和 IP 去重音的论述可见罗梅罗（Romero 1998）。既然如此，合并在截省中产生了辖域平行这一事实并不能作为一个支持合并说法的极具压倒性的证据。

CLM 认为不定词和 wh- 短语之间可能会相互作用，他们承认，这种观点无法解释下面这种例句为何会不合法。

(109)　*Who^x did you see someone^x?

由于他们的体系使用的就是这种约束，因此他们不能从原则上将该例句排除，而只能表示它推导自另外一些属性，这些属性只有显性的 wh- 链才具备。

即使这一问题能够被克服，合并的说法也会遇到一些其他困难。

首先，合并不能处理截省 wh- 短语中描述性内容与其关联词相冲突的情况（1.4 节中的"对比性"截省）。

(110)　a　She has five CATS, but I don't know how many DOGS.
　　　 b　The channel was 15 feet wide, but I don't know how deep.
　　　 c　Abby knew which of the MEN Peter had invited, but she didn't know which of the WOMEN.
　　　 d　We know which streets are being re-paved, but not which avenues.
　　　 e　Max has five Monets in his collection, and who knows how many van Goghs.
　　　 f　There are nine women in the play, but I don't know how many men.
　　　 g　I know how many women are in the play, but I don't know how many men.
　　　 h　She's an absolute idiot: unaware of who she is, or where.

这些都是合并的说法有待解决的问题，因为 wh- 算子所约束的变项会错误地受到两个限制，这与直觉相违背。比如例句（110a）的意思肯定不是我不知道她有多少既是猫又是狗的动物，因为这种动物根本不存在。

其次，可能出现的关联词的范围并不总与预期相符（Romero 1997*a*

专门记录了一些反例）。在她的基础上，我们还可以添加以下几个关联词，它们不能被分析为海姆所定义的不定词：

（111） a More than three of the boys quit, but I can't remember {which/who}.
   b I counted fewer than six sorts, but I couldn't tell which.
   c Most of the boys passed, but I don't know exactly how many.

即使是代词，在正确的条件下，也可以成为截省 wh- 短语的关联词，下面这段荷兰语对话证明了这一点，其中复制的 IP 会包含代词 *er*（Romero 1997*a* 也提供了一些用西班牙语和加泰罗尼亚语造出来的例句，但她指出，由于某些原因这些例句在英语中却不太恰当；有关英语例句的讨论另见 Fukaya 1998: II 注释 6）：

（112） 'Omdat   je   er   nu   gewoon mee   kan   stoppen?'
    because   you   it   now   just   with   can   stop
    ...'Waarmee?' i.e. [Waarmee kan ik nu   gewoon stoppen?]
       what-with   what-with   can I   now just   stop
    ' "Because you can call it quits now?"
    ..."With what?" ' (Zwagerman 1991: 248)

此外，有时合并可能提供了错误的限制：

（113） More than three books were missing, but we didn't know how many.
   a = we didn't know how many books were missing.
   b ?we didn't know how many more than three books were missing.

但是对钟等（Chung *et al.* 1995）的解释而言，最大的问题是仍然没有解释清楚第三章中记录的形式同一性效应。在 CLM 看来，wh- 短语基础生成于标句词短语的指示语内这一点至关重要，缺少移位可以解释为什么缺少孤岛效应。但是形式同一性效应似乎正是判断移位的依据。

首先，如 4.3 节的结论所示，如何对基础生成于标句词短语指示语位置的 wh- 短语进行格核查并不清楚。实际上，有证据显示这种格特征根本不能被核查，这为这些算子在复述结构中的分布做出了解释。但是这种基础生成却正是 CLM 体系的基础论点。

其次，介词悬置概述也很出人意料，因为在合并操作中，我们无法预料到，德语中"光杆"的 wh- 短语不能像在英语中那样约束介词短语中的不定词。相反，介词悬置的事实是发生 wh- 移位的最佳标志。实际上，像 CLM 这样的基础生成分析，在定义与合并相关的约束时，不得不对从介词短语内部移位的限制进行复制。因为合并应该是一种解释性操作，它对细微形态句法事实的敏感是意料之外的。实际上，显性移位下的介词悬置和截省下发现的 wh- 短语的形式之间存在关联，这种关联使任何对合并的重新界定都不可靠：由于将这一条件整合到合并中，然后对它进行跨语言的参数化设置，这两点都与移位的（不同）限制无关，因此我们期待截省下的介词悬置和非省略结构中 wh- 移位下的介词悬置存在跨语言的随机分布。但我们发现事实并非如此，这两者之间反而非常契合。

因此，尽管钟等（Chung et al. 1995）的解释方法有其成功之处，却还是受到了大量问题的困扰。从句法的角度来看，这些问题中最严重的一个就是它不能与第三章中的形式同一性效应兼容。但是，人们会想是否有办法来维持这一解读相较于单一 PF 删除法所具备的优越性。我将在下一节中讨论这一问题。

4.5　IP 复制与 A′ 链一致性

我在本节中提出了一种可能的方法以替代钟等（Chung et al. 1995）的 LF 复制法，试图获得麦钱特（Merchant 2000c）中提出的形式同一性效应。这种方法和 CLM 的方法一样，都是基于一个假设，即省略的同一性条件根本上是一种结构条件，通过复制 LF 的短语标记词来实现。在说明了本方法的基本原则后，我指出了它的不足之处，并说明了为什么我最终认为它不是一个可行的替代方案。

3.1节中给出的语料显示孤岛条件在截省下是无效的,这似乎表明PF删除法不能充分解释孤岛现象。但3.2节中介词裹挟式移位的实际情况表明钟等人(Chung *et al.* 1995)处理LF复制的方法(该方法把不定词理解成一种海姆所定义的变项)不能解释已经证实的语法敏感性。

钟等的方法的一大难题可以追溯到他们采用海姆的方法来分析不定词。在他们看来,关联词没有经历移位,在目标小句中滞留在原位,他们把关联词理解为未被约束的变项。他们只假设存在闭包的操作必须在IP复制前应用到目标小句中,以解释辖域平行。正是这种对海姆理论的依赖,把对上述第二种形式同一性概述所做的任何解释都排除在外。

然而,孤岛不敏感的事实似乎更支持LF复制法而非PF删除法。如何能够在保持移位法优势的同时,继续使截省保持在不定词的辖域?拜尔(Bayer 1996)关于LF层介词悬置的结论提供了一个可能的答案。

在对焦点小品词和疑问词原位滞留进行研究的基础上,拜尔表示语言之间的不同不仅体现在它们是否允许显性A'移位下出现介词悬置,也体现在是否允许LF层隐性A'移位下出现介词悬置(与Aoun 1985: 63–69及其文献的意见相左)。他的结论基于(114)和(115)中的那些语料得出,它们取自英语和希腊语[①](实际上他没有讨论希腊语,但希腊语在相关方面的表现与他用来举例的德语完全相同)。根据假设,特定类型的焦点算子,比如*only*,在它们的非级差解读上,要求其关联词进行LF移位。在允许介词悬置的英语中,这些焦点小品词可以直接与PP内的一个DP相关联,如(114b)所示,因为该DP可以合法地在LF层从PP内部移出来。相反,在不允许介词悬置的希腊语中,焦点小品词必须依附在PP上,如(115a)所示。拜尔认为,如果希腊语中的介词短语在LF层也是孤岛,那么焦点小品词也按此分布。由于辖域因素,焦点小品词+XP必须在LF层移位,所以LF层会发生违反介词悬置的情况,恰好将(115b)排除在

---

① 感谢詹纳基杜和鲁苏为本节中的例句做出判断。

外（目前假设显性移位和隐性移位在这一领域中受到相同的制约）。

(114) a I spoke only to Bill.　　LF: [$_{PP}$ only to Bill]$_1$ I spoke t_1
   b I spoke to only Bill.　　LF: [$_{DP}$ only Bill]$_2$ I spoke [$_{PP}$ to t_2]

(115) a Milisa mono me ton Bill.　LF: [$_{PP}$ mono me ton Bill]$_1$ milisa t_1
    I.spoke only with the Bill
    'I spoke only to Bill.'
   b *Milisa me mono ton Bill. LF: *[$_{DP}$ mono ton Bill]$_2$ milisa [$_{PP}$ me t_2]
    I.spoke with only the Bill
    ('I spoke to only Bill.')

如果我们放弃不定词不能在 LF 层移位这一假设，我们就可以采用上述结果来解决 LF 复制法遇到的形式同一性问题。但我们必须采取下述观点：像其他有辖域的成分一样，不定词是概化量化词（generalized quantifier），由于类型一致的原因，必须在 LF 层移位。在给了不定词辖域后，所得到的 IP 可以用来解决截省中的省略问题。对于像（116a）这样的简单例句，这样做会产生如下推导，推导部分如（116b, c）所示。

(116) a Idha kapjon, alla dhen ksero pjon.
    I.saw someone but not I.know who
    'I saw someone, but I don't know who.'
   b kapjon$_1$ [$_{IP2}$ idha t_1]
    [[kapjon]] = λP[∃x **person**(x) ∧ P(x)]
    [[[$_{IP2}$ idha t_1]]] =λy[**saw(I**, y)]
   c [pjon]$_1$ [$_{IP2}$ **idha** [$_{DP}$$t$]$_1$]

先行小句中的不定词 *kapjon*$_1$ 'someone' 在 LF 层得到了提升（通过适合不定词的任何 QR 版本），它紧邻 IP，该 IP 的较低分段被标记为 IP$_2$。然后在 A′ 链形成后（通过句法下标来表示），IP$_2$ 可以被复制进来，代替截省的 *pjon* 'who' 下缺失的 IP，得到（116c）中的 LF。

这种方法也会产生钟等解读中的辖域平行。如果不定词辖域过低，即

第四章　删除的诞生与消亡

位于复制的 IP 内部，wh- 短语的存在量词就会在其第二个论元中出现空量化现象（兰姆达转换将不可能出现，因此第二个并连语也不会是所需要的 $\langle t \rangle$ 类型）。只有当不定词的辖域在用来解决省略问题的 IP 之外时，才可以使用合适的变项。这种从句法上解决缺失 IP 的纯机械方法当然没有阻止其他成分处于辖域之外并提供一个变项。尽管在一些例句中，这种 IP 可能确实能够提供一个句法上合适的 IP[①]，但我们会以为，其他因素的干扰，可能使随之产生的解读不恰当（即在焦点替换词上有限制；见 Romero 1997a）。为了考察这一方法，此处我们将只关注对省略的结构解析的细小的要求（Rooth 1992a 的"冗余关系 1"；Fiengo and May 1994 的"重构"）。当然，作为一种结构性的解释，这种方法也出现了第一章中所提及的所有问题；但为了便于讨论，我们假设这些问题可以暂时搁置。

我们现在来看一看如何在截省下产生介词匹配效应。尽管我用希腊语做例句，但结果是普适性的。如果拜尔的观点正确的话，像其他 DP 一样，不定词也必须在 LF 层把一个管辖的介词裹挟式移位。这意味着（117a）这种合法例句的产生将按照（117b）和（117c）中给出的步骤进行。首先，量化词提升不定词和介词在先行小句中一起提升至 IP_2 外不定词取得辖域的位置，如（117b）所示。然后得到的 IP_2 被用来解决省略问题，如（117c）所示。

(117)　a　I　Anna milouse me kapjon, alla dhen ksero me pjon.
　　　　　the Anna spoke　with someone　but not I.know with who
　　　　　'Anna was speaking with someone, but I don't know with who.'
　　　b　[me kapjon]$_1$ [$_{IP2}$ i Anna milouse [$_{PP}$ t_1]]
　　　c　[me pjon]$_1$ [$_{IP2}$ **i Anna milouse** [$_{PP}$ t_1]]

在（117c）的表述中，基础生成的疑问词和介词短语 A′ 约束着一个

[①]　尽管这并不明显——据贝盖利和斯托厄尔（Beghelli and Stowell 1997），非不定量词的辖域位置与宽域不定词不同，前者的辖域位置比后者低。

同范畴的句法变项——一个 PP。现在需要做的是让得到的 A′ 链遵从一个条件，该条件要求链中的每一个连接都共享某些基本特征，即这里说的范畴特征。但是如上所见，A′ 链中那些连接之间的一致性不仅限于范畴特征，也延伸到了格（和 φ 特征）上面。我们可以在下述 A′ 链条件中说明这一点：

（118） A′ 链一致性

$\forall \alpha \forall \beta \; [[(\alpha \in C) \wedge (\beta \in C)] \rightarrow (F(\alpha)=F(\beta))]$

其中

a　C = 最大的同标序列 $\langle \alpha_1, \ldots, \alpha_n \rangle$，因此 α_1 处于 A′ 位置上，α_n 是一个语迹，而且

b　$F(x) = \{F | F\ x\ 的一个特征\}$（这里的"特征"至少覆盖了类别、格和 φ 特征）

（118）中的限制表明，A′ 链中每个联结的特征都必须和其他任一个联结的特征相匹配（当然也包括自匹配）。我们可以想到许多对该条件进行说明的方法，这只是方法之一。我们对链中随意选取的任何联结（比如 α_1 或 α_n）实施一致性，都可以得到相同的结果。

现在让我们考察一下（119）这种不合法例句的问题出在哪里。

（119）　*I　Anna milouse　me　kapjon,　alla dhen ksero　pjon.
　　　　 the Anna spoke　with someone but　not　I.know who
　　　　（'Anna spoke with someone, but I don't know who.'）

有两种可能的推导需要考虑。第一，与其合法的英语对应例句一样，我们尝试提供一个合适的 IP，通过关联词 DP *kapjon* 'someone' 的辖域投射，使其能够在省略部位复制，如（120）所示。

（120）　*[kapjon]$_1$[$_{IP2}$ i Anna milouse [$_{PP}$ me [$_{DP}$ t_1]]]

虽然得到的 IP$_2$ 能够解决省略问题，但把 *kapjon* 从它管辖的 PP 中移出却不合法，这违反了在 LF 层起作用的 PP 孤岛条件；参考上文的（115b）。

第二个要考虑的推导满足了 LF 移位限制,这是通过把介词短语裹挟式移位而实现的,如上文(117b)所示,从而得到了(121)中先行小句的 LF。

(121)　[me kapjon]$_i$[$_{IP2}$ i Anna milouse [$_{PP}$ t_1]]

现在,IP$_2$ 是唯一能够用来解决 *pjon* 下省略问题的结构性先行项,把这个 IP$_2$ 复制进去可以得到(122)。

(122)　[pjon]$_i$ [$_{IP2}$ **i Anna milouse** [$_{PP}$ **t$_1$**]]

Pjon 必须与 IP 内的一个语迹形成一个 A′ 链,这里唯一可用的语迹就是 [$_{PP}$ t_1],形成的链是〈[$_{DP}$ *pjon*], [$_{PP}$ t]〉,如(122)中的标引所示。但是这个链违反了(118)中的 A′ 链一致性条件,因为 *pjon* 是 DP 而 t 是 PP,它们的范畴特征没有如(118)中所要求的那样相互匹配。

既然(119)可能有的两个推导方式都不合法,该例句就被排除在外了。这种论证对于所有关联词在介词短语内部的例句都适用。须注意的是,这种解释方法没有把截省例句的不合法归结于和截省 wh- 短语自身相关的一些违规上——DP 截省是完全合法的。相反,不合法的原因是希腊语法不能够提供一个可以解决省略问题的合适的 IP 先行项;因为介词短语对 LF 移位而言是孤岛,介词短语内提供不出 A′ 链一致性所要求的 DP 语迹。

现在我们已经了解了 A′ 链一致性加上拜尔的假设如何能够产生第三章中记录的形式同一性效果了。这一方法的基础是把不定词当成规则的概化量化词,它们通过某种移位操作在 LF 层到达它们的辖域位置。由于不定词的辖域可以投射到孤岛之外(尤见 Farkas 1981),因此合法的先行 IP 得以生成,这些先行 IP 也可以解决涉及从孤岛中提取截省的省略问题。让我们回顾一下例句(103),重述于(123)。

(123)　They want to hire someone who speaks a Balkan language, but I don't remember which.

将不定词 *someone who...* 的辖域固定在 *want* 之下,第一小句就有两种可能的解读,与内嵌的不定词 *a Balkan language* 可能具有的辖域相对应。这两种可能性通过(124a, b)中的 LF 可以体现出来,基本与上文所述(105a, b)中的公式相对应。

(124) a. [a Balkan language]$_1$ [$_{IP}$ they want to hire someone who speaks t_1]
b. [$_{IP}$ they want [[a Balkan language]$_1$ [$_{IP2}$ to hire someone who speaks t_1]]]

只有(124a)中的 LF 提供了一个带合适语迹的 IP,该语迹可被(123)中截省的 *which* 所约束。在(124b)中 IP$_1$ 或 IP$_2$ 都不满足这一点:IP$_1$ 不包括一个未被约束的语迹(因为 t_1 仍然被 [a Balkan language]$_1$ 约束在 IP 内部),而对于 IP$_2$,就算它真有一个合适的解读,它也不能产生(123)所需要的意义(尤其是它失去了 *someone who...* 对 *want* 的从属关系)。

在非孤岛例句中,目前的 LF 复制法正确地产生了所观察到的辖域平行现象。由于用来解决孤岛中截省问题(如(123)所示)的机制与所讨论的用来解决简单例句(如(116)所示)的机制相同,因此形式同一性效应的解释依然成立。

但是对形式同一性"跨越"孤岛的解释要求不定词必须在 LF 层从孤岛中移出。这是一个很不确定的结论,是一个很多人由于各种原因都尽可能去避免的结论(尤见 Winter 1997 和 Reinhart 1997,其最具有说服力的论点来自埃迪·吕斯,埃迪·吕斯观察到复数不定词的分布式解读确实受到了孤岛的限制)。

换言之,这种方法没有弄清楚为什么只有不定词可以从孤岛中移出,并把这一疑问留给了一个尚不明确的孤岛理论,让这一理论来允许这种不可见的辖域移位。同样,在我看来,这种理论能够成功解释这一问题的可能性微乎其微。但是一旦抛弃了这种从句法上解决不定词宽域的方法,我们就只剩下本章中困扰着我们的悖论了。

另一个强烈的反对意见是,(118)中一致性条件的效应通常是从移位操作的定义中推导出来的。移位将一个成分完整地复制下来，没有改变它的任何特征，因此保证了链的一致性。换言之，这种一致性应该是链的一种**推导**属性，而不是一种**规定**属性。须注意的是，这种一致性条件实际上是相当有问题的：它必须要包含一个重要的例外条款，该条款规定一致性条件不适用于在孤岛内部以复述代词为终点的 A′ 链；约束复述代词的算子有许多特征，这些特征可以把它们与截省中的算子区分开来，如上文4.3 节中所见。特征之一就是它们**不能**带格，或者不能出现在介词短语内部，这一点正好和采用（118）这种一致性条件的效应相反。目前，我认为没有办法以一种非规定性的方式来做出必要的区分。

最后，这一方法所依赖的基本假设——拜尔以焦点小品词分布为基础对 LF 移位所做的分析——是否正确还有待商榷（关于这些小品词位置分布限制的一个竞争性解释方案，见 Büring and Hartmann 1999）。正如拜尔本人所说，有一些带显性介词悬置的语言似乎在 LF 移位下没有介词悬置，有一些缺少显性介词悬置的语言在他看来在 LF 层必须有介词悬置，这一点至少与通过和焦点小品词相关联而得出的判断一致。显性移位和隐性移位之间的这种不一致在截省下的形式同一性效应上没有出现。

4.6　小结

本章考察了针对截省结构而提出的五种不同的建议。我已经证明了，每种建议都存在严重的实证性缺陷，主要体现在它们不能解释第三章中列出的核心语料。这是一个很重要的结论，因为它会迫使我们接受一种可能会被认为与传统观点彻底背离的观点。上述分析有时看起来很合理，在说明这些分析的不足之处时，我已经淘汰了一些后续可能会出现的竞争性方案，并且极大地限制了我们的理论选择，为后续章节中的提议打下基础。实际上，我们被逼到了一个角落，一个我们可能不愿意去的角落。下一章的目的就是探究这一角落的本质，通过它的特征揭示不同孤岛条件的本质。

第五章

删除的复活

显然,我们现在处于一个互相矛盾的境地:形式同一性效应和孤岛不敏感性如何能调和?本章我将针对这一难题提出一个双管齐下的解决方案:有些孤岛效应的确是语音形式现象,偏差通过语音形式删除得以修复,然而另外那些明显对孤岛不敏感的情况,如果仔细考察,则是一种假象。

我的分析有两个核心观点:第一,删除对一种同一性条件很敏感,该同一性条件在本质上是语义性的,而不是结构性的,这点我们在第一章中已经指出;第二,截省中的省略,是语音形式删除的结果。

把语义条件和删除路径结合起来,乍一看似乎有些奇怪:一直以来,删除的支持者都主张删除的条件是结构性的,而从语义角度来研究删除条件的理论却往往对句法方面研究得不够。但我认为,这两者在本质上并非互不兼容。相反,这不过表明,省略部位虽然含有句法结构(不发音是由语音形式的删除造成的,该删除操作由第二章中提出的 E 特征所触发),但省略部位之所以是省略部位,还有语义上的原因(理想情况下,这也是由 E 特征来实现的,正如第二章所提到的那样)。

当然,这并不是说省略部位的句法结构和其先行项不起什么作用:语言表达式的意义是其逻辑形式结构特征的函数,所以结构会以某些直接的方式约束其意义。这里我的新观点仅仅是,没有**其他**必须满足的 LF 结构同一性条件,这一观点与已有文献中被广泛接受的假设相反(其中有代表性的文献包括 Rooth 1992a, Fiengo and May 1994, Romero 1998 等)。事实上，正如我们在截省中所看到的那样，这样的逻辑形式同一性条件究竟能否被满足还远没有弄清楚。采用过这种条件的研究者（最有代表性的是 Fiengo and May 1994，他们认为 LF 同一性条件是省略的**充分条件**）主要专注于 VP 省略的研究，但在 VP 省略上很难得到相关证据（载体转换效应是最主要的证据）。另一方面，截省为这个问题提供了更直接的证据：假设存在 LF 同一性条件，这会迫使我们认为在逻辑形式上存在着原本不该存在的结构歧义，或者迫使我们采取逻辑形式修复操作，而这些操作的唯一目的就是为了满足 LF 同一性这一条件。与之相反，如第一章所示，放弃 LF 同一性条件，采取纯语义条件，并不会有任何损失。

第二个观点，从某种意义上说，是对早期省略研究方法的修正，特别是对罗斯（Ross 1969）截省研究方法的修正。但这一观点背后的思维方式不应该被误认为已被广泛接受。相反，这种方法从 20 世纪 80 年代早期就受到冷落，许多研究者或明或暗地表示，省略并不涉及删除。正如我们所看到的那样，删除法有两个主要的竞争对手：第一，在显性句法中，有一个类似代名词的空成分，这一空语类在逻辑形式上被其先行项句法结构的复制体所代替。这一观点的倡导者包括威廉姆斯（Williams 1977）（在某些解读下）、赵（Chao 1987）和洛贝克（Lobeck 1991, 1995），菲恩戈和梅（Fiengo and May 1994）也可能持此观点。第二个竞争对手是纯语义的方法，其倡导者包括达尔林普尔等（Dalrymple et al. 1996）、雅各布森（Jacobson 1992）、哈尔特（Hardt 1993, 1999）和希伯等（Shieber et al. 1996）。尽管在关于省略结构的句法究竟是什么这一问题上，这些作者没有统一明确的观点，但很显然，他们都认为应主要从抽象的语义机制来研究省略，省略部位内部的句法并没有起什么作用。

这些方法所面临的困难，是如何解释有关形式同一性的一些语言事实。如果介词悬置是一个句法特征,据我所知这一假设没有受到任何严重挑战,那么在这些方法下,介词悬置概述就变得尤为神秘莫测。当然,在用删除法对语料进行解读时,无须特别说明:对于介词悬置,无论采用何种理论(假设这一理论是形态句法的),都能解释截省下裹挟式移位的分布,就像在非省略的 wh- 移位下那样。这是采用删除法解释省略的主要动因,也是一个以前从未受到过关注的动因。

鉴于其重要性,让我们简要回顾一下介词悬置概述的相关语料,这些语料成为了非删除法所面对的主要实证性问题。下面这些德语例子来自于 3.2 节。

(1) 德语
    a Anna hat mit jemandem gesprochen, aber ich weiß nicht,
       Anna has with someone spoken but I know not
       *(mit) wem.
       with who
       'Anna spoke with someone, but I don't know (with) who.'
    b *Wem hat sie mit gesprochen?
       who has she with spoken
       ('Who did she speak with?')

上面提及的删除法可以直接解释这些语料,并且预测到了已被证实的相关性。在这一分析框架下,(1a) 中截省的结构将如 (2) 所示:

(2) ...ich weiß nicht, [mit wem]$_2$ [~~Anna t$_2$~~ gesprochen hat]
       I know not with who Anna spoken has

句法上的 A′ 移位生成了语音形式上的表达,如(2)所示,IP 在语音形式上被删除。无论何种理论,只要能解释像(1b)中那样的显性语料,就能无须修改地用于解释截省语料。因为我们已经看到,可供选择的 LF 复制方案在这一点上失败了,所以这是应用删除法的最有力的论据。①

这给我们留下了一个问题，即截省中供删除的 wh- 移位明显对孤岛不敏感。在本章中，我提出这一问题包含两个部分，根据所涉及孤岛的类型，需要两种不同的解决方法。下面是我们所要涉及的一系列孤岛（更详细的列表见 Postal 1996: 他所提供的大部分其他类型的孤岛都归在我的 C 类当中；另见 Goodluck and Rochemont 1992 及 Culicover and McNally 1998 中的论文）：

(3) 孤岛类型
  A 1 选择性（"弱"）孤岛
  B 2 左分支
    3 COMP 语迹效应
    4 派生位置（话题化、主语位置）
    5 并列结构
      (i) 并连语的提取
  C (ii) 从并连语中提取
    6 复杂名词组
      (i) 关系从句
      (ii) 中心语名词的句子性补足语
    7 附加语

正如（3）中标签 A、B、C 所显示的那样，我（暂时）把这些孤岛分为三类。第一类，A 类孤岛，是所谓的"弱"孤岛；但在这里我采取了"选择性"这一更合适的说法。我认为里齐（Rizzi 1990, 1994）和曼齐尼（Manzini 1998）试图从结构上对这些孤岛进行解释的做法不正确，所以这里我采纳的观点来自于绍博尔奇和兹瓦尔兹（Szabolcsi and Zwarts

---

① 但是，从这一系列事实中可以得出对介词裹挟式移位进行正确分析的一个结论。无论我们得到的（1b）在推导过程中出了什么问题，都不能被简单地归结为语音形式上的约束。否则，它也可以从省略来修复，而且，无论在何种方法下，它与截省的关系，都会变得完全无法解释。这就排除了把典型的裹挟式移位同化为乔姆斯基（Chomsky 1995）提出的一般性裹挟式移位的做法。

1993)、鲁尔曼（Rullmann 1995）、库诺和高见（Kuno and Takami 1997）、洪科普（Honcoop 1998）及其他有关学者，这些学者认为孤岛在本质上是语义/语用性的。关于截省和选择性孤岛之间的相互影响，阿尔伯特（Albert 1993）、绍尔兰（Sauerland 1996）、罗梅罗（Romero 1998）和麦钱特（Merchant 2000c）曾进行过考察，共识是这些孤岛不是句法上的，所以我们在截省下观察到的"孤岛"效应并不能为删除问题提供测试基础。在这里我先不考虑此类孤岛，只在 5.4 节中会做简要考察。

第二类，B 类孤岛，我将证明它们的效应的确被 PF 删除消除了（5(i) 可能是个例外，这类孤岛似乎同时具有 LF 和 PF 效应）。在 5.1 节中，我将说明这一结果与截省对孤岛效应的修复作用是相兼容的。

最后一类，C 类孤岛，它们具有一个共同的特征，即都涉及从一个命题域中提取某一成分。我将证明，截省中 wh- 短语从这些孤岛中移出只是一个假象，事实上，内嵌的命题域是用来满足省略的同一性条件的。导致早期研究者认为存在孤岛的解释性效应，可以通过使用独立需要的情态从属机制和 E 类型照应机制来进行解释。因此，截省在确定这些孤岛是否是语音形式层面的现象时起不了什么作用（其他证据的确显示，这些孤岛不是语音形式层面的现象）。[①]

所以我的结论是，截省的删除解读法与截省所赋予的对孤岛条件的明显免疫性是相互兼容的。

5.1 PF 孤岛

5.1.1 左分支提取

我将从讨论最少的孤岛条件之一入手，但我相信有最有力的证据

[①] 其中我没有详细考察的一种孤岛是 wh- 孤岛：这种孤岛和其他类型的命题性孤岛一样，但是某些复杂因素使得孤岛的语料更相关，同时也使得这些语料在解释我们这里所提出的理论时不清晰明了。

表明，该孤岛的效应是在 PF 上产生的，即左分支条件（left-branch condition，简称 LBC）。首先我将考察一系列先前讨论过的情况，然后引出一个新的重要例证，以证明截省并不遵守左分支条件。接下来我会简要概述肯尼迪和麦钱特（Kennedy and Merchant 2000a）所提出的关于左分支条件的 PF 理论，讨论左分支条件效应在 PF 上的证据，证明这一理论也可以对荷兰语中一些新的语言事实做出正确的预测。之后我将证明如何用第一章提出的理论来解释一系列复杂的语言事实。最后我总结了一组新的语言事实，这些事实表明，从定语性程度短语（DegP）中进行的不合法子提取，不遵循这里给出的 PF 解释，继而导致在截省下也不合语法，这说明截省不是孤岛的灵丹妙药。

（4）中所示的是罗斯（Ross 1967）的左分支条件，其中涵盖了一系列不合法的提取，格罗苏（Grosu 1974）证明，这一左分支条件覆盖的语言事实比期望中更多。

(4) 左分支条件（Ross 1967 (4.181) (1986: 127)）
任何一个处在更大名词短语最左边的名词短语，都不能通过转换规则移出该更大名词短语。

从格罗苏的文章以来，左分支条件通常被用来管辖（5）至（7）中那种不合语法的提取；更详细的考察尤见科尔韦尔（Corver 1990）。例（5）是对名词前属格、数量短语和程度词的提取。

(5) a *Whose did he see [___ car] ?
b *How many inches is the monitor [___ wide] ?
c *How is the monitor [___ wide] ?

例（6）是对定语性形容词和单数可数名词、复数可数名词、集合名词和谓词性名词的数量修饰语进行的提取。

(6) a *How detailed does he want [a ___ list] ?
b *How{expensive/fast/big}did she buy [a ___ car] ?

c *How thorough does she write [___ reports]?
　　d *How expensive did he buy [___ {toys/jewelry}]?
　　e *How smart is your brother [a ___ doctor]?
　　f *How good is she [a ___ carpenter]?
　　g *How many did she buy [___ cars]?
　　h *How much did she find [___ gold]?

例（7）是从左分支结构中进行的一种子提取。

（7） a *How does he want [a [___ detailed] list]?
　　b *How did she buy [a [___ {expensive/fast/big}]car]?
　　c *How does she write [___ thorough reports]?
　　d *How did he buy [___ expensive {toys/jewelry}]?
　　e *How is your brother [a [___ smart] doctor]?
　　f *How is she [a [___ good] carpenter]?
　　g *How did she buy [___ many cars]?
　　h *How did she find [___ much gold]?

以上这些例子与（8）和（9）中（大部分）符合语法的裹挟式移位相对照，唯一例外的情况是例（9c, d）中复数可数名词和集合名词定语的裹挟式移位（一个神秘的、从未被成功解释的限制条件：见 Bolinger 1972 的讨论，以及第 186 页脚注①）。

（8） a Whose car did he see?
　　b How many inches wide is the monitor?
　　c How wide is the monitor?

（9） a How detailed a list does he want?
　　b How {expensive/fast/big} a car did she buy?
　　c *How thorough reports does she write?
　　d *How expensive {toys/jewelry} did he buy?
　　e How smart a doctor is your brother?
　　f How good a carpenter is she?
　　g How many cars did she buy?

h How much gold did she find?

关于截省是否遵守左分支条件这一问题，以往文献只是稍有涉及。在罗斯（Ross 1969: 277（74））的基础上，莱文（Levin 1982: 605）对下面例句（其书中例（43））进行了对比：

（10） a *I know he must be proud of it, but I don't know how.

b I know he must be proud of it, but I don't know how proud (of it).

基于这些例句，作者认为截省遵守左分支限制条件。但他们也注意到，（11）那样的例句也是合法的（尤其（11a），参阅 Ross 1969: 284 注释 21 和 L. Levin 1982: 653 注释 10）。

（11） a Someone's car is parked on the lawn—find out whose!

b I should buy some peppers for the dinner, but I don't know how many.

c She found gold, but won't say how much.

但正如他们所指出的那样，上述例句和当前讨论的问题并无关联，因为英语可以在这些语境中允准 NP 省略，即 *Bob's (car) is on the lawn* 和 *Several (peppers) were missing*。因此，没有办法证明（11）这样的例句是左分支提取，而不是简单地从符合语法的问句如 *Whose is parked on the lawn?* 和 *How many should I buy?* 推导而来，这些问句展示的是 NP 省略。[①]

罗斯提供了从谓词性形容词中进行 how 提取的例句，我们可以再补充几个从名词短语中的定语位置进行 how 提取的例句。

（12） a *He wants a detailed list, but I don't know how.

b *She bought an {expensive/fast/big} car, but I don't know how.

c *She writes thorough reports, and wait till you see how!

[①] *How many* 允准 NP 省略，而 *how AP* 却不能，这一事实也驳斥了一个普遍的假设，即前者和后者应被归为一类。肯尼迪和麦钱特（Kennedy and Merchant 2000a）也独立得出了这一结论。

d *He bought expensive {toys/jewelry}, but he wouldn't say how.
e *Your brother is a smart doctor, but it's not clear how.
f *She is a good carpenter, but it's not clear how.
g *She bought many cars but it's not clear how.
h *She found much gold, but she wouldn't say how.

这些例句也许可以用来说明截省的确遵守左分支条件，如同罗斯和莱文所做的那样。但这一结论的得出有些为时尚早。科尔韦尔（Corver 1990）令人信服地指出，(4c)和(6)中发现的偏差仅仅是因为中心语移位的限制。他赞同阿布尼（Abney 1987）提出的扩展的形容词投射，如（13）所示：

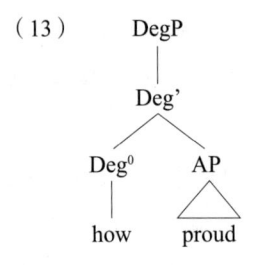

(13)

```
        DegP
         |
        Deg'
        /  \
     Deg⁰   AP
      |     △
     how   proud
```

鉴于这种短语结构，相关例句只表明，从这些语境中无法提取出中心语：

(14) *$[_{Deg0}$ How$]_2$ is he $[_{DegP}[_{Deg0}\ t_2]$ $[_{AP}$ proud of it]]?

因为 how 是中心语，而不是一个短语，所以也不能移位到 SpecCP。洛贝克（Lobeck 1995: 62ff.）也独立地指出，Deg⁰ 中心语不能允准其补足语省略。这就排除了像（15）那样的结构，这一结构和上文中 whose 和 how many 之后的省略类似。

(15) *$[_{DegP}$ how $[_{AP}\ e]]$

在这种情况下，我们不能期待（10a）或（12）那样的截省句像其他语料那样合乎语法。须注意的是，这一结果既可以基于本章中所倡导的移位分析（因为中心语不能移位到指示语位置）而得出，也可以基于原位生成分析（因为中心语不能在指示语位置上生成，且 how 不允许其补足语为空）而得出。

因此，这里的讨论解决了例（5）和（7）中违反左分支的问题，但这并非事情的全貌。

5.1.1.1 截省下的左分支违反

在文献中未注意到的是，可以找到与（6）中相对应的、真正违反了 LBC 的截省例句，如（16）所示。

（16） a He wants a detailed list, but I don't know how detailed.
　　　 b She bought an {expensive/fast/big} car, but I don't know how {expensive/fast/big}.
　　　 c She writes thorough reports, and wait till you see how thorough!
　　　 d He bought expensive {toys/jewelry}, but he wouldn't say how expensive.
　　　 e Your brother is a smart doctor, but it's not clear how smart.
　　　 f She is a good carpenter, but it's not clear how good.

须注意的是，以上这些句子不能简单地理解为 DP 内部省略，因为英语不能允准这类必要的省略①：

（17） a *He turned in a sketchy list, but we need a detailed.
　　　 b *A thorough report is better than a hasty.
　　　 c *Not only is she a carpenter, she's a good!

我对这些例句的看法是，我们的确在处理从 DP 内部进行的对定语性程度短语的提取。我认为这些例句具有以下结构（其中，程度短语的提取跨越了名词性扩展投射的内部最高投射的指示语位置）：

---

① 可对照萨格（Sag 1976a: 334）中一些有问题的例子，它们出自哈里斯（Harris 1965, 1968）和夸克等人（Quirk et al. 1972: 590）。

（18） I don't know [$_{\text{DegP}}$ how detailed]$_1$ ~~he wants [t_1' [a t_1 list]]~~.

换句话说，语音形式上的删除的确修复了原本不合法的定语性形容词短语的提取。① 然而，这一论断并不单单基于以上截省例句，该论断也得到了一些独立事实的支撑，包括一些语言中的 VP 省略、比较结构删除、剥落句和动词空缺等，肯尼迪和麦钱特（Kennedy and Merchant 2000a）曾对此进行讨论，他们基于个体语言的词库特性，提出了解释左分支条件的方法。我们认为，当一种语言可以支持 [+wh] 特征的名词性扩展投射没有特定的功能性中心语时，左分支条件效应就会起作用。这一想法是基于（19）中的语言事实得出的：

（19） a Abby wrote a more interesting novel than Ben {wrote, did, Ø}.
　　　　b *Abby wrote a more interesting novel than Ben wrote [a ___ novel].

例（19a）和（19b）相比，缺少了一些成分。以和截省关系最近的 VP 省略为例，在 VP 省略的删除法下，例（19a）中的 than 小句有（20）所示的结构。

（20） ... than [$_{\text{DegP}}$ Op]$_2$ Ben did [~~write [t_2' [a t_2 novel]]~~].

这个例句中的程度算子已从限定词短语 a novel 中提取出来。尽管如此，经过删除的句子也是合法的，不像例（19b）中没有经过删除的句子那样不合法。肯尼迪和麦钱特（Kennedy and Merchant 2000a）指出，（19b）那样的例句和本书中讨论的英语、希腊语、保加利亚语、波兰语和捷克语疑问句中的左分支 wh- 提取有关联。我们把这一点和各个语言中功能

---

① 例（16c, d），连同复数和集合名词的合乎语法性，表明例（9c, d）中对非省略条件下裹挟式移位的限制也必须有语音形式上的解释，因为这些例子在截省下同它们单数、裹挟式移位的对应成分有相同的地位。这一限制可能附着于某些特征，这些特征可以通过肯尼迪和麦钱特 (Kennedy and Merchant 2000a) 的 F^0 中心语得以实现；可对照本尼斯等人（Bennis et al. 1998）指出的对于相似语料的限制条件。

性词汇的差异联系起来。波兰语和捷克语中（19b）那样的例句以及 *How lengthy did she write a novel?* 这样的定语性问句是合乎语法的。可以假设这些语言的词汇拥有某种元素，这一元素可以实现最高名词性投射的 [+wh] 特征，提取便通过其指示语得以进行。另一方面，英语、保加利亚语和希腊语[①] 不存在类似例（19b）的结构和违反左分支条件的问句，因为它们缺乏这一元素（尽管英语疑问句的中心语的确具有 [-wh] 形式，实现为 *I can't believe he made that long of a film* 和 *How long of a film did you see?* 变体中的 *of*）。那么，在这些语言中，消除这个中心语上不可发音特征组合的唯一方法，要么是将整个名词性短语（构成更为常见的 *How lengthy a novel did she write?*）进行裹挟式移位，要么采用省略操作来删除包含不合语法结构的部分。

将此应用到上文的截省例句中，我们可以得到（21）中的结构：

（21） I don't know [$_{DegP}$ how detailed]$_1$ ~~he wants~~ [$_{FP}$ t_1 $'$ F^0$_{[+wh]}$ [a t_1 list]].

通过 DP 扩展投射（这里标记为 FP）的最高指示语对 [+wh] DegP 进行提取，需要中心语 F^0 具有一个 [+wh] 特征，这可以通过指示语和中心语一致关系实现。核查类似特征的常用方法是对 FP 进行裹挟式移位，在 SpecCP 上核查该特征，这一选择一般来说是可行的（见下文的（47））。

[①] 尽管我没有保加利亚语的相关语料，但是希腊语的语料至少也可以证明这个观点。希腊语可以允许（i）这种形式的截省。

   （i）Proselavan enan psilo andra, alla dhen ksero poso psilo.
       they.hired a.ACC tall.ACC man.ACC but not   I.know how tall.ACC
       'They hired a tall man, but I don't know how tall.'

但遗憾的是，这个例子的合法性并不能揭示事实的真相，因为希腊语，不像英语，可以允准定语性形容词后的名词短语的省略：

   （ii）Enas eksipnos andras   ine protimeros apo enan psilo.
        a.NOM smart.NOM man.NOM is   better   than a.ACC tall.ACC
        'A smart man is better than a tall one.'

关于希腊语名词短语省略的讨论，见 Gianakidou and Merchant 1996, Giannakidou and Stavrou 1999。因此，（i）中 *poso psilo* 的结构可能就是 [$_{DP}$ poso psilo [$_{NP}$ ~~andra~~]]。

然而，令人感兴趣的是，通用 PF 层面删除来实现的省略，为产生合乎语法的语句提供了第二个选项。对包含无法实现的 F^0[+wh] 的 IP 进行删除，就像在 SpecCP 上核查该特征一样，可以使此结构免于语音形式上的崩溃。

基于这种分析，(16) 中截省的合法性就得到了解释。由于不可实现的 [+wh] 的中心语仍然保留在删除部位内部（在此处是 IP），在英语中被理解为词汇空缺的左分支条件则不会被触发。

5.1.1.2 荷兰语（及一些德语）

同样的情况也出现在荷兰语中，下面会讲到一个有趣的现象。荷兰语像英语一样，不允许定语性形容词问句中的 DP 悬置在后面（详细讨论见 Corver 1990: 第十章）。

(22) *Hoe lang(e)   hebben zij [__ een man] aangesteld？
    how tall(AGR) have   they   a   man   hired
    ('How tall a man did they hire?')

但是荷兰语中的定语性形容词的裹挟式移位和英语的还不大一样。标准荷兰语实际上没有裹挟式移位策略，如下所示（特别感谢亨德里克斯的讨论）：

(23) a *Hoe lang(e)   een man hebben zij   aangesteld?
     how tall(AGR) a   man have   they hired
   b *Hoe lang(e)   man hebben zij   aangesteld?
     how tall(AGR) man have   they hired
   c *Hoe een lang(e)   man hebben zij   aangesteld?
     how a   tall(AGR) man have   they hired
   d *Hoe'n lang man hebben zij   aangesteld?
     how a   tall   man have   they hired
   e *Hoe'n lange   man hebben zij   aangesteld?
     how a   tall-AGR man have   they hired

  f Een HOE lange man hebben zij aangesteld? ［回声问句］
   *a how tall-*AGR *man have they hired*
   'A HOW tall man did they hire?'

  但是在一些南部方言中，例（23e）是合乎语法的（这里的语料来自于布拉班特方言；感谢科尔韦尔、马尔德斯和范罗伊的讨论）：

  （24）Hoe'n lange man hebben zij aangesteld ? ［布拉班特语］

  在标准荷兰语中，这一策略是基于 *zo* 'so' 而非 *hoe* 'how' 而建立的，可以同德语和英语中相类似的结构进行比较（比较 Corver 1990: 319 所提供的中部荷兰语例句）。（25a, b）都可以翻译为（25c）。

  （25）a Zo'n lange man heb ik nooit eerder gezien! ［标准荷兰语］
     *so a tall-*AGR *man have I never before seen*
   b So einen großen Mann hab ich nie zuvor gesehen! ［德语］
     so a tall man have I never before seen
   c I've never seen such a tall man before.
   d I've never seen so tall a man before.

  对于例（26a–c）和（26e）中截省的定语性形容词，南部荷兰语和标准荷兰语的可接受度差不多（我所调查的 5 个说标准荷兰语的人中，有一个人认为连（26a）都是不可接受的。在此我对他的判断不予评论）。如上面所示，南部荷兰语和标准荷兰语的区别在于裹挟式移位的可能性上，如（26d）所示。

  （26）Zij hebben een lange man aangesteld, maar ik weet niet
    *they have a tall-*AGR *man hired but I know not*
   a hoe lang.
    how tall
   b *hoe lange.
    *how tall-*AGR

c *hoe lang man.
    how tall man

d hoe'n lange (man)   [* 在标准荷兰语中；比较（23e）]
    how a tall-AGR man
    'They hired a tall man, but I don't know how tall (a man).'

e A: Zij hebben een twee meter lange man aangesteld.
        they have a two meter tall-AGR man hired
    'They hired a two meter tall man.'

    B: Een HOE lange (man)?   [回声问句]
        a how tall-AGR man
    'A HOW tall man?'

基于（24）和（23f）中对应的移位结构的合法性以及凯斯特（Kester 1996）曾讨论过的名词性成分省略，（26d, e）的合法性是可以预料到的。（26）中令人诧异的是（26a）里光杆形容词的合法性，因为其表面上可能的来源语料（（23a, b）或（22））均不合法；同样令人惊奇的是（26b）中形容词的屈折形式并不合法。（26a）和（26b）形成了鲜明的对照：在这种环境下，非中性的名词（*een lang*(e) man* a tall-AGR man）的定语位置需要形容词的屈折形式。

在某种程度上，例（26）中出现的光杆形容词形式是出人意料的。形容词做定语修饰阳性或阴性名词时，通常会以一致形式 *lange* 出现（此处的 *lang* 是中性形式，因此对我们此处的目的并没有太大帮助）。（26a）中的光杆形容词 *lang*，实际上是荷兰语中形容词具有谓词性功能时的形式，此时形容词没有屈折变化，无论该形容词有没有被提问：

（27）a De man is lang(*e).
        the man is tall(AGR)
    'The man is tall.'

    b *Hoe lange is de man?
        how tall-AGR is the man
    ('How tall is the man?')

这也就是说,(26)似乎与(23)或(22)中的定语性形容词疑问句都没有联系,却与(28)中的谓词性疑问句有关:

(28) Hoe lang is de man (die zij hebben aangesteld)?
　　　how tall is the man who they have hired
　　　'How tall is the man who they hired?'

尽管有这种相似之处,但我相信对(26a)中形容词的截省和(28)中形容词性谓词疑问句间的相似性进行探究是毫无收获的。[①] 为了能将(26a)归纳为(28),我们必须大幅度地削减我们用来满足焦点条件的假设(例如,我们不得不忽略定指性限定词的贡献),我们尚不清楚,如果不减少焦点条件,这样的削弱是否能够完成,而且这可能会导致焦点条件不再能做出任何预测。因此,除了表面上缺乏屈折形式外,我们没有理由遵循这一路径。

那么我们接下来该怎么办?上文似乎指出了这样一个结论:荷兰语定语性形容词的屈折变化本身就是语音形式上特征实现原则操作的结果。我坚持认为,(26a)那种荷兰语截省的推导,和对应的英语截省的推导是一样的,都涉及从 DP 内部进行左分支提取,因此为什么被证实的屈折词尾 -e 不出现?这表明 DegP 上的一致特征与其他的强特性一样(见 Kester 1996),可以在语音形式上被删除。这种删除消除了特征实现的必要性,

---

[①] 希腊语支持这个想法。希腊语要求形容词一致,甚至形容词处于谓词位置,例如例(i)(和上文一样,我在这里只注释相关的一致关系,即格的一致;希腊语形容词也要求数和格的变格,但在这里与我们讨论的关系不大)。

(i) Poso psilos ine o andras?
　　how tall.NOM is the.NOM man.NOM
　　'How tall is the man?'

如果"定语性形容词"截省实际上是谓词性形容词的某一形式,我们就可以预测,和事实相反,希腊语中截省的形容词会是(ii)中的主格,而不是我们在第 187 页脚注①中看到的宾格:

(ii) Proselavan enan psilo andra, alla dhen ksero poso psilos.
　　they.hired a.ACC tall.ACC man.ACC but not I.know how tall.NOM
　　('They hired a tall man, but I don't know how tall.')

即使特征实现的依附体本身在删除中可以保留下来。剩下的问题就是为什么屈折形式必须是空缺的。一种可能的解答方案要援引表达的经济原则：在语音形式上所涉及的特征越少越好。另一种可能的解答方案是，这个屈折的混元音（schwa）本身在结构上是出现在 DP 内部的（可能在 DP 中一个形容词性一致投射的中心语上，如 Cinque 1993 所指出的那样；Kester 1996 也对荷兰语的这种现象进行过讨论）：在这种情景下，移位的 DegP 将其屈折词尾悬置在已删除的 DP 内部。无论如何，这里如何实现这种直觉并不重要。关键是要证明缺少屈折形式不一定会迫使我们假定，定语性形容词截省中的 DegP 实际上并不生成于定语位置。相反，这种屈折形式的缺失使我们看到了屈折的本质。

最后，我对所收集的德语对应语料进行了简短的讨论。标准德语和荷兰语一样，不允许任何类型的程度短语与 DP 内部的冠词进行倒装，只有在回声问句解读下，裹挟式移位才有可能发生。（感谢温克勒对这些例句所做的讨论。）

（29） a *Wie groß(en) einen Center haben sie eingestellt?
　　　　 how tall(AGR) a　　 center have　 they hired
　　　　 ('How tall a center did they hire?')
　　　b Einen WIE großen Center haben sie eingestellt?　［回声问句］
　　　　 a-AGR how tall-AGR center have　 they hired
　　　　 'They hired a HOW tall center?'

尽管对相关截省例句的判断并不完全一致（有些说话人并不认为例（30）特别糟糕），但是无论有无屈折变化，截省都不太合乎语法。

（30） ??Sie haben einen großen Center eingestellt, aber ich weiß
　　　　 they have　 a-AGR tall-AGR center hired　　 but　 I　 know
　　　　 nicht, wie groß(en).
　　　　 not　 how tall(-AGR)
　　　　 ('They hired a tall center, but I don't know how tall.')

(比较...aber ich weiß nicht, einen WIE großen. [回声问句]
but I know not a-AGR how tall-AGR)

如果这一判断经受得住进一步的测试,我们就会问为什么会这样。一种可能性是,德语完全缺乏相关的功能性投射(肯尼迪和麦钱特的功能性投射);另一种可能性是,独立于程度短语移位的某一特征本身排除了相关结构(我所想到的一种可能性是无论由于何种原因,某些功能性指示语无法作为提取的中间着陆位置:我们可以和经过中间 SpecCP 的长距离 wh-移位中发现的可接受度降低的情况进行比较)。

尽管需要更多的跨语言证据,我这里只用英语和荷兰语的语言事实来说明,左分支的违反可以在原则上由语音形式删除来补救,并且某些情况下会受个体语言特殊限制条件的限制。

5.1.1.3 定语性形容词截省和焦点条件

然而,这并不意味着所有的定语性形容词截省都是可能的。值得注意的是,当先行小句中没有显性的相关联的形容词时,我们所讨论的这些类型的截省是不可能发生的,如下面语料所示(比较上文(16))。

(31) a *He wants a list, but I don't know how detailed.
  b *She bought a car, but I don't know how {expensive/fast/big}.
  c *She writes reports, and wait till you see how thorough!
  d *He bought {toys/jewelry}, but he wouldn't say how expensive.
  e *Your brother is a doctor, but it's not clear how smart.
  f *She is a carpenter, but it's not clear how good.

这些例句看起来与上文例(6)中所对应的显性左分支提取一样糟糕。但是,鉴于我到目前为止的论证,尤其是我已经论证了左分支提取条件是一种语音形式现象,显性提取不合法的语言事实与(31)中例句的不合法性似乎没有关联。那么,(31)中的例句与(16)中合乎语法的例句有何不同呢?答案并不在省略部位的内部句法:在两种情况中,我们处理的都是合法的左分支提取。很明显，不同点在于潜在的先行词使省略中的提取变得合乎语法。

（31）和（16）之间的对比似乎支持钟等（Chung et al. 1995）提出的"合并"法。或许合并能够拯救这种不可能发生的左分支提取，产生（32）中的推导结果。在（32）中，（32b）是 IP 复制和程度短语合并的结果。（尽管这需要重新定义合并，以使它应用于程度更广的谓词，假设形容词不是海姆所定义的不定指，我们姑且假定这一修改是无伤大雅的。）

（32） a   He wants a detailed list, but I don't know how detailed [$_{IP}$ e].　　　S 结构
　　　　b   ... [how detailed]^x [$_{IP}$ he wants a [detailed]^x list]　　　　LF

但是这种方法具有很强的预测性。既然合并对孤岛（这里是左分支条件）不敏感，那么我们就会期待这样的"形容词性合并"会导致所有孤岛无效。但如下面例句所示，情况并非如此。

（33） a   *She'll be angry if he buys an expensive car, but I don't know how expensive. (对比 It doesn't matter how expensive. [①])

　　　　b   *He got stressed because his boss wants a detailed list, but I don't know how detailed.

　　　　c   *She met a guy who bought an {expensive/fast/big} car, but I don't know how {expensive/fast/big}.

　　　　d   *They want to hire someone who writes thorough reports, and wait till you see how thorough!

　　　　e   *She wants to meet a guy who buys old paintings, but she didn't say how old.

---

① 这种让步截省句的本质在未来的研究中必须得到持续关注。这种截省和与它们相对应的非让步截省有着显著的不同。其不同点在于，让步性截省可以在一系列原本不可及的关联语中实现截省（比较 She won't talk to anyone—it doesn't matter who! 等）。这种对立很明显地表明，在处理截省时不仅要考虑结构，内嵌谓词的语义也必须得到考虑。相关讨论见 Haspelmath 1997: 140–141。

我们不能简单地认为，截省下不可能发生长距离程度短语的提取，如（34）所示：

（34）He said he needed a detailed list, but wait till you hear how detailed!

（16）和（33）之间的对比表明，对于（31）中例句的不合法问题，合并的结构性解决方法并不充分。相反，所期待的对比与焦点条件相左。回顾一下我们在第一章提出的定义，这里重复如下：

（35）**给定**（Schwarzschild 1999）
当且仅当表达式 E 有一个凸显的先行词 A，且有 ∃ 类型转换取模时，A 蕴涵 E 的焦点闭包，表达式 E 为给定。

（36）**IP 省略的省略焦点条件**（施瓦茨柴尔德版本，略微修改）
当且仅当包含 α 的成分为给定时，IP α 才可以被删除或去重音。

（37）**省略给定**
表达式 E 为给定，当且仅当表达式 E 有一个凸显的先行词 A，且有 ∃ 类型转换取模时，
（i）A 蕴涵 E 的焦点闭包，且
（ii）E 蕴涵 A 的焦点闭包。

（38）**IP 省略的焦点条件**
当且仅当 α 为省略给定时，IP α 才可以被删除。

让我们看一下这些定义如何应用于（39）中的这对句子。

（39）a She bought a big car, but I don't know how big.
b *She bought a car, but I don't know how big.

首先，须注意（39a）的读音不是（40b）而是（40a）。

（40）a She bought a big car, but I don't know HOW big.
b *She bought a big car, but I don't know how BIG.

让我们暂且假设，我们所处理的这个句子的结构是（41）。

（41）She bought a big car, but I don't know [HOW$_F$ big] [She bought [t' a [t car]]].

就像在第一章讨论的其他截省的情况一样，目前有两个相互关联的问题需要解决。第一个涉及基于（35）得出的一般焦点条件的应用，而第二个是关于（38）中狭义条件的应用。让我们从前者开始考察。

为了使（41）中的F标记合法，对于CP *(know) whether she bought a big car* 中的问句，必须有可替换项（见第一章的讨论）；换言之，共同基础必须包括先行项A；这一先行项蕴涵下面所示的命题，这一命题通过用程度量化词变项（这里用Q表示）和存在性量化来替换（41）中的HOW$_F$而推导得来：

（42）∃Q [I know [Q (λd.she bought a d-big car)]]

由于 *knowing that she bought a big car* 蕴涵 *knowing whether she bought a big car*，施瓦茨柴尔德焦点条件得到满足。

第二种更狭义的条件以如下的方式得到满足。（39a）中的前半句引入了（43a）中的命题，而被删除的IP中的焦点闭包，假设是DegP内容的重构（见Grosu and Landman 1998），则会如（43b）所示：

（43）a IP$_A$' = ∃d[she bought a d-big car]
　　　 b F-clo(IP$_E$) = ∃d[she bought a d-big car]

由于在这种情况下，程度量化词是焦点，则反向的关系也同样成立，即 IP$_E$' = F-clo(IP$_A$)。因此（38）中省略的焦点条件得到了满足。

另一方面，在（39b）中，先行IP并不提供必要命题（因为IP$_A$' = *she bought a car*），所以焦点条件没有得到满足。

因此，结论是，(16)和(31)①中的对比是焦点条件的结果，并不是省略的特殊操作，也不是提取的句法限制——这是本节中最为重要的一点。

这些必须考虑的因素也不利于上文经过权衡所得出的替选方案，即把(16)中明显的定语性形容词截省视为程度短语做谓词性使用，如(44)所示：

(44) She bought a car, but I don't know how big it is.

首先，(44)的语调是(45a)，而不是(45b)：

(45) a ... but I don't know how BIG it is.
b *... but I don't know HOW big it is.

与(40)相比，删除(44)中的"it is"并不能生成合法截省所要求的语调。事实上，"it is"的删除会错误地得出(31)那样的例句。(44)178中经验证的语调是(46)中焦点标记的结果，它体现了第一章中一般给定条件的效应：由于 big 不是给定的，所以(44)中的 big 必须被标记为焦点（或者，如果默认重音落在内嵌的 AP 上，则包含它的程度短语被标记为焦点）：

---

① 另一方面，(40)中的对比是不同限制条件的结果，即施瓦茨柴尔德（Schwarzschild 1999）的避免焦点条件（AvoidF）：
  （i）避免焦点
     在不违反给定条件假设的情况下，焦点标记要尽可能地少。
例(40a)满足避免焦点条件，因为"knowing that she bought a big car"并不蕴涵"knowing how big a car she bought"。另一方面，例(40b)违反了避免焦点条件（甚至假设 how 上有一个次级的、不能被听到的焦点，以满足给定条件）。在(40b)中，BIG 的焦点标记是多余的，因为前行句提供了一个可以蕴涵(42)的先行项。在(40b)中，如果 BIG 没有被焦点标记，就不会违反给定条件，因为(42)详细表明，被量化的程度词表示的是尺寸（大小）的程度。

(46) She bought a car, but I don't know how [BIG]$_F$ it is.

有关程度短语截省的最后一个问题，由下列例句提出：

(47) a He wants a list, but I don't know how detailed a list.
　　　b She bought a car, but I don't know how {expensive/fast/big} a car.
　　　c ?Your brother is a doctor, but it's not clear how smart a doctor.
　　　d She is a carpenter, but it's not clear how good a carpenter.

在这些例句中，包含程度短语的 DP 进行了裹挟式移位，生成了上文例（9）所看到的合乎语法的模式。这些例句比（31）的例句更合语法，这再次表明，上面的定语性形容词截省，不是迄今尚未发现的 SpecCP 上的名词短语省略或类似省略的结果。这些例句之所以不同是因为要求有不同类型的先行项，以满足焦点条件。请注意，读音又一次为我们提供了线索，这也又一次与上面截省中所看到的情况不同。

(48) a She bought a car, but I don't know how BIG a car.
　　　b *She bought a car, but I don't know HOW big a car.
　　　c *She bought a car, but I don't know how big a CAR.

（48b, c）的不合法是意料之中的。在（48b）中，*big* 不是给定的，因此违反了给定焦点条件。而在（48c）中，*car* 是给定的，违反了避免焦点条件（见 197 页脚注 ①）。（48a）的合法性表示这一焦点标记和（46）中的焦点标记一样（被焦点标记的是程度短语，不是 AP）：

(49) She bought a car, but I don't know [how [BIG]$_F$ a car]$_2$ [she bought t_2]

在这里，*she bought a car* 和 *a car* 都是给定的，而 *big* 却不是。请注意，即使 *a car* 是给定的，它也不能被删除（这种删除会得出（31b）这种不合法的语句）。这表明给定条件对省略来说是必要条件，而不是充分条件，如第一章所述，独立的限制条件（这里指英语中程度短语之后缺少 NP 省略）也起着一定的作用。

然而，我们有理由相信，(49) 中的表达并没有完全表达出这一结构中焦点标记的数量。事实上，当被焦点标记的定语性程度短语被提取时（尽管并不一定只是程度中心语被焦点标记），焦点标记似乎必须渗透到 DP 中（参阅 Drubig 1994 对于焦点短语的理解），这会生成 (50) 这样的结构（这里我也省略了也许必要出现的嵌入的程度短语上的焦点标记）：

(50) She bought a car, but I don't know [how [BIG]$_F$ a car]$_{F2}$ [she bought t_2]

从 (40a) 和 (40b) 的对比来看，这似乎是必要的。这种弥散①与 PF 上不能删除被焦点标记的成分这一自然假设一起排除了 (51) 中的结构，尽管这一结构是满足焦点条件的：

(51) * She bought a car, but I don't know [$_{DegP}$ how [BIG]$_F$]$_1$ [$_{IP}$ she bought [t'_1 a t_1 car]$_F$]

须注意的是，这并不是说定语性形容词上的焦点标记通常都可以弥散到 DP 上：该论述是错误的。对我们而言，仅需要如下条件：当程度短语被提取时，程度短语上的焦点标记被诠释为一种特征，且这一特征必须与 DP 共享（如上面所讨论的 [wh] 特征一样，通过指示语和中心语的一致关系来实现）。尽管这里所涉及的系统错综复杂，难以理解，但我们所提到的解决办法和程度短语上的焦点标记之间，并没有什么内在的互斥性。

然而，也许有另一种方式来解释 (51) 为什么不合法，这种解释方法避免焦点弥散到 DP 上。由于 BIG 是焦点标记，我们可以忽略它接下来的重构（参阅第一章对截省对比的讨论）。不过，我们不能忽视程度短语的提取，因为这一提取会在 DP 内部留下一个语迹。因此，IP$_E$ 的 ∃ 闭包和焦点闭包将会是 (52)，它将空变项约束在与 big 形成对比的级差形容词意义上。

(52) IP$'_E$=F-clo (IP$_E$) = ∃P[she bought a P-car]

---

① 弥散，原文为 percolation，此处指修饰语上 [+F] 特征辐射至其所在整个限定性短语。——译者

但有人可能会说，IP$_A$ 并没有提供这样一个蕴涵。施瓦茨柴尔德（Schwarzschild 1999）注意到，他的"语境蕴涵"概念是模糊不清的，因为什么样的命题能够被包含在共同背景中，以这种方式来满足给定条件，是个开放性问题。在这种情况下，尽管可以从存在一辆车这一论断来推测那辆车存在一种尺寸，但是第二个命题不能被纳入共同背景以满足给定条件：注意，下面这种排序很怪异：#*She ate an apple before she ate a GREEN apple*（比对 *She ate an APPLE before she ate a BANANA*）。不幸的是，在这一点上又出现了许多其他问题，其中最显著的事实是，在先行结构中添加一个被焦点标记的、形成对比的程度短语，并不能改善上面的问题（**She bought an OLD car, but I don't know how BIG*），在这种情况下，对（51）进行纯句法、结构性的解读（依赖于 wh- 提取下的特征传递）就变得没那么有问题了。

由于程度短语在语义上具有复杂性（见 Kennedy 1999），对程度短语中焦点的研究也非常有限，所以很多问题至今还是开放性的，这一点并不奇怪。但是这些特定问题的解决办法，应该和此处所采用的研究省略的方法相融合，并且要符合对截省中程度疑问句的解释，尤其要与一种解释方案相符，即认为删除路径下进行了违反左分支条件的提取。

5.1.1.4　截省下的左分支子提取

最后一组事实表明，并非所有的左分支提取都是相似的。[①] 科尔韦尔（Corver 1990：第九章）注意到，当程度短语处在谓词位置时，可以从程度短语中进行某些度量短语的子提取（大致来说，这些"度量短语"本身是全级差程度短语，相关讨论见 Corver 1990: 237）。他提出一些论据，认为被提取的程度短语来源于谓词内部，并非单纯只是一个 VP 副词（例如，不像 VP 副词那样，它们可以对谓词进行裹挟式移位）。

[①] 感谢科尔韦尔对该部分的讨论并提供荷兰语料。

（53） a How badly was he [___ short of funds]?
　　　 b How easily are there drugs [___ obtainable]?
　　　 c How well was she [___ prepared]?
　　　 d How badly was he [___ burned]?

（54） Hoe　zwaar　is hij [___ behaard]?　　　　　　　［荷兰语］
　　　 how　heavily　is　he　　　haired
　　　 (lit.) 'How heavily haired is he?' [即 How hairy is he?]

这些度量短语不能从定语位置进行提取（Corver 1990: 第十章）：

（55） a *How badly did you meet [a guy [___ short of funds]] ?
　　　 b *How easily did he take [[___ obtainable] drugs]?
　　　 c *How well have you examined [a [___ prepared] student]?
　　　 d *How badly did you treat [a [___ burned] man] ?

（56） *Hoe　zwaar　heeft zij　een [[___ behaarde) man] ontmoet ?　［荷兰语］
　　　　how　heavily　has　she a　　　 haired　　man　met
　　　 (lit. 'How heavily haired a man did she meet?')

正如科尔韦尔指出，这些差异一定与程度短语的不同结构特征有关，程度短语出现在谓词位置上时（此时它们被严格管辖，允许提取）和从定语位置进行子提取时的结构特征不同。肯尼迪和麦钱特（Kennedy and Merchant 2000a）提出的定语性程度短语的提取系统，不能扩展到从定语性程度短语中的提取。至少不存在删除机制能够修复（55）和（56）中的偏差的先验期望。

事实上，截省下的提取，精确地追溯到了在（53）至（54）与（55）至（56）中发生显性提取的可能性。(57)和（58）中的语料表明，对于英语和荷兰语来说，这些度量短语的截省可能来源于谓词性程度短语内部。它们的结构和（53）、（54）中的那些显性的对应句相类似，如下面（59）所示。（我将先行句中有显性程度短语对应成分和没有对应成分的例句合并在一起了，也没有在残余 wh- 短语中标明语调，这些语调与我们上面见到的完全一样，取决于程度短语是否是给定性的。）

(57) a He was (badly) short of funds, but I don't know how badly.
　　　b These drugs are (easily) obtainable, but you don't want to hear how easily.
　　　c She was (well) prepared — guess how well.
　　　d He was (badly) burned, but I don't know how badly.

(58) Hij is (zwaar) behaard, maar ik weet niet hoe zwaar. ［荷兰语］
　　　he is heavily haired but I know not how heavily.
　　　(lit.) 'He is (heavily) haired, but I don't know how heavily.'

(59) He was badly burned, but I don't know HOW$_F$ badly [he was [$_{DegP}$ t_2 burned]].

重要的是，与（55）和（56）相对应的截省句的合法性并没有得到改善：

(60) a *She met a guy (badly) short of funds, but I don't know how badly.
　　　b *He takes (easily) obtainable drugs, but I don't know how easily.
　　　c *They examined a (well)-prepared student — guess how well!
　　　d *They treated a (badly) burned man, but I don't know how badly.

(61) *Zij heeft een behaarde man ontmoet, maar ik weet niet ［荷兰语］
　　　she has a haired man met but I know not
　　　hoe zwaar.
　　　how heavily.
　　　('She met a haired man, but I don't know how heavily.')

这些对比表明，把（55）和（56）那样的子提取排除在外的机制与把定语性程度短语提取排除在外的机制是不同的。根据肯尼迪和麦钱特（Kennedy and Merchant 2000a）的解释，这意味着程度短语本身并不投射焦点投射（FP），度量短语可以通过这个焦点投射的指示语进行提取。这似乎是个令人信服的结论：作为扩展名词性投射的一部分，焦点投射不可能出现在形容词性投射中，且没有任何经验证据证明这一点（*How easily of obtainable a drug is it? 是不合乎语法的，但是 How obtainable of a drug *is it?* 却合法）。

当然，当度量短语对它的定语性依附体程度短语进行裹挟式移位时，所生成的截省就是合乎语法的，因为悬置的有问题的 F^0 被删除了。

（62） a He wants a longer list, but I don't know how much *(longer).
　　　　b ... [$_{DegP}$ how much longer]$_2$ [he wants [$_{FP}$ t'_2 F^0 [a t_2 list]]]

最后，那些在英语中不能被提取的度量短语需要与介词 *by* 连用（见 Corver 1990: 200 中一些简要的讨论和 Abney 1987）：

（63） a ??(By) how{much/many cm} was he too tall to be an astronaut?
　　　　b ??(By) how{much/many pounds} was the packet too heavy to be shipped airmail?

相同的模式也出现在截省中：

（64） a He was too tall to be an astronaut, but I don't know??(by) how {much/many cm}.
　　　　b The packet is too heavy to be shipped airmail, but I don't know??(by) how {much/many pounds}.

这些对比非常重要，因为它们表明，提取上的一些限制，尤其是负责排除左分支子提取的限制，并不是在语音形式上进行操作，因此不受截省中删除的影响。这些对比还表明，截省并不如罗斯或其他研究者所想的那样，是拯救不同孤岛条件的灵丹妙药。另一方面，在截省下可以进行常规的定语性程度短语的提取，这一事实支持了左分支效应是位于语音形式层面这一假设。

5.1.1.5 小结

这一节讨论了一系列关于定语性形容词截省的新的语言事实，指出了这种截省与省略的删除路径兼容。有些语言在语音形式上不存在定语性形容词提取，删除法以上文所论证的方式修补了随之产生的结构。我们看到，语料中复杂的语言事实遵守第一章中所介绍的省略的焦点条件，同时也遵守施瓦茨柴尔德（Schwarzschild 1999）更加宽泛的给定条件。

5.1.2 COMP 语迹效应

我将研究的第二类提取限制是 COMP 语迹效应。其中，*that* 语迹效应是最著名的代表。珀尔马特（Perlmutter 1971）首次注意到了 11 种语言中这种现象的分布情况（尽管他把注意力限制在标句词 *that* 和 *for* 上，这种效应也可以在如 *if* 和 *whether* 这样的 wh- 标句词中发现（如 Hudson 1972 所注意到的），*like* 也有这种效应）。COMP 语迹效应已被广泛讨论（Langendoen 1970; Bresnan 1972; Chomsky and Lasnik 1977; Culicover 1992; Déprez 1994; Browning 1996; Roussou 1998）。（65）中是一些典型的例句。

（65） a　Which senator is it probable (*that) will resign?
　　　 b　*Who did Sally ask {if/whether} was going to fail?
　　　 c　What did Bob want (*for) to be over the door?
　　　 d　How many students does it seem (*like) will past?

尽管意见存在分歧，但 COMP 语迹效应似乎在本质上是一种语音形式现象，虽然这一效应还没有得到充分理解，如珀尔马特（Perlmutter 1971）、乔姆斯基和拉斯尼克（Chomsky and Lasnik 1977）、奥恩等（Aoun *et al.* 1987）、胡克斯特拉（E. Hoekstra 1992）和库利科韦尔（Culicover 1992）所得出的结论（库利科韦尔是以 Bresnan 1977b 发现的副词修复效应为基础；另见 Honegger 1996）。最近，舍纳（de Chene 1995）也提出了 COMP 语迹效应，其研究基础是，当主语语迹出现在一个右节点提升的目标成分内时，产生了修复作用：

（66） a　?That's the meeting which$_i$ I've been thinking that, and Jim's been saying that, t_i could well be canceled.　　　(de Chene 1995: 3 (11a))
　　　 b　?Which gangster did the DA claim that, though he couldn't absolutely prove, [___ was responsible for the killing]?

舍纳（de Chene 1995）还从主语/宾语自小句补足语提取至介词位置的不对称现象出发，论述了 ECP 的不足，这里我就不重复了。虽然他没有进行分析，但他的确得出了这样的结论"寻找新的方法来解决 COMP 语迹效应，其要点在于语音形式方面的语法"（第 4 页）。

麦克洛斯基（McCloskey 1997）基于瑞典语中主语复述代词的分布，也对这一想法做了探究。沿着恩达尔（Engdahl 1984）的思路，他注意到，瑞典语中有一类复述代词只能出现在 COMP 语迹的环境中，如例（67）所示。如果 COMP 语迹效应是一种 ECP 效应，那么这类代词的语音插入将不会影响例句的合法性，其本身是不可提取的。另一方面，如果 COMP 语迹效应是语音形式上的问题，那么可以预测，把语迹作为代词来拼读，可以满足限制条件。

(67) Vilket ord$_3$ visste ingen hur {det$_3$/*t$_3$} stavas? (Engdahl 1985: 13 (12))
which word knew no-one how it is.spelled
'Which word did no one know how it spelled?'

如何准确地理解这一效应并不是我们现在要完成的事，我能做的仅仅是推测 COMP 语迹效应的最终分析应该具备的一般特征。我们或许可以根据某一语言可以在其 C^0 上实现哪些特征来把这种效应形式化，就像我们在上一节为左分支效应所提出的 F^0 一样。这一分析思路很可能可以囊括 COMP 语迹效应的各种管辖分析方法，同时还能继续将结果定位在句法-词汇界面（在"最后插入"模式的词汇插入上）。所以，尽管有证据证明我们是在处理一种"语音"效应，但这并不意味着我们必须如珀尔马特（Perlmutter 1971）最初所提出（而被 Chomsky and Lasnik 1977 进行下去）的那样，退回到表层过滤条件。无论如何，关于这种效应的一个完全成熟的理论对我们来说并不是至关重要的——与我们相关的是类似分析所得出的推测。如果 COMP 语迹效应在相关意义上是"语音"上的，那么我们就不能期望在截省下发现这个效应。下面的例子可以证明我们的预测是对的：

（68） It's probable that a certain senator will resign, but which [it's probable that *t* will resign] is still a secret.

（69） Sally asked if somebody was going to fail Syntax One, but I can't remember who [Sally asked if *t* was going to fail Syntax One] (Chung *et al.* 1995: (86a))

钟等人用这些事实来论证应该用逻辑形式和复制法来解释截省，因为他们把 COMP 语迹效应与违反 ECP 等同起来。但是如果 COMP 语迹效应发生在语音形式上，而不是逻辑形式上，正如其他证据所显示的那样，那么截省缺乏 COMP 语迹效应就不再和删除路径相矛盾了，正如珀尔马特（Perlmutter 1971: 112）所指出的：“如果……[像（65）这样的例句]因其表层限制而不合乎语法，那么随后对其进行截省就可以产生一个合法的句子，而且事实的确如此。"

5.1.3 派生位置孤岛：话题化和主语

第三类孤岛，我将称之为"派生位置"孤岛，包括英语话题化成分和主语（也包括右移位或外置成分）。（这里我将只专注于讨论非句子性主语，尽管我的分析也直接扩展到了句子性主语，假设它们都来源于 VP 内部，这一点我们将在 5.3.2 节中再做讨论。）（70）给出了相关例句：从话题化 XP（a）、被动或非宾格主语（b）、及物或非作格主语（c）中进行提取都是不允许的。

（70） a *Which Marx brother did she say that [a biography of ___], she refused to read?

b *Which Marx brother did she say that [a biography of ___]{is going to be published/will appear}this year?

c *Which Marx brother did she say that [a biographer of ___] {interviewed her/worked for her}?

但相对应的截省句却合乎语法：

(71) a A: A biography of one of the Marx brothers, she refused to read.
      B: Which one?
   b A biography of one of the Marx brothers {is going to be published/will appear} this year—guess which!
   c A biography of one of the Marx brothers {interviewed her/worked for her}, but I don't remember which.

我将这些都纳入到"派生位置"孤岛条件下，因为我认为，所有这些情况都涉及一个经过位移的成分，该成分的表面位置是派生而来的。我的观点是，在合法的截省例句中所看到的提取，是从基础位置进行的提取，而不是从派生位置进行的提取，因为那会导致（70）中那样的例句不合法。

让我们从话题化入手。这里我们可以看到（70a）中的偏差是由宾语的派生位置造成的，而不是由全面禁止从宾语中进行提取而造成的，因为从原位宾语中进行对应的提取是合法的：

(72) Which Marx brother did she say that she refused to read [a biography of ___]?

我认为这一事实是理解对应的截省句为什么合法的关键。我认为这种截省的结构是（73a），而不是（73b）：

(73) A: A biography of one of the Marx brothers, she refused to read.
   a B: Which one [she refused to read a biography of t]?
   b B: *Which one [a biography of t, she refused to read]?

换句话说，没有理由认为形成截省的提取必须来源于与先行小句表层结构完全相同的结构。到目前为止，我认为，删除只受焦点条件控制，而不受任何其他的附加结构要求所控制。像（73）中这样包含话题化宾语的先行结构，也会提供一个必要的语义先行成分，以满足焦点条件。根据焦点条件，（73a）中的截省要求 A 的话语蕴涵 $\exists x[x$ is a Marx brother and she refused to read a biography of $x]$。因此，这个截省句是合法的。

相似的推理也可以适用于主语的情况。(另一种分析方法是，可以把主语孤岛本身看作是一种语音形式效应，但是在这里我不采用这种方法。)让我们从被动句主语开始(在常规假设下，同样的分析也适用于非宾格主语)。(71b)中的截省有(74)中的结构(我忽略了这样一个问题：是否存在额外的中间位置，主语可以经由该位置移至SpecIP，表明此处截省句的主语在其基础位置上)：

(74) ... which$_2$ [$_{IP}$ —— is going to be published [a biography of t_2]]

首先注意，根据对主语孤岛的最新处理方法，从基础位置(在这里是宾语位置)进行提取是合法的。从 SpecIP 中进行提取则被禁止，这并非仅仅因为它是从主语中进行提取(如 Chomsky 1973, Pollard and Sag 1994: 195)，而是因为它不是 L 相关的中心语的补足语的指示语(或不是 L 标记的(Chomsky 1986a: 31)，等等)。这一点得到了罗曼语的证实。在罗曼语中有一个非常著名的从动词前主语与从动词后主语中进行提取的对比(从动词后主语中进行提取是合法的，从动词前主语中进行提取是不合法的)。基于下面的英语例句，我们也可以得出类似的观点。在(75)和(76)的(a)句中，SpecIP 上移置的主语，就其位置而言，对提取形成了一个孤岛；在(b)句中，其基础位置上相同的逻辑"主语"对提取来说不是语障[①]。

(75) a *Which candidate were [posters of t] all over town?
    b Which candidate were there [posters of t] all over town?

(76) a *Which candidate did they say [to get t to agree to a debate] was hard?
    b Which candidate did they say it was hard [to get t to agree to a debate]?

因为我并没有假设先行小句和截省中被删除的 IP 必须具有严格的结构同构，因此像(74)那样的结构会满足焦点条件，并允准被证实的提取。

---

① "语障"的原文为 barrier，指其界限能限制某些现象的语类。——译者

接下来的问题是，既然这种结构的显性对照句是不合法的，那么这种结构在英语中是如何合乎语法的？

（77） *(Guess) [which Marx brother]$_2$ [$_{IP}$ ___ is [$_{VP}$ going to be published [a biography of t_2]]]

对英语中的 SpecIP 不可能为空这一问题的标准答案是扩展投射原则（EPP），实际其本质是 SpecIP 必须得到填充（见 Chomsky 1981）。最近的做法（Chomsky 1995; Alexiadou and Anagnostopoulou 1998）将 EPP 认定为 I^0 上某些特征要求的结果：对于英语来说，乔姆斯基认为 I^0 上有一个"强"EPP 特征。这里"强"的意思是，这种特征在语音形式界面上是不可解释的，因此拼读前必须被核查（这也是系统中强制性显性移位的动因）。从目前的角度来看，这种对 EPP 的理解做出了一个有趣的预测。如果一个"强"特征因为删除的缘故没有达到语音形式界面，那么缺少与之相关联的核查移位也就无关紧要。这正是合法的例（74）和不合法的（77）之间的区别。后者违反了 EPP，因为 I^0 上的"强"特征没有被核查，原封不动地到达了语音形式界面，导致推导崩溃。而（74）中的"强"特征尽管没有被核查，但它和 IP 的剩余部分一起被删除了，因此这个特征没有到达语音形式界面，也就没有导致推导的崩溃。这种对于主语提取的合法性的解释，是以 EPP 的特征实现为基础的，这与我们上面所论述的，在省略下左分支违反的修复作用相类似。

这一解释同样适用于及物动词和非宾格动词的主语，如果内部主语假说是正确的——如果 VP 中存在某些位置，从中 A′ 移位可以提取一个子成分（subconstituent），那么我们期望能够像对待被动和非宾格的主语那样，使主语孤岛无效。因此，（71c）中被删除的结构肯定如下所示：

（78） A biography of one of the Marx brothers interviewed her, but I don't remember which$_3$ [$_{IP}$ ___ [$_{VP}$ ~~a biographer of t_3 interviewed her~~]].

根据人们对 SpecIP 的语障关系所采用的做法，(78) 中提取的合法性可能取决于这个主语是源于 VP 的指示语位置，还是 VP 的附加语位置，看起来似乎更倾向于前者。(这也和另一个问题有关，即语障关系是应该用 θ 管辖（如 Chomsky 1986a: 14–15 中的），还是用 L 相关性（如 Chomsky 1998 所建议的）来表述。不过在这里这两种选择并不重要。)

目前显而易见的问题是，主语在拼读中保持在低位，违反了 EPP，那么这一事实是否对解读有任何进一步的影响？答案是否定的，但值得我们思考的是，这一预测为什么会产生，又为什么没有实现。根据常规的假设，(74) 中的 IP 不应成为进一步移位的依附体。这符合严格循环条件，该条件禁止 A′ 移位先从 IP 中移出然后再从该 IP 内部进行 A 移位（或一般而言，若根据乔姆斯基（Chomsky 1995）的扩展条件进行归纳的话，这一条件可以归纳为，在结构上任何 XP 短语都不能向低于树形图中最高节点的位置移动；最近的研究路径见 Collins 1997）。如果严格循环条件也适用于拼读后移位，那么我们就可以预测，对于 (74) 那类结构中的主语来说，应该有一个辖域冻结效应。

这种预测并没有得到证实。思考 (79) 中的例句，在这些例句中，不定指主语与情态动词和否定词相互作用。

(79) a Five pictures of one of the victims might be distributed to the press, but I can't remember which one$_2$ [$_{IP}$ might be [$_{VP}$ distributed [five pictures of t_2] to the press]].

b Five pictures of one of the victims weren't distributed to the press, but I can't remember which one$_2$ [$_{IP}$ weren't [$_{VP}$ distributed [five pictures of t_2] to the press]].

如果主语 *five pictures of t_2* 被严格循环条件冻结在其基础位置，这甚至发生在拼读之后，那么我们就可以预测，(79b) 仅能允许 ¬∃ 的解读。事实上，¬∃ 和 ∃¬ 两种解读在这里都有可能。后者如 (80) 所示（如果有什么区别的话，后者为优先选择）：

（80） λp[∃x[victim(x) ∧ p = ^[∃₃Y[picture(Y, of x) ∧ ¬ distributed(Y, to the press)]]]]

由于辖域的原因，严格循环条件并不适用，因为在标准假设下，所有量化词提升（QR）实例都与循环条件背道而驰。但我们认为，在拼读之后主语的 A 移位是不可能的，因为驱动这个移位的 I^0 上的"强"特征已经被删除了。但是如果主语 DP 上的格特征仍然需要核查，拼读之后仍然会发生违反自利原则的格驱动 A 移位。（最近一些理论一直致力于把所有的 A 移位简化为特征移位，在这种情况下，主语 DP 可能基础生成于 VP 的外面，相关研究见 Pesetsky 1998*b*, Manzini and Roussou 2000, Hornstein 1999。）

但这些问题很难进行测试。一种可能的方法是测试截省下提取的主语是否可以约束一个更高的代词。如果可以，我们就可以证明，该主语经历了 A 移位，因为 A′ 移位触发了一个弱交叉违反。虽然事实是如此微妙，但我相信有证据表明，这种约束是可能发生的，因此我们有证据表明隐性的短语性 A 移位的确发生了。相关语料见（81）。

（81） a [Every biography of one of the Marx brothers]₁ seemed to its₁ author to be definitive, but I don't remember (of) which (Marx brother).

b [Every soldier from one of the airborne battalions]₂ seemed to his₂ commander to be sick, but I don't know (from) which (battalion).

在这些例句中，跨小句约束是不可能的（即 *Every soldier₂ was sick, but I don't know whether his₂ commander knew）。但是因为这些例句都合乎语法，所以我们有证据认为隐性的短语性 A 移位正在发生。（81b）的推导可以概述如下：

（82） a Spell Out

... which (battalion)₃ [IP [VP seemed to his₂ commander to be [IP [every solider from one of *t*₃]₂ sick]]] b A-movement at LF

　　. . . which (battalion)$_3$ [$_{IP}$ [every soldier from one of t_3]$_2$ seemed to his$_2$ commander [$_{IP}$ t_2' to be t_2 sick]]

在（82b）中，DP$_2$ 由论元移位提升，进而约束 *his*$_2$。假设约束变项照应在逻辑形式上需要成分统制，则移位就是必要的。这种移位并不是简单的 A′ 移位，因为它还能给我们提供一个未经证实的弱交叉效应。

人们可能会期待，通过考察约束三原则 C 的效应，可以对这些情况下的隐性短语移位得出类似的结论。正如（83a）所示，显性的 A 移位可以满足约束三原则 C。这应该与（83b）相比较，在（83b）中，主语保持原位，违反了约束三原则 C。

(83) a Many reports about Clinton$_2$ seemed to him$_2$ to be on TV during the summit.
　　 b *There seemed to him$_2$ to be many reports about Clinton$_2$ on TV during the summit.

用截省的例句进行比较时，可发现并没有约束三原则 C 效应：

(84) One of Albright$_3$'s reports on one of the Balkan countries seemed to her$_3$ to have been leaked to the press, though I don't know which (of the Balkan countries).

与（82）相比，我在（85）中给出了（84）的推导：

(85) a 拼读
　　　　. . . which$_1$ [$_{IP}$ [$_{VP}$ seemed to her$_3$ to have been leaked [one of Albright$_3$'s reports on t_1] to the press]]
　　 b 逻辑形式
　　　　. . . which$_1$ [$_{IP}$ [one of Albright$_3$'s reports on t_1]$_2$ [$_{VP}$ seemed to her$_3$ t_2' to have been leaked t_2 to the press]]

如果这就是所有要说明的内容，那么（84）的合法性就为逻辑形式上的短语性 A 移位提供了另外一个有力论据。因为在逻辑形式上的短语性 A′ 移位，总的来说并不能修复对约束三原则 C 的违反（不过，可参阅 Sauerland 1998、Fox 2000 和 Merchant 2000a 对包含先行词删除的限制条件的讨论）。但让人失望的是，(84) 的情况并不能给我们提供更多的信息，因为我们知道，约束三原则 C 在省略情况下并不能被证实。如我们在第一章所看到的，菲恩戈和梅（Fiengo and May 1994）在讨论 VP 省略的时候已经关注到了这一令人惊异的事实，这一事实在截省的情况下也同样存在，可参阅麦钱特（Merchant 1999a）。比如例（86）：

(86) They said they wanted to hire Abby$_3$, but she$_3$ didn't know why.

如果这一截省是由（87a）得出来的，那么就违反了约束三原则 C。相反，删除的成分如（87b）中所示，这和我们在第一章中所讨论的 VP 省略的语言事实相类似。

(87) a *she$_3$ didn't know why ~~they wanted to hire Abby$_3$~~.
      b she$_3$ didn't know why ~~they wanted to hire her$_3$~~.

既然一般来说，省略情况下没有约束三原则 C 效应，那么（84）的合法性就没法告诉我们主语在逻辑形式上的位置。"载体转换"效应并不能改变基于例（81）所得出的论点。但因为，即使全称量化词的确在一些语境中等同于省略下的代词，而且我们假设，如果代词可以得到正确解读的话，那么代替整个 DP 短语的代词的出现将会消除提取部位，因为代词不能包含提取部位。

请注意，我并没有声称从主语提取出来的截省总要求有一个虚位词（*there* 或 *it*）出现在删除部位，特别是 *there*，不定指主语辖域的可变性反驳了隐藏性 *there* 存在的可能性，因为 *there* 强制其关联项取窄域。而且一些研究者也提出了证据，反驳通过短语性 A 移位来取代 *there*：威廉（Williams 1984）、登迪肯（den Dikken 1995）和佩塞茨基（Pesetsky 1998b）。*there* 和它的关联项之间的关系并不是短语性移位（可能是特征移位，与约束理论、辖域、量化词变项约束都没有关系）。确实，和（82）等价的 *there* 插入并不允许所需的变项约束，这再一次表明，*there* 关联项关系不是逻辑形式上的短语性 A 移位：

（88） There seemed (*to his₂ commander) to be [a soldier]₂ sick.

但是这一事实并不能妨碍上面所提出的分析路径。在截省的例句中，并没有出现 *there*，因此无论是什么阻碍了（88）中的那种短语性移位都无关紧要。

这一分析对迪辛（Diesing 1992）的映射假说（Mapping Hypothesis）也有影响。迪辛（Diesing 1992）认为，逻辑形式层面上 SpecIP 中的内容映射到了量化副词的限定上，而 VP 中的内容则映射到了辖域当中。她采纳了坎普-海姆对不定指名词的分析方法，把不定指名词视为一个开放谓词，提出存在闭包作用于 VP 层面。而且，阶段层面（stage-level，简称SL）谓词的主语基础生成在 SpecVP 中，在拼读之前被提升到 SpecIP 上，并且能够根据情况重构或不重构，而个体层面（individual-level，简称 IL）谓词基础生成于 SpecIP 中，不能在 VP 内部获得解读（也就是说，它们不能从属于存在闭包；SpecVP 被 PRO 占据）。如果迪辛对这几类谓词之间结构差异的猜想正确的话，我们应该在它们的主语是否允许提取方面找到对应的区别。阶段层面谓词的主语应该允许在截省下进行提取，而个体层面谓词，因为基础生成于 SpecIP，则不应该允许这种提取。（89）中的语料展现出了这两种谓词的情况，这些语料并不支持我们所预测出来的差异性，因为它们都是合乎语法的。

（89） a Picture of one of the astronauts weren't available at press time, but I can't remember which one. (SL)

　　　 b Pictures of one of the astronauts weren't visible at press time, but I can't remember which one. (SL 或 IL)

　　　 c Writing samples of one of the astronauts weren't legible, but I can't remember which one. (IL)

> d Pictures of one of the astronauts weren't printable, but I can't remember which one. (IL)
>
> e Eggplants from one of the islands are poisonous—you better find out which one before you go! (IL)

例如，(89e)中的谓词 *poisonous* 为个体层面谓词，应该不允准（90）所示的推导。因为根据假设，提取而来的主语 *eggplants* 不会出现在 SpecVP 中。

(90) *... which one$_1$ [$_{IP}$ [eggplants from t_1]^i are [$_{VP}$ PRO^i poisonous]]

这些思考表明，她所发现的这些效应的正确解释，不可能是她所提出的结构性解释；另见弗尔纳德（Fernald 1994, 2000），他是独立得出这一结论的。

总之，删除这一解释方法和话题化结构是兼容的，因为这些话题化结构和它们那些在省略部位上没有移位时的结构一致。出于相同的原因，这一解释法也和主语兼容，尽管在英语中，主语到 SpecIP 的移位通常不可选。如果 EPP 被应用为一个"强"特征，如乔姆斯基（Chomsky 1995）所示，那么主语孤岛效应的缺失，就是可以预测的，正如我们在左分支孤岛效应下所看到的那样。

由此我们进一步得出了两个有趣的结论：第一，至少存在某种形式的隐性短语性 A 移位；第二，迪辛对阶段层面谓词和个体层面谓词之间差异的结构性解决方案，与在截省条件下从主语中进行提取的解释方法不兼容。

5.1.4 并列结构限制（一）：并连语条件

如（91）所述（Ross 1967 (1986: 98-99), (4.84)）罗斯（Ross 1967）的并列结构限制包括两个子部分。

> (91) 在一个并列结构中，并连语不可以移位；并连语中所包含的任何成分，也不可以移出该并连语。

这两个条件可以用例（92）来说明：（92a）是一个并连语的提取，（92b）是从一个并连语中进行提取。

(92) a *Which senator did they persuade Kennedy and ___ to jointly sponsor the legislation?
　　　b *What movie did Bob both go to a restaurant and see ___ at the Nick that night?

在本节中，我将主要关注第一种类型的提取。我把第一种类型的提取称为"并连语条件"，采取的是波斯塔尔（Postal 1992）的术语（第二种类型将在下一节讨论）。这两种区分最初来源于格罗苏（Grosu 1973），随后得到进一步发展（Grosu 1981: 53-60）。

罗斯（Ross 1969）注意到，截省为并连语条件提供了一些改良。(93) 为他的原本例句 (71)。

(93) Irv and someone were dancing together, but I don't know who.

这些例句的接受度一直存有争议。罗斯在他原始的例句中标记的是"??"，然而拉科夫（Lakoff 1970）做了修改，认为该句完全可以接受。贝克和布雷姆（Baker and Brame 1972）不同意拉科夫的改动，声称"许多说话者认为这个例子是完全不合乎语法的"（第 61 页）。莱文（Levin 1982）给出了下面的例句（94）（在她的书中是（42b）），她并没有做出标注，这表明她也认为该句完全可以接受：

(94) Janet and one of the boys were holding hands, but I don't remember which one.

钟等（Chung et al. 1995）也注意到了这种变异，并提供了（95），他们只是觉得该句稍微有些怪异：

(95) ?They persuaded Kennedy and some other Senator to jointly sponsor the legislation, but I can't remember which one.　(Chung et al. 1995: (83b))

我们可以再加一些例子，如（96）。

(96) a　Ben baked the cake and something else, but I don't know what.
　　 b　Abby was a member of the Students for a Democratic Society and one other organization , but it wasn't clear which.
　　 c　President Kim Dae Jung and a 'senior American representative'—the White House has not said who—will deliver speeches.（《国际先驱论坛报》，2000 年 3 月 29 日，第 2 页）

因此我认为，原则上并连语是可以进行截省的，但要满足一定句法条件。[①]

鉴于我们目前的目标是把截省归纳为删除，这些例句的合法性要求并连语条件的效应是由语音形式上的操作造成的，而不是由作为移位条件的禁止并连语提取这一原则造成的。因此，例（95）的表达应如下所示：

(97)　... but I can't remember which one$_1$ [~~they persuaded Kennedy and t_1 to jointly sponsor the legislation~~]

因此，并连语条件肯定与格罗苏（Grosu 1981: 56）的"空并连语限制"的观点一致。"空并连语限制"指出，并连语在语音上不能为空。并连语条件是一个作用于语音形式的条件，这一论断得到了一些句子的有力支持：有些句子因为空并连语的缘故，看起来有偏差，但这些句子通常不是由我们目前分析下的移位操作派生来的。（Munn 1993 也否认并连语条件是提取的限制。）这些语料可分为四类：空 VP、右节点提升结构、空代

[①] 这种变异性的其中一点与所涉及主语的性质有关。文献中所有的例子都含有一个复数主语（罗斯的"together"，钟等的"jointly"，莱文的"hold hands"）；如果不是复数主语，或谓词有一个强制性分配解读，那么句子有时就会更不合法：

(i) a　*Mark and another boy each won a prize, but I don't remember who.
　　 b　*Some shaft and the coupler were broken—guess which!

这些句子不符合语法，至少驳斥了对并列主语进行连词缩减的分析。（见下文关于并列 VP 的讨论。）但是，如果仅解释为其本身缺乏分配性，并不能充分覆盖语言事实，因为像（96）那样的例子是符合语法的。特别是在（96c）中，有意传达的解读就是分配性的：政要们分别做演讲，而不是联合做一个演讲。

词和空话题，以及不合法的跨界提取。

首先是 VP 省略，正如格罗苏（Grosu 1973, 1981: 53）所指出的，一个空 VP 不能和一个显性 VP 并列。他的例句如（98）所示：

（98） *I couldn't lift this weight, but I know a boy who could [___ and lift a cowbar, too].

在判断这个例句时，我们必须小心，不要在 *and* 前加停顿，因为这样的停顿会使例句变得合乎语法，但这与我们此处讨论的并不相关。相反地，在这种情况下，我们有一个与 *Bob can sing—and dance, too!*（比较 *You should do it, and quickly (too)!*；对这种"附加语 *and*"的讨论见 Progovac 1999）相类似的结构。我们可以通过添加一个"左括号"成分，如 *both* 和 *either*，或者颠倒并连语的顺序，来构建一些这种因素不能起作用的例句。这些例句明显是不合法的。

（99） Bob can judge, and
    a *Abby both can [___ and sing], too.
    b *Abby can [sing and ___], too.
    c *Abby can either [___ or sing].
    d *Abby can either [sing or ___].

尽管有些时候，有人建议英语中的 VP 省略可以被缩减为 VP 话题化（Johnson 1997; Postal 1998: 180），但是为截省和 NP 省略构建类似的论断的话，这种话题化的分析方法不太可行。相关语料如（100）和（101）所示。

（100） a *Abby invited someone, but I don't know who$_2$ [___ and Ben kissed t_2].
        b *Abby invited someone, but I don't know who$_2$ [Ben kissed t_2 and ___].

（101） a *I have five cats, but he has six [___ and dogs]!
        b *I have five cats, but he has six [dogs and ___]!

第二个论据来自于右节点提升结构（Right Node Rising，简称 RNR）

对于并连语条件具有明显的敏感性,这一事实由罗斯(Ross 1967)指出。下面的例句来自于麦考利(McCawley 1988):

(102) *Tom is writing an article on Aristotle and, and Elaine has just published a monograph on Mesmer and, Freud.

如果右节点提升结构事实上是一个韵律删除现象,正如怀尔德(Wilder 1995)和斯温格尔(Swingle 1995)令人信服的论证那样,那么(102)的不合法也必须遵循删除上的限制条件,而不是移位上的限制条件。(尤见 Swingle 1995: 58 注释 34,她把右节点提升作为一种删除理论来分析这类例句。)

另一种论据来自于各种空代词。例如希腊语可以使用空主语,但是它们不能和非空的 DP 并列(据我所知,在各种罗曼语和斯拉夫语中也有类似的现象①)。把并列主语中合乎语法的显性代词和它们对应的不符合语法的空代词进行比较,可以发现并连语的顺序是无关紧要的(感谢詹纳基杜所做的判断)。

(103) a {Aftos/*pro} kai o Pavlos ine adherfia.
         he   pro   and the Paul are siblings
        'He and Paul are siblings.'
      b {Esi /*pro} kai o Pavlos iste adherfia.
         you.sg pro and the Paul are siblings
        'You and Paul are siblings.'

---

① 一个潜在的反例来自爱尔兰语,麦克洛斯基和黑尔(McCloskey and Hale 1984)以及麦克洛斯基(McCloskey 1986)对此做过分析(以及古爱尔兰语,在 McCloskey 1991b 中有过分析)。在这种语言中,可以有(i)所示的结构,在这一结构中,左边的空并连语可以触发一致:

(i) V$_{[\alpha F]}$ [$_{DP}$ pro$_{[\alpha F]}$ Conj DP]...

麦克洛斯基曾跟我建议,即一致成分是左并连语,在韵律上附着在动词上——这一模式对毗邻性敏感,这种分析似乎是可信的,但鉴于篇幅这里不能展开详细的讨论。

c　{Ego/*pro} kai o　Pavlos imaste adherfia.
　　I　pro　 and the Paul　are　siblings
　　'I and Paul are siblings.'

(104) a　O　Pavlos kai {aftos/*pro} ine adherfia.
　　the Paul　and　he　 pro　are siblings
　　'Paul and he are siblings.'

b　O　Pavlos kai {esi　/*pro} iste adherfia.
　　the Paul　and　you.sg pro　are siblings
　　'Paul and you are siblings.'

c　O　Pavlos kai {ego/*pro} imaste adherfia.
　　the Paul　and　I　 pro　are　siblings
　　'Paul and I are siblings.'

类似的论据来自于德语以及东亚语言中不同类型的"话题脱落"结构（见 Huang 1984）。这些结构通常被分析为在小句左缘有一个空算子，在德语中，是在 SpecCP 上。这一算子，尽管满足德语 V_2 的要求，但也不能和一个显性成分并列：

(105) A: Hat er dir　 seine Infos　 gegeben—zum Beispiel,
　　has he you.DAT his　 vitals.ACC given　for example
　　seinen Namen?
　　his　namen.ACC
　　'Did he give you his personal information—for example, his name?'

B: a (*und sein Alter) wollte　er　nicht　sagen.
　　　and his age　wanted　he　not　 say
　　'That (and his age), he didn't want to say.'

b (*Sein Alter und) wollte　er　nicht　sagen.
　　his age and　 wanted　he　not　 say
　　'(His age and) that, he didn't want to say.'

另一种论据来源于一种结构，人们认为在该结构中按跨界（across-the-board）方式进行的提取是合法的，但结果可能会导致一个或两个并连语都为空。正如格罗苏注意到的那样,整个并连结构不能被跨界移除,如例(106a);跨界移位也不能影响一个并连语的次部分和整个并连语,如(106b,c)。这些例子取自加兹达尔等(Gazdar et al. 1985: 178)(另见 Gazdar et al. 1982, Sag and Fodor 1994)。

(106)　a　*Which books did Bob read [___ and ___]?
　　　　b　*I wonder who you saw [___ and [a picture of ___]].
　　　　c　*I wonder who you saw [[a picture of ___] and ___].

下面还有更复杂的例句。在这些结构中,并连语有一个"强化的"作用(Grosu 1981: 55)。这些例句如(107)和(108)所示,它们出自格罗苏(Grosu 1981: 55)。①

(107)　*Here is the picture of Mary which John is looking for ___ and {only/nothing but} ___.

(108)　a　John is growing eagerer and eagerer (to meet Mary) every minute.
　　　　b　*Eagerer though John seemed to be growing ___ and ___, Mary was still reluctant to introduce herself to him.
　　　　　(比较 Eagerer and eagerer though John seemed to be growing...)

既然跨界提取在理论上是可行的,而且跨界提取中的一些条件在这些例句中似乎也得到了满足,那么对于像(106)至(108)这样的例句就应该有一个独立的限制条件。空并连语限制正起到这样的作用。

最后,一种更具推测性的观点是,如果并连语条件是一个语音形式现象,那么我们可以预想能找到一些复述代词,以修复并连语提取造成的一些效应。总的来说,这在一些具有强复述代词的语言中,如爱尔兰语中的

---

① 实际上,如果根据库诺和高见(Kuno and Takami 1997)的**域外提取限制**(Ban on Out-of-Scope Extraction),或者坦克雷迪(Tancredi 1990)的**词汇联合原则**(Principle of Lexical Association),例(107)可能会被排除,像在英语中 *only* 这样的算子在其C成分统制域内,必须与显性成分相联系。

确存在，同时在英语中，这一效应似乎也得到了证实，如（109）。

（109） a That's the guy$_2$ that they were going to kill [you and him$_2$] together.
b Which wine$_3$ would you never serve it$_3$ and sushi together?
(Pesetsky 1998a: 366 注释 28)

但是很难弄清这些结构是否真的表明，移位的语迹可以作为一个代词在孤岛内部被"拼读"，以此作为修补孤岛效应的一种方式（如 Pesetsky 1998a 所提出的那样），也不清楚这些例子是否仅仅运用了一般策略，来解释与基础生成在其 A′位置上的算子有关联的复述代词（相关讨论见 Merchant 1999c）。因此，我们必须要找到一种环境——在这种环境下，我们知道不能采用一般的复述性解释策略，然后去考察复述代词是否即使在这种环境下，也可以作为一个并连语而存在。塞尔斯（Sells 1984）曾讨论过这种环境：当一个关系从句是一个全称量化词限制域的一部分时，复述代词不能与该关系从句算子相关联[1]，如（110）所示[2]：

---

[1] 这一概述存在争议；普林斯（Prince 1990）指出，在关系从句中复述代词实际使用的限制并不是那么明确。

[2] 请注意（i）中的例句。例（i）中这些对比，可以对包含先行词的删除（antecedent-contained deletion，简称 ACD）结构做出一个有趣的预测。

（i） a ?I read the (same) book that Charlie made the claim that you had read it.
b *I read every book that Charlie made the claim that you had read it.

既然复述代词可以改良邻接效应，那么，在某种程度上它们也可以和允准 ACD 的限定词共现（the 在一定程度上允准 ACD: I gave him$_2$ the book Charlie$_2$ wanted me to），我们应该找到一种改良方法，它能够与海克（Haïk 1987）所发现的对邻接效应的改良相媲美。(ii) 中的语料表明的确如此。

（ii） a ?I read the (same) book that Charlie made the claim that you had.
b *I read every book that Charlie made the claim that you had.

这些语料表明，量化词提升后的语迹（甚至以 the 为中心语的 DP 也必须要提升，上段中斜体的例子也显示了这一点，该例子缺乏约束三原则 C 效应）可以等同于一个复述代词，与第一章提到的对"载体转换"效应的语义分析所预期的一样。

（110）*Every guy that you got upset when Betsy started dating him turned out fine in the end.

因此关键性的测试是，确定在这样的关系从句中，复述代词是否可以作为并连语出现。这样的复述代词只能是语音形式上拼读过程中把移位的语迹转换成为代词的结果，因为基础生成的算子和复述代词的常规策略不可行（其原因见 Sells 1984）。相关语料见（111）：

（111）a ?(?)Every guy that you thought {[he and Betsy]/that [Betsy and him]} would make a good couple turned out to be a psycho in the end.
b ?(?)She interviewed every guy that you saw Betsy and him together.

但遗憾的是，似乎很难对这些句子做出判断，它们似乎比（110）好一些，但不如（109a）。由于缺乏更清晰的语料，这一测试的结果仍然不是最终结论。

目前我们已经看到了至少四种空并连语被禁止的情况，没有一种可以令人信服地被分析为与提取相关。这印证了一种假设，即无论空并连语限制的效应可能是什么，空并连语限制都作用于语音表达层面[①]，这与空并连语是否由移位造成无关。如果空并连语限制是在语音形式层面起作用，

[①] 有个遗留问题，在这里我不打算解决，罗德曼（Rodman 1976）和其他人（讨论见 Ruys 1992）已经注意到了这一点，即并连语不能独立形成辖域。如果并连语条件只是语音形式条件，那么并列结构中关于辖域的限制条件就不能遵循量化词提升的限制条件，而是遵循这些结构解读的语义限制条件（见 Winter1998）。

和这一问题相关的是并连语中 wh- 原位的地位问题。尽管菲恩戈、黄、拉斯尼克和莱因哈特（Fiengo, Huang, Lasnik and Reinhart 1988: 81）声称（i）只是略微有些偏差（问号表示他们的判断），

（i）?Who saw John and who?

布雷斯南（Bresnan 1975）、佩塞茨基（Pesetsky 1982: 618）和波斯塔尔（Postal 1992: 23）把相似的例子判断为不可接受（另见 Ginzburg 1992: 171, 他注意到"对于许多说话者来说，[这样的例子] 只能用来重复 [作为回声问句——JM]"）；我倾向于后者的判断。只有当 wh- 原位在逻辑形式上必须移位时，这些事实才是有问题的：如果有问题，且如果并连语条件也应用于逻辑形式层面，后面这些作者的判断才能得到解释。从目前的角度来看，这些事实必须遵循语义机制，而不必遵循移位上的限制。

我们就可以预测，截省可以改良由单个并连语提取而引起的结构缺陷，而且语料事实也正是如此。

5.1.5 小结

以上几节我们考察了截省把成分从各种孤岛中提取出来的能力，这些孤岛包括左分支结构、COMP 语迹语境、派生位置（话题化和主语）和并连语。我认为各种情况中的提取本身都合法，与我们将这些与其对应的显性形式对比而得出的结论不同，语音形式上的删除消除了提取的偏差。我在每种情况下都已说明，有独立的理由相信这些孤岛效应在语音层面起作用。它们的实现方式不同，有些可能比另一些更清晰，这与我们目前对这一现象的理解一样。但是，对于截省语料所支持的假说而言，即"某些孤岛效应不一定是通常意义上的结构性的，而应是语音形式层面的"，这些主张的具体实施并非至关重要。

5.2 截省下的 E 类型照应

在开始讨论下一类别的孤岛之前，需要介绍一些背景知识。这一节主要基于麦钱特（Merchant 1999a）的研究。在本节中，我证明了 IP 先行结构中的一些移位语迹与所删除 IP 中的 E 型代词相同。这将为理解下面章节所要讨论的几种语言事实奠定基础。

5.2.1 问题：截省下的 A′ 语迹

无论采用何种方法来解决 IP 省略，都很容易出现一个问题，即含有 A′ 语迹的 IP 允准了表面上不含 A′ 语迹的 IP 的删除，也就是说，含有语迹的 IP 能够为截省提供一个必要的 IP 先行项。（112）中给出了我自造的例句，（113）至（115）列出了其他研究者已经验证过的句子。

(112)　a　The report details what IBM did and why.

　　　　b　Who did the suspect call and when?

　　　　c　We know which families bought houses on this block, but we don't know which (houses), yet.

　　　　d　It was clear which families had mowed their lawns, but we can only guess with which brands of lawnmower.

　　　　e　The judge had records of which divers had been searching the wreck, but not of how long.

　　　　f　The hospital spokeswoman told us which patients had died, but she wouldn't say when.

　　　　g　The Guinness Book records how long some alligators can hold their breaths, but not which (ones).

　　　　h　Though Abby eventually told us who she saw that night, she never revealed where.

(113)　a　That's a gazebo. But I don't know who built it or why. (听到的对话, Santa Cruz, 15 Sept. 1996)

　　　　b　A ride-along with an officer shows who gets ticketed, and why. (San Jose Mercury News, 9 Aug. 1996)

　　　　c　A chronology was the first step in piecing together what had happened—which had to precede figuring out why. (Robinson 1994: 222)

　　　　d　They didn't have any clear idea of what they were going to try to do, or why. (Robinson 1994: 535)

　　　　e　What's proposed and why. (*San Jose Mercury News*, headline, 28 Nov. 1996)

(114)　a　[The Smart Toilet] is a paperless device that not only accommodates calls of nature, but also 'knows' who's using it and how. (*San Jose Mercury News*, 6 Aug. 1996) b What interveners are able to 'get out of the way', and how? (Szabolcsi and Zwarts 1993: 14)

   c Investigators want to know who is supplying the drugs—and how—since Kevorkian's medical license was suspended in 1991. (*San Jose Mercury News*, 17 Aug. 1996)

(115) a [The police asked] who'd seen him last and where. (Tartt 1994: 294)

   b But R. C. Lahoti, a High Court judge appointed to lead the investigation of the accident, must decide who will decode the recorders and where. (*San Jose Mercury News*, 30 Nov. 1996)

   c He only wanted to know whom they had met, and where. (Robinson, 1996: 515)

甚至多重 wh- 短语也可能出现在先行结构 IP 中：

(116) a We need to know who saw what, and when.

   b This is Washington, where everyone keeps track of who crossed whom and when. (*New York Times Magazine*, 23 July 2000)

   c [He] makes no empirical claims concerning what domain will be opaque for what relations, [or] why. (Szabolcsi and Zwarts 1993: 240 注释 4)

   d You know exactly who will laugh at which particular kind of joke, and for how long. (改编自 de Bernières 1995: 33)

   e He wasn't even certain who within his own family was entitled to what, or why. (Kress 1993: 109)

   f Entitlement, after all, was the entire issue. Who got what, and how, and why. (Kress 1993: 108)

先行项 IP 中量化词提升成分的语迹也可以引起同样的效应：

(117) a　The suspect phoned everyone on this list, but we don't know when.
　　　b　Most gangs will be at the rumble, though it's not clear why.
　　　c　Every boy scout helped, though most didn't know why.
　　　d　(Only a) few boats looked for survivors, though it's not clear why.
　　　e　At least five guerrillas survived the raids, but no one could figure out how.
　　　f　The duke hid exactly six of the jewels, and even Holmes didn't know where.

如果结构性同构要求在先行结构 IP 和被删除 IP 之间保持完全的同一性，我们就会有（118）中的 LF 的表征形式，其中画线部分在 PF 层面被删除；复制法也会产生完全相同的问题。这些 LF 有明显的缺陷，即第二个并列项中的 wh- 语迹不受约束。一般情况下，我们认为一个不受约束的语迹会引起惊人的不合语法现象，但是以下例句表明这种情况并没有发生。

(118) a　… [$_{CP}$ what$_1$ [$_{IP}$ IBM did t_1]] and [$_{CP}$ why [$_{IP}$ <u>IBM did t_1</u>]]
　　　b　[$_{CP}$ who$_2$ did [$_{IP}$ the suspect call t_2]] and [$_{CP}$ when [$_{IP}$ the suspect call t_2]]

解释这些例句可接受性的关键在于它们均有与（119）中的句子相同的解读：这些句子含有与前置非成分统制的 wh- 短语相照应的显性代词，但却没有省略。

(119) a　The report details what$_1$ IBM did and why IBM did it$_1$.
　　　b　Who$_2$ did the suspect call and when did the suspect call him$_2$?
　　　c　Most gangs$_3$ will be at the rumble, though it's not clear why they$_3$'ll be there.
　　　d　Every boy scout$_4$ helped, though most$_5$ didn't know why they$_{4/5}$ helped.

虽然没有人提出过针对（112）至（117）中句子的分析方法，但（119a, b）中的句子在博林格（Bolinger 1978）的一篇重要论文中有过讨论，近期科莫罗夫斯基（Comorovski 1996）也对它们进行了讨论。科莫罗夫斯基只是顺便提了一下，因为她的主要兴趣点不在于此，她只是把所观察到的这类照应链接的可能性归因于现有对 wh- 问题的种种假设。无论这是不是用来验证这种照应链接可行性的正确方法，这种观察都显然没有解决（112）至（117）中的省略句所带来的问题。

特别要注意的是，这些例句似乎都不是某种新颖的、神秘的、从两个并列语中移出第一个 wh- 短语的动词跨界移位操作的结果。这种跨界的解释方法很显然会遇到很多问题（首先是短语结构，还有违反孤岛条件等）。另外，还有许多例句不适用于跨界提取所必需的那类并列结构（更多例句见 Merchant 1999a）。

5.2.2 解决办法：载体转换和 E 类型代词

我要提出的解决办法总的来讲在形式上并不陌生：我会把删除的 IP 与它们前面没有删除的对应成分同化起来。我只是认为（118）中那种被删除的 IP 的逻辑形式，事实上与（119）那种例句的逻辑形式在相关方面完全相同，特别是 wh- 语迹（以及 QR 的语迹）在这些情况下允准代词省略。

正如第一章所提到的，菲恩戈和梅（Fiengo and May 1994）提出并论证了一种用于精准识别这种句法花招的机制："载体转换"（另见 van den Wyngaerd and Zwart 1991, Brody 1995, Kennedy 1997, Giannakidou and Merchant 1998）。"载体转换"本质上规定了省略情况下特定对应成分的类别，（120）给出了其一般形式。对我们而言，载体转换的相关例示可以通过（121）中的图示体现，它说明非代词性成分在省略情况下可以被看作是代词性成分。特别是，像 wh- 语迹这样的算子可以被看作是一个代词性成分，用菲恩戈和梅的术语就是代词性关联成分，如（122）所示。

（120）载体转换（Fiengo and May 1994: 218 ff.）
　　　在省略背景下，名词性成分在其代词性状态方面，可被看作是非区别性的。

（121） $[-代词性] =_e [+代词性]$
（此处 $=_e$ 是指在省略下形成一个等价类别）

（122） $[-a, -p]$（变项或名称）$=_e [-a, +p]$（代词性关联成分 $=^P e$）

菲恩戈与梅竭力论证"载体转换"是句法性的，具有句法效应，而不是简单地与某些更为抽象层面上的语义对应成分相关（如省略的属性照应语处理路径）。他们指出，VP 省略条件下的名称和 wh- 语迹的代词性关联成分不会触发违反约束三原则 C 的情况，却会触发约束三原则 B，并且不遵守孤岛条件，他们认为这些都是句法现象。尽管他们的讨论仅仅局限于 VP 省略，但其中第一、三条属性在截省情况下也可以观察到。当然，如果拒绝了结构同构，我们就没有理由不在省略位置放置常规的代词，这里我就是这么做的。同样的结论也成立。

5.2.2.1 截省下的"载体转换"

让我们从约束理论效应开始，也就是从约束三原则 C 效应的消失开始。例句（123）展现了称谓词违背约束三原则 C 的典型事例。如（124a）所示，移位的 wh- 短语的语迹在一个同标成分统制的代词下得到了复制，但却没有产生偏差，这与之前天真的预期相反，因为从特征上看，称谓词与 wh- 语迹是没有区别的。对于菲恩戈和梅来讲，"载体转换"把语迹变为代词性关联成分，正如（124b）所示的逻辑式，其中变项 t_4 由它的代词性关联成分 $^P e_4$ 来实现。$^P e_4$ 具有 [+ 指代性] 特征，不再受制于约束三原则 C。根据这里所述的理论，这意味着删除的 IP 只是包含了一个代词，如（124c）。

（123） *The detectives wanted to know whether they$_3$ knew why Sue hated the Thompsons$_3$.

（124） a The detectives wanted to know who$_4$ [Sue hated t_4] and whether they$_4$ knew why.

b ... they₄ knew why [**Sue hated** ᴾe₄]

  c ... they₄ knew why [~~Sue hated them₄~~]

约束三原则 B 无法得到检验，因为在截省中，整个 IP 都被省略了，因此没有一个有小句伙伴成分统制代词（clause-mate c-commanding pronoun）的例子能够被构建起来。

其次，我们发现 wh- 短语和受其约束的语迹之间的正常约束关系受到孤岛条件的限制，这种正常约束关系在截省情况下也变得松散了。换言之，一个重构语迹的代词性关联成分可以在孤岛外面找到它的先行词。这在截省情况下完全正确，因为截省首先涉及的是 wh- 孤岛，但是，即便把直接支配截省 IP 的 CP 内嵌到另外一个孤岛中也不会影响这些例句的状态。再者，首先就不应考虑正常约束，因为 wh- 短语不对代词性关联成分进行成分统制。

下面的例句是按如下方法建构的。(125a) 是一个控制语料，说明了从孤岛中进行提取是不合语法的（这里提取的是一个主语；见 Merchant 1999*a* 对其他 24 种孤岛中此类截省句的研究）。(125b) 说明非省略 IP 的 wh- 连接是不可能的。(125c) 列出了没有省略的情况，但有一个与 wh- 先行项连接的代词。这个来自代词性成分的连接使 (125d) 中的截省版的例句合乎语法，如其逻辑形式 (125e) 所示。

(125) a *Which crime₄ did the FBI admit that ⟨solving t₄⟩ will prove difficult?

  b *The FBI knows which truck₄ was rented, but ⟨figuring out from where t₄ was rented⟩ has proven difficult.

  c The FBI knows which truck₄ was rented, but ⟨figuring out from where it₄ was rented⟩ has proven difficult.

  d The FBI knows which truck₄ was rented, but ⟨figuring out from where⟩ has proven difficult.

  e ... figuring out from where [~~it₄ was rented~~] has proven difficult.

因而，现有证据都表明我们是在处理省略部位中的代词。这些效应，连同结构同构条件，均是菲恩戈和梅提出"载体转换"操作的动机。但是，如果所有表征层面上的省略位置都含有一个常规的代词，同样的效果也会马上随之而来，这可以参看第一章内容。接下来，我还是会把所讨论的成分简单地表示为代词，尽管我有时也会继续使用"载体转换"这一行之有效的术语来指称在某种条件下 A′ 语迹允准代词删除的情况，并且把"代词性关联成分"当作在这些条件下被删除的代词。

5.2.2.2 对"载体转换"结果的解读

代词性关联成分和其先行项之间的照应链接必须要与受常规约束的 wh- 语迹或代词区别开来。它们本质上是"驴子句代词"的下位类别：与前置量化表达相照应，而不是受其约束。①

让我们以（126a）及其相关的逻辑式为例，（127）是它们的非省略对应语句（我忽略了 when 的语迹，因为它在这里无关紧要）。

（126） a　Which suspect did Abby call, and when?
　　　　 b　[$_{CP}$ Which suspect$_2$ did [$_{IP}$ Abby call t_2]] and [$_{CP}$ when [$_{IP}$ ~~Abby call him$_2$~~]]

（127） Which suspect did Abby call, and when did she call him?

这里需要直接解决的问题与我们在第一章中提出的与这种语料相关的问题相同：IP 可以被删除这一事实是否遵循焦点条件？正如我们之前所做的那样，考虑到简洁性，我们假设 wh- 移位的语迹，像代词那样也被解释为变项。暂且假定代词和变项可以用同样的规则来解释（回顾第一章中的定义（4）），这种情况下，两者均得出 g(2)。考虑到这一情况，焦点条件得到了满足，因为在这种情况下 IP$_A$ 和 IP$_E$ 满足如下算式：

（128） a　IP$_E'$ = F-clo(IP$_E$) = Abby called g(2)
　　　　 b　TP$_A'$ = F-clo(IP$_A$) = Abby called g(2)

---

① 感兴趣的读者请参考麦钱特（Merchant 1999a）的研究，那里有更多的证据表明将这些代词同化为 E 类型代词是正确的，其依据是这些结构中量化变异性效应的分布。

不管是通过哪种路径对驴子句照应进行解释，这一结果都应该是正确的，因为焦点条件的定义以语义蕴涵而非句子结构为基础，即由 wh- 短语（它的语迹）量化的集合应该是被删除的 IP 中的驴子句代词所挑选出的集合，无论这是如何得以实施的。既然等量去重音在（119）中的情况下是可能的，那么，我可以得出：焦点条件对于"常规"代词和驴子句代词间的差异不敏感（实际上"常规"代词自身不能仅仅被分析为 E 类型代词的一种限制情况）。

有人也许希望省略情境下驴子句照应行为可以更加恰当清楚地阐明驴子句照应现象本身，以帮助我们对以往研究中（见 Heim 1990, Groenendijk and Stokhof 1991, Lappin and Francez 1994, Chierchia 1995）提出的几种备选方案做出决定。遗憾的是，对于这种研究而言，它们似乎会不经任何修改地扩展到此处所展示的语料上，其扩展的程度是这些方法能够成功地解释这些核心语料。

上述事实的确对埃文斯（Evans 1980）和海姆（Heim 1990）采用的 E 类型解释方法提出了一个有趣的问题，该解释方法对代词有个确定的描述，这也是目前最具有解释力的一个方法。语义上看，只要这些描述挑选出正确的个体（正如前期设计那样），焦点条件就会得到满足。尽管如此，如果这一"替换"是从句法上执行的——鉴于上文刚给出的语料——我们还要面临这样的问题：为什么涉及约束理论时，这种语义上定指的描述表现得像一个代词。也许这个问题隶属于一个更大的问题，即如果这种描述确实是句法上的复杂描述，那么它们起初是如何被说成是代词的。

有鉴于此，我将把关于驴子句照应语解释和分析的复杂问题暂且搁置，而采用 E 类型分析路径；基于后面章节的观察，我将继续把驴子句代词解释为（简单）变项，但读者应该记住这是个为了方便而被采用的假设变项。

5.2.3 小结

针对被删除 IP 的先行词中 A′ 语迹的表现所做的研究为一系列结论提

供了证据。首先，我论证了这些语迹与代词是对等的，这满足了第一章所论述的焦点条件。被删除成分是一个代词这一事实解释了与标准变项相关的效应缺失问题，也就是，约束三原则 C 效应和孤岛敏感性被证明无效。我进一步建议把这些代词性关联成分解释为 wh- 短语的 E 类型代词照应成分，与文献中对驴子句照应研究中的其他非成分统制量化词的 E 类型代词照应相同，特别是与在 IP 去重音情况下出现的代词相同。

5.3 命题性孤岛

以此为背景，我现在转向本章开头被称为 C 类的第二类孤岛，这类孤岛有一个共同的区别性特征：在所有情况下，疑问句中的孤岛都包含一个命题性成分。因此，我将这类孤岛称为"命题性孤岛"（propositional islands），但我不打算用这个描述性术语来表示所涉及的孤岛和相关内容的性质。分析这些例子的核心思想是：提取只能在局部进行，只能从内嵌的命题域内进行提取，且孤岛的解读效应（即这种解读受到限制的事实让我们认为一开始就从孤岛内发生了提取）能够通过独立需要的 E 类型照应和情态从属关系机制推导出来。我在这里的目标不是深入探寻对后面这些现象的解释，而是专注于提取的句法层面，尤其要专注于一个事实，即通过运用这些机制，我们可以避免违反孤岛提取的操作。

我首先考虑各种类型的关系从句孤岛，然后再讨论附加语从句和某些违反并列结构限制的情况。

5.3.1 关系从句

这一部分讨论了两种关系从句，即传统的直陈式关系从句和虚拟式关系从句。对于直陈式关系从句，我证明了，从 5.2 节中所得出的结论可知，关系算子的语迹能够允准 IP 中代词的删除，且这一事实能够得出想要的解读。在虚拟关系从句中会出现一些复杂情况，但是这些可以通过情态从属关系解决。此处的分析代表了接下来各节的分析,它们都具有相同的特点。

5.3.1.1 直陈式关系从句

让我们回顾一下,关系从句中的截省是可能的:

(129) a They hired someone who speaks a Balkan language—guess which!
      b They hired someone who speaks a lot of languages—guess how many!

这些与常规提取形成对比,如(130)。

(130) a *Guess which (Balkan language) they hired someone who speaks!
      b *Guess how many (languages) they hired someone who speaks!

我们可以将(129)和(130)做对比,与 5.1 节中的情况一样,它表明关系从句是 PF 孤岛。然而,这个结论不太可能正确——这与上面提到的比较句中左分支提取的改善不同,例如从 than 分句内部的关系从句中进行对等提取仍然是不合法的(比较"导论"中例(5)和第 126 页脚注①):

(131) a *Abby hired someone who speaks a rarer Balkan language than Op_1 Ben did ~~hire someone who speaks~~ [t_1' a t_1 Balkan language].
      b *Abby hired someone who speaks more Balkan languages than Op_1 Ben did ~~hire someone who speaks~~ [t_1 Balkan languages].

与之不同,我的提议是,(129)和(130)之间的平行仅仅是表面上的,(129)中的截省实际上不包含孤岛。相反,我认为它们有如下结构:

(132) a Guess which$_1$ [~~she speaks~~ t_1]!
      b Guess how many$_2$ [~~he speaks~~ t_2]!

因此,它们与(133)中的显性对应项对等。

(133) a They hired someone who speaks a Balkan language—guess which she speaks!

b They hired someone who speaks a lot of languages—guess how many he speaks!

截省示例的解读与未删除的对应部分相同。（134a）中给出了先行小句的意义，（134b）中给出了截省 CP 的意义。（我在此处开始使用世界变体，我将在下一节中阐明这样做的原因；根据 von Stechow 1996 的标记法，此处的 @ 代表现实世界［通常用 W_0 表示］。）

（134） a λw.∃y[**balkan-language**$_@$(y) ∧ ∃x[**speak**$_w$(x, y) ∧ **hire**$_w$(**they**, x)]]
      b ?y[**balkan-language**$_@$(y) ∧ **speak**$_w$(x, y)] =
        λp.∃y[**balkan-language**$_@$(y) ∧ p = λw[**speak**$_w$(x, y)]]

让我们看看带来这些解读的结构是如何满足焦点条件的。让我们回顾一下相关定义：

（135） 省略给定
      表达式 E 为给定，当且仅当表达式 E 有一个凸显的先行项 A，且有 ∃ 类型转换取模时，
      （ⅰ） A 蕴涵 E 的焦点闭包，且
      （ⅱ） E 蕴涵 A 的焦点闭包。

一般的焦点条件要求 [[WHICH$_F$ (Balkan language)]$_1$ she$_6$ speaks t_1]^g，无论 CP 内部的 IP 是否被省略，都要满足给定条件；如罗梅罗（Romero 1998）所示，一个句子，如 *(I know whether) she speaks a Balkan language*，可从（129）中第一个并联语中推断出来，它提供了一个合适的先行项来允准（129）中所示的 F 标记和其在（133）中的非省略的对应部分。有待证明的是，当 CP 内部的 IP 被省略时，该 IP 满足了以给定限制条件为基础的更强的限制条件。因此，让我们仔细考察一下（132a）中删除的 IP。

首先，为方便起见（且显然也是正确的），我们假设 F 标记没有保留在移位的 F 标记成分的语迹上。其次，为了更清晰一些，我们必须假设

一直被我们忽略的 [$_{DP}$ WHICH [$_{NP}$ Balkan language]] 中的 NP 省略在某种程度上对删除的 IP 的意义有贡献。最直接的方法是假设移位复制理论成立，为删除的 IP 生成类似（136）的结果（对语迹的贡献的详细讨论，见 Sauerland 1998）：

(136) [$_{IP}$ she$_6$ speaks [x Balkan language]]

此外，我们让 $[\![she_6^{E\text{-}type}]\!]^g$ = g(6) ∈ D_E。替代 F 标记的内容和未约束变项的存在闭包的结果如下：

(137) IP$_E'$ = F-clo(IP$_E$) = ∃x.g(6) speaks x and x is a Balkan language

(138) 中给出了先行小句的内嵌 IP，它可以作为该从句的先行项，前提是分配给 $she_6^{E\text{-}type}$ 的值与分配给 t_6 的值相同。

(138) $[\![$[$_{IP}$ t_6 speaks a Balkan language]$]\!]^g$ = λw.∃y[**balkan-language**$_@$(y) ∧ **speak**$_w$(g(6), y)]

这为 IP$_A$ 提供了以下内容：

(139) IP$_A'$ = F-clo(IP$_A$) = ∃x.g(6) speaks x and x is a Balkan language

因此，IP$_A$ 和 IP$_E$ 根据需要处于所需的关系中。

先行词中的语迹和省略部位中的代词相同，同样，前一节讨论的疑问句中和 QR 下的 wh-XPs 语迹也相同。不足为奇的是，关系从句中 wh- 移位的语迹会产生同样的效果。同样，除非我们坚持维护删除的 IP 的结构同一条件，否则没有必要明确诉诸载体转换的句法机制。省略部位中的代词只有在其标记与先行项中的语迹相同时，才符合焦点条件下可删除的条件。如前一节所述，这个代词的解读将会是 E 类型代词的解读，因为它不受相关算子的约束。这就预示着，如果一个 E 类型代词在给定条件的上下文中是不合法的，那么截省就会失败，正如显性形式的失败一样。以下例句的偏差说明了这种预测是正确的。

（140） a They hired {*no/??few} people who spoke a lot of languages—guess how many!

b *They didn't hire anyone who speaks a Balkan language, but I don't remember which.

这些与它们显性的对应成分的偏差程度完全一致：

（141） a They hired {*no/??few} people who spoke a lot of languages—guess how many they$^{E\text{-}type}$ spoke!

b *They didn't hire anyone who speaks a Balkan language, but I don't remember which she$^{E\text{-}type}$ speaks.

众所周知，这些情况中的先行结构限定词短语，分别被 no、few 和否定极性词 any 引导，一般不允准 E 类型照应。然而，在有些情况下，E 类型照应语至少（虽然没有与 no 一起）被允准与 few 一起使用，如下面被验证过的例句（如 Evans 1980 的原始例句（5）和（7）所示）。

（142） The May day was still quite chilly and few people were out. I looked at them$^{E\text{-}type}$ idly across the intervening MacArthur Lock...
(Paretsky 1984: 150)

在某种程度上，这种照应是可能的，我们期望依赖这种照应的截省得到相应的改进。这似乎与语料提供者的反应相吻合，他们有时在判断相关例句（（140）中带有 few 的例句）时会有所迟疑，这无疑表明他们正试图构建相关语境来允准照应，但通常效果不佳。①

这些对比也与先行 IP 中的 QR 语迹相同。当量化词提升 DP 允准跨句照应时，截省表现出了（143）至（146）所示的歧义。

---

① 在一些情况下，补足语集合照应是可能的（见 Moxey and Sandford 1993），我把这种可能性放在这里。

（143） Everyone helped, but I don't know why.
   a　= . . . why everyone helped
   b　= . . . why they$^{E\text{-}type}$ helped

（144） Five scouts helped, but I don't know why.
   a　= . . . ?why five scouts helped
   b　= . . . why they$^{E\text{-}type}$ helped

（145） At least three flags will be flown; when will be announced later today.
   a　= . . . ?when at least three flags will be flown
   b　= . . . when they$^{E\text{-}type}$ will be flown

（146） Exactly five officers were fired, but I don't know why.
   a　= . . . why exactly five were fired
   b　= . . . why they$^{E\text{-}type}$ were fired

213 在每种情况下，删除的内容都有系统性的歧义。截省可以被解读为（a）或（b），这代表了删除内容的结构。示例（a）是我们所预期的，因为它们通过以下逻辑完全等同于先行 IP。以（146a）为例，为使截省有该解读，删除的 IP 如（147）所示。

（147）　[$_{IP}$ exactly five were fired]

显然，由于这与先行项相同，因此其删除得到了焦点条件的允准。这里 IP_A 和 IP_E 如（148）所示。

（148） a $IP_E' = \exists_5!x.x$ were fired
    b $IP_A' = \exists_5!x.x$ were fired

（b）解读的可行性也是焦点条件能够使代词等同于语迹的结果。因此，对于（146b），我们有：

（149）　IP_E = [$_{IP}$ they$_2$$^{E\text{-}type}$ were fired] = g(2) were fired

先行词 IP 的低位 IP 分段在 *exactly five officers* 的 QR 后提供了 IP_A：

（150） a　[$_{IP}$ [exactly five officers]$_2$ [$_{IP}$ t$_2$ were fired]]
　　　　 b　IP$_A$ = [$_{IP}$ t$_2$ were fired]

只有在照应语首先得到了解决的情况下，这种对等才能实现（也就是说，仅仅界定一个关联词范围以提供结构上有用的先行 IP 分段是不够的）。如下语料所示，如果先行 DP 向下蕴涵，这种照应链将很困难或不可能。

（151） No one helped, but I don't know why.
　　　　 a　= ... why no one helped
　　　　 b　≠ ... *why they$^{E\text{-}type}$ helped

（152） Few scouts helped, but I don't know why.
　　　　 a = ... why few scouts helped
　　　　 b ≠ ... *why they$^{E\text{-}type}$ helped

（153） Fewer than six states voted for Mondale—the big question is why.
　　　　 a = fewer than six (i.e., so few) voted for him
　　　　 b = ? they$^{E\text{-}type}$ voted for him（即 why those six voted for him at all）

假如只有结构条件起作用的话，这些可以满足上述焦点条件。但这类照应存在的条件不是结构上的，而是语义或语用上的。与（143）至（146）中的不同，这些省略是非歧义性的，这与解决省略或截省的机制没有关系，尤其是它们遵循了 E 类型照应的一般限制条件。

量化的先行词可以允准代词删除这一结论也得到了以下语料的支持（这也表明 Safir 1999 关于 QR 的语迹对载体转换免疫的断言无法维持下去）。

（154） a　I met with every suspect$_1$, though most$_2$, claimed I hadn't.
　　　　 b　Everyone$_1$ helped, though most$_2$ weren't sure why.

这些例句产生歧义的方式与（143）至（146）中的例子相似，这里存在一个有趣的差异，当先行结构中 QR 的语迹等同于一个代词时，这个代词就会受到局部的且成分统治的量化词约束（让我们将该例称为"重新约束"），如（155）所示。（注意，约束理论的测试表明，我们在省略部位有一个代词，而不是一个句法变项：约束三原则 C 失效了，但约束三原则 B 并没有。）

（155） a ...most$_2$ claimed I hadn't [~~met with them$_2$~~].
   b ...most$_2$ weren't sure why [~~they$_2$~~ ~~helped~~].

这不是单纯的精简，且如果重新约束的量化词受到不同的限制，就变得不可能了：

（156） I met with every suspect$_1$, though most cops$_2$ claimed I hadn't.
   a = [met with {every suspect/them$_1$}]
   b ≠ [met with them$_2$]

如果 *in situ* 限制和 [*x suspect*] 一样被解释为定指性描述（见 Sauerland 1998, Fox 2000），这些可能会被用来支持 A′ 复制移位理论。当然，只有当代词本身是此类定指性描述的最小拼读时（如 E 类型代词的传统分析），这一结论才成立，因为在对等的去重音对应部分中，显性代词也存在同样的解释限制：

（157） I met with every suspect$_1$, though most cops$_2$ claimed I hadn't *met with them*$_{\{1/*2\}}$.

有趣的是，这些照应的可能性遵循集合/子集关系（假设：*lifer*′ ⊂ *inmate*′）。对比（158）、（159）的解读与（160）、（161）的解读（同样，正如读者可能会验证的那样，与它们的显性去重音对应部分相等）。

（158） I met with every inmate$_1$, though {many/most} lifers$_2$ said I hadn't.
   a = [met with them$_1$]
   b = [met with them$_2$]

（159） I met with every lifer$_2$, though {many/most} inmates$_1$ said I hadn't.
   a = [met with them$_2$]
   b ≠ [met with them$_1$]

(160) I met with most inmates₁, though many lifers₂ didn't want me to.
  a = [meet with {most/the} inmates]
  b = [meet with them₂]

(161) I met with most lifers₂, though many inmates₁ didn't want me to.
  a = [meet with {most/the} lifers]
  a ≠ [meet with them₁]

当第二个量化词是第一个量化词的子集时，重新约束是可能的（如（158b）和（160b））；否则，重新约束就不可能。

这些语料是否真的应该用移位的复制理论来解释，部分取决于什么才是对照应代词结构的正确分析——重要的是它们是否有内部结构，如果有，这一结构究竟是什么？与更一般的语义-语用解释相比，将这些语料简化为纯粹的结构性解释可能存在一个难题，即"情景性"it 也同样会出现照应解读的可能性，如（162）和（163）中的语料所示。

(162) I met with every inmate₁, though {many/most} lifers₂ didn't like/denied it.
  a it = [that I met with every inmate]
  b it = [that I met with them₂]

(163) I met with every lifer₂, though {many/most} inmates₁ didn't like/denied it.
  a it = [that I met with every lifer]
  b it ≠ [that I met with them₁]

一般认为这个 it 并非通过删除得到（尤见 Bresnan 1971 的论证）。如果这是正确的，那么推理的相似性应该由跨句照应的一般机制来推导出来，而不是由复制理论所编码的结构条件推导出来。另一个显而易见的结论是，甚至连这个 it 也是由一个编码复杂结构的"最小拼读机制"推导出来的（讨论见 Akmajian 1970, Grinder and Postal 1971, Hankamer and Sag 1976, McCawley 1998: 第二章）。[①]

[①] 根据拉科夫（Lakoff 1968）的测试——如果这些代词出现在巴赫-彼得斯的句子（Bach-Peters sentences）中，那么它们必须是非派生代词——这个 it 是非派生的："**The guy who denied *it*** was arrested for *wire-tapping his employee's offices*."。

总之，有大量确凿的证据表明，省略结构的某些解读的可行性与照应语的解决方法、E 类型或其他方面独立需要的机制存在矛盾。

5.3.1.2 虚拟关系从句和情态从属关系

到目前为止，我们一直在关注 DP 中出现的关系从句，这些 DP 在真实世界中都能找到所指对象。在一些直陈/虚拟语气区别较大的语言中，如希腊语、法语和加泰罗尼亚语，这些关系从句中的谓词出现在直陈式中，表明它们出现的 DP 的范围必须超过任何内涵算子（也就是说，描述的内容必须根据说话者的世界来进行评估）。解决上述关系从句的孤岛特征要依赖这一事实，使用 E 类型照应来解决被删除的 IP 中的代词。然而，这种策略不能直接扩展到虚拟关系从句。（关于这些小句的范围属性的讨论，见 Quine 1960; Farkas 1985; Giannakidou 1997, 1998; Quer 1998）这是因为被关系从句（该关系从句中的谓词是虚拟式）所修饰的 DP 的域必须在内涵算子之下，因此不能保证说话者的世界里有一个所指。

一个天真的想法可能会使我们认为，这一事实将意味着在虚拟关系从句中不可能出现跨越关联成分的截省。事实上这是错误的，正如以下希腊语和英语的语料所展示的那样。希腊语中① 内嵌动词前面是虚拟式小品词 na；英语中缺少这些情况下的形态上的虚拟语气，但我们发现了简单的现在时形式。

（164） Theli   na   vri   ena imerologio pu   na   exi grapsi enas
       wants SUBJ find a   diary   that SUBJ has written a
       stratigos tou   Nixon, alla dhen thimame   pjos.
       general of.the Nixon but   not I.remember which
       'She wants to find a diary that a general of Nixon's may have written, but I don't remember which (general).'

---

① 感谢詹纳基杜对本节中希腊语例子的判断和讨论。

（165） Psaxnun kapjon pu na milai mia valkaniki glossa, alla
they.seek someone that SUBJ speaks a Balkan language but
dhe ksero pja.
not I.know which
'They're looking for someone who (would) speak(s) a Balkan language, but I don't know which.'

（166） They want to hire someone who speaks a Balkan language, but I don't know which.

希腊语例句只允许将内涵谓词的不定指 DP 宾语解读为 *de dicto*，而英语则有歧义（尽管就目前而言我们只关注狭域的解读）。因此（165）的先行小句只有（167b）中给出的解读（取模内嵌的不定指成分 *a Balkan language* 的辖域，首先必须具有允准截省的宽域），并且不允许（167a）的解读；我将把注意力集中在这种解读的英语示例上——这一节的其余部分，我们可以忽略宽域的解读。

（167） a $\neq \exists_y [\textbf{Balkan-language}_@(y) \wedge \exists_x [\textbf{person}_@(x) \wedge \textbf{speak}_@(x,y) \wedge \textbf{want}_@$
$(\text{they}, \lambda w[\textbf{hire}_w(\text{they},x)])]]$

b $= \exists_y [\textbf{Balkan-language}_@(y) \wedge \textbf{want}_@(\text{they}, \lambda w[\exists_x[\textbf{person}_w(x) \wedge \textbf{speak}_w$
$(x,y) \wedge \textbf{hire}_w(\text{they},x)]])]$

因为在这些情况下，没有一个个体的存在是蕴涵的，所以认为截省 IP 内的代词指称该个体没有意义。然而，这一难题的关键在于代词性成分在内涵语境中的表现。尤其如罗伯茨（Roberts 1989, 1996）所研究的那样，在某些情况下，只要代词所在的句子包含其中一类合适的情态标记词，照应就有可能跨越句子边界。（168）给出了她的一些例句。

（168） a You should buy a lottery ticket$_1$, It$_1$ might be worth a million dollars.

b He wants to marry a Norwegian$_2$. She$_2$ should like the cold.

c If you (should) see a finch$_3$, stop moving. It$_3$ might get scared off.

情态语境的特性同样适用于疑问句（见 Groenendijk 1998, van Rooy 1998）：

（169）a A patient might come in complaining of pressure in the head. What questions should you ask him?

b Where can I find an Italian newspaper, and how much will it cost?

罗伯茨称这种可能性为"情态从属"，并令人信服地表明，这主要是一种语用现象。对情态从属的准确描述在此处并不重要，只是它是可能的——正是这种可能性允许代词可以在截省中使用。（165）和（166）中的截省相当于下列接连的显性表达。

（170）a ... pja   *(na)   milai.
              which SUBJ speaks

b ... which she {should speak/*speaks}.

这些情况下，一些情态成分是必要的。希腊语中，这种情况必须用虚拟式来补充。想必英语缺乏强的虚拟形态，所以必须使用完整的情态。这与（168）标准情况下和疑问句中必须使用某种情态动词来触发情态从属的事实相同（在英语中，只有首句中的不定指成分是非期待的宽域时，照应语才是可行的）：

（171）a You should buy a lottery ticket. #It is worth a million dollars.

b #Where can I find an Italian newspaper, and how much does it cost?

与英语不同，希腊语也存在同样的对比，希腊语中没有可能发生歧义的语料，因为虚拟关系从句的存在要求首句中内涵算子的不定指成分有狭域解读。

（172）Theli   na   pandrefti mia norvigidha pu   na   exei
       he.wants SUBJ marries   a   Norwegian who SUBJ has

polla lefra.
much money
a Prepi na tis aresi to krio.
    it.is.necessary SUBJ *her pleases the cold*
b #Tis aresi to krio.
    her pleases the cold
'He wants to marry a Norwegian who has a lot of money. She {should like/#likes} the cold.'

那么，再回头看（165）和（166）中的截省，内涵语境中代词在先前内嵌语境中获取先行项的能力将对观察到的语料进行解释。因此，截省只是上述（170）删除了 IP 的版本：

（173） a ... pja₂ ~~pro₆~~ ~~na~~ milai t_2.
          which SUBJ speaks
       b. . . which ~~she₆~~ ~~should~~ ~~speak~~ t_2.

它们大致具有（174）中给出的语义 [①]：

（174） ?y[**balkan-language**$_@$(y) ∧ □ **speak**$_w$(g(6),y)] =
λp∃$_y$[**balkan-language**$_@$(y) ∧ p(@) ∧ p = λw′∀ w[w′Rw → **speak**$_w$(g(6), y)]]

该删除将满足焦点条件，以防有先行项可以生成（175）中的公式。

[①] 我在这里使用休斯和克雷斯韦尔（Hughes and Cresswell 1996）给出的标准定义。假设一个模型是一个有序的三元组 M =⟨W, R, V⟩，其中 R 是 W 的一个可及性关系，W 是一个非空的世界集合，V 是命题变项上的一个赋值函数。当且仅当 V 将值 1 赋给 w 中的 p, V(p,w) = 1，当且仅当 V 将值 0 赋给 W 中的 p, V(p,w) = 0。我们将必要运算符 □ 定义为（i）:
    (i) V(□ϕ, w) = ₁ if ∀ w′ [wRw′ → V(ϕ, w′) = ₁], 否则 V(□ϕ, w) = 0
情态从属只是通过情态基础 *f* 来限制 R（即通过将那些世界 w$_i$ 从不在 ∩ *f*(w) 的 R 的范围中排除）。

(175) $\exists_y[\text{balkan-language}_@(y) \wedge \Box \text{ speak}_w(g(6), y)]$

我们可以假设，关系从句中的虚拟语气词提供了英语中形态上不可见的算子□。① 正是被删除的 IP 中存在的虚拟语气词允准了情态从属的照应语，该虚拟语气词才被解读为某种情态算子。

这得出了（164）至（166）中对截省的预期解读，但这样做并不需要声称孤岛本身存在或在截省中缺失的 IP 中得到了重建。相反，作为这些截省意义的一部分，对"需求世界"的适当限制是情态从属关系的副产品。

正如我们所见，带有直陈式关系从句的截省所涉及的 E 类型照应语对语篇功能是敏感的（见（140）和（141）的讨论）。当先行项不能允准跨句照应时，无论是否存在删除，虚拟关系从句中所需要的情态性从属照应都应被排除。我用最清楚的例子来说明这一事实……希腊语中带有虚拟语气关系从句的强调性否定极性词（关于希腊语强调性 NPI 的辖域属性，见 Giannakidou 1998：第四章，Giannakidou 2000）。即使带有情态成分，这类 DP 也不允准跨句照应。

(176) *Dhen ithelan na proslavoun KANENAN pu na milai mia
not wanted.they SUBJ hire anyone that SUBJ speaks a
valkaniki glossa, alla dhen ksero pja.
Balkan language but not I.know which
('*They didn't want to hire anyone who speaks a Balkan language, but I don't know which.'（比较 140b））

(177) *Dhen ithelan na proslavoun KANENAN pu na
not wanted.they SUBJ hire anyone that SUBJ

---

① 稍微简化一点，这就意味着带有虚拟关系从句的句子将有一个类似于（i）的翻译：
(i) $\exists y[\text{balkan-language}_@(y) \wedge \text{want}_@(\text{they}, \lambda w[\exists y[\text{person}_w(x) \wedge \forall w'[wRw' \to \text{speak}_{w'}(x, y)] \wedge \text{hire}_w(\text{they}, x)]])$

更为细致的论述见 Quer 1998。就我的目的而言，□的语义是什么并不十分重要，只要虚拟关系从句和模态从属触发疑问句中的虚拟意义是一样的就可以。

milai mia valkaniki glossa, alla dhen ksero pja na milai.
speaks a   Balkan   language but not   I.know which SUBJ *speaks*
('*They didn't want to hire anyone who speaks a Balkan language, but I don't know which s/he (would) speak(s).' (比较 141b))

综上所述，只要满足制约（E 类型）照应语分布的独立限制条件，就有可能在关系从句中截省一个关联成分；同样，我们发现不需要对截省做出任何特殊说明。较之于各种只有在省略下才有的操作或允许结构同构条件存在例外的方法，这是目前方法的一个非常吸引人的特点。

5.3.2　附加语和句子主语

以上分析可以直接扩展到附加语成分上，因为这些附加语能够引入情态基础，从而限制后续情态算子的赋值。一个典型的实例是条件句中的条件小句（protasis），在让步、原因和时间附加语中也表现出与条件从句相同的特点（事实上，在真实的用法中，后者更为简单，与上文的直陈式关系从句的实例相同）。

（178）　If Ben talks to someone, Abby will be mad, but I don't remember who.

标准的分析是将 *if* 从句视为（可能是隐性的）量化副词的限制（见 Kratzer 1981, de Swart 1991, von Fintel 1994）。这一分析也同样适应于其他附加语（相关讨论与文献见 Kratzer 1998；Giannakidou and Zwarts, 出版中）。这一形式化分析如（179）所示，与上文考察过的实例相类似。

（179）　$\exists x[\mathbf{person}_@ (x) \wedge \forall w[\mathbf{talk\text{-}to}_w(\mathbf{ben}, x) \rightarrow \mathbf{mad}_w(\mathbf{abby})]]$

（178）中的截省具有（180a）中的结构，可解读为（180b）

（180）　a　... who [~~he talks to ___~~]
　　　　b　?x[**person**$_@$(x) ∧ □ **talk-to**$_w$(**ben**, x)]

此处，情态从属关系必须再一次把□的域限制在那些能够在先行项中满足条件顺序的世界中。这一效应可以被诠释为如下句子"who he would have to talk to [to make Abby mad]"，或解读成略显不自然的句子"who he might talk to in the Abby-mad worlds"。有趣的是，虽然本质上我从截省的基本结构中消除了孤岛，但有一个事实仍然存在疑问，那就是似乎没有任何特别自然的方式来显性表达消失内容的意义。这就与上文涉及的关系从句形成了对比，尤其是在带有显性语气标记的语言中，可能存在相关的非省略变化。从这一点上看，我并不清楚这一问题是否应该得到关注，且不讨论理论，这或许仅仅只是另一个语言更倾向于"经济性"解决方案的案例。与之类似的是 E 类型代词，在 E 类型代词中填入某些显性且明确的描述充其量只是有些冗余。由于这一事实并未阻止分析者假定这种描写事实上是构建出来的，在此我将不再对（180）的显性变化所体现的异常之处展开进一步讨论。或许这一异常与英语中的"虚拟式"有关，英语中的"虚拟式"必须与其世界变项的一个显性约束项同现。我们可能假定英语中的"虚拟式"是条件小句中显性先行词所采用的动词形式（不要与出现在谓词如 require 等的补足语成分中的动词形式混淆，它们也常被称为虚拟式），它基于的是带有显性形态标记的语言中的平行形式。无论英语虚拟式在形态上具有怎样的缺陷，这一对比都可以在这样一个事实中体现出来，即在与上文（169）的语境相同的情况下，非情态成分不能支持情态从属关系。

（181） *Where can I find an Italian newspaper$_4$, and how much does it$_4$ cost?

对于句子主语而言，我们有多种选择。在实际的句子主语实例中，我们根本找不到任何原因去假定主语 CP 中的相关成分能够被提取出来，因为这在语义解释上没有任何差别：

（182） [$_{CP}$ That Maxwell killed the judge] was proven, but it's still not clear with what.

由于主语 CP 在现实世界中是真实的（换言之，V(⟦CP⟧, @) = 1），在语义解释上，我们找不到任何原因认为截省具有（183a）的结构，而非（183b）的结构。

（183） a ... with what₂ [[Maxwell killed the judge t₂] was proven].
b ... with what₂ [[Maxwell killed the judge t₂].

事实上，人们经常注意到，前置句子主语倾向于是事实性的（Kiparsky and Kiparksy 1970: 167），但是，作为在斯韦诺纽斯（Svenonius 1994: 77）的研究中被特别指出的事实，它们不需要是事实性的。当这些句子主语不具有事实性时，我们或需要依靠前文所讨论的语篇从属效应，或需要依靠之前所谈到的发生在 CP 基础位置的成分提取，就如在 5.1.3 节中谈及的非句子主语一样。在这一点上，我并不清楚哪一条证据能够帮助我们做出合理的选择，因此，我将暂时不在它们之中做出选择。

5.3.3 并列结构限制条件（二）：并连语中的提取

相似的考虑还可以在并连语提取的分析中起作用，尤其是 VP 并连语的提取，我将自己的关注焦点限定在此，因为这是最具争议并且让人感兴趣的潜在实例（如果在省略部位中，只有一个单一 CP，仅从一个 CP 并连语或与之类似的成分中进行提取能够遵循前文中有关句子主语的处理方法）。可讨论的相关实例如下所示。

（184） a Bob ate dinner and saw a movie that night, but he didn't say which.
b Bob ate dinner and saw a couple of movies that night, but he didn't say how many.
c Bob saw a movie and ate an expensive dinner that night, but he didn't say how expensive.

我将假定以上例句的结构中包含了 VP 并列关系，而非一些附加在 IP 的并列删减操作（考虑到完整形式的句子 *No-one₂ ate dinner and saw a* movie that night 不能够由句子 * No-one$_2$ ate dinner and he$_2$ saw a movie that night 衍生而来；近期的相关讨论与文献见 Winter 1998）。我将进一步假设并列的 VP 的确是孤岛，这是一个时常会引起热议并且得到波斯塔尔（Postal 1998: 第三章）强烈辩护的假设。

基于以上假设，被删除的 IP 不可能是（185）中的 IP，因为这些 IP 与它们的显性对应部分应该具有相同的地位，如（186）。

(185) a ... Which$_1$ [he ate dinner and saw t_1 that night].
 b ... how many$_2$ [he ate dinner and saw t_2 that night].
 c ... how expensive$_3$ [he saw a movie and ate [t'_3 a t_3 dinner] that night].

(186) a ??Which movie$_1$ did Bob eat dinner and see t_1 that night?
 b *How many movies$_2$ did Bob eat dinner and see t_2 that night?
 c *How expensive a dinner$_3$ did Bob see a movie and eat t_3 that night?

针对这一问题，钟等的解决办法（Chung et al. 1995）是通过合并操作允许约束关系进入一个并连语。对于他们而言，(184a) 那种例句在逻辑形式层面具有如（187）所示的结构（假定载体转换取模）：

(187) ... which^x [he ate dinner and saw [a movie]^x that night].

与萌生操作不同，合并被认为对孤岛条件不敏感，所以（184a）中的截省是完全合乎语法的。但这一解释的问题是下列例句也都完全合乎语法。

(188) a I packed up all the dishes and dumped them without telling her where.
 b He sold his farm and moved away, but no one knows where to.
 c Abby quit and got a new job—guess what as!
 d Ben was sitting in the back and playing the trumpet, but I couldn't tell how loudly.

在钟等（Chung et al. 1995）的体系中，对这些截省的解释必须涉及对孤岛条件敏感的萌生操作。

一种替代方案是主张禁止从并连语中进行提取是一个语音形式效应，如像上文所提到的禁止从并连语中进行提取的讨论一样。^①但是这将会让以下的对比更加难以理解——当主语由限定词 no 主导时，所有类型的截省都不可能发生，无论其是否具有显性关联词。

（189） a *No farmer sold his farm and moved to a certain town—I don't remember which.
       b *No one quit and got a new job—guess what as!
       c * Nobody was sitting in the back and playing one of the horns, but I couldn't tell {which/how loudly}.
       d *Not one critic ate dinner and saw a couple of movies that night, but I don't know how many.

如果从并连语中进行提取本身是可能的，那么这些例句应该与下面的例句是一样的：

（190） Which town did no farmer move to?

的确如此，正如前文中（151）至（153）所示，某些包含向下蕴涵 DP 的 IP 截省是可能的：

（191） No one moved to a certain town—guess which!

（189）中的截省是不合法的这一事实为这一难题提供了解决方法。我提出被删除 IP 包含了一个 E 类型的代词，它由 VP 内部的主语所允准。

---

① 构建能够直接验证这一主张的例句有些困难，尤其是我们不清楚语音层面究竟出了什么问题，才使得语句不合法。在（i）中的例子从某种程度上证实了这一主张，并且表明内嵌的不合法提取位置在省略部位并不能够纠正岛条件违反现象。（（ii）中的例子给出了各种控制语料。）

  （i）　*Abby ate a more expensive dinner than Ben saw a movie and then {ate/did}
  （ii） a　Abby ate a more expensive dinner than Ben did.
     b　Abby ate dinner; Ben saw a movie first and then did.

因此，与其将（192a）作为被删除的 IP 用以解释（184a）的截省，我认为被删除的 IP 事实上应该如（192b）所示。

（192） a ... *which [he_6 ate dinner and saw t that night].
　　　　 b ... which [he_6 saw t that night].

这个 IP 能够被删除是为了防止蕴涵（193）的先行项的存在，其中 g(6) 是一个 E 类型代词，如上文所示。

（193） $\exists x[\mathbf{movie}(x) \wedge \mathbf{saw}(g(6), x, \mathbf{that\text{-}night})]$

并且事实上，我们能够从（184a）的第一个句子推断出（193），Bob_6 ate dinner and saw a movie that night。然而，在（189）的实例中，这样的推断完全不具有可行性，因为 E 类型的解释不可行。截省再次与其带有代词的显性对应部分具有了同样的地位：

（194） a Bob ate dinner and saw a movie that night, but he didn't say which he saw.
　　　　 b *No famer sold his farm and moved to a certain town—I don't remember which he moved to.

因此，在这些语境下，截省的可行性是伴随着 E 类型照应的可行性而存在的。这也正确地预测了"合并"和"萌生"操作的例句之间并没有差别：

（195） Ben was sitting in the back and playing the trumpet, but I couldn't tell how loudly (he was playing it).

这些例句也表明给截省的内容强加一个严格的结构同构限制条件会遇到一定的困难。在此，这种限制条件需要放宽至一定程度，以允许一个 VP 去允准对整个 IP 进行删除。然而，这一困难不会发生在现有的解释中，因为不管提供先行项的短语中多少结构被投射，语义条件都能够被满足。

5.4 选择性("弱")孤岛

从选择性孤岛条件中进行提取的截省具有启发性,因为这再次说明截省对孤岛并不是完全免疫。事实上,如我们将要看到的一样,在选择性孤岛中越过隐性关联语的截省,有时会产生一些用任何句法路径都无法解释的偏差。这一事实也为以往相关研究(Kroch 1989; Comorovski 1989; Szabolcsi and Zwarts 1993; Kuno and Takami 1997; Honcoop 1998)所指出的选择性孤岛是语义或语用现象,而不是句法现象这一观点提供了支持(相反观点见 Rizzi 1990, 1994; Manzini 1998)。

截省和选择性孤岛的问题在阿尔伯特(Albert 1993)、绍尔兰(Sauerland 1996)、罗梅罗(Romero 1998)和麦钱特(Merchant 2000c)的研究中已经有过探讨。这里仅对这些研究中已有的结论进行回顾,并指出一些相关语料与截省句法的删除解释路径是相匹配的。

阿尔伯特(Albert 1993)第一个注意到隐性关联语的截省(隐性论元,或者隐性附加语)体现了对选择性孤岛的系统性敏感度。[①] 这里再次列出阿尔伯特关于隐性论元的某些语料,如(196);(197)来自麦钱特(Merchant 2000c)的研究:

(196) a *Nigel never hunts, but I don't remember what.
      b *No one drank, but I can't say which kind of wine.
      c *The new chef refused to bake, but we don't recall what.
      d *No one talked, but it's not clear to whom.
      e *Mitch refused to go to the party, but we can't remember who with.
      f * Reggie avoids reading novels, but I don't know what about.

[①] 带 why 的截省不在此处的考虑范围之内,此类截省具有一些有趣的特征,但这些特征与我们这里所讨论的相去甚远,如包括否定在内的各种变体(She didn't leave, but I don't know why not.)。相关讨论见 Horn 1978: 164-165, Merchant 2000d。

g *It's hard for Megan to dance, but I don't know who with.

h *Mario denied Sally got in a fight, but it's unclear who with.

i *Judy rarely borrows a car, but I can't recall whose.

(197) a *No nurse was on duty, but we don't know when.

b *A nurse is rarely on duty—guess when!

众所周知，从（196）和（197）的语境中提取某些类型的 wh- 表达式是有偏差的（见上面论著中的例子）。令人惊讶的是，这些例子中，作为截省残留部分的 wh- 短语实际上在显性提取下并没有出现偏差。

(198) a What does Nigel never hunt?

b Which kind of wine did no one drink?

c What does Reggie avoid reading novels about?

(199) a When was no nurse on duty?

b When is a nurse rarely on duty

（198）至（199）中的合法提取与（196）至（197）中不合法的截省之间的对比说明钟等人（Chung et al. 1995）关于孤岛敏感性作为萌生操作其中一个属性的解释有问题：在这些情况中，连接算子和萌生语迹的语链应该合乎语法，因为提取是可能的，然而截省仍然有偏差。

并不是所有的显性关联词截省都有偏差（我们之前已经看到过许多相反的例子），特别是在量化副词出现的情况下。考虑一下（200）中的对比，该例源自阿尔伯特（Albert 1993: 1（1））。

(200) a Sonny always eats around noon, but I don't know what.

b *Sonny rarely eats around noon, but I don't know what.

对于这些，我们可以在下列例句中加入平行对比：

(201) a Ralph bought an old boat, but I don't know how old.

b *No one bought an old boat, but I don't know how old.

（202） Jake {always/*rarely} takes his eggs salty—wait till your hear how salty!

理解这些对比的关键在于隐性关联词的辖域属性：米特沃赫（Mittwoch 1982）和其他学者（更多文献和讨论见 Romero 1998: 38—39）指出，隐性论元和附加语在它们的域内总是采用最窄辖域。如果这一论断是正确的，那么这些对比可以通过先行小句中的隐性量化词和截省句中与 wh- 短语相关联的量化词之间存在的辖域平行来加以解释。例如，在（197a）的第一个小句中，对于 *no nurse* 来说，隐性约束时间变项具有窄域，如（203a）所示，但它不具有（203b）中的解读。要想使（197a）中的截省合乎语法就必须采用（203b）那种解读。

（203） a ¬∃x[**nurse**(x) ∧ ∃t[**on-duty**(x, at t)]]
　　　　b ∃t¬∃x[**nurse**(x) ∧ **on duty**(x, at t)]

这遵循焦点条件，罗梅罗（Romero 1998）对此进行了详细论述。正如她所指出：当干预成分不是向下单显调时，截省是可能发生的（如（200a）、（201a）和（202）），因为这些成分与被删除的 IP 中的 E 类型成分（如上文所示）相同。

因此，重要的不一定是被截省的 wh- 短语的类型，而是关联词（不管是显性的还是隐性的）所采取的小句层面（即在模态范围之外）辖域的可能性。这解释了下列各句在判断上的等级性，其残余的 wh- 短语保持恒定（数量短语通常对孤岛条件提取具有高度敏感性）；产生的截省句的合法性取决于先行小句中数量短语采取小句辖域的能力，这反映了在模态从属语境中某些类型的先行项对照应语的允准能力存在差异。

（204） a He wants to marry someone who speaks {a certain number of/??several/*∅} languages, but I don't know how many.
　　　　b She needs to interview someone who has been in {a predetermined number of/??several/??some/*∅} S. American countries—I don't know how many.

    c We'll get reprimanded if {some special number of/*more than one/*some/*many/*Ø} customers complain, but I forgot how many.
    d He wants to marry someone with {a certain amount of/*Ø} money, but he didn't say how much.

总之，本节所讨论的这些对比说明，截省的可接受性条件与辖域平行的要求存在直接关联，这些条件无法仅从结构条件中推导得出。尽管这些条件并不是句法性的，不能很好地展示省略的句法性质，但这一结论与本章提出的删除路径完全相符。

5.5　小结

本章阐述了适用于截省的、以删除为基础的省略理论能够成功地解释第三章中与孤岛和形式同一性效应相关的语料。形式同一性效应直接遵循这一方法，而显著的孤岛不敏感性在一定程度上要求我们对句法孤岛展开重新思考（至少选择性孤岛不管在何种情况下都不是句法性的）。一方面，我认为在截省条件下一大类孤岛条件——那些包含一个命题域的截省——实际上与孤岛属性无关，因为没有理由假定被删除的内容包含了一个与显性孤岛相类似的成分。另一方面，这也留下了一些有趣的效应，必须将这些效应重新分析成语音层面不合法的必要产物。我针对每一种情况都提出了独立的证据，以证明这是一个具有可信性和一致性的选择。

本章的论述主要是想说明，我们需要一个比以往的假定更为多元化的观点去看待孤岛，各种不同语法因素都可能会引起提取偏差。只有通过观察省略部位的提取，我们才能开始确定语法的哪一部分应该对哪种类型的提取限制条件负责。实际上，我们对其中一些问题的看法已经被显性的、具有声音形式的句法所干扰——对省略背后不具有声音形式的结构，即沉默的句法进行研究是一项艰巨的任务，但这可以使我们获益良多。

结　语

　　当前的研究以在对句法和语义中两个探讨得最深入和最吸引人的领域为基础——省略和 wh- 移位。这两个领域积累了数目众多并能让学者产生兴趣的研究问题，但二者的交集——截省，在很大程度上为学者们所忽略。我认为这一忽略是不幸的，尤其在对截省现象进行调查后发现，它是跨语言中广泛存在的现象，比通常研究的省略现象更为普遍，对其进行研究可以为许多长期存在的困惑和问题提供新的启示。

　　我并非纸上谈兵：本研究选取语料的范围比起通常的研究更为广泛，从而涉及了比以往更多的研究问题。许多意想不到且具有理论挑战性的概述被发掘出来，还有很多概述存在研究的困难，未能从其他类型的省略研究中呈现出来。这其中就包括第三章的形式同一性概述和第二章的截省标句词概述。而且，更让人感兴趣的是，第五章表明我们的孤岛条件概念必须在原有基础上重新精炼，通过分布在各种语法成分中的提取的偏差现象，引向更为多元化的孤岛条件观点。

　　需要记住的重要一点是，我并**没有**提出新的焦点条件，用以对文献中广泛讨论的一般焦点条件进行替换，一般焦点条件同样适用于包含和不包含省略部位的结构。一般焦点条件中的**包含**[①] 条件仍然有效，我并没有提

　　[①] "包含"（containment）一词是作者谈论鲁思（Rooth）的"冗余关系 2"（见第 13 页）时采用的术语。Rooth 称它为"支配性的"（dominating），就此处的理论而言，它与"containing"意思相同，即只有当一个 XP_E 是或者被"包含在"一个短语 XP 中，且该短语中有一个合适的先行词 YP_A 时，该 XP_E 才能被删除。作者认为，只界定这种焦点包含条件（如 Rooth 对焦点的探讨）不足以解释省略的事实。我们需要更多的概念，也就是同一性条件。（感谢麦钱特教授与我讨论，并提供相关解释）——译者

出新观点。我所追求的是此类包含条件必须由一个**同一性**条件作为补充，这一同一性条件只应用于省略自身层面，并且对省略部位以外的成分通常不具敏感性。这一经常被认为是具有句法特性的同一性条件，正是我致力于去证明的，我想证明它可以而且应该用与包含条件非常相似（尽管不是完全相同）的术语表达出来。这是基于省略给定得出的同一性条件的基础，并与基于给定性得出的包含条件相关联。

对省略部位的同一条件进行定义和局部化的优势是：通过这一做法，我们能开始构建一个理论，该理论可以将传统意义上省略位置的"允准"要求和"识别"要求连接起来。正如第二章所指出，这些要求既被 E 特征所施加，它是一种给定的局部特征匹配要求（编码为"允准"），同时这些要求又由一个定义明确的语义条件（省略给定性主导的"识别"条件）所施加。

把基于语义同一性得出的省略理论与不发音但具有完整内部句法结构的省略部位相结合不仅是可行的，而且在事实上也是必要的，这是我在研究中竭力证实的观点。正如这里所提出的那样，一个理论能够把以往省略现象研究中的错误二分性暂时搁置：用语义方法对省略进行解释通常被视为要求在省略的部位没有句法结构的参与，同时省略中存在句法因素的证据通常也被认为其解决方法是以句法结构的同一性为基础。但是，我们也看到这些不同的证据事实上根本不存在竞争关系：它具有完美的一致性，并在事实上对句法上活跃且完整的结构予以支持，由于这些结构的先行项存在语义关系，因此它们是不发音的。这一路径两全其美，对困扰狭义方法的问题，以及虽然有时被提出但尚未得到满意解决的问题（比如"载体转换"问题），展现出了深入的洞察力。虽然在很多方面，本研究只是迈出了第一步，但我乐观地认为，本路径在其基本的理论取向上是正确的，我希望它能够灵活地应对其他省略结构所带来的挑战，就像它能够成功地解释截省现象那样。

参考文献

Abney, Steven (1987). 'The English Noun Phrase in its Sentential Aspect', Ph. D. thesis, MIT.

Ackema, Peter, and Neeleman, Ad (1998). 'Optimal Questions'. *Natural Language and Linguistic Theory*, 16: 443–490.

Adger, David, and Quer, Josep (1997). 'Subjunctives, Unselected Embedded Questions, and Clausal Polarity Items', in K. Kusumoto (ed.), *Proceedings of the 27th Meeting of the North Eastern Linguistic Society*. Amherst, MA: Graduate Student Linguistic Society, 1–15.

Aissen, Judith (1992). 'Topic and Focus in Mayan'. *Language*, 68: 43–80.

Akmajian, Adrian (1970). 'The Role of Focus in the Interpretation of Anaphoric Expressions', in S. Anderson and P. Kiparsky (eds.), *A Festschrift for Morris Halle*. New York: Holt, Rinehart and Winston, 215–226.

Albert, Chris (1993). 'Sluicing and Weak Islands', MS, University of California, Santa Cruz.

Alexiadou, Artemis, and Anagnostopoulou, Elena (1998). 'Parametrizing AGR: Word Order, V-Movement, and EPP-Checking'. *Natural Language and Linguistic Theory*, 16: 491–539.

Anagnostopoulou, Elena (1994). 'Clitic Dependencies in Greek', Ph. D. thesis, Salzburg University.

——van Riemsdijk, Henk, and Zwarts, Frans (1997) (eds.), *Materials on Left Dislocation*. Amsterdam: John Benjamins.

Anderson, Stephen (1996). 'How to Put your Clitics in their Place'. *Linguistic Review*, 13: 165–191.

——(2000). 'Towards an Optimal Account of Second Position Phenomena', in J. Dekkers, F. van der Leeuw, and J. van de Weijer (eds.), *Optimality Theory: Phonology, Syntax, and Acquisition*. Oxford: Oxford University Press, 302–333.

Aoun, Joseph (1985). *A Grammar of Anaphora*. Cambridge, MA: MIT Press.

——and Benmamoun, Elabbas (1998). 'Minimality, Reconstruction, and PF Movement'. *Linguistic Inquiry*, 29: 569–597.

——Hornstein, Norbert, Lightfoot, David, and Weinberg, Amy (1987). 'Two Types of Locality', *Linguistic Inquiry*, 18: 537–577.

Asher, Nicholas, Hardt, Daniel, and Busquets, Joan (1997). 'Discourse Parallelism, Scope, and Ellipsis', in A. Lawson (ed.), *Proceedings of the 7th Conference on Semantics and Linguistic Theory*. Ithaca, NY: Cornell University, 19–36.

Baker, C. L., and Brame, Michael (1972). ' "Global Rules": A Rejoinder'. *Language*, 48: 51–75.

Baltin, Mark, and Postal, Paul (1996). 'More on Reanalysis Hypotheses'. *Linguistic Inquiry*, 27: 127–145.

Bayer, Josef (1984). 'COMP in Bavarian'. *Linguistic Review*, 3: 209–274.

——(1996). *Directionality and Logical Form: On the Scope of Focussing Particles and Wh-in-Situ*. Dordrecht: Kluwer.

Bechhofer, Robin (1976a). 'Reduced Wh-Questions', in J. Hankamer and J. Aissen (eds.), *Harvard Studies in Syntax and Semantics 2*. Harvard University, Cambridge, MA, 31–67.

——(1976b). 'Reduction in Conjoined Wh-Questions', in J. Hankamer and J. Aissen (eds.), *Harvard Studies in Syntax and Semantics 2*. Harvard University, Cambridge, MA, 68–120.

——(1977). 'A Double Analysis of Reduced Wh-Questions', in J. Kegl *et al* (eds.), *Proceedings of the 7th Meeting of the North Eastern Linguistic Society*. Amherst, MA: Graduate Student Linguistic Society, 19–31.

Beck, Sigrid (1996). 'Quantified Structures as Barriers for LF Movement'. *Natural Language Semantics*, 4: 1–56.

Beghelli, Filippo, and Stowell, Tim (1997). 'Distributivity and Negation: The Syntax of *Each* and *Every*', in A. Szabolcsi (ed.), *Ways of Scope Taking*. Dordrecht: Kluwer, 71–107.

Bennis, Hans (1986). *Gaps and Dummies*. Dordrecht: Foris.

——(1995). 'The Meaning of Structure: The *wat voor* Construction Revisited', in M. den Dikken and K. Hengeveld (eds.), *Linguistics in the Netherlands 1995*. Amsterdam: J. Benjamins, 25–36.

—— Corver, Norbert, and den Dikken, Marcel (1998). 'Predication in Nominal Phrases'. *Journal of Comparative Germanic Linguistics*, 1: 85–117.

den Besten, Hans (1978). 'On the Presence and Absence of Wh-Elements in Dutch Com-

paratives'. *Linguistic Inquiry*, 9: 641–671.
——(1989). 'Studies in West Germanic Syntax'. Ph. D. thesis, Tilburg University.
Bissell, Teal (1999). 'Antecedent-Contained Deletion and Null Pronominal Variables'. MA thesis, University of California, Santa Cruz.
Bolinger, Dwight (1972). *Degree Words*. The Hague: Mouton.
——(1978). 'Asking More than One Thing at a Time', in H. Hiz (ed.), *Questions*. Dordrecht: Reidel, 107–150.
Borer, Hagie (1981). 'Parametric Variation in Clicic Constructions'. Ph. D. thesis, MIT.
Bošković, Željko (1995). 'Participle Movement and Second Position Cliticization in Serbo-Croatian'. *Lingua*, 96: 245–266.
Bouton, Lawrence (1970). 'Antecedent-Contained Proforms', in *Papers from the 6th Regional Meeting of the Chicago Linguistic Society*. Chicago: Chicago Linguistic Society, 154–167.
Bresnan, Joan (1971). 'A Note on the Notion "Identity of sense anaphora" '. *Linguistic Inquiry*, 2: 589–597.
——(1972). 'Theory of Complementation in English Syntax'. Ph. D. thesis, MIT.
——(1975). 'Comparative Deletion and Constraints on Transformations'. *Linguistic Analysis*, 1: 25–74.
——(1977a). 'Transformations and Categories in Syntax', in R. E. Butts and J. Hintikka (eds.), *Basic Problems in Methodology and Linguistics*. Dordrecht: Reidel, 261–282.
——(1977b). 'Variables in the Theory of Transformations', in P. Culicover, T. Wasow, and A. Akmajian (eds.), *Formal Syntax*. New York: Academic Press, 157–196.
Brody, Michael (1995). *Lexico-Logical Form: A Radically Minimalist Theory*. Cambridge, MA: MIT Press.
Browne, Wayles (1972). 'Conjoined Question Words and a Limitation on English Surface Structures'. *Linguistic Inquiry*, 3: 222–226.
——(1974). 'On the Problem of Enclitic Placement in Serbo-Croatian', in R. D. Brecht and C. V. Chvany (eds.), *Slavic Transformational Syntax*. Ann Arbor: Michigan Slavic Materials, 36–52.
Browning, M. A. (1987). 'Null Operator Constructions'. Ph. D. thesis, MIT.
——(1996). 'CP Recursion and *that-t* Effects'. *Linguistic Inquiry*, 27: 237–255.
Büring, Daniel (1995). 'On the Base Position of Embedded Clauses in German'. *Linguistische Berichte*, 159: 370–380.
——(1997). *On the Meaning of Topic and Focus: The 59th Street Bridge Accent*. London: Routledge.

——(forthcoming). 'Lee's Phrase It! Focus, Word Order, and Prosodic Phrasing in German Double Object Constructions'. in G. Müller and W. Sternefeld (eds.), *Competition in Syntax*. Amsterdam: John Benjamins.

——and Hartmann, Katharina (1999). 'V$_3$ or not V$_3$?' MS, University of California, Santa Cruz and University of Frankfurt.

Chao, Wynn (1987). 'On Ellipsis'. Ph. D. thesis, University of Massachusetts, Amherst.

——and Sells, Peter (1983). 'On the Interpretation of Resumptive Pronouns', in P. Sells and C. Jones (eds.), *Proceedings of the 13th Meeting of the North Eastern Linguistic Society*. Amherst, MA: Graduate Student Linguistic Society, 47–61.

de Chene, Brent (1995). 'Complementizer-Trace Effects and the ECP'. *Geneva Generative Papers*, 3: 1–4.

Chierchia, Gennaro (1995). *Dynamics of Meaning*. Chicago: University of Chicago Press.

Chomsky, Noam (1972). 'Some Empirical Issues in the Theory of Transformational Grammar', in S. Peters (ed.), *The Goals of Linguistic Theory*. Englewood Cliffs, NJ: Prentice-Hall, 63–130.

——(1973). 'Conditions on Transformations', in S. Anderson and P. Kiparsky (eds.), *A Festschrift for Morris Halle*. New York: Holt, Rinehart, and Winston, 232–286.

——(1981). *Lectures on Government and Binding*. Dordrecht: Foris.

——(1986a). *Barriers*. Cambridge, MA: MIT Press.

——(1986b). *Knowledge of Language*. New York: Praeger.

——(1995). *The Minimalist Program*. Cambridge, MA: MIT Press.

——(1998). 'Minimalist Inquiries: The Framework'. MS, MIT.

——and Lasnik, Howard (1977). 'Filters and Control'. *Linguistic Inquiry*, 8: 425–504.

—— ——(1993). 'Principles and Parameters Theory', in J. Jacobs, A. von Stechow, W. Sternefeld, and T. Vennemann (eds.), *Syntax: An International Handbook of Contemporary Research*. Berlin: De Gruyter, 506–570.

Chung, Sandra, Ladusaw, William, and McCloskey, James (1995). 'Sluicing and Logical Form'. *Natural Language Semantics*, 3: 239–282.

Cinque, Guglielmo (1990). *Types of A' Dependencies*. Cambridge, MA: MIT Press.

——(1993). 'On the Position of Modifiers in the Romance NP'. MS, University of Venice.

——(1999). *Adverbs and Functional Heads: A Cross-Linguistic Perspective*. Oxford: Oxford University Press.

Collins, Chris (1997). *Local Economy*. Cambridge, MA: MIT Press.

参考文献

Comorovski, Ileana (1989). 'Discourse-Linking and the *wh*-Island Constraint', in J. Carter and R.-M. Déchaine (eds.), *Proceedings of the 19th Meeting of the North Eastern Linguistic Society*. Amherst, MA: Graduate Student Linguistic Society, 78–96.
——(1996). *Interrogative Phrases and the Syntax-Semantics Interface*. Dordrecht: Kluwer.
Corver, Norbert (1990). 'The Syntax of Left Branch Constructions'. Ph. D. thesis, Tilburg University.
Culicover, Peter (1992). 'The Adverb Effect: Evidence against ECP Accounts of the *that-t* Effect', in A. Schafer (ed.), *Proceedings of the 23rd Meeting of the North Eastern Linguistic Society*. Amherst, MA: Graduate Student Linguistic Society, 97–111.
——and McNally, Louise (1998) (eds.), *The Limits of Syntax* (Syntax and Semantics 29). San Diego: Academic Press.
Dalrymple, Mary, Shieber, Stuart, and Pereira, Fernando (1991). 'Ellipsis and Higher-Order Unification'. *Linguistics and Philosophy*, 14: 399–452.
Deacon, Terrence (1997). *The Symbolic Species: The Co-Evolution of Language and the Brain*. New York: Norton.
Delin, Judy (1992). 'Properties of *it*-Cleft Presuppositions'. *Journal of Semantics*, 9: 289–306.
Demirdache, Hamida (1991). 'Resumptive Chains in Restrictive Relatives, Appositives, and Dislocation Structures'. Ph. D. thesis, MIT.
Déprez, Viviane (1994). 'A Minimal Account of the *that-t* Effect', in G. Cinque, J. Koster, J.-Y. Pollock, L. Rizzi, and R. Zanuttini (eds.), *Paths towards Universal Grammar: Studies in Honor of Richard S. Kayne*. Washington: Georgetown University Press, 121–135.
Diesing, Molly (1992). *Indefinites*. Cambridge, MA: MIT Press.
den Dikken, Marcel (1995). 'Binding, Expletives, and Levels'. *Linguistic Inquiry*, 26: 347–354.
den Dikken, Marcel, Meinunger, André, and Wilder, Chris (1998). 'Pseudoclefts and Ellipsis', in A. Alexiadou, N. Fuhrhop, P. Law, and U. Kleinhenz (eds.), *ZAS Working Papers in Linguistics 10*. Berlin: Zentrum für Allgemeine Sprachwissenschaft, 21–71.
Dobrovie-Sorin, Carmen (1993). *The Syntax of Romanian*. The Hague: Mouton.
Doron, Edit (1982). 'The Syntax and Semantics of Resumptive Pronouns'. *Texas Linguistics Forum 19*. Austin: University of Texas, 1–48.
——(1990). 'V-Movement and VP-Ellipsis'. MS, Hebrew University of Jerusalem.

——(1999). 'V-Movement and VP-Ellipsis', in S. Lappin and E. Benmamoun (eds.), *Fragments: Studies in Ellipsis and Gapping*. Oxford: Oxford University Press, 124–140.

Dowty, David (1991). 'Thematic Proto-Roles and Argument Selection'. *Language*, 67: 547–619.

Drubig, Bernhard (1994). 'Island Constraints and the Syntactic Nature of Focus and Association with Focus'. *Arbeitspapiere des Sonderforschungsbereichs*, 340/51.

Dryer, Matthew (1997). Handout from Typology Class, Linguistic Society of America Institute, Cornell University, Ithaca, NY.

Engdahl, Elisabet (1984). 'Parasitic Gaps, Resumptive Pronouns, and Subject Extractions'. MS, University of Wisconsin, Madison.

Erceschik-Shir, Nomi (1977). *On the Nature of Island Constraints*. Bloomington: IN: Indiana University Linguistics Club.

——(1992). 'Resumptive Pronouns in Islands', in H. Goodluck and M. Rochemont (eds.), *Island Constraints: Theory, Acquisition, and Processing*. Dordrecht: Kluwer, 89–108.

Evans, Gareth (1980). 'Pronouns'. *Linguistic Inquiry*, 11: 337–362.

Fanselow, Gisbert (1990). 'Scrambling as NP-Movement', in G. Grewendorf and W. Sternefeld (eds.), *Scrambling and Barriers*. Amsterdam: John Benjamins, 113–140.

Farkas, Donka (1981). 'Quantifier Scope and Syntactic Islands', in R. Hendrick, C. Masek, and M. F. Miller (eds.), *Papers from the 17th Regional Meeting of the Chicago Linguistic Society*. Chicago: Chicago Linguistic Society, 59–66.

——(1985). *Intensional Descriptions and the Romance Subjunctive Mood*. New York: Garland.

Fernald, Theodore (1994). 'On the Nonuniformity of the Individual- and Stage-Level Effects'. Ph. D. thesis, University of California, Santa Cruz.

——(2000). *Predicates and Temporal Arguments*. Oxford: Oxford University Press.

Fiengo, Robert, and May, Robert (1994). *Indices and Identity*. Cambridge, MA: MIT Press.

——Huang, C.-T. James, Lasnik, Howard, and Reinhart, Tanya (1988). 'The Syntax of wh-in-situ', in H. Borer (ed.), *Proceedings of the 7th West Coast Conference on Formal Linguistics*. Stanford, CA: Center for the Study of Language and Information, 81–98.

Fillmore, Charles (1965). *Indirect Object Constructions in English and the Ordering of Transformations*. The Hague: Mouton.

——(1986). 'Pragmatically Contolled Zero Anaphora', in V. Nikiforidou, M. VanClay,

M. Niepokuj, and D. Feder (eds.), *Proceedings of the 12th Meeting of the Berkeley Linguistic Society*. Berkeley, CA: Berkeley Linguistic Society, 95−107.

Finer, Daniel (1997). 'Contrasting A′-Dependencies in Selayarese'. *Natural Language and Linguistic Theory*, 15: 677−728.

von Fintel, Kai (1994). 'Restrictions on Quantifier Domains'. Ph. D. thesis, University of Massachusetts, Amherst.

Fox, Danny (1999). 'Reconstruction, Binding Theory, and the Interpretation of Chains'. *Linguistic Inquiry*, 30: 157−196.

——(2000). *Economy and Semantic Interpretation*. Cambridge, MA: MIT Press.

Fukaya, Teruhiko (1998). 'On So-called "Sluicing" in Japanese'. MS, University of Southern California.

Gazdar, Gerald, Pullum, Geoffrey, Sag, Ivan, and Wasow, Thomas (1982). 'Coordination and Transformational Grammar'. *Linguistic Inquiry*, 13: 663−676.

—— Klein, Ewan, Pullum, Geoffrey, and Sag, Ivan (1985). *Generalized Phrase Structure Grammar*. Cambridge, MA: Harvard University Press.

Giannakidou, Anastasia (1997). 'The Landscape of Polarity Items'. Ph. D. thesis, University of Groningen.

——(1998). *Polarity Sensitivity as (Non)veridical Dependency*. Amsterdam: John Benjamins.

—— (2000). 'Negative . . . Concord?', *Natural Language and Linguistic Theory*, 18: 457−523.

——and Merchant, Jason (1996). 'On the Interpretation of Null Indefinite Objects in Greek', in J. Veloudis and M. Karali (eds.), *Studies in Greek Linguistics 17,* Thessaloniki: University of Thessaloniki, 141−155.

—— ——(1998). 'Reverse Sluicing in English and Greek'. *Linguistic Review*, 15: 233−256.

——and Stavrou, Melita (1999). 'Nominalization and Ellipsis in the Greek DP'. *Linguistic Review*, 16: 295−333.

——and Zwarts, Frans (forthcoming), 'Temporal/Aspectual Operators and (Non)veridicality', in A. Giorgi, J. Higginbotham, and F. Pianesi (eds.), *Tense and Mood Selection*. Oxford: Oxford University Press.

Ginzburg, Jonathan (1992). 'Questions, Queries and Facts: A Semantics and Pragmatics for Interrogatives'. Ph. D. thesis, Stanford University.

——(in preparation). 'Questions and the Semantics of Dialogue'. MS, Hebrew University of Jerusalem.

Goodluck, Helen, and Rochemont, Michael (1992) (eds.), *Island Constraints: Theory, Acquisition, and Processing*. Dordrecht: Kluwer.

Grewendorf, Günther, and Poletto, Cecilia (1991). 'Die Cleft-Konstruktion im Deutschen, Englischen, und Italienischen', in G. Fanselow and S. Felix (eds.), *Strukturen und Merkmale syntaktischer Kategorien*. Tübingen: Gunter Narr, 174–216.

Grinder, John, and Postal, Paul (1971). 'Missing Antecedents'. *Linguistic Inquiry*, 2: 269–312.

Groenendijk, Jeroen (1998). 'On Modal Subordination in Questions'. MS, Institute for Logic, Language, and Computation, University of Amsterdam.

——and Stokhof, Martin (1991). 'Dynamic Predicate Logic'. *Linguistics and Philosophy*, 14: 39–100.

Groenendijk, Jeroen and Stokhof, Martin (1997). 'Questions', in J. van Benrhem and A. ter Meulen (eds.), *Handbook of Logic and Language*. Amsterdam: Elsevier, 1055–1124.

Grohmann, Kleanthes (1998). 'Syntactic Inquiries into Discourse Restrictions on Multiple Interrogatives'. *Groninger Arbeiten zur germanistischen Linguistik*, 42: 1–60.

——(2000). 'Prolific Peripheries: A Radical View from the Left'. Ph. D. thesis, University of Maryland, College Park.

Grosu, Alexander (1973). 'On the Nonunitary Nature of the Coordinate Structure Constraint'. *Linguistic Inquiry*, 4: 88–92.

——(1974). 'On the Nature of the Left Branch Condition'. *Linguistic Inquiry*, 5: 308–319.

——(1981). *Approaches to Island Phenomena*. Amsterdam: North-Holland.

—— (1994). *Three Studies in Locality and Case*. London: Routledge.

—— and Landman, Fred (1998). 'Strange Relatives of the Third Kind'. *Natural Language Semantics*, 6: 125–170.

Gunlogson, Christine (in preparation). 'Rising Declaratives'. Ph. D. thesis, University of California, Santa Cruz.

Gussenhoven, Carlos (1983). *On the Grammar and Semantics of Sentence Accents*. Dordrecht: Foris.

Haïk, Isabelle (1987). 'Bound VPs that Need to Be'. *Linguistics and Philosophy*, 10: 503–530.

Hankamer, Jorge (1979). *Deletion in Coordinate Structures*. New York: Garland.

——and Sag, Ivan (1976). 'Deep and Surface Anaphora'. *Linguistic Inquiry*, 7: 391–428.

参考文献

Hardt, Daniel (1992). 'VP Ellipsis and Semantic Identity', in S. Berman and A. Hestvik (eds.), *Proceedings of the Stuttgarter Ellipsis Workshop. Arbeitspapiere des Sonderforschungsbereichs*, 340/29.

——(1993). 'Verb Phrase Ellipsis: Form, Meaning, and Processing'. Ph. D. thesis, University of Pennsylvania.

——(1999). 'Dynamic Interpretation of Verb Phrase Ellipsis'. *Linguistics and Philosophy*, 22: 185–219.

Harris, Zelig (1965). 'Transformational Theory'. *Language*, 41: 363–401.

——(1968). *Mathematical Structures of Language*. New York: Interscience Publishers.

Haspelmath, Martin (1997). *Indefinite Pronouns*. Oxford: Oxford University Press.

Heim, Irene (1982). 'The Semantics of Definite and Indefinite NPs'. Ph. D. thesis, University of Massachusetts, Amherst.

——(1990). 'E-Type Pronouns and Donkey Anaphora'. *Linguistics and Philosophy*, 13: 137–177.

——and Krazter, Angelika (1998). *Semantics in Generative Grammar*. London: Blackwell.

Hendriks, Petra, and de Hoop, Helen (forthcoming). 'Optimality Theory Semantics'. *Linguistics and Philosophy*.

Higgins, F. Roger (1973). 'The Pseudo-Cleft Construction in English'. Ph. D. thesis, MIT.

Hirschberg, Julia, and Ward, Gregory (1991). 'Accent and Bound Anaphora'. *Cognitive Linguistics*, 2: 101–121.

Hirschbühler, Paul (1978). 'The Syntax and Semantics of WH-constructions', Ph. D. thesis, University of Massachusetts, Amherst.

——(1981). 'The Ambiguity of Iterated Multiple Questions', *Linguistic Inquiry*, 12: 135–146.

Hoekstra, Eric (1992). 'On the Parametrisation of Functional Projections in CP', in A. Schafer (ed.), *Proceedings of the 23rd Meeting of the North Eastern Linguistic Society*. Amherst, MA: Graduate Student Linguistic Society, 191–204.

Hoekstra, Jarich (1993). 'The Split CP Hypothesis and the Frisian Complementizer System'. MS, Fryske Akademy, Ljouwert.

——(1995). 'Preposition Stranding and Resumptivity in West Germanic', in H. Haider, S. Olsen, and S. Vikner (eds.), *Studies in Comparative Germanic Syntax*. Dordrecht: Kluwer, 95–118.

——and Marácz, László (1989). 'The Position of Inflection in West Germanic'. *Working*

Papers in Scandinavian Syntax, 44: 75-88.

Höhle, Tilman (1983). 'Akzent in Fragewörtern'. MS, Universität Tübingen.

Hoji, Hajime (forthcoming). 'Surface and Deep Anaphora, Sloppy Identity, and Experiments in Syntax', in A. Barss and T. Langendoen (eds.), *Explaining Linguistics*. London: Blackwell.

——and Fukaya, Teruhiko (1999). 'Stripping and Sluicing in Japanese and Some Implications', in S. Bird, A. Carnie, J. Haugen, and P. Norquest (eds.), *Proceedings of the 18th West Coast Conference on Formal Linguistics*. Somerville, MA: Cascadilla Press, 145-158.

Holmberg, Anders, and Platzack, Christer (1995). *The Role of Inflection in Scandinavian Syntax*. Oxford: Oxford University Press.

Honcoop, Martin (1998). 'Dynamic Excursions on Weak Islands'. Ph. D. thesis, Leiden University.

Honegger, Mark (1996). 'A Phonological Account of the "Adverb Effect" and *That-t* Violations', in *Proceedings of the 1996 Meeting of the Formal Linguistics Society of Mid-America*.

Horn, Laurence (1978). 'Remarks on Neg-Raising', in Peter Cole (ed.), *Pragmatics* (Syntax and Semantics 9). New York: Academic Press, 129-220.

Hornstein, Norbert (1995). *Logical Form: From GB to Minimalism*. Oxford: Blackwell.

——(1999). 'Movement and Control'. *Linguistic Inquiry*, 30: 69-96.

——and Weinberg, Amy (1981). 'Case Theory and Preposition Stranding'. *Linguistic Inquiry*, 12: 55-91.

Huang, C.-T. James (1982). 'Logical Relations in Chinese and the Theory of Grammar'. Ph. D. thesis, MIT.

——(1984). 'On the Determination and Reference of Empty Pronouns'. *Linguistic Inquiry*, 15: 531-574.

Hudson, R. A. (1972). 'Why it is that that *that that* Follows the Subject is Impossible'. *Linguistic Inquiry*, 3: 116-118.

Hughes, G. E., and Cresswell, M. J. (1996). *A New Introduction to Modal Logic*. London: Routledge.

Inoue, Kazuko (1976). *Kenkei bunpoo to nihongo*. Tokyo: Taishukan.

——(1978). *Nihongo-no bunpoo kisoku*. Tokyo: Taishukan.

Jacobson, Pauline (1992). 'Antecedent-Contained Deletion in a Variable Free Semantics', in C. Barker and D. Dowty (eds.), *Proceedings from the 2nd Conference on Semantics and Linguistic Theory*. Columbus, OH: Ohio State University, 193-214.

Johnson, Kyle (1997). 'What VP Ellipsis Can Do, and What it Can't, but Not Why'. MS, University of Massachusetts, Amherst.

Johnston, Michael (1994). 'The Semantics of Adverbial Adjuncts'. Ph. D. thesis, University of California, Santa Cruz.

Joseph, Brian (1980). 'Recovery of Information in Relative Clauses: Evidence from Greek and Hebrew'. *Journal of Linguistics,* 16: 237−244.

Kamp, Hans (1981). 'A Theory of Truth and Discourse Representation', in J. Groenendijk, M. Stokhof, and T. Janssen (eds.), *Formal Methods in the Study of Language.* Amsterdam: Mathematisch Centrum, 277−322.

Karttunen, Lauri, and Peters, Stanley (1979). 'Conventional Implicature', in C.-K. Oh and D. Dineen (eds.), *Presupposition* (Syntax and Semantics 11). New York: Academic Press, 1−56.

Kayne, Richard (1981). 'On Certain Differences between French and English'. *Linguistic Inquiry,* 12: 349−371.

——(1994). *The Antisymmetry of Syntax.* Cambridge, MA: MIT Press.

Keenan, Ed. (1971). 'Names, Quantifiers, and the Sloppy Identity Problem', *Papers in Linguistics,* 4: 211−232.

Kehler, Andrew (1993). 'The Effect of Establishing Coherence in Ellipsis and Anaphora Resolution', in *Proceedings of the 31st Annual Meeting of the Association for Computational Linguistics,* Columbus, OH, 62−69.

——(2000). *Coherence, Reference, and the Theory of Grammar.* Stanford, CA: Center for the Study of Language and Information.

Kennedy, Christopher (1997). 'VP-Deletion and "Nonparasitic" Gaps'. *Linguistic Inquiry,* 28: 697−707.

——(1999). *Projecting the Adjective: The Syntax and Semantics of Gradability and Comparison.* New York: Garland.

——(2000). 'Comparative Deletion and Optimality in Syntax'. MS, Northwestern University.

——and Merchant, Jason (1997). 'Attributive Comparatives and Bound Ellipsis'. Linguistics Research Center Report LRC-97−3, University of California, Santa Cruz.

—— ——(1999). 'Attributive Comparatives and the Syntax of Ellipsis', in F. Corblin, C. Dobrovie-Sorin, and J.-M. Marandin (eds.), *Empirical Issues in Formal Syntax and Semantics 2: Selected Papers from the Colloque de Syntaxe et Sémantique de Paris.* The Hague: Thesus, 233−253.

—— ——(2000*a*). 'Attributive Comparative Deletion'. *Natural Language and Linguistic*

Theory, 18: 89–146.

—— ——(2000*b*). 'The Case of the "Missing CP" and the Secret Case'. MS, Northwestern University and University of Groningen.

Kester, Ellen-Petra (1996). 'The Nature of Adjectival Inflection'. Ph. D. thesis, University of Utrecht.

Kiss, Katalin (1998). 'Identificacional Focus versus Information Focus'. *Language,* 74: 245–273.

Kiparksy, Paul, and Kiparsky, Carol (1970). 'Face', in M. Bierwisch and K. E. Heidolph (eds.), *Progress in Linguistics.* The Hague: Mouton, 143–173.

Kizu, Mika (1997). 'A Note on Sluicing in Wh-in-Sicu Languages'. MS, McGill University.

Klein, Maarten (1977). 'Appositionele constructies in het Nederlands', Ph. D. thesis, Nijmegen University.

Klein, Wolfgang (1993). 'Ellipse', in J. Jacobs, A. von Stechow, W. Sternefeld, and T. Vennemann (eds.), *Syntax: An International Handbook of Contemporary Research.* Berlin: De Gruyter, 763–799.

Kluender, Robert (1998). 'On the Distinction between Strong and Weak Islands: A Processing Perspective', in P. Culicover and L. McNally (eds.), *The Limits of Syntax* (Syntax and semantics 29). San Diego: Academic Press, 241–279.

Koopman, Hilda, and Sportiche, Dominique (1982). 'Variables and the Bijection Principle'. *Linguistic Review,* 2: 139–160.

Kratzer, Angelika (1981). 'On the Notional Category of Modality', in H. Eikmeyer and H. Rieser (eds.), *Words, Worlds, and Contexts.* Berlin: De Gruyter, 38–74.

——(1998). 'Scope or Pseudoscope? Are there Wide-Scope Indefinites?', in S. Rothstein (ed.), *Events and Grammar.* Dordrecht: Kluwer, 163–196.

Kroch, Anthony (1989). 'Amount Quantification, Referentiality, and Long *wh*-Movement'. MS, University of Pennsylvania.

Kuna, Susumu, and Takami, Ken-ichi (1997). 'Remarks on Negative Islands'. *Linguistic Inquiry,* 28: 553–576.

Kuroda, S.-Y. (1968). Review of C. Fillmore, *Indirect Object Constructions in English and the Ordering of Transformations. Language,* 44: 374–378.

Kuwabara, K. (1996). 'Multiple Wh-Phrases in Elliptical Clauses and Some Aspects of Clefts with Multiple Foci', in *Formal Approaches to Japanese Linguistics 2* (MIT Working Papers in Linguistics 29). Cambridge, MA, 97–116.

Ladusaw, William, and Dowty, David (1988). 'Toward a Nongrammatical Account of

Thematic Roles', in W. Wilkins (ed.), *Thematic Relations* (Syntax and Semantics 21). San Diego: Academic Press, 62-74.

Lakoff, George (1968). 'Pronouns and Reference'. Bloomington, IN: Indiana University Linguistics Club. Appears in McCawley (1976), 273-335.

——(1970). 'Global Rules'. *Language*, 46: 627-639.

——(1972). 'The Arbitrary Basis of Transformational Grammar'. *Language*, 48: 76-87.

Langendoen, D. Terence (1970). *Essentials of English Grammar*. New York: Holt, Rinehart, and Winston.

Lappin, Shalom (1996). 'The Interpretation of Ellipsis', in S. Lappin (ed.), *The Handbook of Contemporary Semantic Theory*. Oxford: Oxford University Press, 145-175.

Lappin, Shalom and Francez, Nissim (1994). 'E-Type Pronouns, I-Sums, and Donkey Anaphora'. *Linguistics and Philosophy*, 17: 391-428.

Lasnik, Howard (1999). 'On Feature Strength: Three Minimalist Approaches to Overt Movement'. *Linguistic Inquiry*, 30: 197-217.

——and Saito, Marmoru (1984). 'On the Nature of Proper Government'. *Linguistic Inquiry*, 15: 235-289.

Legendre, Géraldine (1999). 'Morphological and Prosodic Alignment at Work: The Case of South-Slavic Clitics', in K. Shahin, S. Blake, and E.-S. Kim (eds.), *Proceedings of the 17th West Coast Conference on Formal Linguistics*. Stanford, CA: Center for the Study of Language and Information, 436-450.

——(2000), 'Morphological and Prosodic Alignment of Bulgarian Clitics', in J. Dekkers, F. van der Leeuw, and J. van de Weijer (eds.), *Optimality Theory: Phonology, Syntax, and Acquisition*. Oxford: Oxford University Press.

Levin, Beth, and Rappaport, Malka (1988). 'What to Do with θ-Roles', in W. Wilkins (ed.), *Thematic Relations* (Syntax and Semantics 21). San Diego: Academic Press.

Levin, Lori (1982). 'Sluicing: A Lexical Interpretation Procedure', in J. Bresnan (ed.), *The Mental Representation of Grammatical Relations*. Cambridge, MA: MIT Press, 590-654.

Lewis, G. L. (1967). *Turkish Grammar*. Oxford: Oxford University Press.

Lightfoot, David (2000). 'Ellipses as Clitics', in K. Schwabe and N. Zhang (eds.), *Ellipsis in Conjunction*. Tübingen: Niemeyer, 79-94.

Lo beck, Anne (1991). 'The Phrase Structure of Ellipsis', in S. Rothstein (ed.), *Perspectives on Phrase Structure* (Syntax and Semantics). San Diego: Academic Press, 81-103.

——(1995). *Ellipsis: Functional Heads, Licensing, and Identification*. Oxford: Oxford

University Press.

——(1999). 'VP Ellipsis and the Minimalist Program: Some Speculations and Proposals', in S. Lappin and E. Benmamoun (eds.), *Fragments: Studies in Ellipsis and Gapping*. Oxford: Oxford University Press, 98–123.

López, Luis (2000). 'Ellipsis and Discourse-Linking'. *Lingua*, 110: 183–213.

Maling, Joan, and Sprouse, Rex (1995). 'Structural Case, Specifier-Head Relations, and the Case of Predicate NPs', in H. Haider, S. Olsen, and S. Vikner (eds.), *Studies in Comparative Germanic Syntax*. Dordrecht: Kluwer, 167–186.

McCawley, James (1976) (ed.), *Notes from the Linguistic Underground* (Syntax and Semantics 7). New York: Academic Press.

——(1988). *The Syntactic Phenomena of English*. Chicago, IL: Chicago University Press.

——(1998). *The Syntactic Phenomena of English*. 2nd edn. Chicago, IL: Chicago University Press.

McCloskey, James (1979). *Transformational Syntax and Model Theoretic Semantics: A Case Study in Modern Irish*. Dordrecht: Reidel.

——(1986). 'Inflection and Conjunction in Modern Irish'. *Natural Language and Linguistic Theory*, 4: 245–281.

——(1990). 'Resumptive Pronouns, A'-Binding, and Levels of Representation in Irish', in R. Hendrick (ed.), *The Syntax of the Modern Celtic Languages* (Syntax and Semantics 23). San Diego: Academic Press, 199–248.

——(1991*a*). 'Clause Structure, Ellipsis and Proper Government in Irish'. *Lingua*, 85: 259–302.

——(1991*b*). 'A Note on Agreement and Coordination in Old Irish', in S. Chung and J. Hankamer (eds.), *A Festschrift for William Shipley*. Santa Cruz, CA: Syntax Research Center, 105–114.

——(1991*c*). '*There, It,* and Agreement'. *Linguistic Inquiry*, 22: 563–567.

——(1996). 'On the Scope of Verb Raising in Irish'. *Natural Language and Linguistic Theory*, 14: 47–104.

——(1997). 'Resumptive Pronouns'. Handout from talk presented at meeting of the Netherlands Institute for Advanced Study, Wassenaar.

——(2000). 'Quantifier Float and *Wh*-Movement in an Irish English'. *Linguistic Inquiry*, 31: 57–84.

——and Hale, Ken (1984). 'On the Syntax of Person-Number Inflection in Modern Irish'. *Natural Language and Linguistic Theory*, 1: 487–533.

McDaniel, Dana (1989). 'Partial and Multiple Wh-Movement'. *Natural Language and Linguistic Theory,* T: 565–604.

——McKee, Cecile, and Bernstein, Judy (1998). 'How Children's Relatives Solve a Problem for Minimalism'. *Language,* 74: 308–334.

Manzini, Rita (1998). 'A Minimalist Theory of Weak Islands', in P. Culicover and L. McNally (eds.), *The Limits of Syntax* (Syntax and Semantics 29). San Diego: Academic Press, 185–210.

——and Roussou, Anna (2000). 'A Minimalist Theory of A-Movement and Control'. *Lingua,* 110: 409–447.

Marvin, Tatjana (1997). 'Wh-Movement in the Generative Theory with Special Reference to Slovene'. Diploma thesis, University of Ljubljana.

May, Robert (1991). 'Syntax, Semantics, and Logical Form', in A. Kasher (ed.), *The Chomskyan Turn.* Oxford: Blackwell, 334–359.

Merchant, Jason (1998). ' "Pseudosluicing": Elliptical Clefts in Japanese and English', in A. Alexiadou, N. Fuhrhop, P. Law, and U. Kleinhenz (eds.), *ZAS Working Papers in Linguistics 10.* Berlin: Zentrum für Allgemeine Sprachwissenschaft, 88–112.

——(1999*a*). 'E-Type A′-Traces under Sluicing', in K. Shahin, S. Blake, and E.-S. Kim (eds.), *Proceedings of the 17th West Coast Conference on Formal Linguistics.* Stanford, CA: Center for the Study of Language and Information, 478–492.

——(1999*b*). 'Resumptive Operators, Case, and Sluicing'. Paper presented at the 75th annual meeting of the Linguistic Society of America, Los Angeles, CA.

——(1999*c*). 'On the Form of Resumptive-Binding Operators'. MS, University of California, Santa Cruz.

——(2000*a*). 'Economy, the Copy Theory, and Antecedent-Contained Deletion'. *Linguistic Inquiry,* 31: 566–575.

——(2000*b*). 'Antecedent-Contained Deletion in Negative Polarity Items'. *Syntax,* 3: 144–150.

Merchant, Jason (2000c). 'LF Movement and Islands in Greek Sluicing'. *Journal of Greek Linguistics,* 1: 39–62.

——(2000*d*). 'Why No(t)?' MS, University of Groningen.

——(forthcoming). 'Swiping in Germanic', in J.-W. Zwart and W. Abraham (eds.), *Studies in Germanic Syntax.* Amsterdam: John Benjamins.

Mikkelsen, Line (forthcoming). 'Expletive Subjects in Subject Relative Clauses', in J.-W. Zwart and W. Abraham (eds.), *Studies in Germanic Syntax.* Amsterdam: John Benjamins.

Milapides, Michael (1990). 'Aspects of Ellipsis in English and Greek'. Ph. D. thesis, University of Thessaloniki.

Miller, Philip (1991). 'Clitics and Constituents in Phrase Structure Grammar'. Ph. D. thesis, Utrecht University.

Mittwoch, Anita (1982). 'On the Difference between "Eating" and "Eating Something": Activities vs. Accomplishments'. *Linguistic Inquiry*, 13: 113−121.

Moxey, L. M., and Sandford, A. J. (1993). *Communicating Quantities*. Hillsdale NJ: Erlbaum, Hove.

Müller, Gereon (1995). *A-Bar Syntax*. Berlin: Mouton de Gruyter.

——and Sternefeld, Wolgang (1993). 'Improper Movement and Unambiguous Binding'. *Linguistic Inquiry*, 24: 461−507.

Munn, Alan (1993). 'Topics in the Syntax and Semantics of Coordinate Structures'. Ph. D. thesis, University of Maryland, College Park.

Niño, María-Eugenia (1997). 'The Multiple Expression of Inflectional Information and Grammatical Architecture', in F. Corblin *et al.* (eds.), *Empirical Issues in Formal Syntax and Semantics: Selected Papers from the Colloque de Syntaxe et Sémantique de Paris 1995*. Bern: Peter Lang, 127−147.

Nishigauchi, Taisuke (1986). 'Quantification in Syntax'. Ph. D. thesis, University of Massachusetts, Amherst.

——(1998). ' "Multiple sluicing" in Japanese and the Functional Nature of *Wh*-Phrases'. *Journal of East Asian Linguistics*, 7: 121−152.

Nishiyama, Kunio, Whitman, John, and Yi, Eun-Young (1996). 'Syntactic Movement of Overt Wh-Phrases in Japanese and Korean'. *Japanese/Korean Linguistics 5*. Stanford, CA: Center for the Study of Language and Information, 337−351.

Oppenrieder, Wilhelm (1991). 'Preposition Stranding im Deutschen? Da will ich niches von hören!', in G. Fanselow and S. Felix (eds.), *Strukturen und Merkmale syntaktischer Kategorien*. Tilbingen: Gunter Narr, 159−173.

Partee, Barbara, and Bach, Emmon (1981). 'Quantification, Pronouns, and VP Anaphora', in J. Groenendijk, M. Stokhof, and T. Janssen (eds.), *Formal Methods in the Study of Language*. Amsterdam: Mathematisch Centrum, 445−481.

Perlmutter, David (1971). *Deep and Surface Structure Constraints in Syntax*. New York: Holt, Rinehart, and Winston.

Pesetsky, David (1982). 'Paths and Categories'. Ph. D. thesis, MIT.

——(1987). 'Wh-in-situ: Movement and Unselective Binding', in E. Reuland and A. ter Meulen (eds.), *The Representation of (In)definiteness*. Cambridge, MA: MIT Press,

98–129.

——(1998*a*). 'Some Optimality Principles of Sentence Pronunciation', in P. Barbosa, D. Fox, P. Hagstrom, M. McGinnis, and D. Pesetsky (eds.), *Is the Best Good Enough?* Cambridge, MA: MIT Press, 337–383.

——(1998*b*). 'Phrasal Movement and its Kin'. MS, MIT.

Pollard, Carl, and Sag, Ivan (1994). *Head-Driven Phrase Structure Grammar*. Chicago: University of Chicago Press.

Pollmann, T. (1975). 'Een regel die subject en copula deleert?' *Spektator*, 5: 282–292.

Postal, Paul (1992). 'The Status of the Coordinate Structure Constraint'. MS, IBM.

——(1996). 'Islands'. Paper presented at Western Conference on Linguistics 96, University of California, Santa Cruz. Revised version to appear in M. Baltin and C. Collins (eds.), *The Handbook of Syntactic Theory*. Oxford: Blackwell.

——(1998). *Three Investigations of Extraction*. Cambridge, MA: MIT Press.

Potts, Christopher (1999). 'Vehicle Change and Anti-Pronominal Contexts'. MS, New York University.

Potsdam, Eric (1998). *Syntactic Issues in the English Imperative*. New York: Garland.

Prince, Ellen (1978). 'A Comparison of WH-clefts and IT-clefts in Discourse', *Language*, 54: 883–906.

——(1990). 'Syntax and Discourse: A Look at Resumptive Pronouns', in *Proceedings of the 16th Meeting of the Berkeley Linguistic Society*. Berkeley, CA: Berkeley Linguistics Society, 482–497.

Progovac, Ljiljana (1999). 'Events and Economy of Coordination'. *Syntax*, 2: 141–159.

Prüst, Hub (1993). 'Gapping and VP Anaphora'. Ph. D. thesis, University of Amsterdam.

——and Scha, Remko (1990*a*). 'VP Ellipsis Induces Clausal Parallelism', in R. Bok-Bennema and P. Coopmans (eds.), *Linguistics in the Netherlands 1990*. Dordrecht: Foris, 123–132.

——(1990*b*). 'A Discourse Perspective on Verb Phrase Anaphora', in M. Stokhof and L. Torenvliet (eds.), *Proceedings of the 7th Amsterdam Colloquium*. Institute for Logic, Language, and Information, University of Amsterdam, 451–474.

——van den Berg, Martin, and Scha, Remko (1994). 'Discourse Grammar and Verb Phrase Anaphora'. *Linguistics and Philosophy*, 17: 261–327.

Pullum, Geoffrey (1991). *The Great Eskimo Vocabulary Hoax and Other Irreverent Essays on the Study of Language*. Chicago: University of Chicago Press.

——and Zwicky, Arnold (1997). 'Licensing of Prosodic Features by Syntactic Rules: The Key to Auxiliary Reduction'. Paper presented at the annual meeting of the Linguistic Society of America, Chicago.

Puskás, Genoveva (1999). *Word Order in Hungarian: The Syntax of A'-positions*. Amsterdam: John Benjamins.

Quer, Josep (1998). 'Mood at the Interface'. Ph. D. thesis, Utrecht University.

Quine, W. V. O. (1960). *Word and Object*. Cambridge, MA: MIT Press.

Quirk, R., Greenbaum, S., Leech, G., and Svartvik, J. (1972). *A Grammar of Contemporary English*. London: Seminar Press.

Reinhart, Tanya (1995). 'Interface Strategies'. OTS working papers 95-102, Utrecht University.

Reinhart, Tanya (1997). 'Quantifier Scope: How Labor is Divided between QR and Choice Functions'. *Linguistics and Philosophy*, 20: 335-397.

Reis, Marga (1985). 'Satzeinleitende Strukturen im Deutschen: Über COMP, Haupt- und Nebensätze, *w*-Bewegung und die Doppelkopfanalyse', in W. Abraham (ed.), *Erklärende Syntax des Deutschen*. Tubingen: Günter Narr, 271-311.

van Riemsdijk, Henk (1978). *A Case Study in Syntactic Markedness: The Binding Nature of Prepositional Phrases*. Dordrecht: Foris.

——(1983). 'The Case of German Adjectives', in F. Heny and B. Richards (eds.), *Linguistic Categories: Auxiliaries and Related Puzzles 1*. Dordrecht: Reidel, 223-252.

——(1997). 'Left Dislocation', in E. Anagnostopoulou *et al.* (1997), 1-12.

Rizzi, Luigi (1990). *Relativized Minimality*. Cambridge, MA: MIT Press.

——(1994). 'Argument/Adjunct (A)symmetries', in G. Cinque, J. Koster, J.-Y. Pollock, L. Rizzi, and R. Zanuttini (eds.), *Paths towards Universal Grammar: Studies in Honor of Richard S. Kayne*. Washington: Georgetown University Press, 367-376.

——(1995). 'The Fine Structure of the Left Periphery'. MS, University of Geneva.

Roberts, Craige (1989). 'Modal Subordination and Pronominal Anaphora in Discourse'. *Linguistics and Philosophy*, 12: 683-721.

——(1996). 'Anaphora in Intensional Contexts', in S. Lappin (ed.), *The Handbook of Contemporary Semantic Theory*. Oxford: Blackwell, 215-246.

Rodman, Robert (1976). 'Scope Phenomena, "Movement Transformations", and Relative Clauses', in B. Partee (ed.), *Montague Grammar*. New York: Academic Press, 165-176.

Romero, Maribel (1997*a*). 'Recoverability Conditions for Sluicing', in F. Corblin *et al.* (eds.), *Empirical Issues in Formal Syntax and Semantics: Selected Papers from the Colloque de Syntaxe et Sémantique de Paris 1995*. Bern: Peter Lang, 193-216.

——(1997*b*). 'The Correlation between Scope Reconstuction and Connectivity Effects', in E. Curtis, J. Lyle, and G. Webster (eds.), *Proceedings of the 16th West Coast Conference in Formal Linguistics*. Stanford, CA: Center for the Study of Language and Information, 351−366.

——(1998). 'Focus and Reconstruction Effects in Wh-Phrases'. Ph. D. thesis, University of Massachusetts, Amherst.

Rooth, Mats (1985). 'Association with Focus'. Ph. D. thesis, University of Massachusetts, Amherst.

——(1992*a*). 'Ellipsis Redundancy and Reduction Redundancy', in S. Berman and A. Hestvik (eds.), *Proceedings of the Stuttgarter Ellipsis Workshop*. Arbeitspapiere des Sonderforschungsbereichs 340, No. 29.

——(1992*b*). 'A Theory of Focus Interpretation'. *Natural Language Semantics,* 1: 75−116.

——(1996). 'Focus', in S. Lappin (ed.), *The Handbook of Contemporary Semantic Theory*. Oxford: Blackwell, 271−297.

van Rooy, Rob (1998). 'Modal Subordination in a Dynamic Semantics'. MS, Institute for Logic, Language, and Computation, University of Amsterdam.

Rosen, Carol (1976). 'Guess What About?', in A. Ford, J. Reighard, and R. Singh (eds.), *Papers from the 6th Meeting of the North Eastern Linguistic Society*. Montreal: Montreal Working Papers in Linguistics, 205−211.

Ross, John R. (1967). 'Constraints on Variables in Syntax'. Ph. D. thesis, MIT.

——(1969). 'Guess Who?', in R. Binnick, A. Davison, G. Green, and J. Morgan (eds.), *Papers from the 5th Regional Meeting of the Chicago Linguistic Society*. Chicago: Chicago Linguistic Society, 252−286.

——(1986). *Infinite Syntax! Norwood*, NJ: Ablex.

Roussou, Anna (1998). 'Features and Subject Dependencies: *that-t* Phenomena Revisited'. MS, University of Wales, Bangor.

Rudin, Catherine (1985). *Aspects of Bulgarian Syntax: Complementizers and Wh-Constructions*. Columbus, OH: Slavica Publishers.

Rullmann, Hotze (1995). 'Maximality in the Semantics of WH-Constructions'. Ph. D. thesis, University of Massachusetts, Amherst.

Ruys, Eddy (1992). 'The Scope of indefinites'. Ph. D. thesis, Utrecht University.

Safir, Ken (1999). 'Vehicle Change and Reconstruction in A'-Chains'. *Linguistic Inquiry*, 30: 587−620.

Sag, Ivan (1976*a*). 'Deletion and Logical Form'. Ph. D. thesis, MIT.

——(1976*b*). 'A Note on Verb Phrase Deletion'. *Linguistic Inquiry, 7:* 664−671.

——and Fodor, Janet D. (1994). 'Extraction without Traces', in *Proceedings of the 13th West Coast Conference on Formal Linguistics*. Stanford, CA: Center for the Study of Language and Information, 365–384.

Sauerland, Uli (1996). 'Guess How?', in J. Costa, J. Goedemans, and R. van Vijver (eds.), *Proceedings of the 4th Conference of the Student Organization of Linguistics in Europe*. Leiden: Student Organization of Linguistics in Europe, 297–309.

——(1998). 'The Meaning of Chains'. Ph. D. thesis, MIT.

Schwabe, Kerstin (2000). 'Coordinate Ellipsis and Information Structure', in K. Schwabe and N. Zhang (eds.), *Ellipsis in Conjunction*. Tübingen: Niemeyer, 247–269.

Schwarzschild, Roger (1999). 'Giveness, AvoidF, and Other Constraints on the Placement of Accent'. *Natural Language Semantics*, 7: 141–177.

Sells, Peter (1984). 'Syntax and Semantics of Resumptive Pronouns'. Ph. D. thesis, University of Massachusetts, Amherst.

Shieber, Stuart, Pereira, Fernando, and Dalrymple, Mary (1996). 'Interactions of Scope and Ellipsis'. *Linguistics and Philosophy*, 19: 527–552.

Shimoyama, Junko (1995). 'On "Sluicing" in Japanese', MS, University of Massachusetts, Amherst.

Shlonksy, Ur (1988). 'Complementizer-Cliticization in Hebrew and the Empty Category Principle'. *Natural Language and Linguistic Theory*, 6: 191–205.

von Stechow, Arnim (1996). 'Against LF Pied-Piping'. *Natural Language Semantics*, 4: 57–110.

Suñer, Margarita (1998). 'Resumptive Restrictive Relatives: A Crosslinguistic Perspective'. *Language*, 74: 335–364.

Svenonius, Peter (1994). 'Dependent Nexus: Subordinate Predication Structures in English and the Scandinavian Languages'. Ph. D. thesis, University of California, Santa Cruz.

de Swart, Henriëtte (1991). 'Adverbs of Quantification: A Generalized Quantifier Approach'. Ph. D. thesis, University of Groningen.

Swingle, Kari (1995). 'On the Prosody and Syntax of Right Node Raising'. Qualifying paper, University of California, Santa Cruz.

Szabolcsi, Anna, and Zwarts, Frans (1993). 'Weak Islands and Algebraic Semantics for Scope Taking'. *Natural Language Semantics*, 1: 235–284.

Takahashi, Daiko (1994). 'Sluicing in Japanese'. *Journal of East Asian Linguistics*, 3: 265–300.

Takami, Ken-ichi (1992). *Preposition Stranding: From Syntactic to Functional Analyses*.

Berlin: Mouton de Gruyter.

Tancredi, Chris (1990). 'Not Only *Even*, but Even *Only*'. MS, MIT.

——(1992). 'Deletion, Deaccenting, and Presupposition'. Ph. D. thesis, MIT.

Taraldsen, Knut Tarald (1986). '*Som* and the Binding Theory', in L. Hellan and K. Koch Christensen (eds.), *Topics in Scandinavian Syntax*. Dordrecht: Reidel, 149–184.

Tomioka, Satoshi (1995). '[Focus]$_F$ Restricts Scope: Quantifiers in VP Ellipsis', in M. Simons and T. Galloway (eds.), *Proceedings of the 5th Conference on Semantics and Linguistic Theory*, Ithaca, NY: Cornell University, 328–345.

——(1996). 'On the Mismatch between Variable Binding and Sloppy Identity', in J. Camacho, L. Choueiri, and M. Watanabe (eds.), *Proceedings of the 14th West Coast Conference on Formal Linguistics*. Stanford, CA: Center for the Study of Language and Information, 541–556.

——(1997). 'Focusing Effects and NP Interpretation in VP Ellipsis'. Ph. D. thesis, University of Massachusetts, Amherst.

——(1999). 'A Sloppy Identity Puzzle'. *Natural Language Semantics*, 7: 217–241.

Trissler, Susanne (1993). 'P-Stranding im Deutschen', in F.-J. d'Avis *et al.* (eds.), *Extraktion im Deutschen l* 247–291. Arbeitspapiere des Sonderforschungsbereichs, 340/34.

Vat, Jan (1981). 'Left Dislocation, Connectedness, and Reconstruction'. *Groninger Arbeiten zur germanistischen Linguistik,* 20. Reprinted in Anagnostopoulou *et al.* (1997), 67–92.

Vikner, Sten (1991). 'Relative *der* and other C^0 Elements in Danish'. *Lingua*, 84: 109–136.

——(1995). *Verb Movement and Expletive Subjects in the Germanic Languages.* Oxford: Oxford University Press.

Wahba, Wafaa Abdel-Faheem Barran (1984). 'Wh-Constructions in Egyptian Arabic'. Ph. D. thesis, University of Illinois, Urbana-Champaign.

Webelhuth, Gert (1992). *Principles and Parameters of Syntactic Saturation.* Oxford: Oxford University Press.

Wilder, Chris (1995). 'Some Properties of Ellipsis in Coordination'. *Geneva Generative Papers*, 2: 23–61.

Williams, Edwin (1977). 'Discourse and Logical Form'. *Linguistic Inquiry*, 8: 103–139.

——(1984). '*There-Insertion*'. *Linguistic Inquiry*, 15: 131–153.

——(1986). 'A Reassignment of the Functions of LF'. *Linguistic Inquiry*, 17: 265–299.

Wiltschko, Martina (1993). 'ProPPs im Deutschen'. MA thesis, Universität Wien.

Winkler, Susanne (1997). 'Ellipsis and Information Structure in English and German: The Phonological Reduction Hypothesis'. *Arbeitspapiere des Sonderforschungsbereichs*, 340/121.

Winter, Yoad (1997). 'Choice Functions and the Scopa! Semantics of indefinites'. *Linguistics and Philosophy*, 20: 399−467.

——(1998). 'Flexible Boolean Semantics'. Ph. D. thesis, Utrecht University.

vanden Wyngaerd, Guido, and Zwart, Jan-Wouter (1991). 'Reconstruction and Vehicle Change', in F. Drijkoningen and A. van Kemenade (eds.), *Linguistics in the Netherlands 1991*. Amsterdam: John Benjamins, 151−160.

—— ——(1999). 'Antecedent-Contained Deletion as Deletion', in R. van Bezooijen and R. Kager (eds.), *Linguistics in the Netherlands 1999*. Amsterdam: John Benjamins, 203−216.

Zwart, Jan-Wouter (1993). 'Dutch Syntax: A Minimalist Approach'. Ph. D. thesis, University of Groningen.

语言索引

所有索引所标页码为英文版页码，即本汉译版的边码。

A

Akan 阿坎语 2
Amharic 阿姆哈拉语 79 注 ①
Arabic 阿拉伯语 131
    Egyptian 埃及语 130 注 ①
    Moroccan 摩洛哥语 94, 99

B

Basque 巴斯克语 90–91, 94, 100
Bavarian 巴伐利亚语 67–69, 77
Brabants 布拉班特语 170–171
Bulgarian 保加利亚语 65–66, 94, 97, 109–110, 168

C

Catalan 加泰罗尼亚语 94, 97, 151, 216
Chinese 汉语 84
Czech 捷克语 90–91, 94, 96, 100, 132, 143–144, 168

D

Dagaare 达加尔语 2
Danish 丹麦语 62–63, 64 注 ①, 68, 77, 92–93, 123
Dutch 荷兰语 20–21, 46, 62–63, 74–75, 78, 79–80, 94–95, 110–113, 123–124, 145, 151, 163, 169–174, 180–182

E

East Asian languages 东亚语言 197
English 英语 2, 8–9, 22, 41–42, 43–46, 56–59, 63–65, 70, 72, 78, 86–88, 92, 102, 104, 112–115, 117–124, 127–130, 132–136, 141 注 ②, 150–151, 153, 164–169, 170, 172, 174–196, 198–203, 205–206, 209–218, 221–228

F

Finnish 芬兰语 2, 90–91, 102, 103
Flemish, West 佛兰德语，西部 145
French 法语 92 首个注 ①, 94, 98, 216
Frisian 弗里斯兰语 74–75, 78–80, 92–93, 95 注 ②, 102, 123, 145

G

German 德语 22–23, 42–44, 46–49, 51–53, 62–63, 78, 89–91, 94, 95 注 ①②, 100, 102–105, 108–109, 110–113, 123–124, 125, 132, 136–141, 151, 153, 156, 161, 170, 173–174, 197
    另见 Swiss German
Germanic 日耳曼语 92, 123
Greek 希腊语 43, 557 末个注 ①, 90–91, 94, 100, 102–105, 110–113, 126–127, 132, 144–145, 153–156, 168, 172 注 ①, 196–197, 216–220

H

Hebrew 希伯来语 80, 94, 99, 130
Hindi 印地语 46, 48–49, 82 注 ①, 84–85, 90–91, 100 注 ①

Hungarian 匈牙利语 81-82, 84, 90-91, 100 注 ①, 102, 103, 125-126

I

Icelandic 冰岛语 92-93

Irish 爱尔兰语 46, 49-50, 71, 76, 80, 130-131, 196 注 ①, 198

Italian 意大利语 94, 99

J

Japanese 日语 79 注 ①, 84, 90, 110-112, 116

K

Korean 朝鲜语 84

L

Lezgian 列兹金语 102, 103

Luxemburgish 卢森堡语 67

M

Macedonian 马其顿语 65-66

N

Norwegian 挪威语 64 注 ①, 68-69, 77, 92-93, 123

O

Old Irish 古爱尔兰语 196 注 ①

P

Persian 波斯语 94, 97

Polish 波兰语 90-91, 94, 96, 100, 102-106, 132, 143, 168

R

Romance 罗曼语 187, 196

Romanian 罗马尼亚语 20, 125-126

Russian 俄语 90-91, 94, 96, 100, 102-106, 132, 142-143

S

Scandinavian 斯堪的纳维亚语 62, 92, 102

Serbo-Croatian 塞尔维亚-克罗地亚语 65-66, 94, 97, 100

Slavic 斯拉夫语 65, 142-144, 196

Slovene 斯洛文尼亚语 65-66, 76, 78, 80, 90-91, 94, 97, 100

Spanish 西班牙语 94, 98, 130 注 ①, 151

Swedish 瑞典语 92-93, 123

Swiss German 瑞士德语 94 注 ①, 95 注 ①, 141 注 ②

T

Turkish 土耳其语 84-85, 100 注 ①, 103, 110-112

Tzotzil 索西语 50 注 ①

W

West Flemish 西佛兰德语，见 Flemish, West

Y

Yiddish 意第绪语，依地语 94, 95-96

姓名索引

A

Abney, S. 阿布尼 166, 182
Ackema, P. 阿克玛 112
Adger, D. 阿杰 44
Aghaei, B. 阿盖伊 97
Agouraki, Y. 阿古拉基 94, 144
Aissen, J. 艾森 50 注 ①
Akmajian, A. 阿克马健 216
Albert, C. 阿尔伯特 149, 162, 226-227
Alexiadou, A. 亚历克西娅杜 94, 187
Aloni, M. 阿洛尼 99
Anagnostopoulou, E. 阿纳格诺斯托普洛 94, 187
Anderson, S. 安德森 66, 72 注 ①
Aoun, J. 奥恩 146, 153, 290
Asher, N. 阿舍 4, 17, 26
Avrutin, S. 阿夫鲁京 96, 142

B

Bach, E. 巴赫 216 注 ①
Baker, C. L. 贝克 29 首个注 ①, 34 注 ①, 114-115, 193
Baltin, M. 巴尔廷 102
Bayer, J. 拜尔 67, 141, 153-158
Bechhofer, R. 贝克霍弗 65, 111 注 ①
Beck, S. 贝克 47 注 ①
Beghelli, L. 贝盖利 154 注 ①
Benmamoun, E. 本马莫恩 146
Bennani-Meziane, M. 本纳尼-梅齐亚纳 99

Bennis, H. 本尼斯 74, 167 末个注 ①
Bernstein, J. 伯恩斯坦 135
Besten, H. den 贝森 74
Bhatt, R. 巴特 48, 82 注 ①, 100 注 ①
Bissell, T. 比斯尔 130 注 ①
Bolinger, D. 博林格 112, 164, 203
Bošković, Ž. 博斯科维奇 66
Bouton, L. 布顿 129
Brame, M. 布雷姆 29 首个注 ①, 34 注 ⓪, 114-115, 193
Bresnan, J. 布雷斯南 183, 200 注 ①, 216
Brody, M. 布罗迪 204
Browne, W. 布朗 65, 111 注 ①
Browning, M. 布朗宁 135 注 ①, 183
Büring, D. 布林 13, 48, 94, 158
Busquets, J. 布斯克茨 4, 17, 26

C

Chao, W. 赵 146, 160
Chene, B. de 舍纳 183-184
Chierchia, G. 基耶尔基亚 207
Chomsky, N. 乔姆斯基 4, 24, 56, 64 注 ①, 73, 114, 115, 161 注 ①, 183-184, 187-188, 193
Chung, S. 钟 5, 6, 33-34, 88, 123, 146-152, 174, 185, 194, 223-224, 227
Cinque, G. 桑克 77, 148, 173
Cocchi, G. 科基 99
Collins, C. 柯林斯 188

Comorovski, C. 科莫罗夫斯基 203, 226
Corver, N. 科尔韦尔 95, 163, 166, 167 末个注 ①, 169–170, 180–182
Cresswell, M. 克雷斯韦尔 219 注 ①
Culicover, P. 库利科韦尔 183

D

Dalrymple, M. 达尔林普尔 26, 160
Damir, M. 达米尔 99
Danopoulos, K. 达诺普洛斯 94
Delin, J. 德林 119
Demirdache, H. 德米尔达赫 141 注 ②
Déprez, V. 德普雷 183
Dianova, S. 迪亚诺娃 97, 109
Diesing, M. 迪辛 192–193
Dikken, M. den 迪肯 34 注 ①, 59 注 ①, 167 末个注 ①, 191
Dobrovie-Sorin, C. 多布罗维耶-索林 20, 125
Doron, E. 多伦 71, 99, 146
Dowty, D. 道蒂 35
Drubig, B. 德吕比 179
Dryer, M. 德莱尔 92

E

Elordieta, A. 埃洛迪埃塔 100
Engdahl, E. 恩达尔 184
Erteschik-Shir, N. 埃尔特斯基克-希尔 115–116, 119
Evans, G. 埃文斯 207, 212

F

Fanselow, G. 范泽洛 47
Farkas, D. 法卡斯 81, 156, 216
Fernald, T. 弗尔纳德 192
Féry, C. 费里 98
Fiengo, R. 菲恩戈 7, 11, 13, 16 注 ①, 17, 24–25, 29 首个注 ①, 129, 154, 160, 191, 200 注 ①, 204–206

Filip, H. 菲利普 96
Fillmore, C. 菲尔莫尔 34 注 ①, 119
Finer, D. 芬纳 130
Fintel, K. von 芬特尔 221
Fodor, J. 福多尔 197
Fox, D. 福克斯 4, 17, 20, 29 末个注 ①, 32, 99, 149, 191, 214
Francez, N. 弗朗西斯 207
Fukaya, T. 深谷 9 注 ①, 84, 151

G

Gazdar, G. 加兹达尔 197
Gerbrandy, J. 格布兰迪 75, 95
Giannakidou, A. 詹纳基杜 24, 80 注 ②, 94, 110 注 ①, 111 注 ①, 126, 144, 153 注 ①, 168 注 ①, 196, 204, 216, 220, 221
Ginzburg, J. 金兹伯格 40, 54, 200 注 ①
Godjevac, S. 戈杰瓦茨 97
Grate, D. 格拉特 110 注 ①
Grewendorf, G. 格雷文多夫 125
Grinder, J. 格林德 216
Groenendijk, J. 格罗嫩迪克 122, 207, 218
Grohmann, K. 格罗曼 114
Grosu, A. 格罗苏 20, 125, 134 注 ①, 135 注 ①, 163, 177, 193, 195–198
Gunlogson, C. 贡洛森 64
Gussenhoven, C. 古森霍芬 95 注 ①
Gutierrez, R. 古铁雷斯 98

H

Haan, G. de 汉恩 92
Haeberli, E. 黑伯利 94 注 ①
Haïk, I. 海克 69, 199 注 ①
Hale, K. 黑尔 196 注 ①
Hankamer, J. 汉卡默 119, 216
Hardt, D. 哈尔特 4, 16 注 ①, 17, 23, 26, 115 注 ①, 160

Harris, Z. 哈里斯 167 首个注①
Hartmann, K. 哈特曼 158
Haspelmath, M. 哈斯佩尔玛斯 175 注①
Heim, I. 海姆 61, 147, 192, 207
Hendriks, H. 亨德里克斯 95, 169
Hendriks, P. 亨德里克斯 26, 95
Higgins, F. R. 希金斯 59 注①
Hirschberg, J. 赫希伯格 15
Hirschbühler, P. 赫希比勒 58 注①, 92 首个注①, 98
Hoeksema, J. 霍克西马 95, 101
Hoekstra, E. 胡克斯特拉 183
Hoesktra, J. 胡克斯特拉 69, 74–75, 92, 95 注①, 124, 141, 145
Höhle, T. 霍勒 51
Hoji, H. 保司 8 注①, 84
Hollebrandse, B. 霍利布兰德斯 95
Holmberg, A. 霍姆伯格 73
Honcoop, M. 洪科普 162, 226
Honegger, M. 霍尼格 183
Hoop, H. de 胡普 26
Horn, L. 霍恩 226 注①
Hornstein, N. 霍恩斯坦 102, 114, 183, 189
Huang, J. 黄 5, 197, 200 注①
Hudson, R. 赫德森 183
Hughes, G. 休斯 219 注①

I

Inoue, K. 井上 84
Ito, J. 伊藤 64 注①

J

Jacobson, P. 雅各布森 160
Johnson, K. 约翰逊 13, 58 注①, 113 注①, 195
Johnston, M. 约翰斯顿 20

K

Kamp, H. 坎普 147, 192

Karttunen, L. 卡尔图宁 120, 147
Kayne, R. 凯恩 79 注①, 102
Keenan, E. 基南 2
Kehler, A. 凯勒 15 注①
Kennedy, C. 肯尼迪 24, 29 末个注①, 60 注③, 69, 72, 113, 117–118, 163, 165 注①, 167–169, 173, 180, 181–182, 204
Kester, E.-P. 凯斯特 134, 171–173
Kiparksy, P. 塞浦路斯 222
Kiss, K. 基斯 122, 126
Kizu, M. 木津 84
Klein, E. 克莱因 197
Klein, M. 克莱因 65, 116, 120
Klein, W. 克莱因 22, 80 注②
Kluender, R. 克鲁德 5
Koopman, H. 库普曼 71
Kratzer, A. 克拉策 61, 221
Krizhanskaya, D. 克里扎斯卡娅 96
Kroch, A. 克罗赫 226
Kuno, S. 库诺 162, 198 注①, 226
Kuroda, S.-Y. 黑田 34 注①
Kuwabara, K. 桑原 84

L

Labelle, M. 拉贝尔 98
Ladusaw, W. 拉杜索 5, 6, 33–34, 88, 123, 146–152, 174, 185, 194, 223–224, 227
Lakoff, G. 拉科夫 114–115, 193, 216 注①
Landman, F. 兰德曼 177
Langendoen, T. 兰根多恩 183
Lappin, S. 拉平 207
Lasnik, H. 拉斯尼克 4, 20, 74, 183–184, 200 注①
Legendre, G. 勒让德尔 66, 72 注①
Levin, B. 莱文 33
Levin, L. 莱文 87, 165–166, 194

Lewis, G. 刘易斯 111 注①
Lightfoot, D. 莱特富特 80 注①, 19, 183
Lobeck, A. 洛贝克 7, 43, 55-60, 67-70, 77, 134, 146, 160, 166
López, L. 洛佩斯 10

M

McCawley, J. 麦考利 25, 196, 216
McCloskey, J. 麦克洛斯基 5, 6, 33-34, 42, 49, 71, 76, 80, 88, 122, 123, 128, 130, 131, 133, 146-152, 174, 184, 185, 194, 196 注①, 223-224, 227
McDaniel, D. 麦克丹尼尔 52, 135
McKee, C. 麦基 135
Maling, J. 马林 139
Manzini, R. 曼齐尼 162, 189, 226
Maracz, L. 马拉奇 69
Marvin, T. 马文 66, 76, 80, 97
May, R. 梅 5, 7, 11, 13, 15 注①, 17, 24-25, 29 首个注①, 129, 154, 160, 191, 204-206
Meinunger, A. 迈宁格 94
Merchant, J. 麦钱特 19, 20, 24, 29 末个注①, 32, 64 注①, 69, 72, 80 注②, 84, 111 注①, 116-118, 121 注①, 123, 135 注①, 152, 163, 165 注①, 167-169, 173, 181-182, 191, 198, 200, 204-206, 226-227
Mester, A. 梅斯特 94, 110 注①
Mikkelsen, L. 米克尔森 64 注①, 68, 77, 92
Mittwoch, A. 米特沃赫 227
Mokrosinska, D. 莫克罗辛斯卡 96, 143
Monachesi, P. 莫纳凯西 99
Mora, J. 莫拉 98 注①
Moxey, L. 莫克西 212 注①
Mulders, I. 马尔德斯 95, 170
Müller, G. 米勒 47, 48, 52, 75, 140-141
Munn, A. 芒恩 195

N

Neeleman, A. 尼利曼 112
Niño, M. 尼尼奥 2
Nishigauchi, T. 西口池 5, 84, 112, 113
Nishiyama, K. 西山 84

O

Oppenrieder, W. 奥本里德 141 注①

P

Pereira, F. 佩雷拉 26, 160
Perlmutter, D. 珀尔马特 79, 183-185
Pesetsky, D. 佩塞茨基 114, 121, 146, 189, 191, 198, 200 注①
Peters, S. 彼得斯 120, 216 注①
Pilátová, A. 皮拉托娃 143
Platzack, C. 普拉扎克 73
Poletto, C. 波莱托 125
Pollard, C. 波拉德 187
Pollmann, T. 波尔曼 116
Postal, P. 波斯塔尔 89, 102, 112 注①, 161, 193, 195, 200 注①, 216, 223
Potsdam, E. 波茨坦 70
Potts, C. 波茨 24
Prince, E. 普林斯 119, 130 注①, 199 注①
Progovac, L. 普罗戈瓦茨 195
Prüst, H. 普鲁斯特 4, 26
Przepiórkowski, A. 普里齐奥科夫斯基 96
Pullum, G. 普鲁姆 80 注①, 112 注①, 197
Puskas, G. 普斯卡斯 81, 126 注①

Q

Quer, J. 克尔 4, 97, 98, 216, 220 注①
Quirk, R. 夸克 167 注①

R

Rappaport, M. 拉帕波特 33
Reinhart, T. 莱因哈特 147 注①, 157, 200 注①
Reis, M. 赖斯 51-52

Riemsdijk, H. van 里姆斯迪克 40, 42, 45, 54, 95, 101, 123, 139, 141 注 ②
Rizzi, L. 里齐 59, 68, 75, 162, 226
Roberts, C. 罗伯茨 217-218
Rodman, R. 罗德曼 200 注 ①
Romero, M. 罗梅罗 4, 6, 13, 20, 29-32, 36, 37, 113 注 ①, 149, 150-151, 154, 160, 162, 210, 226-228
Rooth, M. 鲁思 4, 6, 10, 13, 15, 30 注 ②, 154, 160
Rooy, R. van 罗伊 95, 170, 218
Ross, J. R. 罗斯 3-5, 8 注 ①, 40, 41-42, 45-46, 55-56, 65, 86-87, 89, 92, 108-115, 123, 129, 132, 160, 163, 165-166, 183, 193-194, 196
Rott, H. 罗特 94, 136
Roussou, A. 鲁苏 94, 153 注 ①, 183, 189
Rudin, C. 鲁丁 66, 109-110
Rullmann, H. 鲁尔曼 110 注 ①, 162
Ruys, E. 吕斯 95, 157, 200 注 ①

S

Sadock, J. 萨多克 95
Safir, K. 萨菲尔 24, 214
Sag, I. 萨格 2, 19, 29, 57 注 ①, 119, 167 首个注 ①, 187, 197, 216
Saito, M. 萨伊托 20
Sandell, K. 桑德尔 92
Sandford, A. 桑福德 212 注 ①
Sauerland, U. 绍尔兰 20, 32, 128 注 ①, 149, 162, 191, 210, 214, 226
Scha, R. 沙阿 4, 26
Schürcks-Grozeva, L. 舒尔克斯-格罗泽娃 109
Schwabe, K. 施瓦贝 37 注 ①
Schwarzschild, R. 施瓦茨柴尔德 14-16, 28, 30, 37, 175, 177 注 ①, 179, 183

Sells, P. 塞尔斯 146, 199
Shieber, S. 希伯 26, 160
Shimoyama, J. 下山 84
Shlonksy, U. 隆克西 80
Spaelti, P. 斯佩尔蒂 94 注 ①
Sportiche, D. 斯波尔蒂什 71
Sprouse, R. 斯普劳斯 139
Stavrou, M. 斯塔夫鲁 168 注 ①
Stechow, A. von 施特肖 211
Steinberg, E. 斯坦伯格 95
Sternefeld, W. 斯特恩菲尔德 47, 75
Stockhof, M. 施托克霍夫 122, 207
Stowell, T. 斯托厄尔 154 注 ①
Suñer, M. 苏涅尔 130 注 ①
Svenonius, P. 斯韦诺纽斯 64 注 ①, 92, 222
Swart, H. de 斯沃特 221
Swingle, K. 斯温格尔 196
Szabolcsi, A. 绍博尔奇 129 注 ①, 202, 226

T

Takahashi, D. 高桥 84, 110, 113 注 ①
Takami, K. 高见 101-102, 162, 198 注 ①, 226
Tancredi, C. 坦克雷迪 4, 10, 58 注 ①, 198 注 ①
Taraldsen, T. 塔拉尔森 68
Thráinsson, H. 萨恩森 92
Tomioka, S. 富冈 4, 8 注 ①, 17, 122
Trissler, S. 特里斯勒 140-141

V

Vat, J. 勿 139
Vikner, S. 维克纳 62, 68, 77
Vries, O. 弗里斯 92

W

Wahba, W. 沃赫拜 130 注 ①
Ward, G. 沃德 15
Webelhuth, G. 韦贝尔胡特 48 注 ①
Weinberg, A. 温伯格 102, 183

Whitman, J. 惠特曼 84

Wilder, C. 怀尔德 59 注 ①, 196

Williams, E. 威廉姆斯 57-58, 160, 191

Williams, G. 威廉姆斯 42

Wiltschko, M. 维尔奇科 141

Winkler, S. 温克勒 10, 15, 58 注 ①, 80 注 ②, 94, 136, 173

Winter, Y. 温特 99, 157, 200 注 ①, 223

Wittgenstein, L. 维特根斯坦 1

Wyngaerd, G. vanden 温格 204

Y

Yi, E.-Y. 易 84

Z

Zwart, J.-W. 兹瓦尔特 67, 69, 74-75, 204

Zwarts, F. 兹瓦兹 129 注 ①, 162, 202, 221, 226

Zwicky, A. 兹维基 80 注 ①

主题索引

A

∃-type shifting ∃ 类型替换 14, 27, 30
A′-chain uniformity A′ 链一致性 152–158
ACD, 见 antecedent-contained deletion
across-the-board movement 跨界移位 197–198, 203–204
active/passive alternation 主动/被动变换 15 注①, 34–35
actives, 见 active/passive alternation
adjectives, embedding questions 形容词, 内嵌疑问句 44–45
 另见 attributive adjectives
adjuncts 附加语 19, 20, 120–121
 PP adjunct remnants 介词短语附加语剩余成分 103–104
 另见 islands, adjuncts
aggressively non-D-linked wh-phrases in sluicing, 见 sluicing, with *the hell*
agreement 一致:
 case, 见 form identity, case
 complementizer 标句词 67–69
 on Dutch adjectives 荷兰语形容词 171–172
 subject-verb 主谓 2
 with a CP host of sluicing 截省的 CP 依附体 42
 with *wh*-operators *wh*- 算子 57–59
analyticity 分析性 102
anaphoricity of F-marking 焦点标记的照应性 37
antecedent-contained deletion 包含先行词的删除 199 注 ②
argument structure 论元结构:
 alternations under ellipsis 省略下的变换 33–35
 另见 active/passive alternation
ATB, 见 across-the-board movement
attributive adjectives 定语性形容词 88, 164–180
 另见 islands, left branches
AvoidF 避免焦点条件 177 注①, 179

B

Binding Theory 约束理论 24, 190–191, 204–205, 214

C

Case and Resumptive-binding Operator Generalization 格和复述约束算子概述 146
case 格:
 agreement, 见 form identity, case-matching
 driving LF A-movement 触发逻辑层面 A 移位 189
 on resumptive-binding operators 复述约束算子 132–146
checking, 见 feature checking
clefts 分裂句, 分裂结构 59, 119–120, 125–126
 underlying sluicing 底层的截省,

289

见 pseudosluicing
clitic-doubling 附着成分复现 20
clitics 附着词, 附着成分:
 auxiliaries as 助动词作为 80 注 ①
 in the COMP domain 在标句词域内 65-66, 69, 72 注 ①
COMP domain in sluicing 截省中的标句词域 61-82
comparatives 比较句, 比较结构 68, 72, 107 注 ①, 115 注 ①, 117-118, 167-169, 209
complementizers 标句词:
 agreement with 一致 67-69
 lack of in sluicing 截省句中缺少 56, 74-82
 licensing IP-ellipsis 允准 IP 省略 59-61
 另见 COMP domain in sluicing
Complex NP Constraint 复杂名词短语限制 87
 另见 islands, complex NPs
COMP-trace effect 标句词语迹效应 62, 78-81, 88, 183-185
concessive sluices 让步截省句 175 注 ①
conditionals as islands 条件句作为孤岛条件 90 注 ①, 221
Conjunct Condition 并连语条件 193-200
contrast sluices, 见 sluicing, contrast sluices
Coordinate Structure Constraint 并列结构限制 86, 193-200, 223-226
 另见 islands, coordinate structures
coordination underlying multiple sluicing 多重截省下的并列结构 111 注 ①
copy theory of movement 复制移位理论 210-211, 214-216
copying vs. deletion, 见 deletion vs. copying
correlates, 见 sluicing
CP 标句词短语:
 ellipsis of 省略 117-118
 as host of sluicing 作为截省依附体 40-54

positional restrictions on 位置性限制 45-50

D

deaccenting 去重音 4, 10, 17, 23, 25, 33-34, 38, 56, 149, 215
 adjacent to an ellipsis site 省略部位的邻接 58
deletion vs. copying 删除与复制 5, 55, 146, 152, 159-163
derived position islands, 见 islands, derived positions
distressing, 见 deaccenting
deviance from identity under ellipsis 省略下同一性偏差 19-25
 另见 vehicle change
D-linked wh-phrases 语篇关联 wh- 短语 20
donkey pronouns, 见 E-type anaphora
double objects 双宾语 34 注 ①
Doubly-Filled Comp Filter 双重标句词填入过滤条件 74, 78

E

E feature E 特征 60-61, 231
economy 经济性 1, 73, 172, 222
e-GIVENness 省略给定:
 definition of 定义 26
 in sluicing 在截省句中 29-37, 176-180, 210-214, 231
 in VP-ellipsis 在动词短语省略中 26-29
ellipsis 省略:
 argument structure alternations under 论元结构变换 33-35
 semantic approaches to 语义研究路径 2, 10-38, 159-160
 varieties of deviance from identity under 与同一性有偏差的变体 19-25
 另见 vehicle change; deletion vs. copying;

NP-ellipsis; sluicing; VP-ellipsis
elliptic conjunctions 省略连词 107 注①
else 35–36, 122
EPP, 见 extended projection principle
E-type anaphora E 类型照应 200–208, 210–214, 220–221, 222, 225, 228
exceptives 例外成分 22, 107 注①
existential type-shifting, 见 ∃-type shifting
expletives 虚位词：
 there 191
 wh- 52 注①
extended projection principle 扩展投射原则 187–188, 193
extraposition 外置 45–46, 185

F
F-closure 焦点闭包 26–37, 29 末个注①, 177–180
 definition of 定义 14
 另见 Focus condition
feature 特征：
 checking 核查 59–61, 73–74, 169, 187–189
 uniformity 一致性 155
 F-marking 焦点标记 13–15, 26 注①, 37 注①, 176–180
focus 焦点 13–15
 另见 F-closure; Focus condition
Focus condition 焦点条件 26, 38
 applied to sluicing 应用于截省 29–38, 174–180, 186, 207, 210–214, 219
 applied to VP-ellipsis 应用于动词短语省略 26–29
 general definition of 一般性定义 38
 另见 R-focus condition; S-focus condition
form identity 形式同一性：
 case-matching 格匹配 42–45, 89–91, 108–109, 151

Generalization I 概述 I 91
Generalization II 概述 II 92
in other elliptical constructions 在其他省略结构中 107 注①
preposition-stranding 介词悬置 91–107, 109, 151–152
fragment answers 片语答句 107 注①, 119–120
fragments 片语 40

G
gapping 空缺句, 空缺结构 107 注①, 113 注①, 167
gerunds 动名词 22
GIVENness 给定 14–16, 30–31, 34
 definition of 定义 14
government 管辖 57–61

H
Heavy XP Shift 重 XP 转移 47

I
identification of ellipses 省略识别 2, 6, 61, 231
identity 同一性：
 deviance from under ellipsis, 见 vehicle change function, 见 partial identity function
 in form, 见 form identity
imperatives 祈使式 22
implicational bridging 隐含连接 15, 29
implicit arguments 隐性论元 18, 227
 另见 sluicing, with implicit correlates
indirect object, 见 double objects
individual-level predicates 个体层面谓词 192–193
infinitivals 不定式 22
inversion 倒装：
 of auxiliary with subject, 见 I-to-C movement
 of *wh*-words with prepositions, 见 swiping
IP copy, 见 LF-copying

IP-ellipsis, 见 sluicing
islands 孤岛：
  adjuncts 附加语 88, 90 注 ①, 221–222
  classification of 分类 162
  complex NPs 复杂名词短语 87, 88
  coordinate structures 并列结构 86, 88, 193–200, 223–226
  COMP-trace 标句词语迹 88, 183–185
  derived positions 派生位置 88, 185–193
  embedded questions 内嵌疑问句 88, 163 注 ①
  left branches 左分支 87, 88, 163–183
  PF-islands PF 孤岛 161–200
  propositional islands 命题性孤岛 208–228
  relative clauses 关系从句 4–6, 87, 90 注 ①, 208–221
  repair by resumptives 被复述词修复 128–146, 198–199
  selective ('weak') 选择性（"弱"）87, 149, 162, 226–228
  sentential subjects 句子性主语 87, 88, 221–222
  subjects (non-sentential) 主语（非句子性）88, 185–193, 205–206
  syntactic ('strong') 句法（"强"）86–89
  topicalizations 话题化 88, 185–186
  wh- 88, 163 ①
isomorphism, 见 structural isomorphism
I-to-C movement I 到 C 的移位 63–65, 69, 73–74

L

Left Branch Condition 左分支条件 87, 163–183
  另见 islands, left branches; sluicing
LF, 见 Logical Form
LF-copying LF 复制 6, 146–158, 160–161

LF-movement LF 移位：
  A-movement A 移位 189–190
  A′-movement A′ 移位 153–158, 189–190, 200 注 ①
licensing 允准：
  alternatives to government approaches 管辖路径的替代方案 60–61
  general considerations 总则 2, 6, 231
  of IP-ellipsis IP 省略 55–61
  of VP-ellipsis 动词短语省略 60
Logical Form 逻辑形式 11

M

Mapping Hypothesis 映射假说 192–193
merger 合并 147–152, 174, 223–225, 227
Minimal Link Condition 最小链接条件 114
modal subordination 情态从属 216–222, 228
multiple sluicing, 见 sluicing, multiple
multiple wh-movement under sluicing 截省结构下多重 wh- 移位, 见 sluicing, multiple

N

negative polarity items 否定极性词 29 首个注 ①, 212, 220
NP-ellipsis 名词短语省略 30 注 ①, 43, 134, 147 注 ②, 165, 167, 168 注 ①, 178, 195–196, 210
NPIs, 见 negative polarity items
null complement anaphora 空补足语照应 119
Null Conjunct Constraint 空并连语限制 195–200

O

Optimality Theory 优选论 112–113

P

parallelism 平行：
  clausal 小（从）句的 4
  scopal 辖域的 17, 29, 147–151, 153–158, 227–228

partial identity function 部分恒等函数 61
partial sluicing 部分截省 57-58
participles 分词 22
passives, 见 active/passive alternation
PF, 见 Phonological Form
PF crash PF 崩溃 73-74, 169
PF deletion, 见 deletion vs. copying
PF-islands PF 孤岛 161-200
Phonological Form 语音形式 5
pied-piping 裹挟式移位：
    by degree words 通过程度词 164-167, 170-171
    by prepositions 通过介词 92, 135-136, 161 注①
polarity, 见 negative polarity items
positions available to CP hosts of sluicing 截省中 CP 依附体的位置 45-50
preposition inversion in sluicing, 见 swiping
preposition-stranding 介词悬置, 见 sluicing, preposition-stranding under; form identity, preposition-stranding
presupposition 预设 16 注②, 61
prime notation, definition of 主要符号, 定义 27
Principle B 约束三原则 B 204-205, 214
Principle C 约束三原则 C 24, 190-191, 204-205, 214
Procrastinate 拖延原则 112
pronominal correlate 代词性关联成分 204-205
propositional islands 命题性孤岛 208-228
prosody 韵律 50, 121
pseudoclefts 假分裂句 59 注①
pseudogapping 假空缺 29 末个注①, 35, 72, 113 注①
pseudosluicing 假截省 101 注①, 115-127

P-stranding, 见 sluicing, preposition-stranding under

R

rebinding 重新约束 214-215
reconstruction 重构 13, 17, 154
redundancy relations 冗余关系 13, 154
relative clauses 关系从句：
    free relatives 自由关系从句 59 注①
    indicative relatives 直陈式关系从句 208-216
    lack of IP-ellipsis in 缺少 IP 省略 59
    subjunctive relatives 虚拟关系从句 216-221
    另见 islands, relative clauses
remnant XPs 残余成分 XP 29 末个注①
resumptive pronouns 复述代词 128-146, 184, 198-199
resumptive-binding operators 复述约束算子 128, 132-146
R-focus condition 鲁思焦点条件 13
Right Node Raising 右节点提升 195-196
RNR, 见 Right Node Raising
R-pronouns R 代词 95 注①, 123-124, 140-141

S

scopal parellelism in ellipsis 省略中的辖域平行 17, 29, 147-51, 153-158, 227-228
scrambling 挪移 47-48, 84-85
segments, ability to license ellipsis 分段, 允准省略的能力 19, 213
selectional restrictions 选择限制条件 41-42
semantics 语义学：
    approaches to ellipsis 省略的研究方法, 见 ellipsis, semantic approaches to
    background on 背景 11-12
    of the E-feature 省略特征的 61
Sentential Subject Constraint 句子主语限制 87

另见 islands, sentential subjects
S-focus condition 施瓦茨柴尔德的焦点条件 14
situational *it* 情景性 *it* 215–216
sloppy identity 宽泛同一性 8, 129
sluicing 截省：
    case-matching in 格匹配 89–91
    concessive 让步 175 注①
    contrast sluices 对比截省 36–37, 150
    etymology of 词源 3 注①
    and islands, 见 islands
    lack of I-to-C movement in 缺少 I 到 C 的移位 63–65
    lack of sloppy identity in 缺少宽泛同一性 8
    left branches 左分支 127, 163–183
    in matrix clauses 在主句中 63–65
    multiple 多重 85, 109–114
    'partial' "部分" 57–58
    preposition-stranding under 在以下条件下的介词悬置 91–107, 151–152, 153–156, 161
    with *if/whether* 带有 *if/whether* 56, 80 注②
    with implicit correlates 带隐性关联词 3, 19, 120–121, 148–149, 226–228
    with inverted prepositions, 见 swiping
    with *the hell* 带有 *the hell* 64 注①, 121–122
    with *wh*-expletives 带有 *wh*- 虚位成分 52 注①
    Sluicing-COMP generalization 截省 COMP 概述 62
sprouting 萌生操作 146–149, 224–225, 227
stage-level predicates 阶段层面谓词 192–193
stress-shift in German 德语中的重音转移 51–53
Strict Cycle Condition 严格循环条件 188–189

Stripping 剥落句剥落结构 107 注①, 167
strong islands, 见 islands, syntactic
structural isomorphism 结构同构 17–19
    problems for 问题 19–25, 225–226
Subject-Auxiliary Inversion, 见 I-to-C movement
subjects, 见 islands, subjects
subjunctive relatives, 见 relative clauses, subjunctive relatives
Superiority 优先条件 113–114
swiping 附带（省略）结构 64, 121 末个注①, 123–124

T

that-trace effect, 见 COMP-trace effect
topicalization islands, 见 islands, topicalizations
topic-drop 话题脱落 197
traces 语迹 20, 26 注①, 28, 32, 112, 201–208, 210–216

V

V_2 第二动词 20–21, 62–63, 69, 197
vehicle change 载体转换 11, 12, 24–25, 28–29, 38, 129, 191, 199 注②, 204–207, 211, 214, 223, 231
verb second, 见 V_2
veridicality 真实性 220–221
VP-ellipsis 动词短语省略 2–3, 4–6, 8–9, 10–11, 13–19, 167–168, 199 注②, 204, 214–216
    in coordinte structures 在并列结构中 195–196, 224 注①
    crosslinguistic rarity of 跨语言罕见的 2–3
    sloppy identity in 宽泛同一性 8 注①
    wh-movement in *wh*- 移位 58, 114–115

W

Wackernagel clitics, 见 clitics in the COMP domain
weak crossover 弱交叉 189–190
weak islands, 见 islands, selective

wh-expletives, 见 expletives, *wh*-
wh-in-situ languages *wh*- 原位语言 84-85
wh-islands *wh*- 孤岛, 见 islands, *wh*-
wh-movement *wh*- 移位 20
    in sluicing 在截省中 92-107
    in VP-ellipsis 在动词短语省略中 58, 114-115
    另见 sluicing, multiple
whom 92 末个注 ①, 124 注 ①, 133 首个注 ①
whose 133-134, 165
wh-traces, 见 traces

译后记

The Syntax of Silence: Sluicing, Islands, and the Theory of Ellipsis 是牛津大学出版社理论语言学研究系列丛书中的一本。对此书的翻译源起于2018年，当时我在芝加哥大学语言学系跟随 Jason Merchant 教授做博士后研究，其间系统学习了 Jason 和 Anastasia 教授夫妇开设的《句法分析》《句法学和语义学》等课程。在学习之余，我全身心投入到此书的翻译工作中。如今商务印书馆决定将其出版，介绍给国内语言学界同仁，定名为《沉默的句法——截省、孤岛条件和省略理论》。

当代理论语言学的主要任务之一是在声音和意义之间进行理论构建。省略作为一种涉及句法、语义、语用、篇章、认知等不同维度的复杂语言现象，是典型的句法语义界面研究对象，也是国外理论语言学研究的重点。《沉默的句法》提出的省略理论是国外句法语义界面研究的经典理论，对该领域研究有理论指引和操作范例作用。其影响力从其被引频次及所引语料可见一斑。截至2021年3月18日，经google学术搜索查询，该书已被引用2679次，是句法语义界面研究，特别是省略研究的国内外必引文献和经典文献之一。作为跨语言研究的典范，全书涉及24个不同语种的语料，兼顾了理论探索和跨语言实证研究，是无可置疑的经典之作。为此，本人在美学习期间，就下定决心要将此书翻译出来，介绍给国内句法研究学界，以期对国内相关研究助益一二。

听闻商务印书馆正在论证是否将本书译介到中国，一些国际上句法研究尤其是省略研究的大家，纷纷来信力荐此书，以下是三位著名学者来信中的推介语：

译后记

  获悉 Jason Merchant 的书将翻译成中文出版，我要说真是太棒了！这里附上我在《语言》期刊上发表的一则评论。在那则评论中我写道："自罗斯（Ross 1969）的那篇开创性文章以来，本书是最重要的截省省略结构研究，也是有史以来对这引人关注的省略结构最详细的研究。"在我看来，12 年后上述说法依然成立。任何对省略现象感兴趣的人都必须读 Merchant 的书。

——马里兰大学语言学系终身教授 Howard Lasnik

  对于一般的语言省略现象，尤其是截省的研究，Jason Merchant 的书至关重要。他书中的发现以及提出的相关解释塑造了过去 15 年截省研究的进程。他对省略先行条件的表述最受人们青睐，部分原因在于他将阐释与截省的句法分析联系起来。他的著作具有语言学理论方面的重要历史价值，同时也是一部罕见的跨语言详尽研究典范。此外，清晰的写作风格和论述方式也使该书颇具教学价值。在一个备受关注的研究领域，该书虽已存在多年，但仍具有新颖性。它提出的大多数问题在今天仍然备受关注，提出的解决策略仍然适用。

——马萨诸塞大学安姆斯特分校语言学系终身教授 Kyle Johnson

  Jason Merchant 在 2001 年出版的著作《沉默的句法》是对 21 世纪理论语言学最重要和最持久的贡献之一。该书重点研究的是省略现象，即说话者在讲话时省略了多余的内容，具体而言，就是 "Someone wrote a book, but I don't know who." 这种截省结构。此后出版的每一部关于省略现象的著作，无论用哪种语言撰写，都必然会提及《沉默的句法》中的主张与假设。这本书彻底改变了我们对省略进程的思考方式，并为该领域研究范围的不断扩大奠定了基础。

——斯坦福大学语言学系教授 Vera Gribanova

  在此背景下，我更加坚定了将此书翻译好的决心。但是理想和现实间总是有着不小的差距。在翻译过程中，我遇到了许多困难，时间紧张，杂务繁忙，无法沉心静气专注翻译工作等，但其中最大的问题还是相关知识有所欠缺。该书是省略研究的专业书籍，专业术语多，表述书面化、专门化，较为艰深。因此要翻译好，首先要自己理解准确，而准确的理解是建立在研读相关文献，系统掌握相关知识的基础上，因此本书的翻译过程，更是一个自我学习的过程。其间我对一些关键术语的理解，如 vehicle

297

change 和 modal subordination 等，在作者 Jason 教授的指导下，也在不断加深。试举两例：

> 特征转换是 Fiengo 和 May（1994）引进的术语，目的是为了解决 NP 先行结构的形式（例如名称）与省略部位的不完全一致问题，如一个名称可以被一个相对应的代词所代替。在这一理念下，名称、代词、定指性描述都是指数的不同载体，例如：
> They arrested Alex_1, though he_1 didn't know why 〈they arrested him_1_〉.
> 在上例中，指数 1 可以被 Alex、he 和 him 所指代，即这些 NP 都指向同一个个体（名称 Alex）。但事实上，指数变换的载体非常重要，正如 Fiengo 和 May（1994）的研究一样，在先行结构中 Alex_1 和被删除的 TP 中的 him_1 不完全一样，因为如果一样的话，him_1 将会被 Alex_1 所取代。这违反了约束三原则中的 C，因为 he_1 成分统制 him_1。有鉴于此，Fiengo 和 May 提出了在省略部位中指数的"载体"（vehicle）可以"转换"（change）的假说。

又如：

> 情态从属指在一定的句法环境下，情态动态的语义解释会受限，例如：
> Beth can buy a banana, and it might cost $1.
> 情态动词 might 的语义解释（其量化范围）受其并连语 can 语义解释的限制，即 might 的语义解释从属于 can 的语义解释，情态从属语境使正常情况下不可能的照应关系变得可能，如上例中 it 回指前句中的 banana。

在本书的翻译过程中，这种对原文理解的困惑不时出现，但每次 Jason 教授都及时给予我指导和解答。记得 Jason 教授常对我说的一句话是"Happy to answer more questions, as always!"。此外 Jason 教授还为我提供了专用办公室和必要的办公条件，并时不时邀请我去家里小聚，让我在国外的学习、工作和生活变得丰富多彩，在此我要对 Jason 教授表示深深的谢意。

译后记

在本书的翻译过程中,我还得到了很多朋友的帮助,特别是马秀杰博士,她也关注省略问题,也觉得该书是国内学者了解国外省略研究前沿的必读书目。她毕业之后,来到北京外国语大学工作,与我成为同事,我们经常相互探讨和学习。在本书翻译过程中,秀杰博士在百忙之中对全书进行了校译,并就术语翻译与我时常讨论,使我收获颇多。此外,我还要感谢上海交通大学赖欣祺博士,欣祺老师多次与我讨论,帮我解疑答惑,使我受益匪浅。

我还要对我的硕士生王竹和访学的王磊老师表示由衷的感谢,他们现在分别在北京外国语大学和北京语言大学攻读博士学位,当初都参与了部分初稿的翻译工作。

此外,本书的翻译为北京外国语大学青年学术创新团队项目的阶段性成果之一,得到北京外国语大学卓越人才支持计划资助。

最后,由于本人学术水平和视野有限,书中难免有纰漏,敬请各位专家学者批评指正!

张天伟

2021 年 4 月

语言学及应用语言学名著译丛书目

句法结构(第2版)	〔美〕诺姆·乔姆斯基	著
语言知识:本质、来源及使用	〔美〕诺姆·乔姆斯基	著
语言与心智研究的新视野	〔美〕诺姆·乔姆斯基	著
语言研究(第7版)	〔美〕乔治·尤尔	著
英语的成长和结构	〔丹〕奥托·叶斯柏森	著
言辞之道研究	〔英〕保罗·格莱斯	著
言语行为:语言哲学论	〔美〕约翰·R.塞尔	著
理解最简主义	〔美〕诺伯特·霍恩斯坦〔巴西〕杰罗·努内斯〔德〕克莱安西斯·K.格罗曼	著
认知语言学	〔美〕威廉·克罗夫特〔英〕D.艾伦·克鲁斯	著
历史认知语言学	〔美〕玛格丽特·E.温特斯 等	编
语言、使用与认知	〔美〕琼·拜比	著
我们思维的方式:概念整合与思维的隐含复杂性	〔法〕吉勒·福柯尼耶〔美〕马克·特纳	著
为何只有我们:语言与进化	〔美〕罗伯特C.贝里克 诺姆·乔姆斯基	著
语言的进化生物学探索	〔美〕菲利普·利伯曼	著
叶斯柏森论语音	〔丹〕奥托·叶斯柏森	著
语音类型	〔美〕伊恩·麦迪森	著
语调音系学(第2版)	〔英〕D.罗伯特·拉德	著

韵律音系学	〔意〕玛丽娜·内斯波 〔美〕艾琳·沃格尔	著
词库音系学中的声调	〔加〕道格拉斯·蒲立本	著
音系与句法：语音与结构的关系	〔美〕伊丽莎白·O.塞尔柯克	著
节律重音理论——原则与案例研究	〔美〕布鲁斯·海耶斯	著
语素导论	〔美〕戴维·恩比克	著
语义学（上卷）	〔英〕约翰·莱昂斯	著
语义学（下卷）	〔英〕约翰·莱昂斯	著
做语用（第3版）	〔英〕彼得·格伦迪	著
语用学原则	〔英〕杰弗里·利奇	著
语用学与英语	〔英〕乔纳森·卡尔佩珀 〔澳〕迈克尔·霍	著
交互文化语用学	〔美〕伊什特万·凯奇凯什	著
应用语言学研究方法	〔英〕佐尔坦·德尔涅伊	著
复杂系统与应用语言学	〔美〕戴安娜·拉森-弗里曼 〔英〕琳恩·卡梅伦	著
信息结构与句子形式	〔美〕克努德·兰布雷希特	著
沉默的句法：截省、孤岛条件和省略理论	〔美〕贾森·麦钱特	著
语言教学的流派（第3版）	〔新西兰〕杰克·C.理查兹 〔美〕西奥多·S.罗杰斯	著
语言学习与语言教学的原则（第6版）	〔英〕H.道格拉斯·布朗	著
社会文化理论与二语教学语用学	〔美〕雷米·A.范康珀诺勒	著
法语英语文体比较	〔加〕J.-P.维奈 J.达贝尔内	著
法语在英格兰的六百年史（1000—1600)	〔美〕道格拉斯·A.奇比	著
语言与全球化	〔英〕诺曼·费尔克劳	著
语言与性别	〔美〕佩内洛普·埃克特 萨利·麦康奈尔-吉内特	著
全球化的社会语言学	〔比〕扬·布鲁马特	著
话语分析：社会科学研究的文本分析方法	〔英〕诺曼·费尔克劳	著
社会与话语：社会语境如何影响文本与言谈	〔荷〕特恩·A.范戴克	著

图书在版编目(CIP)数据

沉默的句法:截省、孤岛条件和省略理论/(美)贾森·麦钱特(Jason Merchant)著;张天伟译.—北京:商务印书馆,2023
(语言学及应用语言学名著译丛)
ISBN 978-7-100-20735-5

Ⅰ.①沉⋯ Ⅱ.①贾⋯ ②张⋯ Ⅲ.①省略(语法)—研究 Ⅳ.①H043

中国版本图书馆 CIP 数据核字(2022)第 102175 号

权利保留,侵权必究。

语言学及应用语言学名著译丛
沉默的句法
截省、孤岛条件和省略理论
〔美〕贾森·麦钱特 著
张天伟 译

商 务 印 书 馆 出 版
(北京王府井大街36号 邮政编码100710)
商 务 印 书 馆 发 行
北京市白帆印务有限公司印刷
ISBN 978-7-100-20735-5

2023年2月第1版 开本 880×1230 1/32
2023年2月北京第1次印刷 印张 10¼
定价:78.00元